MIDDLE LEVEL
EDUCATION

Recent Titles in
Bibliographies and Indexes in Education

MIDDLE LEVEL EDUCATION

An Annotated Bibliography

Samuel Totten, Toni Sills-Briegel,
Kathleen Barta, Annette Digby,
and William Nielsen

*Prepared under the auspices of the Center for
Middle Level Education, Research, and Development,
University of Arkansas, Fayetteville,
College of Education*

Bibliographies and Indexes in Education, Number 16

Greenwood Press
Westport, Connecticut • London

Library of Congress Cataloging-in-Publication Data

Middle level education : an annotated bibliography / Samuel Totten . . .
   [et al.].
       p.   cm.—(Bibliographies and indexes in education, ISSN
   0742–6917 ; no. 16)
       "Prepared under the auspices of the Center for Middle Level
   Education, Research, and Development, University of Arkansas, Fayetteville,
   College of Education."
       Includes bibliographical references and indexes.
       ISBN 0–313–29002–4 (alk. paper)
       1. Middle schools—United States—Bibliography.   I. Totten,
   Samuel.   II. University of Arkansas, Fayetteville.   Center for
   Middle Level Education, Research, and Development.   III. Series.
   Z5815.H56M53   1996
   [LB1623.5]
   016.373.2′36′0973—dc20   96–6136

British Library Cataloguing in Publication Data is available.

Library of Congress Catalog Card Number: 96–6136
ISBN: 0–313–29002–4
ISSN: 0742–6917

First published in 1996

Greenwood Press, 88 Post Road West, Westport, CT 06881
An imprint of Greenwood Publishing Group, Inc.

Printed in the United States of America

The paper used in this book complies with the
Permanent Paper Standard issued by the National
Information Standards Organization (Z39.48–1984).

10 9 8 7 6 5 4 3 2

To:

All of the enthusiastic and excellent Arkansas-based middle level educators whom I have had the great pleasure to work with over the past seven years.

Totten

Alice Rollow for her friendship and support over the years and to my O'Callaghan Middle School team members: Sylvia, Shelley, and Grant.

Sills-Briegel

Jason, Kathryn, Michael, Kristen, and David in the hopes that they will benefit from our knowledge of middle level education.

Barta

Gary, Jeremy, and Christy Digby for their patience and support.

Digby

My wife, four children, and *all* the students who came into my classrooms.

Nielsen

Contents

CONTENTS

CONTENTS

Introduction

1. Overview of Middle Level Education

Samuel Totten and Toni Sills-Briegel

Over the past decade or so, there has been a major push in the United States to develop strong middle level programs (for any combination of grades five through eight or nine) in our nation's schools (California State Department of Education, 1987; Carnegie Council on Adolescent Development, 1989; National Middle School Association, 1992). The key purpose of such school programs is to meet the unique needs (intellectual, social, emotional, and physical) of early adolescents (age 10 to 15 years). As the authors of *Turning Points: Preparing American Youth for the 21st Century*, a major document on the need to transform the education of young adolescents, note:

> Young adolescents today make fateful choices, fateful for them and for our nation. The period of life from ages 10 to 15 represents for many young people their last best chance to choose a path toward productive and fulfilling lives.
>
> This time [early adolescence] is of immense importance in the development of the young person. *Biologically, young adolescents experience puberty, a period of growth and development more rapid than in any other phase of life except infancy* (italics added).
>
> Middle grade schools—junior high, intermediate, or middle schools—are potentially society's most powerful force to recapture millions of youth adrift (Carnegie Council on Adolescent Development, 1989, pp. 20, 21, 32).

Probably no more effective phrase has been coined to describe the plight of these young adolescents than "caught in the middle" (California State Department of Education, 1987). Too old to be children, yet too young to take on the responsibilities of adulthood, this unique group of young people requires careful attention as they begin to step, sometimes with uncertainty, towards adulthood. Many argue that no more challenging group of students faces a teacher.

Middle level students are just like other students except that every adjective describing them should be prefaced by either "more" or "less," i.e., more happy, more sad, more sensitive, less sensitive, less studious, more arduous. While other students, both elementary and secondary, have relatively predictable ranges of responses both academically and emotionally, at *different* moments the same middle level student tends to go off the scale at either end. Teachers must be unpredictable themselves to capture their students' attention. Working with such young people demands high energy levels and creative and flexible minds to generate lesson plans to capture the voracious imaginations of some students, and entice the perennially bored into activity. The one constant in a middle level classroom is that nothing expected will happen. Teachers need huge repertoires of strategies and the flexibility to change from one plan to another within moments.

Middle level students test every statement, every lesson, every event against themselves. They test their bodies, their minds, their emotions in search of new possibilities *and* for limits. And each individual has his or her own set of limits. Teachers must allow as wide a range as possible, yet be able to set limits that allow everyone to advance unhindered. While teaching self control in social and emotional matters, teachers must encourage a wild abandon intellectually. Students must be motivated to read, to write, to communicate in all sorts of meaningful and intriguing ways, to learn to play with numbers, and to ponder their place in their school, their community, and the world.

Unique Aspects/Components of an Exemplary Middle Level Program

What is most important in regard to middle level programs is not the grade configuration or the name of the school, but the philosophy to which a school adheres as well as the instructional and extracurricular programs it has in place to meet the needs of its students. This point cannot be stressed too strongly. An exemplary middle level program (or middle school), then, is one in which the social, emotional, physical, and intellectual needs of its students are consciously, enthusiastically, and systematically addressed by the administrators, teachers, and programs. As middle level advocates frequently point out, *an ideal middle school is one where the school fits the student rather than where the student fits the school.* Over and above that, many of these schools either have in place or are working towards developing such middle level components as: a core curriculum that is interdisciplinary in nature, challenging, and imbued with depth vs. perfunctory coverage; interdisciplinary teaming; advisor/advisee programs; exploratory programs; flexible and block scheduling; and a comprehensive health program.

Recent Thrusts of Middle Level Education

While the concept of middle schools is not new (indeed, it has been in existence since the early 1960s [1]), the thrust over the past decade is notable for

---

[1] As middle level pioneer John Lounsbury noted in 1985: "Although some

several reasons. First, there has been a direly needed reevaluation of the unique needs of early adolescents in order to develop programs that meet their specific needs in not only the academic/intellectual sphere but also the social, emotional, and physical spheres. Undoubtedly, this has been a result of several key factors: the new and increasing problems society is faced with, including those directly impacting young people (e.g., broken homes, latch-key situations, violence in our homes, streets, and schools, ever-increasing poverty, homelessness, drop-out rates) as well as those caused by them (e.g., gang involvement, violence by and against the young and others); the results of research vis-à-vis the education, health, and welfare of young adolescents by those in schools of education as well as other fields (e.g., social services, health, juvenile crime); and the ardent desire by educators to develop efficacious programs so that middle schools and junior highs are no longer simply "holding areas" but places of great stimulation and care. Second, the development of new and stronger middle level programs has become part and parcel of the current educational reform movement under way in the United States. Third, not only are educators at the public school level and university level deeply involved in the development of strong middle level programs, but many other parties are as deeply involved: various philanthropic organizations; youth service and other community organizations; health, juvenile, and social service organizations; state education departments; various political leaders at both the state and federal levels; and concerned parents. Fourth, there has been an increasing call for *and* focus on the development of a strong research base vis-à-vis various facets of middle level education. Fifth, there is possibly more innovation taking place in the area of middle level education than at any other level.

All of these efforts to reform educational programs for young adolescents were (and still are) badly needed. As the authors of *Turning Points* trenchantly asserted in 1989:

> A volatile mismatch exists between the organization and curriculum of middle grade schools, and the intellectual, emotional, and interpersonal needs of young adolescents.... Today, as young adolescents move from elementary to middle or junior high schools, their involvement with learning diminishes and their rates of alienation, drug abuse, absenteeism, and dropping out begin to rise. The warning signals are there to see.
>
> The ability of young adolescents to cope is often further jeopardized by a middle grade curriculum that assumes a need for an intellectual moratorium during early adolescence. Some

---

people have viewed the middle school as a new and independent idea, it is really a part of the on-going reorganization effort, the latest point of emphasis in the continuing effort to mesh human development and educational ideals with financial realities, administrative necessities, and tradition. And even as the term middle school was being introduced [in the mid-1960s], the junior high school was evidencing clear signs of both a renaissance and a reformation....Junior high schools, then have existed for three quarters of a century, middle schools for one-quarter of a century." (p. 2)

educators consider the young adolescent incapable of critical, complex thought during rapid physical and emotional development.

Minimal effort, they argue, should be spent to stimulate higher levels of thought and decision making until the youth reaches high school and becomes teachable again. Existing knowledge seriously challenges these assumptions. Yet many grade schools fail to recognize or to act on this knowledge....Furthermore, many middle grade schools pay little attention to the emotional, physical, and social development of their students (Carnegie Council for Adolescent Development, 1989, p. 32).

A great deal has been accomplished in the years since *Turning Points* was published, but visits to many middle level schools and junior highs today make it obvious that one cannot be sanguine about the current state of affairs when it comes to meeting the specific and dire needs of young adolescents. Simply stated, much work still needs to be done. That said, the most positive aspect of all this is that middle level education does not seem to be one of the many educational fads that are here today and gone tomorrow. Thousands of highly dedicated, intelligent, and hard-working educators across the nation are arduously attempting to change the focus, programs, climate, and running of schools for the express purpose of meeting the unique needs of early adolescents.

Conclusion

As one will readily ascertain by both the number of citations in this volume and the eclectic nature of the works highlighted, middle level education is the focus of a great deal of activity on many fronts. Much of the activity is quite impressive, and those educators and others who are at the forefront of the middle level movement should be commended.

What the middle level movement needs most at this juncture is a stronger research base, more solid commitment from and support by both federal and state governments as well as colleges of education, and the willingness of all parties (educators at the middle level and in colleges of education, government agencies, health, juvenile and social services, youth organizations, and parents) to join together in an effort to strengthen current efforts and to develop even more innovative and synergistic efforts in the future. Perhaps, then, this society and its schools will truly begin to meet the unique needs of our early adolescents.

References

California State Department of Education (1987). *Caught in the middle: Educational reform for young adolescents in California public schools.* Sacramento, CA: Author.

Carnegie Council for Adolescent Development (1989). *Turning points:*

Preparing American youth for the 21st century. New York: Carnegie Corporation of New York.

Lounsbury, John H. (1984). "Prologue." In John H. Lounsbury (Ed.) *Perspectives: Middle school education.* Columbus, OH: National Middle School Association.

National Middle School Association (1992). *This We Believe.* Columbus, OH: Author.

2. Structure of the Bibliography

Subject and Scope

Over the past thirty years, much has been written about the unique cognitive and affective needs of young adolescents as well as efforts of educational systems to meet those needs through relevant curricula and appropriate learning experiences. This annotated bibliography focuses on practical aspects of middle level education and on research related to adolescence and middle level practices. It includes essays, articles, and reports on various aspects of middle level programs, community service projects, classroom activities, curricular issues, and other related topics. This volume also contains research reports on a wide variety of issues ranging from the role of peer pressure upon young adolescents to professional development programs for middle level teachers. Also included are essays, articles, and reports on school climate, organizational structures, student achievement and evaluation, effective teaching strategies in content areas, and parental involvement. (For a complete listing and description of topics, refer to *Overview of Bibliographic Topics*.)

This bibliography was developed for the express purpose of providing a comprehensive, up-to-date reference tool for teachers, administrators, researchers, parents, professionals in health-related fields, and other community members interested in various facets of middle level education. To accomplish that purpose, we have included works (articles, essays, newsletters, monographs, bibliographies, reports, dissertations, conference papers and proceedings, book review, videotapes, books, and textbooks) that a diverse readership will find of interest. Also in an effort to provide a *comprehensive* bibliography, we have included the best work, the weakest works, and those that fall in between the two extremes. Works that appear to be weak in content and/or usefulness are identified as such by a statement specifying the perceived weaknesses. We have also included names of organizations and other resources that provide on-going support for people involved in middle level education.

The emergence of middle level schools in the 1960s resulted in a minimal number of immediate publications, most of which were accounts of personal experiences, outlines of teaching strategies and lesson plans, state reports, and general statements on the nature and needs of young adolescents. Since the publication of works such as *The Middle School We Need* in the mid-1970s, the middle level movement has experienced an explosion of growth and popularity, resulting in a significant number of publications, ranging from personal narratives to research-based reports. To assist readers interested in tracing the development of the middle school movement from its early stages to the present and to provide readers with a comprehensive overview of the middle level movement, we have included seminal works from the 1960s as well as from each subsequent decade. It should be noted, however, that the majority of the annotations deal with the works that have appeared since the 1980s.

Sources of References

When compiling this bibliography, we consulted standard sources. Those most frequently consulted were the *Current Index to Journals in Education, Dissertation Abstracts, Education Index, The ERIC Sources in Education,* and the *Library of Congress Subject Catalog.* We also used a variety of data bases in our search, including Colorado Alliance of Research Libraries (CARL), Educational Resources Information Center (ERIC), Online Computer Library Center, (OCLC), and Subject Content Oriented Retriever for Processing Information On-Line (SCORPIO).

Scholarly and professional journals in the field of education were the major sources of items included in the bibliography. To a significant extent, we also used journals focusing on health education, nursing, and psychology. Annotations are included for each themed issue as well as for individual articles in each of the issues.

3. Overview of Bibliographic Topics

The publication of *Turning Points* (Carnegie Council on Adolescent Development, 1989) called national attention to the special opportunity afforded middle level schools to "recapture millions of youth adrift" (p. 8) if such were designed with the special needs of young adolescents in mind. The topics selected for inclusion in the bibliography represent an attempt to profile the components that make for a true middle level experience broadly defined as those schools that attempt to serve the unique developmental needs of the young adolescent through "interdisciplinary teaming, advisor/advisee programs, exploratory programs, flexible scheduling, etc." (Totten & Snider, 1994, p. 6). The second document that influenced the selection of topics for the bibliography was *Fateful Choices* (1992). It called attention to the major areas of risk to the health and safety of children during the middle years.

The bibliography begins with a section entitled **General Issues** addressing such things as the research agenda for middle level, reform issues, professionalism, history, philosophy, effectiveness, and organizational culture. The remainder of the bibliography contains references on topics that can be meaningfully arranged under the eight major Carnegie recommendations for "transforming middle grade schools" (Carnegie Council on Adolescent Development, 1989, p. 9). Where useful, citations were organized into subgroups of research, practical, and general for several of the topics.

The first two recommendations of *Turning Points*, 1. "School should be a place where close, trusting relationships with adults and peers create a climate for personal growth and intellectual development" (Carnegie Council on Adolescent Development, 1989, p. 37); and 2. "Decisions concerning the experiences of middle grade students should be made by the adults who know them best" (p. 54), are supported by topics including philosophy, early adolescent development, middle level programs, middle level administration, middle level facilities, interdisciplinary team organization, and advisor/advisee programs.

Philosophy. In an effort to highlight the broad overall features that make middle level education unique in meeting the needs of young adolescents, both classic and current pieces are included. Such common ground can serve as the focus for subsequent decisions of structure and content.

Early adolescent development. Articles in this extensive section bring home the rationale for middle level programs that address the unique cognitive, physical, social, emotional needs of this age group. Selected articles on gender issues are also included. A number of the research-based selections were developed under the auspices of the Center for Early Adolescence in Carboro, North Carolina. It is hoped that additional study of many of these sources will be the stimulus and grounding for future innovations in middle level programs.

Middle level programs. Entries in this section examine examples of middle level programs in action, curriculum issues, efforts to make the transition to a middle level program, organizational culture, school climate, and summer institutes.

Middle level administration. The importance of committed leadership in the successful implementation of a middle level program is the focus of articles in this section. Characteristics of effective leaders in middle level settings and the role of leaders in ensuring success are highlighted.

Middle level facilities. These references describe how such things as building design can support the implementation of middle level programs.

Interdisciplinary team organization. According to Totten and Snider (1994) interdisciplinary team organization "*constitutes the basic building block for effective middle level schools*" [italics in the original] (p. 8). Readers will find articles that address the process of using interdisciplinary teams and selected research on affective and academic outcomes.

Advisor/advisee. Identified as "one that creates a setting where all students are well known by at least one adult in a school" (Totten & Snider, 1994, p. 9), advisor/advisee programs stand as one of the unique middle level features that tries to build in developmental support for the emerging adolescent's search for identity. Articles reviewed include a small number of research articles examining attitudes and several resources that could be used to develop topics for advisory programs.

The third recommendation in *Turning Points*, 3. "Every student in the middle grades should learn to think critically through mastery of an appropriate body of knowledge, lead a healthy life, behave ethically and lawfully, and assume the responsibilities of citizenship in a pluralistic society" (Carnegie Council on Adolescent Development, 1989, p. 42) is supported by topics related to curriculum.

Core curriculum and other key subject areas. Standard subject-related divisions are used to organize the material as it applies to middle level settings. Many entries address implementation of standards established by such groups as the National Council for Teachers of Mathematics. Selections on whole language are also included.

Integrated curriculum. Efforts to get at concept development through the exploration of relationships between and among core subjects along with whole language applications are among the most widely tried learning strategies in middle level settings.

Behavior and classroom management. This topic occupies planning and classroom time for many teachers; articles in this section illustrate how the unique features of middle level programs can provide the context for implementing strategies to help students get along in groups. In recognition of the impact of affective issues on schooling during early adolescence, the section on behavior and classroom management strategies focuses on such affective outcomes as anger, and self-esteem. Motivational strategies for this age group are included. Affective issues are acknowledged to be central during the middle level years. The traditional issues of attendance, discipline, and retention are approached from the middle level point of view.

Exploratory and elective subjects. Giving early adolescents the opportunity to investigate possible interest areas in an atmosphere that according to Totten and Snider (1994) is supportive and fun is the intention of a good exploratory program. The selections in the section offer readers imaginative ways to bring students and teacher together to try out different knowledge bases and skills.

Social issues, community service, and service learning at the middle level. The annotations in this section demonstrate the capacity for collaboration that can be of mutual benefit for all those that participate. As partners in providing the opportunity for young adolescents to plumb the depths of their talents and capacity to contribute to improving the quality of life for those less fortunate, middle level schools and community agencies can collaborate in creative ways that will be of mutual benefit to participants

Topics related to organizational and pedagogical processes support the fourth *Turning Points* recommendation, 4. "All young adolescents should have the opportunity to succeed in every aspect of the middle grade program, regardless of previous achievement or the pace at which they learn" (Carnegie Council on Adolescent Development, 1989, p. 49).

Flexible and block scheduling. Key to giving teachers the freedom to determine the best way to individualize approaches that ensure success is the ability to determine schedules on a daily and weekly basis. Ideally decisions regarding such scheduling options would be left to those who work directly with the students, teachers, or teams of teachers.

Pedagogical issues and strategies. Annotations in this section address application of both standard and innovative approaches to instruction at the middle level. Among these are grouping, learning styles, metacognition, critical thinking, problem-solving, questioning strategies, constructivism, cooperative learning, interdisciplinary instruction, interdisciplinary units, portfolios, and learning centers.

Educational technology. The entries in this section focus on the use of such technologies as computers, calculators, and videos to achieve the academic outcomes in middle level settings.

Special needs. Included in this section are entries that describe approaches to working with at-risk, gifted and talented, and special education students at the middle level.

Multicultural issues/concerns. Entries in this section show how diversity issues can be incorporated using the unique features of middle level programs.

Assessment. Included in this section are references that describe methods of both individual and program evaluation. Innovative assessment methods, such as portfolios that are designed to showcase desired the unique outcomes of middle level experience, are highlighted.

Achievement. Of special concern are innovative ways to measure the special outcomes that result from a developmental focus in education at the middle level, such as those in the affective domain. Traditional outcome measures are also highlighted. Several of the research studies reviewed examine the effect of the key features of middle level programs on traditional outcome measures, such as cognitive achievement in the basic skills and

The fifth recommendation in *Turning Points*, 5. "Teachers in middle grade schools should be selected and specially educated to teach young adolescents" (Carnegie Council on Adolescent Development, 1989, p. 58), underscores the importance of teacher preparation and staff development for middle level educators.

Middle level teacher preparation issues. Articles annotated in this section provide a framework to consider the current issues of certification at the state level. Efforts by teacher preparation programs to carve out specific tracks in middle level education are profiled.

Middle level teacher inservice and staff development. A range of articles points out the need for ongoing staff development especially for settings that are in transition from traditional organizations to middle level. Students of change theory will be interested in some of the case reports of settings where the transition from traditional junior high programs to middle level programs was completed.

The need for interdisciplinary collaboration is underscored in *Turning Points* by the sixth recommendation. 6. "Improve academic performance through fostering health and fitness" (Carnegie Council on Adolescent Development, 1989, p. 9).

Counseling. The role of mental health professionals in supplementing the efforts of staff to make the middle level experience meaningful for the young adolescent is explored. Particular emphasis on the importance of support for the development of positive self-concepts and prevention of suicide is offered.

Health issues. Early adolescence is identified as a time of choicemaking regarding lifestyle or risk behaviors that can have profound influence on future health and development. Annotations included in this section incorporate a wide range of health risks faced by today's young adolescents that can be prevented with the development of strong interpersonal skills. Topics of general health, health education, sexuality issues, nutrition, safety, substance abuse, tobacco-related issues and school health services are profiled (Hechinger, 1992). Collaboration among professionals is necessary to reach the goals set forth in *Turning Points*; so for that reason articles from journals related to the health professions were reviewed.

The last two *Turning Points* recommendations involve the whole community in overseeing the development of young people: 7. "Families and middle grade schools must be allied through trust and respect if young adolescents are to succeed in school" (Carnegie Council on Adolescent Development, 1989, p. 66); and, 8. "Schools and community organizations should share responsibility for each middle grade student's success" (p. 70).

Family and community. Articles that focus on innovative methods for drawing on the resources of families and the community offer readers effective models to consider in their own settings.

Middle level resources: A final section on resources completes

the bibliographic entries. Items selected for annotation in the resource section
include organizations chartered to support the development of middle level
programs; state reports on efforts to implement middle level programs; journals,
both national, state, and regional; and newsletters of various organizations that
specifically address middle level issues.

References

Carnegie Council on Adolescent Development. Task Force on Education of
    Young Adolescents. (1989). *Turning points: Preparing American
    youth for the 21st century.* New York: Author.

Hechinger, F. M. (1992). *Fateful choices: Health youth for the 21st Century.*
    New York: Carnegie Corporation.

Totten, S., & Snider, D. (1994). Middle level education terms and concepts:
    Some confusions cleared up. *Mid South Middle Level Education
    Journal, 1*(1), 5-12).

I

General Issues

A. GENERAL - RESEARCH

1.   Belcher, H. L. (1982). An analysis of the development of middle grade education, 1880-1980 (Doctoral dissertation, University of Toledo, 1982). *Dissertation Abstracts International, 43,* 2214A.

Identifies factors including pressures and forces related to political, social, economic, and educational concerns that helped mold the philosophy, functions, structure, and curriculum of both the junior high school and middle school. Discusses five major conclusions about middle level education as determined by the study.

2.   Binko, J., & Lawlor, J. (1986). Middle schools: A review of current practices—how evident are they? *NASSP Bulletin: The Journal of Middle Level and High School Administrators,* 70(491), 81-87.

The authors describe the findings of a study they conducted during inservice sessions at four middle schools in which participating teachers and administrators were asked to use a Q-sort technique to rank 37 practices that had been deemed vital to middle level programs. They discuss their findings as well as the implications of such.

3.   Brown, J. G., & Howard, A. W. (1972). Who should teach at schools for the middle years? *The Clearing House,* 46(5), 279-283.

Reports the findings of a study designed to examine the perceptions of middle level administrators with regard to competencies, attitudes, characteristics, and academic background common to effective middle level teachers.

4.   Compton, M. F. (1983). Television viewing habits of early adolescents. *The Clearing House,* 57(2), 60-62.

Reports the results of a study designed to investigate the amount of time young adolescents spend in watching television. Concludes that the amount of time spent does not decline during adolescence.

5.   Epstein, J., & Mac Iver, D. J. (1990). *Education in the middle grades: Overview of national practices and trends*. Columbus, OH: National Middle School Association. 94 pp.

Education in the Middle Grades reports on a comprehensive survey conducted by the Center for Research on Elementary and Middles Schools at the Johns Hopkins University of 2400 middle level principals in regard to the degree that their schools had implemented programs that are frequently recommended for the middle grades. Among the components that were addressed in the survey and study are the following: between-class ability grouping, homeroom and advisory periods, teaming, curriculum, instruction, and remedial instruction. It concludes with a summary of practices and trends as well as an overall evaluation of programs. Not only are the findings fascinating and of great significance, but they are reported in a clear and concise manner.

6.   George, P. S., & Anderson, W. (1989). Maintaining the middle school: A national survey. *NASSP Bulletin: The Journal for Middle Level and High School Administrators*, 73(521), 67-74.

Discusses the findings of a survey (of 154 administrators who are reportedly leaders of some of the nation's best middle level programs) which asked the respondents to share the strategies they have used successfully to keep the middle level programs under their charge healthy, strong, and ongoing. The primary focus of the piece was on "maintenance strategies: implementation" (e.g., participatory decision making, leadership and philosophical vision, staff development, evaluation and public relations) and "maintenance strategies: post implementation" (awareness of vulnerability, networking, continual school improvement, vigilance, etc.).

7.   George, P. S., & Oldaker, L. L. (1985). *Evidence for the middle school*. Columbus, OH: National Middle School Association. 39 pp.

This booklet is comprised of two main parts: in Part I, "Research in Middle Level Education" ("A Review of Research Activities," "A New Research Strategy," and "Recent Research Findings"), George presents a brief overview of research efforts regarding middle level education. In this section he refers "outlier studies," or those studies whose focus is "on the careful scrutiny of the most successful examples of a subject that could be found, those that lay outside the boundaries of the mediocre.
          Outlier studies concentrate on attempting to learn what makes the best become the best. In Part II, "A Survey of the Effectiveness of Middle Level Schools" ("The Design of the Study," "Represen-tations of the Exemplary Middle School" and "Summary and Conclusions"), George and Oldaker describe and discuss a study they conducted of "130 middle schools which had been deemed particularly successful or exemplary." Among the key findings of the researchers is that "results indicate that middle schools which manage to receive a reputation as highly successful are very similar in terms of the components of

the program," i.e., team organization, teacher-based guidance activities, flexible use of time, faculty participation in decision making, and other tenets of the middle school concept.

8.   Gordon, J. S., Markle, G. C., Johnston, J. H., & Strahan, D. B. (1979). A Delphi study to determine needed middle school research. *Middle school research: Selected studies 1977-1979. Volume II* (pp. 49-57). Fairborn, OH: National Middle School Association.

The authors concluded that the participants (middle level teachers, middle level administrators, university personnel, and parents, all of whom were members of the National Middle School Association) in their study claimed that the greatest need for research was in the areas of staffing, appropriate curriculum, and scheduling. Also perceived as being direly needed was pre-service and inservice education for middle level personnel.

9.   Grant, R. (1987). A career in teaching: A survey of middle school teachers' perceptions with particular reference to the careers of women teachers. *British Educational Research Journal, 13*(3), 227-39.

Reports on a survey of teachers' perceptions of a school promotional system. Compares male/female status in education and comments upon the lack of women in higher level positions. The majority of female teachers see themselves as disadvantaged in the educational marketplace.

10.   Holifield, J. R. (1981). An analysis of junior high/middle school teachers' perception of factors affecting teacher job stress and principals' perception of ways to alleviate or manage teacher job stress (Doctoral dissertation, Ball State University, 1981). *Dissertation Abstracts International, 42,* 1401A.

Top two job stressors were caused by students. Two through ten job stressors included: uncooperative parents, maintaining self-control when angry, too much paperwork, lack of public faith and support, misunderstanding or misinterpretation resulting from ineffective communication, verbal abuse by students, too much time required on activities unrelated to actual teaching, and conflict of concurrent demands of home and job responsibilities. Includes methods principals use to relieve teacher stress and suggests methods for teachers to relieve their own stress.

11.   Hultsman, W. Z. (1992). Constraints to activity participation in early adolescence. *The Journal of Early Adolescence, 12*(3), 280-299.

"This study examined why early adolescents do not become involved in, or drop out of, organized recreation activities in which they have an interest or had previously been involved. The subjects were 940 fifth through eighth graders in a large metropolitan area of a southwestern state. Early adolescent involvement in new activities was perceived to be constrained by parents denying permission to join, lack of skills, and lack of transportation. Loss of interest, dislike for leaders, moving, and feeling too old were perceived reasons for ceasing participation. Results also suggested that early adolescents perceived constraints somewhat differently than do adults. Opportunities should capitalize on circumstances crucial to early adolescent development. Activity providers should focus marketing efforts on constraints identified by this age group as well as extolling the benefits and satisfactions derived from activities, to provide a continuity of challenge and interests as individuals move through various life stages."

12.   Irvin, J. A. (Ed.) (1992). *Transforming middle level education: Perspectives and possibilities*. Needham Heights, MA: Allyn and Bacon. 412 pp.

The express purpose of this volume is to synthesize an ever-increasing body of research vis-à-vis middle level education. The volume is comprised of four parts and twenty chapters: Part One. Chapter 1. Perspectives on the Middle School Movement by John H. Lounsbury; Chapter 2. A Portrait of Diversity: The Middle Level Student by Joe Milgram; Chapter 3. Young Adolescents' Perceptions of School by Linda R. Kramer; Chapter 4. Youth as Cultural and Economic Capital: Learning How to Be by J. Howard Johnston; Chapter 5. A New Paradigm of Schooling: Connecting School, Home and Community by Frances K. Kochan.
        Part Two. Developing a Sense of Responsiveness. Chapter 6. Climate and Culture as Mediators of School Values and Collaborative Behavior by J. Howard Johnston; Chapter 7. Developing a Sense of Mission in Middle Schools by Robert Shockley; Chapter 8. The Process of Change: Developing Effective Middle School Programs by Robert C. Spear; Chapter 9. Interdisciplinary Teaming and the Social Bonding of Middle Level Students by Joanne M. Arhar; Chapter 10. Teacher Advisory: The Fourth R by Neila A. Connors; Chapter 11. Exploratory Programs in the Middle Level School: A Responsive Idea; Chapter 12. Maintaining Middle Schools by James P. Garvin.
        Part Three: Developing a Sense of Relevance. Chapter 13. Middle Level School Curriculum: Defining the Elusive by Conrad F. Toepfer, Jr; Chapter 14. Appropriate Grouping Practices for Middle Level Students by Robert C. Spear; Chapter 15. Motivation: Moving, Learning, Mastering and Sharing by Julia Thomason and Max Thompson; Chapter 16. Developmentally Appropriate Instruction: The Heart of the Middle School by Judith L. Irvin; Chapter 17. Meeting the Needs of Young Adolescents Through Cooperative Learning by Karen D. Wood; Chapter 18. Humanizing Student Evaluation and Reporting by Gordon F. Vars.
        Part Four. Developing a Support System for Continued Improvement. Chapter 19. Middle Level Teacher Preparation and Certification by C. Kenneth McEwin; and, Chapter 20. Turning Points and Beyond: Coming of Age in Middle Level Research. Each of the twenty chapters in this volume is annotated separately in this bibliography.

13.   Irvin, J. L. (1992). A research agenda for middle level education: An idea whose time has come. *Current Issues in Middle Level Education*, *1*(1), 21-29.

In this piece Irvin, the editor of *Research in Middle Level Education* and a member of the National Middle School Association's Research Committee, provides a succinct overview of the history of research vis-à-vis middle level concerns, various efforts to disseminate research findings on the middle level, a description of various research studies regarding middle level concerns, and suggestions for setting a research agenda for the 1990s and beyond.

14.   Johnston, J. H., & Markle, G. C. (1986). *What research says to the middle level practitioner*. Columbus, OH: National Middle School Association. 103 pp.

A compilation of articles on research that originally appeared in the *Middle School Journal* between 1979 and 1989. All of the pieces constitute a summary of research rather than original research. The volume is comprised of three sections: I. Organization of the Middle School, II. Teaching Middle School Students, and III. Needed Research. Part I includes the following seven chapters: Middle Grade Organization, Effective Schools, Effective Middle Level Principals, Teacher Behavior, Teacher Thinking, Teacher Stress, and, Promotion & Retention.
        Part II includes fourteen chapters: Motivating Students; Classroom Management; Classroom Groups; Peer Relationships in the Classroom; Ability Grouping; Diagnostic Prescriptive Teaching; Classroom Time; Developing Problem Solving Skills; Critical Thinking; Attitude Development; The Teacher's Effect on Pupil Self-Concept and Related School Performance - Part I; Self Concept and School Performance - Part II; Instructional Questions; and Computer-Assisted Instruction. Many of the articles are far too short and lacking in depth to be really useful to the practitioner. Furthermore, many of the pieces are dated, and are—due to the fact that it was published in 1989 and no fault of the authors—bereft of key research which raises key questions about the earlier research.
        Finally, a great deal of new research has been published since 1989 on many of the aforementioned topics, and teachers and administrators would be wise to seek out that work in order to obtain that research which is on the "cutting-edge." As Johnston and Markle point out in their last section, "Needed Research," "unfortunately, the present 'state of the art' in middle school research is not well developed." That is still true today. While progress is certainly being made, there are still many key middle level components, programs and concerns that have not been addressed by researchers.

15.   Larson, R. W., & Richards, M. H. (1991). Boredom in the middle school years: Blaming schools versus blaming students. *American Journal of Education, 99*(4), 418-443.

The authors use time sampling data from 392 middle level (grades 5-9) students from working-class and middle-class suburbs of Chicago to show high rates of boredom within and outside of school. High boredom correlates with high ability and with oppositional behavior (when ability is controlled), but not with onset of adolescence.

16.   Lipsitz, J. (1990). *Successful schools for young adolescents*. New Brunswick, NJ: Transaction Books. 223 pp.

A highly regarded book in the field. Thomas Sergiovanni, for one, described this book as "...the most meaningful description of school effectiveness I've seen—a credit to quality research, qualitative research and a remarkably insightful writing style." In Part I ("Expanding the Definition of Effectiveness") Lipsitz presents a framework for examining successful middle-grade schools." In Part II ("Case Studies of Successful Middle-Grade Schools") she presents detailed and fascinating case studies of four different successful middle-grade schools (one in Alamance County, North Carolina; one in Detroit, Michigan; one in Louisville, Kentucky; and one in Shoreham, New York). Her conclusions in Part III ("Recurrent Themes in Successful Middle-Grade Schools") are particularly insightful and useful.

17.   Mac Iver, D. J. & Epstein, J. L. (1993). Middle grades research: Not yet mature, but no longer a child. *Elementary School Journal*, *93*(5), 519-533.

Provides a critique of the latest (as of 1992) research on various facets of middle level education. In doing so, the authors look at the following issues: grade span, school size and grade size, grouping and regrouping practices, departmentalized and semidepartmentalized staffing, curriculum and instruction, "responsive practices" (e.g., advisory groups, interdisciplinary teams, "extra help programs" for students who have fallen behind academically), transition and articulation practices, and projected trends in the areas of research and practice.

18.   Nafpaktitis, M., Mayer, G. R., & Butterworth, T. (1985). Natural rates of teacher approval and disapproval and their relation to student behavior in intermediate school classrooms. *Journal of Educational Psychology*, *77*(3), 362-367.

Results showed higher rates of approval of off-task behavior were associated with lower rates of on-task behavior. The lowest rates of teacher disapproval were associated with highest rates of student on-task behavior.

19.   Pedersen, J., & Totten, S. (1992). The status of middle schools in the state of Arkansas: A survey of superintendents and principals. *Current Issues in Middle Level Education*, *1*(2), 39-64.

Discusses a survey that the authors conducted, under the auspices of the Arkansas Middle Grade Policy and Practice Task Force, in order to assess the current status of middle level education in the State of Arkansas. The survey was sent to all superintendents and principals administering schools with grade levels five to nine. The authors state that the results of the survey suggest that schools in Arkansas are doing little in the way of program development for the transescent and there seems to be no plan at the present time by the majority of schools to move to a true middle level program/school. The authors suggest that steps must be taken with the state to provide training for administrators, teachers and parents in regard to middle level philosophy as well as how sound middle level programs are in meeting the needs of transescents. The appendix includes a copy of the survey used for the study.

20. Sierer, T. M. (1989). The concerns and attitudes of early adolescent middle school students in transition to high school. In David B. Strahan (Ed.), *Middle school research: Selected studies 1989* (pp. 30-46). Columbus, OH: Research Committee of the National Middle School Association.

In this study "a total of 192 eighth grade and 190 ninth grade students were surveyed to obtain information on attitudes toward the middle school experience and concerns of transition to high school. Results were factor analyzed and indicated such factors as need for self-direction, confidence about academic performance, friendship, belongingness in school, poor progress with schoolwork, general dislike of school, and positive attribution. Those students who experienced a difficult transition indicated lack of acceptance by both classmates and teachers as the primary cause for the inability to adjust. ANOVAs were used to test for effects of grade level, past perceived achievement (GPA), gender, and whether or not an older sibling attended the same school for each of the factors identified."

21. Sparapani, E. F., Abel, F. J., & Edwards, P. (1992). A survey of middle grades teaching. *Current Issues in Middle Level Education*, *1*(2), 7-28.

The authors discuss the results of a survey of middle level and junior high teachers located in four states of the eastern United States concerning their understanding of the middle level concept. Among the most disturbing findings are the following: Most teachers do not seem to understand the difference between a junior high school and a middle school, even though they believe middle schools are a more appropriate setting for the transescent; most teachers agree that transescents should be involved in community projects, but seldom seem to provide for such activities; and most teachers agree that a strong connection between parents and the school is important, but make few opportunities to get parents involved. The piece concludes with a set of recommendations. The appendix includes a copy of the survey used in the study.

22. Strahan, D. B. (1992). Turning points and beyond: Coming of age in middle level research. In Judith L. Irvin (Ed.), *Transforming middle level education: Perspectives and possibilities* (pp. 381-399). Needham Heights, MA: Allyn and Bacon.

In this piece Strahan discusses answers to the following questions in regard to research on middle level education: How does middle level research relate to the rest of education? What is the current status of research in the middle level zone? and How can we improve middle level research?

23. Thornburg, H. D. (1984). Middle level education: A researcher speaks. *Action in Teacher Education*, *6*(3), 65-72.

Thornburg surveyed the status of research on middle level education as it stood in the early- to mid- 1980s, and called for changes in teacher preparation for future middle level teachers as well as the development of middle level curricula based on the sociological implications of the aforementioned research.

24.   Van Zandt, L. M., & Totten, S. (1995). The current status of middle level education research: A critical review. *Research in Middle Level Education, 18*(3), 1-25.

This essay provides both a review of the research literature in middle level education as well as examines the breadth and depth (quantity and quality) of such research. In doing so, it discusses the early reviews of middle level education research, presents a review of selected middle level practices (e.g., interdisciplinary teaming, advisory groups, cooperative learning, interdisciplinary curriculum, exploratory curriculum, flexible/block scheduling), and concludes by providing recommendations for future research efforts.

B. GENERAL - PRACTICAL

25.   Carroll, J. H., & Christenson, C. N. (1995). Teaching and learning about student goal setting in a fifth-grade classroom. *Language Arts, 72*(1), 42-49.

Discusses the importance of goal-setting activities for middle level students. Lists several suggestions for language arts teachers to use in assisting their students with setting short- and long-term goals.

26.   Doda, N., George, P., & McEwin, K. (1987). Ten current truths about effective schools. *Middle School Journal, 18*(3), 3-5.

Ten reminders of what good teachers seem to instinctively understand. A good hand-out for discussion in a pre-teaching methods class. Items discussed include class size, class climate, teacher/student "quality" time, reward systems, teacher fellowship, active teaching, concrete lessons, humor, thinking big—but teaching small, and caring for students. The authors state that what works to make middle school effective is fairly clear and simple to implement.

27.   George, P. S. (1991). Student development and middle school organization: A prolegomenon. *Midpoints, 1*(1), 1-12.

In this paper, George discusses the various options open to educators as they go about developing and organizing their middle level program. "Looking at issues of supportive interpersonal structure and teacher subject specialization the author provides a model of student development and school organization." George goes on to say that "Such a model should be helpful in the design of new buildings and programs, in more effective deployment of teachers into various sorts of interdisciplinary collaboration, in the evaluation of middle level schools, and in prediction and solution of problems of the school which might be traceable to organizational roots."

28.   Hanson, M. (1992). *How to conduct a school recovery support group*. San Antonio, TX: ECS Learning Systems, Inc. 72 pp.

Appropriate for middle school and high school. Based on a 12-step concept, this book shows how to begin and run a recovery support group. Provides instructions, group session activities, explanation of relapse, ways to involve parents.

29.   Lawrence, J. R. S. (1995). Yellow school bus. *English Journal, 84*(2), 31-32.

A brief, but enlightening, article that offers suggestions for "surviving" the first year of teaching. Written by a middle level language arts teacher, the article will be helpful to first-year teachers in understanding that their experiences are common among novice teachers.

30.   Mayer, L. (1995). Bringing 'em up right: Making school transitions a success. *Schools in the Middle, 4*(4), 41-42.

Describes a program that uses early site visits and big brothers/big sisters to help middle level students move into high school.

31.   Mid-Continent Regional Educational Laboratory. (1990). *Young adolescents and middle level education: A review of current issues, concerns, and recommendations*. Aurora, CO: Mid-Continent Regional Educational Laboratory.

32.   Quattrone, D. F. (Fall 1990). Carnegie's middle school ideals: Phases of program development. *Journal of Curriculum and Supervision, 6*(1), 52-61.

Initially, Quattrone provides an overview and brief critique of Carnegie's report entitled *Turning Points* (including what he deems "competing priorities" in the report), and then he presents a plan of action in regard to how schools can implement the concepts found in *Turning Points* in an integrated versus a piecemeal fashion. Educators at all levels should find Quattrone's concerns and insights worthy of serious consideration.

33.   Stavro, S. (1993). Surviving the storm before the calm. *Middle School Journal, 24*(5), 60-62.

Offers a list of 20 practical suggestions for surviving the "storms" often encountered by middle level teachers.

C. GENERAL - GENERAL

34.   Alexander, W. M. (1984). The middle school emerges and flourishes. In John H. Lounsbury (Ed.), *Perspectives: Middle school education* (pp. 14-29). Columbus, OH: National Middle School Association.

Discusses the rationale for the development of middle level programs, the administrative problems and policies faced by the middle school movement, the growth of the middle level movement, and the organization of instruction in middle schools.

35.   Alexander, W. M. (1987). Toward schools in the middle: Progress and problems. *Journal of Curriculum and Supervision, 2*(4),314-329.

Discusses the following issues: a brief historical overview of the attempts by schools to develop programs to meet the unique needs of young adolescents, the key differences between a junior high and a middle school, the unique philosophy and programs of the middle level school, the current status of middle level programs vis-à-vis the development of exemplary middle level programs, and current problems that need to be addressed in order to strengthen the middle level movement.

36.   Alexander, W., & McEwin, C. K. (1986). Middle level schools—Their status and their promise. *NASSP Bulletin: The Journal for High School and Middle School Administrators, 70* (486), 91-95.

The authors discuss the status of middle level programs of 1986 and conclude by addressing the question "Are middle schools successful?"

37.   Arnold, J. (1990). *Visions of teaching and learning: 80 exemplary middle level projects.* Columbus, OH: National Middle School Association. 150 pp.

Organized by categories and subjects, this books presents descriptions of successful, ongoing middle level projects.

38.   Billings, R. L. (1977). Musts for a middle school. *The Clearing House, 49*(8), 377-379.

Reports the results of a study designed to gather data about criteria common to effective middle schools. Addresses issues such as scheduling and teaming.

39.   Bondi, J., & Wiles, J. (1986). School reform in Florida. *Educational Leadership, 44*(1), 45-46.

Tough Florida standards create problems for middle schools and raise dropout rates in high schools. Middle schools appear to be extensions of high schools, with pressure on teachers to prepare students for a college-bound curriculum.

40.   Brod, P. (1969). The middle school in practice. *The Clearing House, 43*(9), 530-532.

Discusses the unique characteristics of middle schools with an emphasis upon the role of counselors, philosophy of middle school movement, and methods of meeting the needs of young adolescents. Provides comparative data for readers interested in tracing the evolution of middle schools during the past several years.

41.   Capelluti, J., & Stokes, D. (Eds.). (1991). *Middle level education: Programs, policies, and practices*. Reston, VA: National Association of Secondary School Principals. 68 pp.

This booklet highlights exemplary projects and practices being implemented at the middle level. Topics include curriculum, evaluation, guidance, leadership, and organization.

42.   Center for Human Resources, The, Heller Graduate School, Brandeis University. (1990). *Future options education: "Not another handbook" handbook on how to help young people in the middle-grades aspire and achieve*. Waltham, MA: Author. 120 pp.

This guidebook was developed for the express purpose of of providing insights into the types of strategies that middle-grades teachers and schools could implement in order to stimulate young adolescents to pursue higher expectations, whether college, post-high-school training, or skilled jobs after high school graduation. The nine chapters of the guide are entitled as follows: 1. What is "Future Options Education?"; 2. The Core of Future Options Education; 3. Personalized Adult Attention; 4. Assessing Students; 5. The Future Options Plan; 6. Comprehensive Future Options Education Initiatives; 7. Organizing a Future Options Education Initiative; 8. "Selling" Future Options Education to Others; and 9. Evaluating Future Options Education Initiatives.

43.   Chiara, C., & Johnson, E. (1972). Is the middle school doomed for failure? *The Clearing House*, *46*(5), 288-292.

Traces the development of the middle level movement. Encourages middle level educators to examine the history of the junior high school and to apply knowledge gained from "past mistakes and victories" in the establishment and organization of middle level schools.

44.   Clark, S. N., & Clark, D. C. (1992). *Schools in the middle: A decade of growth and change*. Reston, VA: National Association of Secondary School Principals. 207 pp.

This volume is comprised of three main parts: Part 1. "Successful Middle Level Schools: What They Are and What They Could Be"; Part 2. "Middle Level Schools: Programs and Curriculum"; and Part 3. "Creating Responsive Middle Level Schools: School Restructuring and Leadership." All of the pieces that are included herein originally appeared in NASSP's *Schools in the Middle* newsletter. Among some of the more thought provoking pieces included herein are: "Four Climates of Effective Middle Level Schools," "Common Denominators in Effective Middle Schools," "Planning Gifted/Talented Middle Level School Programs: Issue and Guidelines," "Interscholastic Athletics and Middle Level Education: To Have or Not to Have?" "What Values Are We

Teaching, Should We Teach, at the Middle Level?" "Time on Task: Implications for Middle Level Instruction," "Staff Development Programs for Middle Level Schools," "Leadership in the Middle Level School: An Imperative for Excellence."

45.   Dickinson, T., & Butler, D. A. (1992). The things they bring with them. *Current Issues in Middle Level Education, 1*(1), 3-7.

In this thought provoking piece, the authors discuss what middle level teachers need to bring to class in order to effectively meet the unique needs of young adolescents. Among the "things" they suggest are the following: a sense of gritty determination to engender success for all their students; a desire to discover and try various methods in order to reach all of their students; a love of learning, knowledge, and their students; and a questioning attitude about self, purpose, process, etc. This is an excellent article that experienced teachers can use to refresh and refocus themselves and an outstanding one for future teachers to ponder as they consider whether or not they wish to teach young adolescents.

46.   Fibkins, W. L. (1985). What makes a middle school excellent? *Principal, 64*(4), 50-51.

Lists nine factors that set good schools apart from poor ones. Compares two middle schools cited for excellence by President Ronald Reagan and Secretary of Education Terrell Bell.

47.   Flinker, I., & Pianko, M. (1971). The emerging middle school. *The Clearing House, 46*(2), 67-72.

Discusses the unique needs of young adolescents and the attempt to meet those needs through middle schools. Addresses issues such as organizational structures and resistance to change.

48.   Fox, J. H., Jr. (1977). Middle school: Surviving, refining and growing in the future. In P. S. George (Ed.), *A look ahead* (pp. 17-24). Columbus, OH: National Middle School Association.

Examines several forces that affect middle level education. Specifically discussed are public skepticism, the need for a balanced curriculum, and the historical foundations of middle level education Also emphasizes the need for evaluation of middle school programs.

49.   Fullan, M. (1991). *The new meaning of educational change.* New York: Teacher's College Press. 416 pp.

Providing insights into the change process, this book recommends powerful strategies that make true improvement possible.

50.   Garvelink, R. H. (1974). The anatomy of a good middle school. *The*

Clearing House, *48*(2), 100-102.

Discusses the characteristics of effective middle level schools. Specifically discussed are the underlying philosophy of the middle school movement, curriculum issues, student-teacher relationships, and flexible scheduling.

51. George, P. (1988). Education 2000: Which way the middle school? *The Clearing House*, *62*(1), 14-17.

Discusses the future of the middle school movement by addressing the following issues: shifting social priorities and enrollments, co-curricular challenges, school building problems, grouping, advisor-advisee programs, and teacher education.

52. George, P. S. (1973). Unresolved issues in education for the middle years. *The Clearing House*, *47*(7), 417-419.

Discusses selected issues related to implementing and maintaining middle level schools.

53. George, P. S. (1983). Confessions of a consultant: Middle school mistakes we made. *Middle School Journal*, *14*(4), 3-6.

Discusses errors made in two areas: program development and program implementation. Program development problems include lack of teacher preparation for advisor-advisee programs. Interdisciplinary teaming should have been required. Differences between team teaching and team organization should have been clarified. Problems in program implementation included a need for more effective staff development, greater interaction between university and middle schools, and allowing middle school concepts to develop over time.

54. George, P. S. (1984). Middle school instructional organization: An emerging consensus. In John H. Lounsbury (Ed.) *Perspectives: Middle school education* (pp. 52-67). Columbus, OH: National Middle School Association.

Discusses how and why middle level school programs should be organized. In doing so, George discusses successful team organization as well as advisory groups and alternatives to age grouping.

55. George, P. S. (Ed.). (1977). *A look ahead*. Columbus, OH: National Middle School Association.

Features a collection of fifteen essays focusing on a variety of issues relevant to middle level education (present, past, and future). Written by nationally recognized middle level educators, the essays are categorized as follows: (1) Optimism, pessimism, and the future, (2) Issues and answers, (3) The people in the school, and (4) Curriculum and instruction. Although published in 1977, the book addresses many issues that remain at the forefront of middle level education.

56.   George, P. S., Stevenson, C., Thomason, J., & Beane, J. (1992). *The middle school—And beyond*. Alexandria, VA: Association for Supervision and Curriculum Development. 166 pp.

This volume, by four noted middle level education teacher educators and researchers, provides an overview of middle level education, a rationale as to the vital significance of middle level education in the lives of young adolescents, ideas on how to develop and implement sound middle level schools, and examples of successful programs. The book is comprised of seven chapters: 1. Toward the Middle School; 2. Teachers and Students: Relationships and Results; 3. Middle School Organization: Values Underlying Practices; 4. Middle School Organization: Practices Reflecting Values; 5. Letting Go: Visions of the Middle School Curriculum; 6. Middle School Leadership; and, 7. Beyond the Middle School.

57.   Georgiady, N. P. (1977). The middle school today—prologue or epilogue, pp. 75-81. In P. S. George (Ed.), *A look ahead*. Columbus, OH: National Middle School Association.

Discusses the number of middle level schools and the impact that they existence has had upon the educational community. Also stresses the need for appropriate professional development for administrators and faculty.

58.   Glickman, C. D. (1987). Unlocking school reform: Uncertainty as a condition of professionalism. *Phi Delta Kappan, 69*(2), 120-122.

The realization that no one knows the best way to effect school reform releases educators to explore the unknown and find solutions in progress which meet their own needs.

59.   Goerss, K. V., & Associates. (1993). *Letters from the middle*. Columbus, OH: National Middle School Association. 40 pp.

Written by practicing middle level educators as a guide to a future middle level teacher, this booklet provides advice, encouragement, and practical ideas for anyone who is preparing for and/or already teaching young adolescents. Written in the form of letters, the teacher/writers address such topics as: celebrating the middle, picturing the middle level teacher, words of wisdom about classroom discipline and self-discipline, homework, being an advisor, teaming, instructional strategies, cooperative learning, making parents partners and being a professional.

60.   Hornbeck, D. W., & Arth, A. A. (1991). 1990s: Challenge of the century for middle level educators. *NASSP Bulletin: The Journal for Middle Level and High School Administrators*, 75(536), 94-100.

The authors review significant developments in the middle level education movement and also issue challenges for consideration as well as suggestions for the future.

61.   Hough, D. (1995). The elemiddle school: A model for middle grades reform. *Principal, 74*(3), 6-9.

The author argues that schools that include both primary and middle grades may be better for preadolescents than middle or junior high schools.

62.   Huber, J. D. (1976). Reincarnation of the one room schoolhouse—The American middle school. *The Clearing House, 49*(3), 103-105.

An analysis of the middle school movement. Emphasis is upon philosophy, physical facilities, and instructional methods.

63.   Johnson, M. (Ed.) (1980). *Toward adolescence: The middle school years* (Seventy-Ninth Yearbook of the National Society for the Study of Education). Chicago: University of Chicago Press.

This book is comprised of a series of articles on middle grades education. Among the topics that are discussed are the needs of early adolescents, the ideal middle level program, cognition, the family of young adolescents, juvenile justice, and moral development of early adolescents.

64.   Klingele, W. E., & Siebers, R. J. (1980). The uncomfortable middle school. *The Clearing House, 53*(9), 412-414.

Discusses the philosophy of middle level education. Traces the historical development of middle level schools with an emphasis upon problems and solutions to those problems. Concludes that the middle level philosophy and practices may be desirable for all students, regardless of age and grade level.

65.   Koerner, T. (1989). Reform plans, and implications for principals discussed by the chairman of task force on education of middle grade students. *NASSP Bulletin: The Journal for Middle Level and High School Administrators, 73*(518), 64-75.

An interesting and wide-ranging discussion of the Carnegie report entitled *Turning Points*.

66.   Kohut, S., Jr. (1988). *The middle school: A bridge between elementary and secondary school*. Washington, DC: National Education Association. 32 pp.

A research-based report that presents an overview of what the middle school is, the type of curriculum and instructional practices that work best, the unique demands on the faculty and administrators, and methods for evaluating programs.

67.   Kuhlmann, J. (1992). Hiring the right teacher: Focus on the interview. *Schools in the Middle: Theory Into Practice, 2*(2), 19-21.

Discusses the importance of ascertaining whether a candidate for a middle level teaching position has the requisite interpersonal skills to work with young adolescents as well as a solid understanding of the needs of today's young adolescents.

68.   Lane, W. (1993). Strategies for incorporating humor into the school climate. *Schools in the Middle*, *2* (4), 36-38.

Discusses the need for making humor an integral part of a school environment. Specifically presented are practical suggestions for incorporating "fun" into faculty meetings. Success in making fun a part of each day at a middle school in Annandale, Virginia, has led to increased teacher morale and lower stress levels.

69.   Levine, D. U., Levine, R. F., & Eubanks, E. E. (1984). Characteristics of effective inner-city intermediate schools. *Phi Delta Kappan*, *65*(10), 707-711.

Examines four areas of reform efforts in four inner-city schools: organizational arrangements facilitating improved reading, emphasis on higher-order skills, emphasis on personal development, and high institutional expectations.

70.   Lewis, A. C. (Ed.). (1989). High Support [Special issue]. *High Strides*, *1*(3).

Explores the issues related to "caring" for young adolescents. Six articles included in the themed issue are "On Caring," "Climate, and Chance," "Five Big Cities Slated to Launch Creative Middle School Planning," "Teachers See Results as Advisors," "New Carnegie Report Targets Middle Grades as 'Last, Best Chance,'" "Care Teams: Safe Places to Talk about Scary Issues," "Becoming 'Adequate' in School and in Life," "Rescue Teams at Work a Robinson," and "Fixing the Heart as well as the Body." Includes thirty suggestions for showing support for urban young adolescents.

71.   Lewis, A. C. (Ed.). (1991). Diversity [Special issue]. *High Strides* *3*(4).

Includes eight articles with an emphasis on diversity in the classroom. Concepts discussed are a definition of "multi-cultural," implications for teacher education programs, case study of Harriet Tubman Middle School in Oregon, cooperative learning in an English as a Second Language classroom, and strategies for diminishing biases.

72.   Lewis, A. C. (Ed.). (1992). Barriers to reform [Special issue]. *High Strides*, *4*(3).

Investigates barriers that often hinder progress with an emphasis on testing, time, and student turnover. Also includes statistics on alcohol use, sexual behavior, and AIDS cases among young adolescents.

73.   Lounsbury, J. H. (1984). Epilogue—unfinished business: An agenda

for the next decade. In John H. Lounsbury (Ed.), *Perspectives: Middle school education* (pp. 169-175). Columbus, OH: National Middle School Association.

Suggests an agenda for the National Middle School Association for the decade spanning the mid-1980s to the mid-1990s. Among the suggestions are to seek the continued growth of the National Middle School Association, establish middle level programs in all schools that contain middle level grades, extend efforts to educate the general public about the nature of early adolescents, achieve recognition of both the humane and the academic responsibilities of middle schools, break the hammerlock of departmentalization as the sole basis for organizing the curriculum, secure leadership committed to the middle school in state departments of education, achieve distinctive middle grades teacher certification and teacher education in every state, and promote the involvement of parents in the development of improved middle level programs.

74.   Lounsbury, J. H. (1991). *As I see it.* Columbus, OH: National Middle School Association. 102 pp.

Written by a former editor of the *Middle School Journal* and a major figure/leader in the field of middle level education, this compilation of pieces was selected from his column, "As I See It," in the *Middle School Journal*. Among the eclectic array of pieces included herein are the following: "Moving the school in the middle from the bottom to the top"; "Just what should every early adolescent know?"; "Homework: Is a new direction needed?"; "The school as teacher"; "Interdisciplinary teaming—destination or way station?"; "The middle school—the exploratory school"; "Middle level education: Progress, problems, and promises"; and "What values are we teaching, should we teach, at the middle level?"

75.   Lounsbury, J. H. (1992). Perspectives on the middle school move-ment. In Judith L. Irvin (Ed.), *Transforming middle level education: Perspec-tives and possibilities* (pp. 3-15). Needham Heights, MA: Allyn and Bacon.

Provides a brief historical overview of the development of a "special" school for early adolescents. In doing so, Lounsbury addresses the following concerns: Why and how the junior high came to be, early developments and status of the junior high school, contributions of the junior high school, handicaps to the development of the junior high school, the emergence of the middle school, handicaps to the development of the middle school, and the future of the middle level movement.

76.   Lounsbury, J. H. (Ed.). (1984). *Perspectives: Middle school education.* Columbus, OH: National Middle School Association. 182 pp.

This volume, whose contributors constitute many of the most noted educators in the field of middle level education, contains a host of essays that present a solid overview of many different aspects of middle level education. The titles and authors of the fifteen chapters are: 1. Prologue" by John H. Lounsbury; 2. "The Junior High School: Successes and Failures" by George E. Melton; 3. "The

Middle School Emerges and Flourishes" by William M. Alexander; 4. "The Nature of Transescents" by Donald H. Eichhorn; 5. "The Functions of Middle Level Schools" by Gordon F. Vars; 6. "Middle School Instructional Organization: An Emerging Consensus" by Paul S. George; 7. "Balance in the Middle School Curriculum" by Mary F. Compton; 8. "Selecting Appropriate Instructional Strategies" by Alfred A. Arth; 9. "The Generics of Middle School Teaching" by Nancy Doda; 10. "Administering a Middle School" by Elliot Y. Merenbloom; 11. "Preparing Teachers for the Middle School" by C. Kenneth McEwin; 12. "Staff Development and In-Service Education" by Conrad F. Toepfer, Jr.; 13. "A Synthesis of Research Findings on Middle Level Education" by J. Howard Johnston; 14. "The Development of the National Middle School Association" by Winston Pickett; and, 15. "Epilogue — Unfinished Business: An Agenda for the Next Decade" by John H. Lounsbury. A majority of the chapters have been separately annotated and appear in this volume under the appropriate section/heading.

77.   Lounsbury, J. H., & Clark, D. C. (1990). *Inside grade eight: From apathy to excitement*. Reston, VA: National Association of Secondary School Principals. 168 pp.

"In March 1989, eighth grade students in 162 schools were shadowed for one day to examine eighth grade education from the student's point of view. *Inside Grade Eight* provides a snapshot of middle level education today and offers an agenda for middle level education for the 1990s."

78.   Lounsbury, J. H., & Johnston, H. J. (1988). *Life in the three six grades*. Reston, VA: National Association of Secondary School Principals. 144 pp.

The authors discuss the results of a shadow study of sixth graders across the nation. They report on what a sixth grader's school day is like, how programs for sixth grades differ, and how our knowledge of the nature and needs of sixth graders match the programs actually provided.

79.   Malinka, R. (1977). The middle school trends and trouble spots. In P. S. George (Ed.), *A look ahead* (pp. 49-60). Columbus, OH: National Middle School Association.

Includes the author's personal observation about emerging trends in middle level education, a discussion of concerns and potential problems, and suggestions for ensuring a bright future for middle level programs.

80.   Maynard, G. (1986). The reality of diversity at the middle level. *The Clearing House*, 60(1), 21-23.

Challenges middle level educators to consider the needs of young adolescents when organizing, planning, and implementing instructional programs and activities. Specifically addressed is the need to consider the diversity represented by middle level students.

81.   McEwin, C. K., & Thomason, J. (1989). *Who they are, how we teach: Early adolescents and their teachers*. Columbus, OH: National Middle School Association. 26 pp.

In this booklet, the authors examine the middle grades learner, characteristics of effective middle grade teachers, and implications for instruction. The authors stress the need to take into full recognition the developmental needs of young adolescents as teachers go about developing curriculum, choosing teaching and learning strategies, and implementing classroom instruction.

82.   McLesson, B., & Koval, M. (1993). Jackie Robinson Middle School: Providing for students in an urban setting. *Journal of the New England League of Middle Schools, 6* (3), 16-20.

A case study of Jackie Robinson Middle School, a magnet school in Milwaukee, Wisconsin. Specifically outlined is the organizational structure designed with the needs of the students as the first priority. Includes examples of interdisciplinary units and individualization through hands-on experiences, FAVE (Fine Arts and Vocational Education), and exploratory courses.

83.   Mills, R. F., & Pollack, J. P. (1993). Collaboration and teacher change in the middle school. *The Clearing House, 66*(5), 302-304.

Examines the unlimited possibilities for innovation if middle level teachers worked together cooperatively for educational change and reform. Provides data from one such collaborative effort by two middle school teachers. Claims that collaboration can be a challenging addition to teachers' professional lives.

84.   National Association of Secondary School Principals. (1987). *Developing a mission statement for the middle level school.* Reston, VA: Author. 46 pp.

Presents a "nuts and bolts" approach to developing a statement of purpose for a middle level program.

85.   National Association of Secondary School Principals. (1993).*Schools in the middle: A decade of growth and change.* Reston, VA.

A collection of thirty *Schools in the Middle* newsletters published between 1981 and 1990. Addresses a variety of topics relevant to middle level education.

86.   Oestreich, A. H. (1969). Middle school in transition. *The Clearing House, 44*(2), 91-95.

Discusses the organizational structure of middle schools. Provides useful data for tracing the development of middle schools.

87.   Pickett, W. (1984). The development of the National Middle School Association. In John H. Lounsbury (Ed.) *Perspectives: Middle school*

education (pp. 157-168). Columbus, OH: National Middle School Association.

Discusses the genesis of the National Middle School Association, the various stages it has gone through over the years and the impact that has had on the organization, and the benefits to the members of the organization.

88.   Pickett, W. D. (1982). The emergence of the National Middle School Association (Doctoral dissertation, East Tennessee State University, 1982). *Dissertation Abstracts International, 43,* 3241A.

Provides an historical record of NMSA during its first decade, critically analyzes the Association, and examines NMSA's past experiences in order to provide information concerning its future.

89.   Read, J. E., & Burkhardt, R. (1992). It's not just a job. *New Mexico Middle School Journal, 2,* 20-23.

Encourages middle level teachers to take advantage of opportunities to influence the direction of middle level education by becoming part of a learning community. Opportunities for service include becoming active in a professional organization, submitting an article to a professional journal, and making presentations at workshops.

90.   Russ, P. (1993). Partners in education: A university-middle school mentorship program. *The Clearing House, 66*(5), 285-287.

Discusses a partnership arrangement between Tulane University and Live Oak Middle School in New Orleans, Louisiana. Emphasizes the mutual benefits of such a partnership and presents suggestions for establishing and maintaining an active partnership.

91.   Sinks, T. A., et al. (1976). The middle school trend: Another look in the upper Midwest. *The Clearing House, 49*(2), 52-56.

Analyzes the early middle school movement in Illinois, Indiana, Iowa, Minnesota, Wisconsin, and Ohio. Focuses on organizational structures, curricular issues, and instructional strategies. Useful data for researchers interested in tracing the development of the middle school.

92.   St. Clair, R. (1984). In search of excellence at the middle level. *NASSP Bulletin: The Journal for Middle Level and High School Administrators, 68*(473), 1-5.

Compares and contrasts the U.S. Department of Education's criteria for excellent middle schools with the National Association of Secondary School Principals' criteria, and finds that there is a huge discrepancy.

93.   Steltzer, W. N., Jr. (1979). An orientation program for a middle school. *The Clearing House, 52*(9), 52-54.

Provides an overview of an orientation program for students entering middle level schools in the Avon Grove School District. Encourages parents and students to visit the school several times during the year preceding the actual time of enrollment. Offers suggestions for making a transition from an elementary school setting to a middle level setting.

94.   Stewart, W. J. (1976). What causes a middle school to be ineffective. *The Clearing House*, *49*(1), 23-25.

Examines the causes of failure for many middle schools and offers practical suggestions for addressing the problems.

95.   Swiger, J. R. (1987). A resource guide and tentative model for middle school implementation (Doctoral dissertation, Seattle University, 1987). *Dissertation Abstracts International, 48,* 1359A.

Reviews the literature dealing with the historical development of the middle school concept. Identifies appropriate procedures for the transition to middle school programs and includes a case study of a successful transition as an example.

96.   Tadlock, M., & LoGuidice, T. (1994). The middle school concept in small rural schools: A two year inquiry. *Middle School Journal, 26*(1), 3-6.

While there are positives for being small and rural, roadblocks to the implementation of middle level organizational components certainly exist. Specific solutions to several "roadblocks" arc suggested. The authors recommend more networking, improved technology, improved professional development of teachers, and an increase in resources.

97.   Taylor, E. E. (1992). The first year of RE: Learning at Laurel Central Middle School. *NASSP Bulletin: The Journal for Middle Level and High School Administrators*, *76*(541), 22-24.

A principal describes his middle school's involvement in the Coalition of Essential School's project and the successes that have resulted from such participation.

98.   Thomason, J. T., & Grebing, W. (1990). *We who laugh, last.* Columbus, OH: National Middle School Association. 58 pp.

A collection of humorous incidents and stories from the middle level with contributions from middle level educators from across the nation. Aside from simply being humorous, staff developers and teacher educators could use various anecdotes from this booklet in order to highlight particular points about the needs of young adolescents, teaching young adolescents, etc.

99.   Toepfer, C. F., Jr., Lounsbury, J. H., Arth, A. A., & Johnston, J. H. (1986). What we wish people knew about middle level education [Special

issue]. *The Clearing House, 60*(1).

A special issue devoted to middle level issues. Begins with an editorial directed
to parents and educators to create an awareness of selected key issues. Includes
articles on a wide range of topics with an emphasis on meeting the diverse needs
of young adolescents.

100.   Totten, S., & Snider, D. (1994). Middle level terms and concepts:
Some confusions cleared up. *Mid South Middle Level Education Journal, 1*(1),
5-12.

The authors discuss the fact that many middle level terms and concepts are
misused by various parties when discussing middle level education. They then
set out to examine the misconceptions as well as provide correct
definitions/descriptions of key terms and concepts. Among the terms and
concepts they address are: middle school, middle level, and middle grades; early
adolescent and young adolescent; interdisciplinary team organization;
advisor/advisee; flexible/block scheduling; exploratory; and cooperative
learning.

101.   Trubowitz, S. (1986). Stages in the development of school-college
collaboration. *Educational Leadership, 43*(5), 19-21.

Lists and discusses the following stages: Hostility and skepticism, lack of trust,
period of truce, mixed approval, acceptance, regression, renewal, and continuing
progress. Emphasizes that the process of a school and college working together
is one of constant change.

102.   *Turning Points: State Network News* . (1992). Special Issue: Middle
Grade Reform at Turning Points, *3*(1).

Discusses the status of middle grade reform in the United States as of October
1992.

103.   Vars, G. F. (1984). The functions of middle level schools. In John H.
Lounsbury (Ed.), *Perspectives: Middle school education* (pp. 39-51). Columbus,
OH: National Middle School Association.

Discusses the differences between the various functions of junior high school
and middle schools as espoused in various publications on the education of
intermediate students. Vars concludes that "most recent proposals are found
wanting, hence the call for renewed attention to all the functions that were first
synthesized by William T. Gruhn in 1940."

104.   Watland, A. E. (1988). Professionalism and job satisfaction
perceptions of middle school teachers in Alaska, Norway, and Wales. *The
Clearing House, 61*(8), 358-362.

Focuses on teacher professionalism. Argues that all teachers, regardless of ethnic background and heritage, view teaching as a profession. Also discusses the relationship between professionalism and job satisfaction.

105.   Wavering, M. J. (Ed.). (1995). *Educating young adolescents.* New York: Garland Publishing, Inc.

A volume of fifteen chapters covering general concepts of middle level programs (philosophy, leadership, organization, and teacher characteristics), general characteristics of young adolescents (growth and development) and key components of middle level programs (core and exploratory curriculum; advisor-advisee; and community service).

106.   Whisler, J. S. (1990). *Young adolescents and middle level education: A review of current issues, concerns, and recommendations.* Aurora, CO: Mid-continent Regional Educational Laboratory (McREL). 34 pp.

This monograph addresses a host of concerns, including, but not limited to, problems faced by today's adolescents, characteristics of the young adolescent (physical, intellectual, emotional/psychological, social, moral and ethical development), meeting young adolescents' developmental needs, general recommendations for middle level education, and characteristics of effective middle schools.

107.   Wiles, J. W. (1977). The middle school: Issues and action plans. In P. S. George (Ed.), *A look ahead* (pp. 61-66). Columbus, OH: National Middle School Association.

Discusses critical needs related to middle level education. Identified needs include bridging the gap between theory and practice, applying appropriate and practical implementation strategies, and developing an effective evaluation system.

108.   Wiles, J., & Bondi, J. (1986). *Making middle school work.* Reston, VA: Association of Supervision and Curriculum Development.

Discusses characteristics of effective middle schools. Includes practical suggestions for developing and implementing middle level programs. Also includes numerous examples of forms and letters that can be adapted by middle level educators and administrators for use in their own settings.

109.   Williams, G. L. (1972). The middle school reform in Italy. *The Clearing House*, *46*(4), 245-249.

Describes the Italian middle level system as it made a successful transition from independent vocational and academic schools to a consolidated organizational structure. Also discusses the effects of the change upon the high school system.

II

Philosophy of Middle Level Education

110.   Eichhorn, D. H. (1987). *The middle school.* Columbus, OH: National Middle School Association. 116 pp. [Originally published in 1966.]

A classic in the field and grounded in Piagetian development, *The Middle School* advances "the idea that the basis of this 'new school' should be the intellectual development or readiness of its client, the young adolescent. While an accepted concept today, this was a major statement of school philosophy in 1966 when the text was first published. More than a historical document from the 1960's, *The Middle School* remains a visionary blueprint of educational reform." Among the issues it addresses are physical growth, mental growth, cultural forces, middle school environment, guidance services and activities, and administration.

111.   Irvin, J. L., Valentine, J. W., & Clark, D. C. (1994). Essential elements of a true middle school: What should be vs. what is. *Middle School Journal,* *26*(1), 54-58.

Acknowledges that middle level education has come of age and developed a unique identity, yet states that much is yet to be accomplished. Lists ten essential elements for a true middle school and discusses status and need for improvement of each.

112.   National Middle School Association. (1992). *This we believe.* Columbus, OH: Author. 40 pp.

This booklet provides the philosophical foundation in regard to why educators need to create schools that are developmentally responsive to young adolescents. Among the issues it addresses are the rationale of the middle school, characteristics of young adolescents, and definitions of a middle school.

III

Early Adolescent Development

A. EARLY ADOLESCENT DEVELOPMENT - RESEARCH

113.   Becker, H. J. (1987). *Addressing the needs of different groups of early adolescents: Effects of varying school and classroom organizational practices on students from different social backgrounds and abilities* (Report No. 16). Baltimore: Johns Hopkins University, Center for Research on Elementary and Middle Schools.

114.   Boulton, M. J. (1992). Participation in playground activities at middle school. *Educational Research, 34*(3), 167-182.

Eight and 11-year-old children's playground behavior was studied using direct observation techniques. Older children spent more time playing rule games compared to younger children who spent significantly more time playing alone. A second study explored the feelings of children who were excluded from play groups. Older boys seemed to be responsible for segregated (by age and sex) play on the playground.

115.   Dornbusch, S. M., Petersen, A. C., & Hetherington, E. M. (1991). Projecting the future of research on adolescence. *Journal of Research on Adolescence, 1*(1), 7-17.

Highlights recent major trends in research on adolescence and offers suggestions for needed studies. Suggested studies include 1) the influence of biology especially reproductive change processes, 2) qualitative work on the influence of the environment, 3) developmental trajectories of different subgroups, 4) more longitudinal studies, 5) influence of community factors on adolescent adjustment, and 6) evaluation of programs and interventions.

116.   Feldmann, S. S., & Elliott, G. (1990). *At the threshold: The developing adolescent.* Cambridge, MA: Harvard University Press. 642 pp.

Another of the many projects supported by the Carnegie Corporation of New

York, this edited volume provides a picture of the developing adolescent in multiple contexts including families, peer groups, schools, leisure, and work. The editors candidly point out that by highlighting research that summarizes what is known about adolescents, the variability of their experiences is muted. The review of research begins with a grounding in the profound physiological changes of puberty that are eventually interpreted in a cultural context. In the section on adolescent thinking, the authors remind readers that development occurs in many realms simultaneously creating a "complex web" (p. 89).

Part Two emphasizes the importance of context in influencing adolescent development. The chapter on schools found a paucity of research that would justify the current movement toward middle schools. A major strength of the volume is the identification of areas needing further research. In particular the review of research on contexts uncovered a lack of information on leisure time and the influence of neighborhoods and communities.

Part Three examines several of the key psychosocial issues of adolescence including family and peer relationships, motivation and achievement, sexuality, identity development, and coping. In an outstanding chapter on adolescent health, the authors make a strong case for examining the mortality and morbidity of adolescents from "preventable social, environmental, and behavioral factors" (p. 433) including accidents, suicide, homicide, substance abuse, sexual activity, and sexual abuse. Interestingly, mental health needs are one of the highest health concerns of this age group. Overall the reference supports the need for comprehensive approaches to supporting developing adolescents in their passage to adulthood rather than isolated, single focus interventions.

117.   Garrod, A. (Ed.). (1993). *Approaches to moral development : New research and emerging themes*. New York: Teachers College Press.

A collection of essays examining issues related to moral development of children, adolescents, and young adults with a focus on age- and gender-related perspectives.

118.   Hillman, S. B., Wood, P. C., Becker, M. J., & Altier, D. T. (1990). Young adolescent risk-taking behavior: Theory, research and implications for middle schools. In Judith L. Irvin (Ed.), *Research in middle level education: Selected studies 1990* (pp. 39-50). Columbus, OH: National Middle School Association.

In this piece the authors discuss risk-taking behavior and developmental issues of early adolescence as well as ways in which middle school administrators and teachers can develop and implement curricular changes to meet the needs of adolescents.

119.   Jones, J. P. (1992). Using realistic fiction to enhance social decision making in middle grades students (Doctoral dissertation, University of North Carolina at Greensboro, 1992). *Dissertation Abstracts International, 53*, 3163A.

Students read six novels and compared characters' decisions to their own using a systematic decision making model. Data analysis indicated growth toward a systematic approach to decision making and an increased awareness of consequences. Eighty-six percent of students thought realistic fiction was a good consultant source for difficult social decisions.

120.   Lerner, R. M. (1993). *Early adolescence: Perspectives on research, policy, and intervention.* Hillsdale, NJ: Lawrence Erlbaum Associates, Inc. 552 pp.

"This volume brings together a broad group of scholars from a diverse array of disciplines—behavioral health, child and adolescent development, communications, counselor education, economics, family studies, health education, marketing, nursing, occupational studies, policy, psychology, and sociology. Each writes integratively about cutting-edge research issues pertinent to various facets of the study of early adolescence.
        All contributors speak to the idea of interdisciplinary integration as a means of advancing knowledge in particular focus areas of early adolescence; all approach their topic with an orientation to integrating levels of organization. In so doing, they testify to the importance of two interrelated integrations—multidisciplinary and multiprofessional—for furthering understanding of young adolescents. Their aim is to show the actual and potential integration of the research base with issues of policy intervention. Accordingly, all authors are committed to making their presentations useful for this tripartite audience."

121.   Lerner, R., Petersen, A. C., & Brooks-Gunn, J. (1991). *Encyclopedia of adolescence. Volume I (A-L) and Volume II (M-Index).* New York: Garland Publishing. 601 pp. and 620 pp., respectively.

A massive and impressive work which provides authoritative articles on a wide array of subjects/topics vis-à-vis various cognitive, social-emotional, and physical concerns.

122.   Lewis, M. E. R. (1988). A description of eight shy middle school students (Doctoral dissertation, University of Florida, 1988). *Dissertation Abstracts International, 49,* 3604A.

Shyness is a universal problem and affects more than half the students of middle school age. Twelves themes emerged from data: reluctance to initiate, low visibility, inhibited body language, obedience, introverted behavior, irrational self-perceptions, social anxiety, self-consciousness, a distrust of strangers, minimal risk-taking, a need for clarity, and inadequate social skills. Offers suggestions for modifying behaviors.

123.   Lipsitz, J. (1977). *Growing up forgotten: A review of research and programs concerning early adolescence.* Lexington, MA: D. C. Heath, Lexington Books. 267 pp.

Review of the research on schools and the young adolescent prior to 1977.

Identifies the misfit between knowledge about the developmental needs of early adolescents and school configurations. Includes a section on the early development of middle schools and the lack of a research base demonstrating effectiveness. Strong emphasis on organizing school settings and strategies based on developmental needs. Longitudinal studies with consideration of gender and cultural influences were highly recommended. A key concept of the works reviewed revealed high variability of young adolescents especially regarding physical changes of puberty.

124.   McGurk, H. (Ed.) *Childhood social development: Contemporary perspectives*. Hillsdale, NJ: Lawrence Erlbaum Associates, Inc. 256 pp.

"Bringing together work by an eminent group of British and American developmental psychologists, this volume provides an account of research in action and debate in progress in a selection of areas of childhood social development where significant progress is underway. Addressing issues in social development from infancy to adolescence, topics examined include interactions between biological and social factors in sex role and social development, the development of friendships and peer relationships, the role of peer interaction in social and cognitive development, and the influence of cultural artifacts in the social and cognitive development of children."

125.   National Research Council [U.S.]. Panel to Review the Status of Basic Research on School-Age Children. (1984). *Development during middle childhood: The years from six to twelve*. In W. Andrew Collins, (Ed.). Washington, DC: National Academy Press.

Summarizes research in several developmental areas of childhood including physical, cognitive, and self-understanding as well as environmental contexts of the family, peers, and the school. Includes a chapter on cross-cultural perspectives. Recommendations for research are given in the areas of social relationships and competence.

126.   Petersen, A. C. (1993). Presidential address: Creating adolescents: The role of context and process in developmental trajectories. *Journal of Research on Adolescence, 3*(1), 1-18.

Provides support for the current lines of research on adolescence emphasizing the need for more complex models to explain behavior. Highlights the influence of cultural context on risk behavior. Recommends research on interventions delivered early enough to prevent or delay experimentation in risk behavior.

127.   Shrum, W., Cheek, Jr., N. H., & Hunter, S. McD. (1988). Friendship in school: Gender and racial homophily. *Sociology of Education, 61*(4), 227-239.

Examined similarity among peers, with respect to race and gender. The relationship between homophily and grade increased racially from elementary to middle school and decreased from middle school onward. Gender homophily remained stable earlier and then decreased from middle school onward. Reinforced theories that the middle school years can be an important time in shaping social attitudes.

128. Simmons, R. G., & Blyth, D. A. (1987). *Moving into adolescence: The impact of pubertal change and school context.* New York: Aldine de Gruyter. 441 pp.

"The purpose of the book is to study the transition from childhood into early and middle adolescence in order to investigate change along a wide variety of psychosocial dimensions with a particular focus on the self-image" (p. 3). The book describes a five year longitudinal study of 621 children in Grade 6. Independent variables were age, gender, pubertal timing and timing of school transition. Seventy dependent variables in the following five categories were measured: establishing self-image, intensifying peer relationships, establishing independence, planning for the family, and dealing with conformity/deviance issues. Identified types of children at risk during the period of early adolescence including "girls, students experiencing many life changes simultaneously (including early developing girls), children who are allowed earlier independence from parents, children who have been victimized by peers, and children with certain disadvantages prior to the transition" (p. 359). Although children in the sample were not in middle schools, several grade configurations, were present (K-6 and K-8). Authors were supportive of middle school configurations stating that "an earlier transition would be easier for children, especially if they are smaller in size than the usual junior high school" (p. 358). Stressed the need to research outcomes related to size of school and early transition.

129. Smulyan, L. (1986). Adolescence in theory and practice: A key to understanding middle level students. *The Clearing House, 60*(2), 53-55.

Reports the results of a study designed to examine theories of young adolescence in the context of a middle-level English classroom. Findings indicate that gender differences and self-identity have a significant impact upon students' responses.

130. Susman, E. J., Feagans, L. V., & Ray, W. J. (Eds.). (1992). *Emotion, cognition, health, and development in children and adolescents.* Hillsdale, NJ: Lawrence Erlbaum Associates.

A small volume on the behavioral aspects of health promotion. Based on "a conference on emotion and cognition as antecedents and consequences of health and disease processes in children and adolescents" (p. 1). Contains useful chapters on the emerging field of health behavior research; risk-taking in adolescents; ego development of adolescents with diabetes; and development of concepts of wellness, illness, health, and disease. A research-based volume of interest to health professionals who work with adolescents.

131. Williams, M. M. (1992). How a value is treated in middle schools:

The early adolescents' perspective (Doctoral dissertation, Boston University, 1992). *Dissertation Abstracts International*, *53*, 3518A.

This study investigated how the teaching and learning of the moral value, respect for others, occurred in sixth, seventh, and eighth-grade classrooms in three types of schools: inner city, suburban, and private. Students, teachers, parents, and administrators were surveyed, observed, and interviewed to determine how respect for others was treated. Little difference was found in the way respect for others was taught across schools, yet large differences were found in the way it was taught within schools in different classrooms. Respect for others was not learned well by students taught formally. Respect was learned best through modeling, quality teaching, and a positive moral climate. The role of the teacher appeared to be very important in creating and maintaining a positive moral climate in the classroom.

132.   Winegar, L. T., & Valsiner, J. (Eds.). (1992). *Children's development within social context*. 2 volumes. Hillsdale, NJ: Lawrence Erlbaum Associates, Inc. 224 pp. and 288 pp., respectively.

Volumes I of this two volume set is subtitled "Metatheory and Theory." Volume II is subtitled "Research and Methodology." "These companion volumes bring together research and theoretical work that addresses the relations between social context and the development of children. They allow for the in-depth discussion of a number of vital meta-theoretical, theoretical, and methodological issues that have emerged as a result of increased investigation in these areas. For example: Which methodological and statistical procedures are appropriate and applicable to studies of social context and processes of development? Should the nature of social context be reconceptualized as something more than different levels of some social independent variable? Are theories of development that do not consider social context incomplete?"

B. EARLY ADOLESCENT DEVELOPMENT - PRACTICAL

133.   Compton, M. F. (1977). Physical needs of students and the future of the middle school. In P. S. George (Ed.), *A look ahead* (pp. 105-115). Columbus, OH: National Middle School Association.

Argues for increased attention to unique physical needs of young adolescents. Includes a brief history of the medical science model and its impact upon educational systems.

134.   Eichhorn, D. H. (1984). The nature of transescents. In John H. Lounsbury (Ed.), *Perspectives: Middle school education* (pp. 30-37). Columbus, OH: National Middle School Association.

Discusses the physical and cognitive characteristics of transescents and then discusses the implications they have for curriculum and instructional concerns.

135.   Garvin, J. P. (n.d.). *Learning how to kiss a frog—Advice for those who*

work with pre- and early adolescents. Topsfield, MA: New England League of Middle Schools.

Highly acclaimed, this book presents a clear explanation of the unique characteristics of early adolescence.

136. Heath, S. B., & McLaughlin, M. W. (1991). *Identity and inner-city youth*. New York: Teachers College Press.

Discusses the importance of neighborhood organizations in assisting young adolescents in building self-esteem and positive outlooks. Addresses issues of collaboration among organizations, roles of gangs, historical roles of gender and ethnicity, and frameworks used by adolescents to construct self-identity.

137. Hill, J. P. (1980). *Understanding early adolescence: A framework.* Carroboro, NC: Center for Early Adolescence. 52 pp.

"This guide to the age group helps the reader to see young adolescents in their daily environment—family, school, peer group, and community. The vital set of developmental tasks and changes that young adolescents work through in each of these settings is also discussed."

138. Manning, M. L. (1993). Cultural and gender differences in young adolescents. *Middle School Journal, 25*(1), 13-17.

Synthesizes the findings of studies designed to investigate cultural and gender differences of young adolescents. Focuses on culture and friendship patterns, cultural and identity development, and gender and sex roles attitudes and behaviors. Includes ten suggestions for utilizing differences among young adolescents as strengths upon which to base learning experiences.

139. Presseisen, B. (1982). *Understanding adolescence: Issues and implications for effective schools*. Philadelphia, PA: Resources for Better Schools. 60 pp.

Presseisen delineates the nature of adolescence as it relates to the implications for educational practice, particularly effective schooling.

140. Scales, P. C. (1991). *Portrait of young adolescents in the 1990s*. Carrboro, NC: University of North Carolina at Chapel Hill, Center for Early Adolescence.

Provides a statistical and developmental profile of today's 10 to 15 year olds in the areas of "health status, family lives, education, and experience in the community" (p. 2) to help people develop more responsive policies and programs. Summarizes the developmental needs as "positive social interaction with adults and peers; structure and clear limits; physical activity; creative expression; competence and achievement; meaningful participation in families, schools, and communities; and, opportunities for self-definition" (pp. 13-14). Examines program and policy implications for the healthy development of young adolescents. Includes an excellent summary of previous reports on adolescent development.

141.   Sheiman, D. L., & Slonim, M. (1988). *Resources for middle childhood: A sourcebook*. New York: Garland Publishing Co. 138 pp.

Provides introductory essays and annotated bibliography of resources for the following topics related to children ages six to 12: physical, psychosocial, and cognitive development; family interactions; play; peer relationships; schooling; and the societal impact on middle childhood. The resource should be of interest to both parents and teachers. Contains many references from the popular press that are suitable for parents.

C. EARLY ADOLESCENT DEVELOPMENT - GENERAL

142.   Children's Defense Fund. (1991). *The adolescent and young adult fact book*. Washington, DC: Author. 164 pp.

"This comprehensive reference on America's 10- to 24-year old details: family income, education of parents, where youths live, family types, health status, mortality, causes of death, school enrollment, educational attainment, sexual activity, child-bearing, family formation, employment and earnings, drug and alcohol use, crimes and victimization, and far more."

143.   Eichorn, D. H. (1977). Middle school learner characteristics: The key to alternative programs. In P. S. George (Ed.), *A look ahead* (pp. 88-104). Columbus, OH: National Middle School Association.

Emphasizes the need for middle level programs to be student-centered by eliminating conditions that hinder the learning process for young adolescents. Specifically compares the graded-age model with the developmental grouping model.

144.   Johnston, J. H. (1992). Youth as cultural and economic capital: Learning how to be. In Judith L. Irvin (Ed.) *Transforming middle level education: Perspectives and possibilities* (pp. 46-62). Needham Heights, MA: Allyn and Bacon.

In this chapter Johnston discusses the following issues: socialization of youth, children as resources/liabilities, the school's role in socialization, membership in the social group, learning to work, social heterogeneity and urbanization, collaboration and collective action,

145.   Kaplan, L. J. (1984). *Adolescence, the farewell to childhood*. New York : Simon and Schuster. 400 pp.

A psychoanalytic narrative on the period of adolescence em-phasizing the "life-history approach" (p. 19). Examines the "major historical issues surrounding the significance of the adolescent phase in the evolution of human morality" (p. 18) and the "unique dilemmas and innovative solutions of adolescence" (p. 18).

146.   Kramer, L. R. (1992). Young adolescents' perceptions of school. In Judith L. Irvin (Ed.) *Transforming middle level education: Perspectives and possibilities* (pp. 28-45). Needham Heights, MA: Allyn and Bacon.

In her essay, Kramer discusses such issues as (1) the kinds of teachers young adolescents prefer, (2) how perceptions of teacher attitudes influence student behavior, (3) students' interpretations of instructional processes, and (4) students' definitions of the ideal learning environment. The chapter is based on selected research studies and interviews conducted by the author with young adolescents across five states. Woven throughout the chapter are the words and insights of the young adolescents Kramer interviewed.

147.   Lefstein, L. M., & Lipsitz, J. (1986). *Programs for young adolescents*. Carrboro, NC: Center for Early Adolescence. 173 pp.

A catalog of 27 programs across the United States that have been found to be particularly successful for youth workers and program planners searching for models of effective out-of-school programming for young adolescents. These high-quality programs effectively respond to the developmental needs of 10- to 15-year olds and encompass a variety of settings. Ideas about program planning, fundraising, publicity, inservice training, facilities, program evaluation, and staffing are also offered.

148.   Lefstein, L. M., Kerewsky, W., Medrich, E. A., & Frank, C. (1982). *Young adolescents at home and in the community*. Carrboro, NC: Center for Early Adolescence. 92 pp.

This monograph provides an indepth examination of the issue of afterschool care for young adolescents. Among other concerns, the essays address the need for services that respond to the developmental needs of the age group, governmental youth policy, and effective afterschool programs for young adolescents.

149.   Lipsitz, J. (1986). *After school: Young adolescents on their own*. Carrboro, NC: Center for Early Adolescence. 86 pp.

This report examines the policy implications of the so-called latchkey issue and its effects on the age group known as early adolescents. It also discusses public policy initiatives that have addressed public responsibility for adolescent socialization, current government policies that either enhance or impede healthy growth of young adolescents, and possible options for the future.

150.   Martin, T. (1993). "Turning Points" revisited: How effective middle-grades schools address developmental needs of young adolescent students. *Journal of Health Education, 24*(Suppl. 6), 24-27.

Comments on how schools can help address student needs for "diversity, self-exploration and self-definition, meaningful participation in school and community, positive social interaction with both peers and adults, physical activity, competence and achievement, and structure and clear limits" (p. 24). Reiterates the recommendations found in Turning Points.

151.   McEwin, C. D., & Thomason, J. T. (1989). *Who they are—How we teach: Early adolescents and their teachers*. Columbus, OH: National Middle School Association.

Discusses the characteristics (intellectual, physical, emotional, and social) of middle level students. Also discusses the characteristics of effective middle level teachers and implications of teacher/student characteristics upon instruction and curriculum.

152.   Milgram, J. (1992). A portrait of diversity: The middle level student. In Judith L. Irvin (Ed.), *Transforming middle level education: Perspectives and possibilities* (pp. 16-27). Needham Heights, MA: Allyn and Bacon.

Discusses the unique physical, social, and emotional characteristics of young adolescents as well as key concerns regarding their cognitive development.

153.   Moyer, D. H. (1976). Aggressive and delinquent adolescent behavior patterns: Effective curriculum adjustments in the middle school. *The Clearing House*, *49* (5), 203-209.

Focuses upon two types of adolescent behavior, aggressive and delinquent. The author offers suggestions for addressing these problems through developing and implementing curriculum relevant to the needs of young adolescents.

154.   Phelps, P. H. (1991). The middle child and the middle level student: Kindred spirits. *Becoming*, 2(2), 13-15.

Compares the characteristics and feelings of a middle child in a family with those of a middle level student. Specifically discussed are the following commonalities: desires to be needed, displays a facade of toughness, competes for attention, often feels trapped, experiences self-doubt, exhibits sensitivity to issues of fairness, seeks structure, and desires a personal identity.

155.   Ricken, R. A. (1985). *Love me when I'm most unlovable: The middle school years*. Reston, VA: National Association of Secondary School Principals. 24 pp.

A collection of prose and poetry written by early adolescents. Provides insights into their unique thoughts and feelings.

156.   Ricken, R. A. (1987). *Love me when I'm most unlovable. Book two: The kids' view*. Reston, VA: National Association of Secondary School Principals. 32 pp.

Ricken examines the wants, needs, hopes, and fears of middle level students through poetry and prose. Among the topics addressed are teachers, parents, friends, and school.

157.   Smith, A. (1981). Piaget's model of child development: Implications for educators. *The Clearing House, 55* (1), 24-27.

Discusses the philosophical base and importance of including "hands on" activities in middle school classroom. Emphasizes that the majority of young adolescents continue to function at the concrete operations stage as described by Piaget and that curriculum and class activities should be designed to meet the specific developmental needs of students.

158.   Takanishi, R. (Ed.). (1993). *Adolescence in the 1990s.* New York: Teachers College Press.

A collection of essays targeting key issues related to adolescent education and development, including parent-school involvement, transition from school to work settings, interdisciplinary studies, collaboration between social services and educational institutions, and establishment of learning communities. Recommended for teachers, administrators, policy makers, and community leaders.

159.   Thornburg, H. (1971). Learning and maturation in middle school age youth. *The Clearing House, 45*(3), 150-155.

Discusses developmental stages applicable to young adolescents. Also analyzes the need for middle school educators to select instructional practices that will meet those needs.

160.   Thornburg, H. D. (1986). Is the beginning of identity the end of innocence? *The Clearing House, 59*(5), 217-219.

Discusses the characteristics common to young adolescents. Emphasizes the need for educators and parents to become aware of the developmental stages of middle level students and to design relevant programs and activities.

D. PHYSICAL DEVELOPMENT

161.   Hutson, B. A. (1985). Brain growth spurts—What's left by the middle school years? *Middle School Journal, 16*(2), 8-10.

Provides background information on brain growth theory and controversy and summarizes two major points: the patterns of growth in brain weight, and how much brain growth is left for spurts at middle school. The author concludes that since growth in head circumference is over sixty percent complete by birth and nearly ninety-five percent complete by age 11 or 12, little is left to distribute to predicted spurt periods during the middle school years. Suggests that middle school curricula designed to accommodate spurts in brain growth (or the lack of them) may not be valid.

162.   Smolak, L., Levine, M.P., & Gralen, S. (1993). The impact of puberty and dating on eating problems among middle school girls. *Journal of Youth and Adolescence*, 22(4), 355-368.

Report of a portion of a longitudinal study of middle school girls. Variables included "pubertal and dating status, body dissatisfaction, weight management, and eating disordered attitudes" (p. 355). The results indicate that girls who experience the events of early menarche and dating have greater body dissatisfaction and may be at greater risk for developing eating disorders.

E. SOCIAL DEVELOPMENT

163.   Beane, J. A. (1986). The self-enhancing middle-grade school. *School Counselor*, 33(3), 189-195.

Provides arguments for the role of school personnel in "enhancing the self-perceptions of middle graders" (p. 190). The need for such support is based on the continued breakdown of the family, the relationship between self-esteem and educational outcomes, and the affective goals of middle schools. Factors influencing self-esteem include "the character of the teachers, the nature of the learning activities, and the social nature of middle graders" (p. 191). Concludes with recommendations for the changing role of counselors in raising awareness of self-esteem issues, providing staff development, contributing to curriculum planning, and developing support networks.

164.   Clark-Lempers, D. S., Lempers, J. D., & Ho, C. (1991). Early, middle, and late adolescents' perceptions of their relationships with significant others. *Journal of Adolescent Research, 6(3)*, 296-315.

The authors used self-report data from 1,110 adolescents to examine their perception of their social world using the Network of Relationships Inventory, a Likert-type scale of attributes (affection, admiration, reliable alliance, intimacy, nurturance, instrumental aid, conflict, companionship, and satisfaction with the relationship). Subjects considered their relationships to parents, same-sex best friend, sibling, and teacher. Of special interest to educators is the section on perception of teachers. Overall "the present data corroborate the conclusion that teachers do not exert much influence on adolescent lives in general" (p. 311). Rankings of significance decreased over time for all relationships. The authors offer explanations for this trend.

165.   Clasen, D. R., & Brown, B. B. (1987). Understanding peer pressure in middle school. In David B. Strahan (Ed.) *Middle school research selected studies 1987* (pp. 65-75). Columbus, OH: Research Committee of the National Middle School Association.

This study examined how adolescents perceive peer pressure. "A sample of 368 middle schools students who had been identified by peers as belonging to one of six major school groups responded to a questionnaire measuring perceptions of peer pressure in five years: involvement with peers, school involvement, family involvement, conformity to peer norms, and misconduct. Findings showed that peer pressure differed in strength by domain and that the degree to which pressures were felt varied by crowd. Results provided insight into adolescents' perceptions of peer pressure in middle school and prompted suggestions for helping young adolescents manage peer pressure more effectively."

166. Lockledge, A., Andres, K., Price, A., & Williams, M. (1994). The social lives of young adolescents. *Middle Ground* , (Fall), 3-5.

Results of a study of students grades six - eight in reference to how they use their time outside of school. Friends' homes were the site of most out-of-school activities with an emphasis on "talking" (p. 4). There was a reported drop in participation in school-sponsored activities between sixth and eighth grade.

F. EMOTIONAL DEVELOPMENT

167. Butte, H. P. (1993). Developing curriculum to reduce emotional stress in middle schoolers. *Middle School Journal*, *24*(4), 41-46.

Argues that in light of the fact of the growing number of middle level students who are exhibiting psychological stress of some kind, the entire school (and not just the counseling and special education staff) needs to address this major concern. Butte discusses proposes a curriculum-based solution and then goes on to discuss current curricular approaches to stress, necessary conditions for affective instruction, and suggestions for teachers and curriculum developers.

168. D'Onofrio, J., & Klesse, E. (1990). *Adolescent stress*. Reston, VA: National Association of Secondary School Principals. 24 pp.

The purpose of this book is to provide insights into the causes and types of stress that take place during the adolescent years and to offer tips about how to reduce that stress.

169. Strubbe, M. A. (1989). An assessment of early adolescent stress factors. In David B. Strahan (Ed.), *Middle school research: Selected studies 1989* (pp. 47-59). Columbus, OH: Research Committee of the National Middle School Association.

"This study examined the frequency and intensity of early adolescent experiences with stress. A sample of 3,382 middle level students from thirteen states responded to the Early Adolescent Stress Inventory. Using a five-point scale, subjects indicated their levels of experienced stress on forty-three items. Findings revealed that many sources of early adolescent stress were chronic in nature, related to developmental tasks, pertained to academic achievement and differentially affected young adolescents. The transescent at greatest risk for both experiencing more sources of stress and reacting more stressfully to them was an eighth grade female enrolled in special education."

G. GENDER ISSUES

170.   Blake, S. (1993). Are you turning female and minority students away from science? (What Research says). *Science and Children, 30*(7), 32-35.

The author discusses how females and minorities are currently underrepresented in science-related employment. Average science proficiency for nine-year-old boys and girls (except in the physical sciences) is the same. The performance gap becomes evident in the middle level grades (age 13) where boys have a higher achievement in science than the girls.

The performance gap between white and black children begins in the elementary grades (age nine). Studies show that teachers give boys more wait time than girls for answering questions. Girls (especially black girls) receive less feedback than boys do. Research findings indicate that girls learn better in a cooperative, rather than a competitive, environment. The author provides guidelines for structuring science activities that motivate and respond to the interests of all middle level students.

171.   Canner, J., Simmons, E. S., & Steinberg, A. (1994). Sex differences in middle school students' attitudes toward school. *Research in Middle Level Education, 18*(1), 105-115.

Used cross-sectional data from selected middle school students on a measure of "Quality of School Life" (p. 108) to compare changes from sixth to eighth grade. Examined differences between boys and girls. Found that while girls had significantly higher scores in sixth grade, their scores declined over the three years of middle school.

172.   Dubas, J. S. (1991). The effects of pubertal development on achievement during adolescence. *American Journal of Education, 99*(4), 444-460.

The author investigated the roles of pubertal timing and pubertal status on school achievement for 115 boys and 137 girls. These students were followed through grades 6, 7, and 8. Late-maturing boys were found to have the lowest school achievement, whereas late-maturing girls had the highest school achievement. Follow-ups at grade 12 indicate few long-term effects.

173.   Kastor, E. (1993). The eternity of being 12: Chelsea Clinton brings middle level to the White House. *Schools in the Middle, 2*(4), 30-35.

Focuses on the concerns and issues facing young adolescent females. Includes a discussion on concerns about parents, boy/girl relationships, physical development and maturation, and need for love and acceptance. Includes the voice of young adolescents through numerous quotations.

174.   Mee, C. S. (1995). Middle school voices on gender identity. *Women's*

Educational Equity Act Publishing Center Digest, pp. 1-2, 5-6.

Focused on selected results related to gender issues from interviews with 2,000 middle school students. Noted pattern in girls' difficulty in identifying "the best thing about my gender" (p. 1) and in boys' difficulty in identifying "the worst thing about my gender" (p. 2).

Related these results to previous gender research. Included several quotes from student responses. Offered several recommendations to break through the gender bias including "teach media literacy and critical viewing skills...address harassing behaviors between and within genders...examine how language is used in the classroom" (p. 6).

175.   Watson, B. (1994-1995). Creating gender-sensitive middle schools: A challenge for administrators. *NCMSA Journal, 16*(1), 35-37.

The authors describe ways to implement a gender equity program in a middle school setting. Strategies address the moral climate, grouping procedures, materials, teacher responses to students, use of integrated units, evaluation strategies, and responses to behavioral problems.

IV

Middle Level Programs

A. MIDDLE LEVEL PROGRAMS - RESEARCH

176.   Alexander, W. M., & McEwin, C. K. (1989). *Schools in the middle:
Status and progress.* Columbus, OH: National Middle School Association.

This booklet reports the results of a national survey whose purpose was to
ascertain the extent and type of middle school practices being developed and
implemented in middle schools across the U.S. Among the middle school
practices discussed are advisor-advisee, exploratory curriculum, interdisciplinary
curriculum, teaming, and varied instruction.

177.   Allen, H. A., & Splittgerber, F. (1980). The middle school as
perceived by teachers, principals and national leaders. *Middle school
research: Selected studies 1980* (pp. 1-16). Fairborn, OH: Research
Committee and Publications Committee of the National Middle School
Association.

This research study was comprised of two components: (1) an information
survey to collect and describe the working of middle schools from national
leaders, coordinators in state departments of education, principals and teachers
in exemplary middle schools, and (2) an attitudinal questionnaire to collect
information about the perceptions of the national leaders, coordinators,
principals and teachers toward certain functions and characteristics of the
middle school relating to students, teachers, principals, curriculum, facilities,
and organization.

178.   Beckman, V. C. (1979). A study to determine the current level of
implementation of eighteen basic middle school principles in the state of
Missouri. *Middle school research: Selected studies 1977-1979. Volume II* (pp.
43-48). Fairborn, OH: National Middle School Association.

In this study Beckman examined the extent to which 147 middle schools in the
state of Missouri had implemented basic middle school principles. The key
finding was that "the schools with the titles of elementary school, middle school,

and junior high school were more similar than different in terms of implementation of the basic middle school principles."

179.   Bohlinger, T. (1979). The current status of Ohio middle schools implementation of eighteen middle school characteristics. *Middle school research: Selected studies 1977-1979. Volume III* (pp. 17-23). Fairborn, OH: National Middle School Association.

Bohlinger states that he conducted this study in order to ascertain whether those schools called middle schools were in reality adhering to the middle level philosophy or were "middle" in name only. He notes that while Alexander only found a total of three middle schools in existence in 1968 that by 1974, 219 schools were referring to themselves as middle schools.
        The key finding in this study was that grades 6-8 and grades 5-8 in Ohio's public schools had not implemented the eighteen basic middle school characteristics to a great degree (a total composite score of 50.5% represents the average implementation for all grades 6-8 and 5-8 in the state's public schools).

180.   Bough, M., et al. (1973). The middle school: A five state survey. *The Clearing House*, *47*(3), 162-166.

Presents the results of a survey designed to gather data on middle schools in Minnesota, Wisconsin, Iowa, Illinois, and Indiana.   Contains useful comparative data.

181.   Brown, E. L. (1993). *A change process for developing exemplary middle schools*. Dissertation completed at the University of Southern California. (Copies available exclusively from Micrographics Department, Doheny Library, USC, Los Angeles, CA 90089-0182).

"The purpose of this study was to understand what elements of exemplary middle school reform as depicted in the California State Department of Education's *Caught in the Middle* (1987) were implemented in identified exemplary middle schools and how these elements were implemented within the context of the post-1983 educational reform agenda. The study assessed the extent of the schools' intention to implement and their actual implementation of each element. A focus of the study was the interaction between state policy direction and the local implementation processes. The design of the study was based on a comparative case survey research design. Detailed, descriptive individual case studies were compiled for each of the selected eight middle schools; the case studies were then analyzed both vertically within the site and horizontally across the sites."

182.   Coffland, J. A. (1976). Reexamining the middle school: A student survey. *The Clearing House*, *49*(4), 154-157.

Reports the findings of a study designed to ascertain the feelings and perceptions of middle level students with regard to teachers, instructional programs, curriculum, and school organization.

183.   Cooper, D. (1970). Unshackled education. *The Clearing House*, *45*(1), 22-25.

A case study of a middle level program in Lexington, North Carolina. Emphasis is upon flexible scheduling, blocking of periods, and individualization of instruction.

184.   DeMedio, D. L., & Mazur-Stewart, M. (1986-1987). Kansas educators reflect on middle grades education. *KAMLE Karavan: Journal of the Kansas Association for Middle Level Education*, *1*, 20-21.

The authors report on their study concerning the opinions of Kansas teachers and principals working in grades five through eight toward middle grades education. The researchers discuss earlier studies conducted in Michigan and Ohio, their procedures, their findings and conclusions.

185.   Earle, J. (1989). *The steps to restructuring: Changing Seattle's middle schools*. Alexandria, VA: National Association of State Boards of Education. 36 pp.

Presents information on the first two years of Seattle's middle school reform effort in which the district restructured its ten middle schools. The author states that the findings "for the school, district, and community, and state levels are offered not just to help readers understand Seattle's experience, but in the hope that other urban districts undertaking similar restructuring efforts, will find it useful as well."

186.   Erb, T. O. (1979). A comparative study of junior high school and middle schools in the state of Kansas. *Middle school research: Selected studies 1977-1979. Volume I* (pp. 41-48). Fairborn, OH: National Middle School Association.

Erb concludes that in the spring of 1979 both the middle schools and junior high schools in Kansas looked more like mini-high schools than the ideal middle school. He notes, however, that there was a slight movement on the part of certain middle schools toward the implementation of middle school theory and certain components such as teachers playing a greater role in guidance, faculty organizing into teams, homebases being established, and more exploratory curriculum opportunities being offered.

187.   George, P. S., & Shewey, K. (1994). *New evidence for the middle school* (2nd ed.). Columbus, OH: National Middle School Association. 126 pp.

Results of a 1993 survey of successful middle schools are presented and analyzed along with a review of earlier research studies.

188.   Henrie, L. M. (1992). A comparative study of the effect of school

structure at the intermediate level on student achievement, attitude, attendance, and discipline (Doctoral dissertation, East Texas State University, 1992). *Dissertation Abstracts International*, *53*, 675A.

This study explored the effectiveness of the middle school instructional organization upon seventh-grade student achievement, attitude, and discipline referrals. Two schools were compared. One school was organized according to the middle school philosophy. Teachers and students were organized into teams, and an advisory period was scheduled each day. The other school was organized departmentally. Standardized instruments were used to determine achievement and attitude. Attendance and discipline referral information was gathered from school records. Analysis of the data showed that the middle school structure had a positive effect on achievement and attitude of the students. Attendance and discipline did not appear to be affected by the implementation of the middle school philosophy. One apparent weakness of the study is that it lasted only one year, not sufficient time to assess adequately long term effects of middle school practices.

189.   Hough, D. & Irvin, J. (1995). Does it work? *Middle School Journal*, *26*(3), 69-70.

The authors discuss the status of research on middle level education as well as the question "Does it [middle schools] work?" They argue that for such a relatively young program, the research available is both numerous and fairly strong. In regard to the question, "Does it work?," the authors discuss the complexity of that question but offer some hopeful answers.

190.   Hough, D. (1991). Setting a research agenda for middle level education. *Crossroads: The California Journal of Middle Grades Research*, *1*(1), 4-10.

"In this article, Dr. Hough frames organizational, philosophical, and curriculum issues that undergird the need for substantive research that will guide middle level education in the years to come."

191.   Lewis, A. C. (1991). *Gaining ground: The highs and lows of urban middle school reform 1989-1991*. New York: The Edna McConnell Clark Foundation. 125 pp.

A major and significant report on twelve middle schools in five different urban school systems (Baltimore, Louisville, Milwaukee, Oakland, and San Diego) and the way they have have embraced creativity and flexibility as they developed middle level programs to meet the unique and complex challenges posed by their communities as well as to meet the unique needs of their students. As the foreword states: "These educators have learned that if middle school youth are to be successful, cities must become communities. Such a community embraces change, nurtures diversity, expects responsibility to and from the community, and fosters collaboration... In their struggle for reform, the school systems in this book...realize that the challenge is not limited to 'moving around the same old furniture within the house of poverty.' They know that urban middle schools must be transformed by altering values, as well as by changing fundamental policies and practices." Anne Lewis presents a scenario of each of the schools — their problems, the personnel involved in the projects, the student population, the communities they are located in, the ways the schools went about making key changes, and the results of the efforts as evidenced in both the classroom and in the students' lives, et al.

192.   Moeller, T. E., & Valentine, J. W. (1981). Middle schools for the eighties: Programmatic characteristics. *Middle School Journal, 12*(4), 26-27, 30.

Considers the question, "What should be the programmatic characteristics of the middle school of the eighties?" Data gathered from a survey instrument are reported according to the following categories: learning environment, curriculum and course offerings, strategies and modes of learning, scheduling, reporting of student progress, guidance program, personnel involved in teaching students.

193.   Munsell, W. R. (1985). The extent to which identified programmatic characteristics of middle level education are implemented in the middle schools of Colorado. In David Strahan (Ed.), *Middle school research: Selected studies 1985* (pp. 34-67). Columbus, OH: Research Committee of the National Middle School Association.

Among the key findings of this research are the following: for the most part, the middle schools in Colorado were not (as of 1985) implementing middle level components as recommended in the literature; there was not a significant difference between middle schools and junior highs in regard to the implementation of the middle level philosophy or middle level components; both middle level and junior high principals' perceptions of the need to implement middle level programs were higher than those of the middle level and junior high teacher respondents, and middle school respondents differed significantly from junior high school respondents in regard to their perception of the extent to which the middle level school should implement such components as flexible scheduling and interdisciplinary team organization.

194.   Pook, M. E. (1981). A study of the relationship of teacher job satisfaction and the level of implementation of recommended middle school practices. In Thomas Owen Erb (Ed.), *Middle school research: Selected studies 1981*(pp. 99-107). Columbus, OH: Research Committee of the National Middle School Association.

Among the conclusions of this study are: 1. Overall job satisfaction of middle school faculty does not vary significantly in low, medium, or high implementation schools; 2. Teacher satisfaction with the curriculum in middle schools increases as the degree of implementation of middle school practices increase; 3. Teachers in high implementation schools are more satisfied with the community support of education than teachers in low implementation schools;

4. Teachers in high implementation middle schools are more satisfied with school facilities than teachers in low implementation schools; 5. Teachers are more dissatisfied with their teaching load in high implementation schools than low implementation schools; and, 6. Teachers who prefer teaching at the middle level are more satisfied in their work than teachers who prefer teaching at other levels.

195.   Schmidt, D. J. (1984). A comparative study of organizational curricular practices and innovations in middle/intermediate schools and junior high schools in the Rocky Mountain Region. In Hershel D. Thornburg and Stefinee E. Pinnegar (Eds.), *Middle school research: Selected studies 1984* (pp. 28-33). Columbus, OH: National Middle School Association.

Among the findings were: Although middle/intermediate schools had implemented more middle level concepts/components than did junior high schools, the differences were not statistically significant; middle school/ intermediate school and junior high schools tended to be more similar in their approaches to instruction than they they were different; both course work in middle level philosophy and attendance at professional meetings seemed to be factors in the openness to innovation among among middle level administrators; and the increased availability of information about middle level philosophy and practices appeared to have had a positive influence on the programs of both the middle/intermediate and junior high schools in the region.

196.   Trusty, J. (1992). An examination of possible predictors of alienation from school in elementary and middle school students (Doctoral dissertation, Mississippi State University, 1992). *Dissertation Abstracts International, 53,* 2242A.

Student levels of alienation from school increase significantly between the fifth and sixth grade and appear to stabilize in the sixth to eighth grades. Gender and school variables emerged as the most consistent predictors of alienation from school.
        African-Americans were less alienated than whites and lower socioeconomic status students were less alienated than higher socioeconomic status students. Most results followed predicted directions.

197.   Waggoner, V. C., & McEwin, C. K. (1993). Middle level practices in European international and Department of Defense schools. *Middle School Journal, 24* (5), 29-36.

Presents the results of an international study designed to investigate middle level programs and practices in international and Department of Defense schools in Europe during the 1989-90 school year. The purpose of the study was to gather data to support change in international middle level education.
        Presents results and recommendations in the following areas: enrollment, organization, activities, core subjects, grouping patterns, exploratory courses, advisory programs, scheduling, instructional plans, teacher preparation, and personnel.

B. MIDDLE LEVEL PROGRAMS - PRACTICAL

198.   Bracey, G. (1993). Teachers design their own school. *High Strides*
5(3), 1.

Traces the development of a middle level school in Indianapolis, Indiana, from
inception to curriculum planning and implementation. Focuses upon the
characteristics that reflect the middle level philosophy.

199.   Clark, D. C., & Clark, S. N. (1990). *Schools in the middle, theory into
practice: Restructuring middle schools—strategies for using "Turning Points."*
Reston, VA: National Association of Secondary School Principals.

200.   Davidson, J., & Pulver, R. (1991). *Literacy assessment for the middle
grades—Leader's manual and user's manual.* Carrboro, NC: Center for Early
Adolescence. 132 pp. and 182 pp., respectively.

The Literacy Assessment for the Middle Grades is a self-assessment and
planning process that provides a means to take comprehensive look at a school's
literacy policies and practices. "Designed to improve the literacy supports that
schools provide for young adolescents, this process can help middle-grades
schools to increase their understanding of the reading and writing needs of
young adolescents and the best ways to meet these needs; to develop a shared
vision to drive the school's planing around reading and writing issues; and to
create a blueprint for action."

201.   Dorman, G. (1987). *Improving middle-grade schools: A framework
for action.* Carrboro, NC: Center for Early Adolescence. 108 pp.

The author of the Center for Early Adolescence's Middle Grades Assessment
Program (MGAP) "documents the experiences of eleven middle-grades schools
involved in the MGAP school improvement process. Contains valuable
information for educators working to improve middle and junior high schools
and discusses how schools can develop programs that are both academically
effective and developmentally responsive."

202.   Dorman, G., Lipsitz, J., & Verner, P. (1985). Improving schools for
young adolescents. *Educational Leadership, 42*(6), 44-49.

The Middle Grades Assessment Program is advocated as an effective method of
improving education in middle schools. A case study of Francisco Middle
School demonstrates how the program builds a mindset, momentum, and support
for change among the teaching staff.

203.   Fore, D. L. (1995). Charting its own future: Oakland's Jingletown
Middle School joins charter crusade. *High Strides, 7*(5), 1, 4-5.

Profiles the efforts of one urban middle school "to establish its own curriculum,
student evaluations, class sizes and school hours" (p. 4). Highlights different

viewpoints toward such charter schools.

204.   George, P. S. (1987). *Long-term teacher-student relationships: A middle school case study*. Columbus, OH: National Middle School Association. 28 pp.

Presents evidence that middle level students benefit from programs designed to keep students and teachers together for more than a year.

205.   Laven, D., & McKeever, W. (1989). Program Quality Review in California middle schools. *Thrust, 18*(5), 45-47.

The authors report on their school's use of California's tool for assessing its state's middle level programs. They discuss both the review handbooks and the review process itself.

206.   National Association of Secondary School Principals. (1988). *Assessing excellence: A guide for studying the middle level school*. Reston, VA: Author. 62 pp.

Developed by the NASSP Council on Middle Level Education, this document outlines how a faculty can assess all or part of a middle level program.

207.   Raebeck, B. S. (1990). Transformation of a middle school. *Educational Leadership, 47*(7), 18-21.

Describes major changes accomplished as one school switched from a junior high school, subject-centered philosophy to that of a student-centered, middle school philosophy. Discusses student management systems and school rules. Places emphasis on simplicity and decision-making by both faculty and students.

208.   Rottier, J., & Whooley, J. E. (1986). An instrument for evaluating middle grade instructional programs. *Middle School Journal, 17*(3), 20-24.

The authors have developed an instrument based on the "essential elements" presented in the National Middle School Association publication, *This We Believe*. They suggest that information gained can be used to help planners establish program improvement priorities as well as improve the nature of educational practices, the nature of learning, and societal expectations. Includes instructions on the use of the instrument and analysis and interpretation of data. Respondents are asked to select answers on a scale of 1 to 6 (strongly disagree to strongly agree) in two areas: "current situation" and "ideal situation." Approximately 58 statements in 11 categories are considered.

209.   Thomason, J., & Williams, B. (1982). Middle schools are for me. *Educational Leadership, 40*(2), 54-58.

Describes a plan for middle school reorganization which balances theory, administration, and practice.

210.   Totten, S. (in press). The development of a new middle level school program via a university/school district partnership. *Schools in the Middle.*

The author discusses how University of Arkansas, Fayetteville, faculty members worked closely with public school personnel in order to design a totally new middle level program in a school that had traditionally mixed the junior high and high school students (grades 7-12).

C. MIDDLE LEVEL PROGRAMS - GENERAL

211.   Curtis, T. E. (1977). The middle school tomorrow: Three perennial problems. In P. S. George (Ed.), *A look ahead* (pp. 67-74). Columbus, OH: National Middle School Association.

Examines the rationale for middle level programs, presents a need for curriculum designed to meet the unique developmental characteristics of young adolescents, and emphasizes the necessity of evaluating and analyzing existing middle level programs.

212.   Dettre, J. R. (1973). The middle school should be a separate and equal entity. *The Clearing House, 48* (1), 19-23.

Provides a rationale for middle level programs. Advocates elementary, middle, and secondary school structures.

213.   Eichhorn, D. (1966). *The middle school.* Reston, VA, and Columbus, OH: National Association of Secondary School Principals, and National Middle School Association. 116 pp.

A classic in the field. In this book, Eichhorn provided the first comprehensive overview regarding the need for a unique type of educational program at the middle level. In the book Eichhorn proposes two concepts that he argues are "fundamental to planning, developing, and operating a middle school: a direct model relationship between the learner's characteristics and the school program (socio-psychological model); and transescence," which he defined as "the stage of development which begins prior to the onset of puberty and extends through the early stages of adolescence." The book is comprised of nine chapters: 1. The Emerging Middle School, 2. Physical Growth, 3. Mental Growth, 4. Cultural Forces, 5. Middle School Environment, 6. Educational Program, 7. Guidance Services and Activities, 8. Administration, and 9. Conclusions and Recommendations. It also contains a glossary and a short bibliography.

214.   Erb, T. O. (1986-1987). Effective middle grades programs: No checklists for excellence. *KAMLE Karavan: Journal of the Kansas Association for Middle Level Education, 1, 7.*

Argues that sound middle level programs focus on characteristics of excellence (personalized places, flexible use of time, visionary leadership, and academic focus), not on checklists. Also warns against quick fix solutions to complex problems. He goes on to explain what he means by each of the aforementioned "characteristics of excellence." What is particularly interesting is how he drives home both the need for middle level programs to be personalized places that exude an ethos of caring as well as have a strong academic focus.

215.   Erb, T. O. (1987-1988). The difference between a junior high and middle school is in your head. *KAMLE Karavan: Journal of the Kansas Association for Middle Level Education, 2,* 18-19.

Drives home the point that the key difference between junior highs and middle schools "is defined by a state of mind about what is the main purpose of middle grades education." Erb goes on to illustrate his point by setting up scenarios and providing both a junior high perspective and a middle school perspective.

216.   Garvin, J. P. (1992). Maintaining middle schools. In Judith L. Irvin (Ed.), *Transforming middle level education: Perspectives and possibilities* (pp. 193-201). Needham, MA: Allyn and Bacon.

Garvin argues that in order to maintain organizational change at the middle level, the following components need to be in place: 1. philosophical commitment from the school board and superintendent; 2. leadership with effective interpersonal abilities that is informed, committed, courageous, and energetic; 3. a strong faculty; 4. a mission statement; 5. sufficient transition time; 6. realistic expectations; 7. in-service; and, 8. attention to key team issues.

217.   Gatewood, T. E. (1977). Less than optimistic (but realistic) view of the middle school. In P. S. George (Ed.), *A look ahead* (pp. 7-16). Columbus, OH: National Middle School Association.

Discusses the obstacles, including political and administrative, that face middle level educators. Emphasizes the need for middle level programs to consist of accountability and valid assessment measures.

218.   George, P. S. (1977). The challenge before us. In P. S. George (Ed.), *A look ahead* (pp. 156-158). Columbus, OH: National Middle School Association.

Offers the following suggestions for ensuring the continued success of middle level programs: (1) Educators must realize the unique, vital role of middle schools within the educational system, and (2) Everyone involved in middle level education should replace skepticism and blame with a willingness to work together in developing and implementing student-centered programs.

219.   Gibson, J. T. (1978). The middle school concept: "An albatross?" *The Journal of Teacher Education, 29*(5),17-19.

Gibson delineates the basic differences between a junior high school and a middle school by examining what each school tends to emphasize.

220.   Gritzmacher, H., & Larkin, D. (1993). A comparison of middle level and special education. *Middle School Journal, 25*(1), 28-32.

Compares the components of a successful middle level program to those typically associated with special education programs. Specifically discussed are learner-centered instruction, bridging, interdisciplinary teaming, adviser/advisee programs, block scheduling, and exploratory courses. Concludes with a challenge for middle level educators and special educators to continue collaboration for successful inclusion of all students in to the middle level environment.

221.   Henson, K. T. (1986). Middle schools: Paradoxes and promises. *The Clearing House, 59*(8), 345-347.

Compares the history of middle level schools with that of junior high schools with an emphasis upon why the middle level school will continue to succeed. Concentrates upon the paradoxical nature of middle schools and their apparently successful future.

222.   Howlett, P. (1989). *THRUST* interview: Middle school principal Susan VandeVeer. *Thrust, 19*(1), 32-34.

A middle school principal who is in the process of establishing (with her faculty) a "model middle school" in California discusses the following issues: 1. middle school structure and how it meets the unique needs of young adolescents, 2. how "choice" boosts the student success rate, and 3. the principal's role in implementing radical change.

223.   Lawton, E. (1992). *The effective middle level teacher*. Reston, VA: National Association of Secondary School Principals.

Addresses the characteristics of young adolescents and effective middle level teachers and the implications that those characteristics have upon middle level programs.

224.   Leake, D. (1992). Milwaukee's African American Immersion Middle School: Meeting special needs. *Schools in the Middle: Theory into Practice, 1*(4), 27-30.

Discusses the purpose and focus of Milwaukee's African American Immersion Middle School (the primary one being to attempt "to eliminate the negative attitudes and influences that impede the academic success of black students").

225.   Lewis, A. C. (1990). *Making it in the middle: The why and how of excellent schools for young urban adolescents*. New York, NY: The Edna McConnell Clark Foundation. 77 pp. [Foreword by Deborah Meier.]

In this booklet, Lewis not only examines many of the key problems educators face in urban schools systems as they attempt to educate young adolescents, but also describes how some educators in these systems are solving them. Among the commonalities that she cites as being crucial in developing exemplary schools for young adolescents are the following: high content, high expectations, and high support. Particularly interesting is the chapter entitled "Ideas into Action."

226.   Lewis, A. C. (1991). *Gaining ground: The highs and lows of urban middle school reform 1989-1991*. New York: The Edna McConnell Clark Foundation.

A report on the first two years of an education reform project established by the Edna McConnell Clark Foundation and implemented in five urban school systems: Baltimore, Louisville, Milwaukee, Oakland, and San Diego.

227.   Lewis, A. C. (1993). *Changing the odds: Middle school reform in progress*. New York: The Edna McConnell Clark Foundation.

A report on the second two years of an education reform project established by the Edna McConnell Clark Foundation and implemented in five urban school systems: Baltimore, Louisville, Milwaukee, Oakland, and San Diego.

228.   Lipsitz, J. (1984). *Successful schools for young adolescents*. New Brunswick, NJ: Transaction Books. 223 pp.

Highly acclaimed, "this book establishes a framework for identifying and examining effective middle-grades schools—a framework that considers adolescent development, school effectiveness research, and public policy concerns. Presents in-depth case studies of four successful middle-grades schools that foster healthy social development and learning."

229.   Lounsbury, J. H. (1977). Assuring the continued success of the middle school. In P. S. George (Ed.), *A look ahead* (pp. 148-153). Columbus, OH: National Middle School Association.

Emphasizes the need for student-teacher collaboration in designing middle level programs that meet the unique needs of adolescents. Also discusses the need for middle level educators to move toward student-centered programs and away from departmentalized, subject-centered curriculum.

230.   National Association of Secondary School Principals. (1985). *An agenda for excellence at the middle level*. Reston, VA: Author. 24 pp. A statement on the characteristics that should be evident in all middle level programs.

231.   National Association of Secondary School Principals. (1989). *Middle level education's responsibility for intellectual development*. Reston, VA: Author. 56 pp.

"Issues central in planning middle level school programs to improve students' intellectual development are examined in this monograph, developed by NASSP's Council on Middle Level Education."

232.   National Association of Secondary School Principals. (1991). *Promising programs in the middle grades.* Reston, VA: Author. 72 pp.

This monograph presents an examination of programs that look promising for improving education in the major academic areas at the middle level. It includes a directory of promising programs and a questionnaire to guide discussion about a school or district's present programs and needed directions.

233.   Shockley, R. (1992). Developing a sense of mission in middle schools. In Judith L. Irvin (Ed.), *Transforming middle level education: Perspectives and possibilities* (pp. 93-101). Needham Heights, MA: Allyn and Bacon.

In this piece Shockley discusses the following concerns: common denominators found in most clearly defined mission statements, culture building and the school mission, the role of school leadership, and the school mission as it relates to faculty development.

234.   Spear, R. C. (1992). The process of change: Developing effective middle school programs. In Judith L. Irvin (Ed.), *Transforming middle level education: Perspectives and possibilities* (pp. 102-138). Needham Heights, MA: Allyn and Bacon.

A detailed essay on the crucial issue of the change process. Among the many issues Spear addresses are the following: issues of individual change and the role of a teacher in an exemplary middle school, the Concerns Based Adoption Model (CBAM), issues of organizational change, stages of organizational change, staff development, and a case study of a school going through the process of change.

235.   Stelle, A., & Wallace, H. (1979). Meeting learning needs of the young adolescent. *Thrust, 8*(3), 25-27.

Discusses why and how various middle level school districts in California developed "middle grade schools." It also focuses on some of the problems the districts encountered and how they worked to overcome them.

236.   Toepfer, C. F. (1977). The middle school as multiple school: A means for survival. In P. S. George (Ed.), *A look ahead* (pp. 139-147). Columbus, OH: National Middle School Association.

Discusses the need for personalizing middle level programs to meet the unique needs of each student population. Also addresses the need for collaboration among teachers and students in the development and implementation of programs.

237.   Toepfer, C. F., Jr. (1991). To improve middle level instructional

programs.. *Becoming*, 2(2), 6-12.

Focuses upon the need to tailor middle level programs to the needs of young adolescents. Discusses critical issues that middle level educators should consider when developing and implementing programs. Specifically discussed are diversity, organization, readiness, accelerated programs, and integrated curriculum.

238.   Vars, G. F. (1977). Emphasizing student involvement: A key to the future. In P. S. George (Ed.), *A look ahead* (pp. 130-138). Columbus, OH: National Middle School Association.

Emphasizes the need for student-teacher collaboration and planning and the necessity of encouraging and accepting student input on all aspects of middle level programs.

239.   Wilson, M. T. (1969). What is a middle school? *The Clearing House, 44*(1), 9-11.

Discusses components of an effective middle school with emphasis upon grouping, individualization of instruction, evaluation procedures, and team teaching. A good resource to compare middle level programs of the 1990s with those of the 1960s.

240.   Yoder, Jr., W. H. (1982). Middle schools vs. junior high misses the point. *Educational Leadership, 40*(2), 50.

Argues that names are less important than programs. Middle level children are no more unique than elementary or high school students and require no programs beyond those which should be available to other age groups.

D. CURRICULUM - RESEARCH

241.   Brodhagen, B., Weilbecker, B., & Beane, J. (1992). Living in the future: An experiment with an integrative curriculum. *Dissemination Services in the Middle Grades*, ELI, P. O. Box 863, Springfield, MA.

Reports the results of a study on the effects of integrated curriculum and student-teacher planning upon culturally and academically diverse students.

242.   Resnick, D. P., & Resnick, L. B. (1985). Standards, curriculum, and performance: A historical and comparative perspective. *Educational Researcher, 14*(4), 5-20.

American curriculum appears to be weak for two reasons: a lack of stringent course requirements, and weak content and poor instruction within course. Emphasis on the basics has limited instruction to elementary levels. Improved educational standards will require demanding studies that go beyond the basics. Discusses the power of textbook companies based on public demand to control curriculum. Considers new forms of educational assessment and the advantages and disadvantages of tracking for higher standards.

E. CURRICULUM - PRACTICAL

243.   Beane, J. A. (1993). Problems and possibilities for an integrative curriculum. *Middle School Journal*, *25* (1), 18-23.

Addresses key issues involved in developing and implementing an integrated curriculum. Specifically discussed are the role of subject matter, subject areas, planning, classroom life, and rational for an integrated curriculum.

244.   Egan, K. (1992). *Imagination in teaching and learning: The middle school years*. Chicago: The University of Chicago Press. 178 pp.

Egan discusses the imaginative life of the "typical" eight- to fifteen-year old and offers practical advice on how the imagination can be engaged in learning. The book contains a host of concrete examples of curriculum design and teaching techniques structured to appeal specifically to children in their middle years.

245.   Far West Laboratory for Educational Research and Development. (1992). *Toward a Community of Learners: A Regional Newsletter on Authentic Instruction for the Middle Grades*, Volume 1.

The inaugural volume of this newsletter sets out its purpose (a vehicle for providing educators with insights as to how one could develop and implement "authentic curriculum and instruction" as well as how to develop and nurture a "community of learners"). In order to illustrate what they mean by those terms, the authors analyze the workings of a writers' workshop at the middle level. A fascinating and valuable discussion.

246.   Garvin, J. P. (1989). *Merging the exploratory and basic subjects in the middle level school: Practical suggestions that work*. Topsfield, MA: New England League of Middle Schools. 22 pp.

A very brief overview of how to integrate exploratory curriculum and activities (e.g., "music, art, home economics, technical arts, health, computers, physical education, drama, business, languages, library, etc.") into the academic core curriculum.

247.   James, M. A. (1992). The shibboleths of reform. *Current Issues in Middle Level Education*, *1*(1), 31-39.

Describes a pilot middle level curriculum reform project which was prompted by Beane's ideas on curriculum, Jacobs' ideas on interdisciplinary units, and Hass' ideas of students as "a source for curriculum direction. The result was the development and implementation of two "true" interdisciplinary units, inspired teachers and students working together, and a situation where the participants in the pilot project conducted a five day intensive middle school institute in which

120 other middle level teachers took part.

248.   Lewbel, S. (1993). From an interdisciplinary to an integrative
approach: The first year. *Journal of the New England League of Middle
Schools, 6* (3), 12-15.

Discusses the change process at Rochambeau Middle School in Connecticut.
Using James Beane's *Rhetoric to Reality: A Middle School Curriculum* and
Carnegie's *Turning Points* as guides, faculty and administrators made a
commitment to move from an interdisciplinary approach to an integrative
curriculum. Analyzes the atmosphere within the school setting, curricular
changes, and long-range plans.

249.   Lewis, A. C. (Ed.). (1989). High content [Special issue]. *High
Strides, 1* (2).

Offers examples of middle level curricula designed to engage students as active
learners. Concludes that existing curricula in many middle level schools do not
challenge students and are not relevant to their needs.

F. CURRICULUM - GENERAL

250.   Arnold, J. (Ed.). (1990). *Visions of teaching and learning:
Eighty exemplary middle level projects.* National Middle School Association.
150 pp.

In this book Arnold has selected "exemplary projects" that are thought
provoking, actively engage learners, and incorporate quality instructional
practices. The seven chapters of the volume are: 1. Multidisciplinary-
Interdisciplinary Projects, 2. Social Studies Projects, 3. Language Arts Projects,
4. Science/Math Projects, 5. Allied Arts/Exploratory Projects, 6. Special
Population Projects, and 7. Community Service Projects.

251.   Beane, J. A. (1990). *A middle school curriculum: From rhetoric to
reality.* Columbus, OH: National Middle School Association. 72 pp.

Challenging the standard approach to curriculum taken at the middle level,
Beane not only critiques the subject curriculum but offers a proposal for
developing age-appropriate curriculum. As John Lounsbury states in the
foreword: "To date middle level education, despite all its important and needed
organizational changes, has seemed to lack a clear vision of what might be, of
what attributes our graduates should possess or a philosophically and
educationally valid conception that would make it possible to put its rhetoric
regarding the developmental needs of early adolescents into reality. The need
for such a vision has now been met. In this genuinely significant volume, James
Beane has thoughtfully and thoroughly reviewed the past, exposed for analysis
the separate subject approach, and outlined a proposal for a new general
education program that would truly transform the middle level school. This
program would reflect the known needs of early adolescents, and it would also

deal forthrightly with the equally important needs of contemporary society." The book is comprised of five chapters and a epilogue: 1. The Middle School Curriculum Question; 2. Curriculum Views in the Middle School Movement; 3. The General Education Question at the Middle Level, 4. A Middle School Curriculum, 5. Implementing the "New" Curriculum; and, Epilogue. A Challenge to the Middle School Movement.

252.   Beane, J. A. (1993). What is an integrative curriculum? Let's be clear about what we mean and why it is important. *Journal of the New England League of Middle Schools, 6 (3)*, 2-4.

Discusses the meaning of an integrated curriculum. Also presents the benefits of developing and implementing such a curriculum at the middle level. Reiterates that curriculum should be designed to meet the needs of early adolescents.

253.   Bergmann, S. (1986). Making decisions about the tough topics. *The Clearing House*, *60*(1), 24-26.

Emphasizes the need for middle level students to participate in meaningful discussions about topics relevant to their needs and concerns. Includes suggestions for teaching decision making skills.

254.   Brazee, E., & Capelluti, J. (1993). Focus on middle level curriculum: An integrative curriculum for middle level: A recent rationale. *Journal of the New England League of Middle Schools, 6* (3), 21-27.

Explains why an integrated approach receives broad-based support from professionals in business, medicine, and other areas. Also examines a rationale for integrative curriculum, common beliefs and their impact upon innovation, and the congruence between an integrative curriculum and the middle level philosophy.

255.   Compton, M. F. (1984). Balance in the middle school curriculum. In John H. Lounsbury (Ed.), *Perspectives: Middle level education* (pp. 68-78). Columbus, OH: National Middle School Association.

Discusses the following issues: "What is balance in the curriculum?" "What aspects need to be balanced in the curriculum?"; ways to achieve balance in the curriculum; and, an alternative curriculum plan which "places together in a cluster those curricular areas which seem logically to fit together." In regard to the latter recommendation, Compton suggests the following: "One part, 'humanities,' might include language, music, art, and social science. A second part, "technology," might include science, industrial art, mathematics, and home living. A third cluster of equal importance might include the exploratory areas typically found in activities programs, mini-courses, club activities, and the areas of health, physical education, and leisure.

256.   Dickinson, T. (Ed.) (1992). *Readings in middle level curriculum: A continuing conversation*. Columbus, OH: National Middle School Association.

Contains reprints of twenty-one articles that appeared in the *Middle School Journal*. Provides an excellent collection of resources on middle school curriculum.

257.   Dickinson, T. (Ed.) (1993). *Readings in middle school curriculum: A continuing conversation*. Columbus, OH: National Middle School Association. 232 pp.

A collection of essays on middle level curricular issues. Includes reprints of landmark articles originally published in the *Middle School Journal*.

258.   Drake, S. M. (1993). *Planning integrated curriculum: The call to adventure*. Alexandria, VA: Association for Supervision and Curriculum Development.

Discusses the processes involved in planning and implementing an integrated curriculum. Traces the change process from initial thinking about changing the focus of the curriculum to actually doing so. The chapter "The Struggle to Change" addresses many of the practical concerns faced by middle level educators: school calendar, time, extensive planning time required, lack of resources, staff turnover, leadership, evaluation, and parental involvement. Offers useful suggestions for addressing these problems and others often encountered in any change process. Also discusses three frameworks within which an integrated curriculum can be successfully implemented: multidisciplinary, interdisciplinary, and transdisciplinary. An excellent resource for all middle level educators.

259.   Ediger, M. (1992). Middle school curriculum. *New Mexico Middle School Journal*, 2, 12-15.

Focuses on the need for middle level students to experience reality through relevant curricula. Includes goal statements designed to assist middle level teachers and administrators in developing and implementing a curriculum that meets the interests, needs, and abilities of middle level students. Also investigates the philosophical bases of curriculum with emphasis upon realism, experimentalism, existentialism, and idealism.

260.   Epstein, J., & Salinas, K. C. (1992). *Promising programs in the middle grades*. Reston, VA: National Association of Secondary School Principals. 108 pp.

In their preface, the authors state that: "Educators in the middle grades are searching for promising programs to improve the education of all students, and particularly of educationally disadvantaged students. In 1989, we canvassed the field for curricula that help middle grades teachers and administrators improve all students' opportunities for learning. More than 200 programs were reviewed, including many recommended by the U.S. Department of Education's Program Effectiveness Panel (PEP), those recognized as effective Chapter 1 programs, and other programs described in journals, conferences, and informal publications.

The search focused on programs that bring high content to the major academic subjects for educationally disadvantaged students in the middle grades. Promising programs either emphasize *new access* to existing high content or *new high content*. The programs offer learning opportunities that prevent learning problems from developing or that treat learning problems. Students may be expected to make average progress or accelerated progress in one year's time in programs that aim to be equally or more effective than others. Programs aim to teach basic skills faster and better, or to teach basic and advanced skills in ways that deepen students' thinking, understanding, and knowledge.

From the academic subject programs reviewed, we identified about 80 that had promising components for middle grades educators. None could be labeled 'effective' because of serious measurement and evaluation problems. The programs include examples that look promising for improving math, reading, writing, and language arts, thinking skills, science, and social studies in the middle grades."

261.   Furniss, J. M. (1993). Teaching ethics in high school. *The Clearing House*, 66(6), 327-328.

Discusses the impact that media has had upon young adolescents and argues that, as a result, the teaching of ethics should be an integral part of each middle school program.

262.   Hawkins, M. L., & Graham, M. D. (1994). *Curriculum architecture: Creating a place of our own*. Columbus, OH: National Middle School Association. 111 pp.

In his preface John H. Lounsbury notes that "With style, boldness, and a hard-to-deny sense of reality, this book provides an important but often overlooked perspective on the business of designing a curriculum for young adolescents. Its central message surfaces frequently and with clarity. Each school must create its own curriculum based on its own study of its students, its community, its faculty, and with the real involvement of the students themselves. The task is to design 'a place of our own'...This volume offers both an important point of view and guidance in taking the big step beyond organizational change to the necessary alteration of the school's culture, its values, and its collective beliefs."

263.   Jenkins, J. M., & Tanner, D. (Eds.). (1992). *Restructuring for an interdisciplinary curriculum*. Reston, VA: National Association of Secondary School Principals.

Highlights curricular issues of secondary and middle level schools. Includes a noteworthy chapter on a program in a model California middle school.

264.   Jenkins, K. D., & Jenkins, D. M. (1992). Curriculum imperatives for 21st century middle schools. *Current Issues in Middle Level Education*, 1(1), 49-65.

The authors persuasively argue that despite all sorts of calls for curriculum reform, the curriculum at the middle level has changed very little—if at all— over the past several generations. They assert that the curriculum at the middle level needs to become more relevant to the developmental characteristics of middle level students. They delineate some suggestions that they see as assisting in bringing about a curriculum that is both unique and appropriate for students at the middle level. They also suggest specific activities that they think are needed to help bring about the changes.

265.   Lewis, A. C. (Ed.). (1989). High expectations [Special issue]. *High Strides*, *1*(6).

A collection of articles with an emphasis on curricular concerns. Reiterates the idea that middle level curricula must be relevant for and meet the needs of young adolescents. Profiles the characteristics of a typical urban middle level student and examines the impact that meeting the needs of that student will have upon middle level programs.

266.   Lock, C. R. (1984). Involving students in curriculum development. *The Clearing House*, *57* (6), 261-262.

Discusses the need for a relevant curriculum that meets the needs of young adolescents. Discusses strategies for developing and implementing such a curriculum, with an emphasis upon student involvement.

267.   National Association of Secondary School Principals. (1991). *Promising programs in the middle grades*. Reston, VA: Author. 72 pp.

This monograph presents an examination of programs that look promising for improving education in the major academic areas at the middle level. It includes a directory of promising programs and a questionnaire to guide discussion about a school or district's present programs and needed directions.

268.   Toepfer, C. F. Jr. (1992). Middle level school curriculum: Defining the elusive. In Judith L. Irvin (Ed.), *Transforming middle level education: Perspectives and possibilities* (pp. 205-243). Needham Heights, MA: Allyn and Bacon.

After decrying the point about the lack of attention that has been paid to the *what* of the middle school (meaning the curriculum), Toepfer examines and discusses the following issues: middle grades organizational changes in which he provides a historical perspective, the middle level concept, developmental issues of young adolescents, middle level curricular functions (integration, exploration, guidance/advisement, differentiation, socialization, articulation), readiness to learn, the need for a middle level curricular focus, curriculum organization (advantages of interdisciplinary learning, grouping and cooperative learning), and middle level curriculum models and approaches.

269.   Vars, G. F. (1992). Integrative curriculum. *Current Issues in Middle Level Education*, *1*(1),   66-78.

In this piece, Vars discusses the history of the effort towards intergrative curriculum and posits suggestions that educators ought to consider so that they avoid some of the mistakes of past efforts. In doing so, he addresses the following: terminology, the core curriculum, origins of the movement towards integrative curriculum, a very succinct statement regarding research vis-à-vis integrative curriculum and his advice to those undertaking the implementation of integrative curriculum.

G. TRANSITION TO THE MIDDLE LEVEL - RESEARCH

270.   Backes, J. S. (1993). Moving toward the middle. *Current Issues in Middle Level Education, 2* (2), 12-26.

Examines the transition of Agassiz Junior High School in Fargo, North Dakota, to a middle school. Using the Delphi Technique, administrators and teachers evaluated characteristics of middle schools in reference to the existing program at Agassiz Junior High and the extent to which change would be required to implement middle level concepts. Although the article presents the results of the self-study, the emphasis is upon the change process involved in transitioning from a junior high school concept to a middle level concept.

271.   Pate, P. E., Mizelle, N. B., Hart, L. E., Jordan, J., Matthews, R., Matthews, S., Scott, V., & Brantley, V. (1993). The Delta Project: A three-year longitudinal study of middle school change. *Middle School Journal, 25*(1), 24-27.

Describes the Delta Project, a change program designed by middle level teachers in rural Georgia. As part of the project, changes were made in the curriculum, methods of instruction, and organizational structures. Provides a rational for the project; traces the development of the project; describes the organizational, curricular, and instructional components of the project; and highlights the collaborative efforts resulting from the project.

272.   Sierer, T. M. (1989). The concerns and attitudes of early adolescent middle school students in transition (Doctoral dissertation, Temple University, 1988). *Dissertation Abstracts International, 49,* 2486A.

The author used a cross-sectional, descriptive research design to study the attitudes of eighth and ninth-graders toward the middle school experience and concerns of transition to high school. Those students who experienced difficult transition indicated being unaccepted by both classmates and teachers as the primary cause of the inability to adjust. Eighth graders were consistently more positive toward school than ninth graders. Male achievers, regardless of grade, generally had a more positive attitude toward math and science than any other group of students. Female achievers generally had a more positive attitude toward social studies and English than any other group of students.

273.   Stone, D., Wiles, J. C., & Bondi, J. C. (1980). Transition to a middle school: A study of change. *Middle School Research: Selected Studies 1980* (pp.

27-33). Fairborn, OH: Research Committee and Publications Committee of the
National Middle School Association.

The authors studied the change process involving a school in Hillsborough
County, Florida, that changed over from a "seventh-grade center" to a middle
school (grades six and seven combined). The study addressed the following:
who initiated the change, the types of curricular and instructional programs that
were decided upon and why, the actual changes that occurred, the attitudes of
teachers and students to the change, and the impact of the change on student
achievement.

H. TRANSITION TO THE MIDDLE LEVEL - PRACTICAL

274.   Baltzer, R. (1995). Two-teacher teaming: Relationships and
ownership. *Journal of the New England League of Middle Schools, 8*(2), 16-18.

The authors report on the successful use of two-teacher teams as a way to reduce
the student teacher ratio in a setting that was in transition from a junior/senior
high system to a middle school. The change allowed at least two adults to learn
the unique needs of a small group of students.

275.   Bilodeau-Jones, M, & Bossie, J. (1993). Integrated studies in a multi-
age classroom at the middle level: You can get there from here! *Journal of the
New England League of Middle Schools, 6* (3), 8-11.

Traces the transition of an elementary school from a traditional format to one
that encourages innovations through the Integrated Studies in a Multi-Age
Classroom (ISMAC) model. Specifically discussed are organization, mini-
courses, interdisciplinary studies, language arts/fine arts/exploratory, and student
learning styles and responsibilities.

276.   Bondi, J. (1977). Addressing the issues: The middle school a positive
change in American education. In P. S. George (Ed.), *A look ahead* (pp. 25-35).
Columbus, OH: National Middle School Association.

Includes practical suggestions for developing and implementing effective middle
school programs. Also discusses the importance of well-prepared administrators
and appropriate professional development opportunities for faculty.

277.   Ebersold, D. (1991). From junior high to middle schools: Organizing
for change. *The Transescent, 16* (1), 7-8.

Discribes a school that made a successful transition from a junior high school to
a middle level school. The principal outlines the process and procedures by
which the administration, faculty, and staff made the transition. Offers many
useful, practical suggestions for developing and implementing middle level
practices.

278.   Filby, N. N., Lee, G. V., & Lambert, V. (1990). *Middle grades*

reform: A casebook for school leaders. San Francisco, CA: Far West Laboratory for Educational Research and Development and California Association of County Superintendents of Schools. 115 pp.

The express purpose of this volume is to assist local educators in the process of school improvement by providing access to the best ideas in research and practice and support for local improvement efforts—in this case, the development of exemplary middle level programs. In the introduction, the authors state that "There are two things to think about when implementing middle grades reform: one is the idea of 'what' a middle school really is; the other is 'how' does one lead a school into and through the change process? This book focuses especially on the "how." Research on school change and the experiences of California educators provide some guidance on successful reform efforts." It is replete with practical ideas, suggestions, and questions worthy of serious consideration. Woven throughout are the unique insights from administrators who have been successful in developing sound middle level programs.

279.   Garvelink, R. H. (1976). Creating a good middle school: Through revolution or evolution? *The Clearing House*, *49*(4), 185-86.

Outlines eight key steps in making a successful a transition from a junior high school structure to a middle level organization.

280.   Garvin, J. P. (1990). *A sane transition to the middle school program*. Newburyport, MA: Garvin Consultant Association. 88 pp.

This booklet, by a noted middle level educator, presents a blueprint in regard to how the transition can be made from a traditional junior high to an ideal middle level program. As its table of contents suggests, it provides a year-by-year plan of action: 1. Prerequisites, 2. Getting Started, 3. Designing the Program - Year 2; 4. Opening the School - Year 3; 5. Continuing to Grow - Year 4; 6. Affirming the Process—Year 5. It concludes with a set of tables and explanations of such items as scheduling, staffing models, etc., and a bibliography.

281.   Quattrone, D. F. (1989). A case study in curriculum innovation: Developing in interdisciplinary curriculum. *Educational Horizons*, *68*(1), 28-35.

A case study of a junior high school in Greenwich, Connecticut, that made a successful transition from a junior high school philosophy to that of a middle school. Summarizes the planning process used by administration and faculty in making the transition.

282.   Steltzer, W. N., Jr. (1979). An orientation program for a middle school. *The Clearing House*, *52* (9), 52-54.

Provides an overview of an orientation program for students entering middle level schools in the Avon Grove School District. Encourages parents and students to visit the school several times during the year preceding the actual

time of enrollment. Offers suggestions for making a transition from an
elementary school setting to a middle level setting.

283.   Williamson, R., & Johnston, J. H. (1991). *Planning for success:
Successful implementation of middle level organization.* Reston, VA: National
Association of Secondary School Principals. 98 pp.

This is a highly useful booklet which provides a step-by-step plan on how to go
about developing a middle level program. Among its key strengths is a focus on
the need to ensure that there is collaborative planning, insights on how to cope
with dissent and resistance, and pitfalls to be aware of and to avoid. The
appendices include a host of documents that teachers and administrators will be
able to use and/or adapt to their own situation (e.g., planning checklist, parent
survey, student survey, planning timeline, pilot evaluation form, implementation
plan, communication plan/schedule, decision matrix, etc.).

I. TRANSITION TO THE MIDDLE LEVEL - GENERAL

284.   Cramp, J. W. (1987). Who's responsible for the transition from middle
to high school? *NASSP Bulletin: The Journal for Middle Level and High School
Administrators, 71*(501), 145-147.

A very interesting and thought-provoking piece on the need for high schools to
accommodate and meet the unique needs of young adolescents.

285.   Di Virgilio, J. (1970). Switching from junior high to middle school?
The Clearing House, 44(4), 224-226.

Compares program of junior high schools to those of middle level schools.
Concludes that middle level schools offer a positive learning environment for
young adolescents. Focuses upon activities that are relevant and sensitive to the
academic and social needs of middle level students.

286.   Lewis, A. C. (Ed.). (1992). Risk takers [Special issue]. *High
Strides, 4*(4).

A themed issue devoted to six urban middle schools that "have radically changed
the structure of the school day, curriculum, teaching, and in some cases, the
school building in order to give their students a top-notch education." Concludes
that even though the six schools have different programs, they have similar
characteristics: commitment to mission of school, support for change,
willingness to take risks, and commitment of faculty and staff. Schools
recognized for their achievements are City Magnet School, Lowell,
Massachusetts; Chattanooga School for the Arts and Sciences; Frederick
Douglass Academy, Harlem; Peter Burnett Academy, San Jose, California; and
The Saturn School, St. Paul, Minnesota.

287.   Sklarz, D. P. (1982). A primer for middle school transition. *The
Clearing House, 55*(5), 197-198.

Discusses a model for making a successful transition from a junior high structure to a middle level system. Emphasizes the roles of research, organizational structures, and teacher training in effective middle level structures.

288.   Williams, G. L. (1972). The middle school reform in Italy. *The Clearing House*, *46*(4), 245-249.

Describes the Italian middle level system as it made a successful transition from independent vocational and academic schools to a consolidated organizational structure. Also discusses the effects of the change upon the high school system.

J. ORGANIZATIONAL CULTURE

289.   Ashton, P., Doda, N., Webb, R. B., Olejnik, S., & McAuliffe, M. (1981). Middle school organization, teacher job satisfaction, and school climate. In Thomas Owen Erb (Ed.), *Middle school research: Selected studies 1981*. Columbus, OH: Research Committee of the National Middle School Association.

The results of this study suggest that the middle school's inclusion of team organization as well as its emphasis on the affective domain may have the potential for improving and/or increasing teacher job satisfaction.

290.   Daniel, L. G., & Blount, K. D. (1992). The Middle School Description Survey: A quantitative instrument for measuring organizational culture in middle schools. *Research in Middle Level Education*, *16*(1), 13-34.

This study "presents results of an effort to establish the psychometric integrity of the The Middle School Description Survey (MSDS), an instrument designed to measure middle school educators' perceptions of an idealized middle school organizational culture. As a part of the present study, selected items from an original 61-item pool were rewritten to eliminate ambiguity. In addition, original MSDS items that had not performed well during previous trial administrations were eliminated, and new items were added. The resulting 53-item instrument was completed by a nationwide random sample of 264 middle and junior high school principals. Data from this sample were subjected to factor analytic methods in order to address the instrument's construct validity. An anticipated structure of five factors was identified. On the basis of these analyses, conclusions are made regarding the continued usefulness of the instrument as a measure of organizational culture in middle schools."

291.   Klingele, W. E. (1985). Middle level education: Do we need it? *The Clearing House*, *58*(8), 334-336.

Compares the traditional "eight-four" organizational structure with the middle school organizational structures. Concludes that the middle level structure is more desirable, mainly because such a structure better meets the needs of young adolescents and offers increased opportunities for innovation and risk-taking.

292.   McEwin, C. K., & Jenkins, D. M. (1992). Where does the sixth grade belong? Programs and practices in three school organizational plans. *Current Issues in Middle Level Education, 1*(1), 8-19.

In this study, the authors sought answers to the following questions: Which, if any, grade organizational plan best serves sixth grade students? Are sixth graders experiencing schooling differently depending on their placement in 6-8 middle schools, K-6 elementary schools or K-8 schools? Are young adolescents provided equal access to developmentally responsive programs regardless of their placement? Does grade organization really make a difference? Where do sixth graders really belong? While no definitive answers are provided, the authors state that "...analysis of the data indicates that sixth grade youth enrolled in 6-8 middle schools are much more apt to experience the kind of schooling needed."

293.   McPartland, J. M. (1987). *Balancing high quality subject-matter instruction with positive teacher-student relations in middle grades: Effects of departmentalization, tracking and block scheduling on learning environments.* (Report #15). Baltimore, MD: Center for Research on Elementary and Middle Schools.

Reports the results of a study designed to identify the "best" organizational structure for effective middle level schools. Specifically, discussed are the effects of self-contained classroom instruction vs. departmentalization on student-teacher relationships and quality of instruction.

294.   White, G. P. (1993). Revolution in the middle: Recasting the middle level learning system. *Middle School Journal, 25*(1), 8-12.

Argues that middle level educational systems should be reformed with primary attention on the needs of young adolescents. Reform efforts should include rethinking curriculum; instruction and assessment; viewing organization as a means, not an end; and broadening the definitions of teachers. Presents useful, practical suggestions for accomplishing lasting educational reform.

K. SCHOOL CLIMATE

295.   Beane, J. A. (1986). A human school in the middle. *The Clearing House, 60*(1), 14-17.

Describes a model school climate that addresses the social and academic needs of young adolescents. Analyzes attempts of critics to eliminate those characteristics that contribute to an effective middle school climate and structure.

296.   Hoversten, C. D. (1992). Sustaining and impinging factors on teaching satisfaction of effective middle level teachers (Doctoral dissertation, University of Northern Iowa, 1992). *Dissertation Abstracts International, 53*, 3737A.

Commitment to teaching was sustained through a strong sense of mission, relationships with students, a supportive administrator, and positive feedback.

297.   Lewis, A. C. (Ed.). (1990). Climate/Discipline [Special issue]. *High Strides*, 2(4).

A special double issue that addresses numerous concerns related to school climate and classroom management. Specifically discussed are grading practices, tracking, and peer mediation programs.

298.   Montoya, A. L., & Brown, N. L. (1989). School climate in the middle school. In David B. Strahan (Ed.), *Middle school research: Selected studies 1989* (pp. 7-18). Columbus, OH: Research Committee of the National Middle School Association.

The researchers of this study set out to determine if there was a difference in the "relationship between perceptions of school climate held by students, teachers, and principals in middle and elementary school settings." The article describes the methods of the study, an analysis of the findings, and implications of the study. The appendix includes a copy of an instrument called the "School Climate Inventory."

299.   Thomas, D. D., & Bass, G. R. (1992). An analysis of the relationship between school climate and the implementation of middle school practices. *Research in Middle Level Education*, 16(1), 1-12.

"This study was designed to examine the relationship between the level of implementation of recommended middle school practices and school climate in Oklahoma middle schools. The Middle School Practices Index was sent to all middle school principals in the state. MSPI scores were used to identify one group of schools with high levels of implementation of recommended middle school practices and another group with low levels of implementation. Faculty from these two groups of schools were surveyed using the NASSP School Climate Survey. An analysis was performed to identify relationships between the implementation of middle school practices and school climate. Perceptions of school climate by teachers in the high implementation schools were higher on 7 of the 10 school climate indicators. Two of those differences were found to be significant at the .05 level. A correlational analysis found 19 significant relationships between middle school practices and school climate indicators. Based upon this analysis, it was concluded that a positive school climate is related to a high level of implementation of middle school practices."

300.   Wilmore, E. L. (Summer 1992). The "affective" middle level school: Keys to a nurturing school climate. *Schools in the Middle: Theory into Practice*, 1(4), 31-34.

Discusses three keys to effective school climate: an excellent curriculum and instruction, which should also be enjoyable; an outstanding student affairs program in which there are ample opportunities for all students; and solid parental support.

L. IMPLEMENTATION OF MIDDLE LEVEL PROGRAMS

301.   Alexander, W. M. (1977). Alternative futures for the middle school.
In P. S. George (Ed.), *A look ahead* (pp. 36-48). Columbus, OH: National
Middle School Association.

Discusses the need for flexible, evolving middle level programs by addressing
characteristics such as innovative, student-centered, and ever-changing. Also
emphasizes the need for adequate planning and appropriate program evaluation
components.

302.   Clark, S. N., & Clark, D. C. (1994). *Restructuring the middle level
school: Implications for school leaders*. New York: State University of New
York Press. 316 pp.

An excellent resource for middle school teachers and administrators. Focuses on
nature and needs of young adolescents, curriculum, instruction, assessment,
models of successful programs, collaboration, professional development, and
issues and trends in middle level education.

303.   Clark, T. A., Bickel, W. E., & Lacey, R. A. (1993). *Transforming
education for young adolescents: Insights for practitioners from the Lilly
Endowment's Middle Grades Improvement Program, 1987-1990*. New York:
Education Resources Group, Inc. 55 pp.

Based on extensive documentation of the Lilly Endowment's Middle Grades
Improvement Program in over 60 Indiana middle schools, this monograph
presents findings about needs assessment and planning, adolescent development,
parent and community involvement, staff and organizational capacity building,
and empowering teachers.

304.   Hon, J. E., Klemp, R. M., & Shorr, A. A. (1992). Middle schools in
transition: A cooperative approach. *New Mexico Middle School Journal, 2*,
25-31.

Summarizes the findings of two studies that investigated the implementation of
the middle level philosophy and concepts in the Los Angeles Unified School
District.
          Results indicated that schools implementing at least one middle level
concept reported increased attendance rates, reduced absences, reduced
suspensions, and fewer transfers.

305.   Lewis, A. C. (Ed.). (1993). Middle school still drifting. *High Strides,
5*(3), 2.

Reports the results of a survey designed to investigate the extent to which middle
level schools have implemented selected components of middle level programs.
Concludes that "best practice ideas about educating young adolescents are still
mostly on paper."

306. Raebeck, B. S. (1992). *Transforming middle schools: A guide to whole-school change*. Lancaster, PA: Technomic.

Outlines strategies, models, and procedures for implementing effective middle level programs. Addresses problems often faced by middle level educators involved in change, includes a strong research/knowledge base, and offers suggestions for involving the entire school in planning and implementing a long-term strategic plan. Other issues discussed include student morale, organization, teaming, scheduling, curriculum, grading/evaluation, grouping, and leadership.

307. Tadlock, M., & Barrett-Roberts, J. (1995). *Middle level education in small rural schools*. Columbus, OH: National Middle School Association. 64 pages.

Provides stories of two rural schools who successfully implemented middle level programs.

308. Wiles, J., & Bondi, J. (n.d.). *Planning Steps for Developing Middle Schools*. Tampa, FL: Wiles, Bondi & Associates. [Wiles and Bondi and Associates, Inc., P.O. Box 16545, Tampa, FL 33687.] Not paginated. Approximately 200 pages.

In this booklet, the authors provide instruments and information which address the various components of an effective middle school and ideas vis-à-vis analysis, design, implementation, and evaluation. It includes a good number of documents/findings generated by actual school districts and schools across the United States that have developed middle level programs. The articles, diagrams, charts, suggestions are xeroxed from various sources. The booklet would be much more useful/helpful and easy to use if it had a table of contents and/or index.

309. Yokoi, I. (1993). A school that works. *High Strides*, 5 (3), 4-5.

A case study of James A. Foshay Middle School in Los Angeles, California. Specifically discussed are reasons for the positive impact that the school has had upon students within its district.

V

Middle Level
Administration

A. MIDDLE LEVEL ADMINISTRATION - RESEARCH

310.   Allen, H. A., Splittgerber, F. L., & Ryan, J. P. (1979). Principals'
attitudes about the characteristics and functions of the middle school, pp. 13-21.
In *Middle school research: Selected studies 1977-1979. Volume II*, (pp. 239-
252). Fairborn, OH: National Middle School Association.

Among the conclusions of this national study (The National Middle School
Study) are the following: Stress on basic skills and the development of students'
self-concept received stronger support than quantitative goal statements dealing
with academic achievement, survival skills, discipline, and citizenship. From the
principals' perspective a successful middle school teacher should be able to
support guidance and counseling services. Principals did not support teachers'
involvement in staff selection even though the middle school concept
emphasizes team planning and teaching. The emphasis at the national level on
training to better anticipate emerging adolescent needs was not seen as being
necessary to be a successful middle school teacher. Transition was not placed in
the top choices of the principals. A copy of the instrument and the breakdown of
the responses are included in the appendix.

311.   Barrett, P. A. M. (1991). A national study of the middle school
principalship including an analysis of the effect of the middle school principal's
training and experience (Doctoral dissertation, East Texas State University,
1991). *Dissertation Abstracts International, 52,* 1582A.

Most middle school principals obtain on-the-job rather than formal training for
their position. Principals consider inter-disciplinary teams and teachers
committed to the middle school concept to be essential elements for middle
schools. Significant differences existed among principals' perceptions of middle
schools characteristics in relationship to their prior administrative experiences,
but not teaching certificate, teaching experience, or administrative certificate.

312.   Bauck, J. M. (1987). Characteristics of the effective middle school
principal. *NASSP Bulletin: The Journal for Middle Level and High School*

Administrators, *71*(500), 90-93.

Using data collected in a NASSP study of the middle level principalship, the author, in part, addresses such issues as the principal's participation in professional organizations, educational background, length of tenure on the job, outlooks, interactions with people, and views of parental/community involvement.

313.   Chiusolo, J. L., & Sloan, C. A. (1993). A profile of middle/junior high school principal leadership styles and political games. *The AIMS Journal*, *8* (1), 59-70.

Reports the results of a study designed to investigate the relationship between the "predominant leadership style and the level of the school principal with the type and intensity of political games played in the schools based on teacher perception." Includes recommendations for principals and an extensive list of related terms and definitions.

314.   Greenleaf, W. T. (1983). Profile of the middle school principal. *Principal*, *62*(4), 30-33.

An analysis of responses to a questionnaire surveying attitudes and characteristics of 300 middle school principals. Principals agreed that the most important characteristics of a middle school are "transitional nature, the attention to basic skills, the need for a professional counselor, the provision of creative experiences, a program of community relations, and a broad range of specialized student services."

315.   Johnson, M. A. (1992). Principal leadership, shared decision making, and student achievement. *Research in Middle Level Education*, *16*(1), 35-61.

"The purpose of this study was to determine the type of leadership that exists and the degree to which shared decision making and collaboration are present on campuses where middle level students are successful.... Thirty-six middle schools in Texas were selected on the basis of sustained high or low-performance for a three-year period on state criterion-referenced tests. The sample of 18 high- and 18 low-performing campuses was matched on the basis of five variables resulting in two relatively homogeneous groups. The student populations of the campuses were largely poor and minority. Decision making patterns of the principals and the presence of organizational centralization (top-down control) were analyzed to provide a comprehensive understanding of the relationship of these variables to student achievement. Data collection methods consisted of a combination of surveys, analysis of faculty handbooks containing rules and regulations for teachers, extensive phone interviews with principals, and on-site visitations to four of the schools. The principles of quality, cooperation and non-coercion appeared to be significantly greater on high-performing campuses.... Additionally, both teachers and principals on high-performing campuses indicated significantly less central control over campus matters by positions of authority outside the campus organization. The study supported assertions that the traditional, centrally controlled system of education is a system that compensates for individual weaknesses while failing to capitalize on individual strengths "(Levine, 1985). Strong support was found for the restructured middle school which offers an effective organizational design to support the expressed priorities of teachers in this study to control decisions concerning their own classrooms, curriculum, and instruction.

316. Keefe, J. W., Clark, D. C., Nickerson, N. C. Jr., & Valentine, J. (1983). *The middle level principalship. Volume II: The effective middle level principal.* Reston, VA: NASSP. 104 pp.

"This report of the national Study of Schools in the Middle includes a discussion of personal and professional traits of effective principals, job tasks and problems, and middle level educational issues. Several effective principals are also profiled."

317. Meyer, C. F., & Van Hoose, J. J. (1979). A study of the perceptions of performance of middle school principals by selected teachers and principals. In *Middle school research: Selected studies 1977-1979.* Volume III, pp. 31-41. Fairborn, OH: National Middle School Association.

Among the findings of this study were the following: "The majority of the performance skills practiced by the middle school principals are not congruent with what they should be practicing, as perceived by the middle school principals themselves. The teachers perceived all of the skills being practiced by the middle school principals as significantly different from the manner in which they should be practiced. There is a significant difference in what the middle school principals perceive they are practicing and what the teachers perceive they are practicing, on a large majority of the skills. There is a significant difference in what middle school principals perceive they should be practicing and what teachers perceive they should be practicing, on a majority of the skills. Directional trends have merged, evidenced in the data with the teachers and principals both stating that what should be practiced rank higher than what is practiced."

318. Sams, P. A. H. (1987). Leadership styles of successful middle school principals. (Doctoral dissertation, The University of North Carolina at Greensboro, 1987). *Dissertation Abstracts International, 48,* 1080A.

Based on responses to Elias Porter's *Strength Deployment Inventory* and the *Job Interactions Survey,* significant findings were found. In general, successful leadership hinged on the principal's capacity to "bind vision to goals, goals to commitment, and commitment to practices."

319. Stillerman, K. P. (1992). Successful North Carolina middle school principals' visions. *Research in Middle Level Education, 16*(1), 63-78.

"The purpose of this research was to discover how five successful school principals in North Carolina define vision and their perception of how they communicate vision in their schools.... Five principals, nominated by a panel of middle school experts as being among the most successful middle grades practitioners in the state, participated in the study. A set of guiding questions was used to interview each principal. In addition, site visits were conducted for the purpose of observation and informal interview of teachers, counselors, assistant principals, and students. Written documents, such as teacher and student handbooks, school improvement plans, and memos from the principals were examined. The final data were reported as narratives or portraits of the principals and their visionary leadership. The research indicated that successful middle school principals are visionary leaders. It further revealed that vision is an iterative process, shaped the principal's own set of values, school culture, consensus on effective middle school practice, and district expectation."

320.   Valentine, J. W. (1984). A national study of schools in the middle — perspectives on five issues. *NASSP Bulletin: The Journal for High School and Middle School Administrators*, 68(473),12-18.

Valentine reports on NASSP's "National Study of Schools in the Middle." In doing so, he reports on what he considers the most significant and interesting findings as they relate to the daily activities of the middle level principal.

321.   Valentine, J. W., Clark, D. C., Irvin, J. L., Keefe, J. W., & Melton, G. (1993). *Leadership in middle level education, Vol. I: A national survey of middle level leaders and schools*. Reston, VA: National Association of Secondary School Principals.

The first of two volumes in the national Study of Leadership in Middle Level Education. Reports data from a sample of middle level principals on personal and professional traits of principals, their job tasks and problems, school programs, and selected educational issues. More specifically, the study examines characteristics of principals and programs that influence school operation. Also discusses key trends and beliefs that affect student success. Includes 119 tables.

322.   Valentine, J., Clark, D. C., Nickerson, N. C. Jr., & Keefe, J. W. (1982). *The middle level principalship. Volume I: A study of middle level principals and programs*. Reston, VA: National Association of Secondary School Principals. 168 pp.

This report of the National Study of Schools in the Middle presents data from a national survey of middle level principals' personal and professional traits, job tasks, and problems; student, staff, and community characteristics; school programs; and educational issues.

B. MIDDLE LEVEL ADMINISTRATION - PRACTICAL

323.   Alley, R. A. (1993). Behind the science: Principals set the stage for middle level performance. *Schools in the Middle*, 2(4), 43-44.

Using a theater analogy, the author describes the importance of middle level administrators in "directing" a "production" that meets the needs of middle level students. Includes a list of characteristics often exhibited by effective middle level administrators.

324.   Filby, N. N., Lee, G. V., & Lambert, V. (1990). *Middle grades reform: A casebook for school leaders*. San Francisco, CA: Far West Laboratory for Educational Research and Development and California Association of County Superintendents of Schools. 115 pp.

The express purpose of this volume is to assist local educators in the process of school improvement by providing access to the best ideas in research and practice and support for local improvement efforts—in this case, the development of exemplary middle level programs. In the introduction, the authors state that "There are two things to think about when implementing middle grades reform: one is the idea of 'what' a middle school really is; the other is 'how' does one lead a school into and through the change process?" This book focuses especially on the "how." Research on school change and the experiences of California educators provide some guidance on successful reform efforts. It is replete with practical ideas, suggestions, and questions worthy of serious consideration. Woven throughout are the unique insights from administrators who have been successful in developing sound middle level programs.

C. MIDDLE LEVEL ADMINISTRATION - GENERAL

325.   Aronstein, L. W., Marlow, M., & Desilets, B. (1990). Detours on the road to site-based management. *Educational Leadership, 47*(7), 61-63.

Describes a series of critical, though ordinary, incidents which occurred as a faculty moved through a restructuring process to site-based management.

326.   Bauck, J. M. (1987). Characteristics of the effective middle school principal. *NASSP Bulletin: The Journal for Middle Level and High School Administrators, 71*(500), 90-93.

Using data collected in a NASSP study of the middle level principalship, the author, in part, addresses such issues as the principal's participation in professional organizations, educational background, length of tenure on the job, outlooks, interactions with people, and views of parental/community involvement.

327.   Chiusolo, J. L., & Sloan, C. A. (1993). A profile of middle/junior high school principal leadership styles and political games. *The AIMS Journal, 8* (1), 59-70.

Reports the results of a study designed to investigate the relationship between the "predominant leadership style and the level of the school principal with the type and intensity of political games played in the schools based on teacher perception." Includes recommendations for principals and an extensive list of related terms and definitions.

328.   George, P. S. (1990). From junior high to middle school—principals' perspectives. *NASSP Bulletin: The Journal for Middle Level and High School Administrators*, 74(523), 86-94.

George argues that with the proper support, junior high school principals can make a successful transition to a middle school organization. He shares the perspectives of principals who successfully made the transition. Among the issues addressed are: new principals' concerns, the principal as an instructional leader, initiating a middle level program, principals' perceptions of interdisciplinary teaming, decision making in the middle school, and implications for school districts.

329.   Johnson, M. A. (1992). Principal leadership, shared decision making, and student achievement. *Research in Middle Level Education*, 16(1), 35-61.

"The purpose of this study was to determine the type of leadership that exists and the degree to which shared decision making and collaboration are present on campuses where middle level students are successful.... Thirty-six middle schools in Texas were selected on the basis of sustained high or low-performance for a three-year period on state criterion-referenced tests. The sample of 18 high- and 18 low-performing campuses was matched on the basis of five variables resulting in two relatively homogeneous groups. The student populations of the campuses were largely poor and minority. Decision making patterns of the principals and the presence of organizational centralization (top-down control) were analyzed to provide a comprehensive understanding or the relationship of these variables to student achievement. Data collection methods consisted of a combination of surveys, analysis of faculty handbooks containing rules and regulations for teachers, extensive phone interviews with principals, and on-site visitations to four of the schools. The principles of quality, cooperation and non-coercion appeared to be significantly greater on high-performing campuses.... Additionally, both teachers and principals on high-performing campuses indicated significantly less central control over campus matters by positions of authority outside the campus organization. The study supported assertions that the traditional, centrally controlled system of education is a system that compensates for individual weaknesses while failing to capitalize on individual strengths "(Levine, 1985). Strong support was found for the restructured middle school which offers an effective organizational design to support the expressed priorities of teachers in this study to control decisions concerning their own classrooms, curriculum, and instruction.

330.   Keefe, J. W., Clark, D. C., Nickerson, N. C. Jr., & Valentine, J. (1983). *The middle level principalship. Volume II: The effective middle level principal*. Reston, VA: NASSP. 104 pp.

"This report of the national Study of Schools in the Middle includes a discussion of personal and professional traits of effective principals, job tasks and problems, and middle level educational issues. Several effective principals are also profiled."

331.   Merenbloom, E. Y. (1984). Administering a middle school. In John H. Lounsbury (Ed.), *Perspectives: Middle school education* (pp. 98-108). Columbus, OH: National Middle School Association.

Discusses the major tasks of middle school administration: translating theory into practice, discussing the basis for adopting the middle school concept, establishing effective communication with constituency groups, coordinating continuous staff development, articulating with feeder schools, insuring that the curriculum responds to the needs of the student, creating a flexible school organization, monitoring the effectiveness of the teaching teams as well as the daily instructional program, and maintaining the commitment to the early adolescent and the middle school concept.

332.   Meyer, C. F., & Van Hoose, J. J. (1979). A study of the perceptions of performance of middle school principals by selected teachers and principals. In *Middle school research: Selected studies 1977-1979*. Volume III, pp. 31-41. Fairborn, OH: National Middle School Association.

Among the findings of this study were the following: "The majority of the performance skills practiced by the middle school principals are not congruent with what they should be practicing, as perceived by the middle school principals themselves. The teachers perceived all of the skills being practiced by the middle school principals as significantly different from the manner in which they should be practiced.
        There is a significant difference in what the middle school principals perceive they are practicing and what the teachers perceive they are practicing, on a large majority of the skills. There is a significant difference in what middle school principals perceive they should be practicing and what teachers perceive they should be practicing, on a majority of the skills. Directional trends have merged, evidenced in the data with the teachers and principals both stating that what should be practiced rank higher than what is practiced."

333.   Shockley, R. (1986-1987). The effective middle level school administrator. *KAMLE Karavan: Journal of the Kansas Association for Middle Level Education, 1*, 7-9.

Discusses the need for the middle level principal to have a solid understanding of the unique needs of young adolescents and how that translates into school policies and programs, to take on the role of "cultural leader" (whereby s/he defines, strengthens and articulates the values and beliefs that the middle school has an unique identity"), to be an instructional leader, and to be pro-active and not re-active.

334.   Totten, S., Snider, S., & Jones, M. (1995). The Critical Role of the Principal at the Middle Level. *Current Issues in Middle Level Education, 4*(1), 85-93.

Among the issues the authors discuss are leadership, leadership at the middle level, the principal's role in staff development, the critical need for a sense of mission, and the need for indepth preparation for middle level principals.

335.   Spinder, J. P., & George, P. S. (1984). Participatory leadership in the middle school. *The Clearing House*, *57*(7), 293-295.

Discusses the need for middle level teachers to be involved in the decision-making process. Argues that principals can function more effectively by using a site-based management model than by using the traditional "top-down" model of leadership.

336.   Stillerman, K. P. (1992). Successful North Carolina middle school principals' visions. *Research in Middle Level Education*, *16*(1), 63-78.

"The purpose of this research was to discover how five successful school principals in North Carolina define vision and their perception of how they communicate vision in their schools.... Five principals, nominated by a panel of middle school experts as being among the most successful middle grades practitioners in the state, participated in the study. A set of guiding questions was used to interview each principal. In addition, site visits were conducted for the purpose of observation and informal interview of teachers, counselors, assistant principals, and students. Written documents, such as teacher and student handbooks, school improvement plans, and memos from the principals were examined. The final data were reported as narratives or portraits of the principals and their visionary leadership. The research indicated that successful middle school principals are visionary leaders. It further revealed that vision is an iterative process, shaped the principal's own set of values, school culture, consensus on effective middle school practice, and district expectation."

337.   Totten, S., Snider, D., Jones, M., & Sewall, A. (in review). The need for specially prepared middle level administrators.

In this piece the authors discuss the following: the dearth of attention that has been directed to the need for specially prepared middle level administrators; the importance of a strong educational leader at the middle level; current efforts by schools of education to prepare middle level administrators; and the knowledge, skills and dispositions needed to serve as an effective educational leader at the middle level.

338.   Valentine, J. W. (1984). A national study of schools in the middle — perspectives on five issues. *NASSP Bulletin: The Journal for High School and Middle School Administrators*, *68*(473),12-18.

Valentine reports on NASSP's "National Study of Schools in the Middle." In doing so, he reports on what he considers the most significant and interesting findings as they relate to the daily activities of the middle level principal.

339.   Valentine, J. W., Clark, D. C., Irvin, J. L., Keefe, J. W., & Melton, G.

(1993). *Leadership in middle level education, Vol. I: A national survey of middle level leaders and schools.* Reston, VA: National Association of Secondary School Principals.

The first of two volumes in the national Study of Leadership in Middle Level Education. Reports data from a sample of middle level principals on personal and professional traits of principals, their job tasks and problems, school programs, and selected educational issues. More specifically, the study examines characteristics of principals and programs that influence school operation. Also discusses key trends and beliefs that affect student success. Includes 119 tables.

340.   Valentine, J., Clark, D. C., Nickerson, N. C. Jr., & Keefe, J. W. (1982). *The middle level principalship. Volume I: A study of middle level principals and programs.* Reston, VA: National Association of Secondary School Principals. 168 pp.

This report of the National Study of Schools in the Middle presents data from a national survey of middle level principals' personal and professional traits, job tasks, and problems; student, staff, and community characteristics; school programs; and educational issues.

VI

Middle Level Facilities

341.   Jones, M., & Totten, S. (forthcoming). Designing and building a new middle school: One district's plan of action. *Schools in the Middle*.

The authors discuss the steps that were taken in order to initiate, develop and implement a new middle level program in Springdale, Arkansas. In doing so, they talk about the critical need to work early on with the school personnel and the architect of the new building, the need to constantly stay student focused, the value in visiting other middle level programs, and the value in preparing a document to guide implementation of the overall program.

342.   Magid, M. K. (1976). A community designs its school. *The Clearing House*, *49*(4), 157-159.

Describes the physical design and facilities of Woodrow Wilson Middle School, a model middle school located in Oakland California. Describes a collaborative effort involving school representatives, parents, and community representatives to design a building that enhances student learning.

VII

Interdisciplinary Team Organization (ITO)

A. INTERDISCIPLINARY TEAMING - RESEARCH

343.   Arhar, J. (1992). A research agenda for interdisciplinary teaming: Looking through the lens of school restructuring. *Research in Middle Level Education*, 15(2), 1-7.

This piece serves as an introduction to this special issue (on interdisciplinary teaming) of *Research in Middle Level Education*. Discusses the significance of interdisciplinary teaming, the fact a systematic research program on interdisciplinary teaming is still in its infancy, and a set of suggestions vis-à-vis a research agenda.

344.   Arhar, J. (Guest Editor). (1992). Special Issue of *Research in Middle Level Education*. "Interdisciplinary Team Organization." *15*(2).

This special issue contains five essays (four of which are studies on interdisciplinary teaming). The five pieces are as follows: Joanne Arhar's "A Research Agenda for Interdisciplinary Teaming: Looking Through the Lens of School Restructuring"; Rebecca A. Mills, et al's "The Influence of Middle Level Interdisciplinary Teaming on Teacher Isolation: A Case Study"; Thomas E. Gatewood, et al's "Middle School Interdisciplinary Team Organization and Its Relationship to Teacher Stress"; Greg P. Stefanich, et al's "A Longitudinal Study of Interdisciplinary Teaching and Its Influence on Student Self-Concept"; and, "Sally N. Clark and Donald C. Clark's "The Pontoon Transitional Design: A Missing Link in the Research on Interdisciplinary Teaming." Each piece is separately annotated in this bibliography.

345.   Arhar, J. M. (1990). Interdisciplinary teaming as a school intervention to increase the social bonding of middle level students. In Judith L. Irvin (Ed.), *Research in middle level education: Selected studies 1990* (pp. 1-10). Columbus, OH: National Middle School Association.

"Eleven teamed and eleven non-teamed schools representing urban and suburban districts from four major regions of the country participated in this study.

Approximately 2500 seventh graders in teamed middle level schools were compared to 2500 seventh graders in non-teamed middle level schools on the three measures of social bonding: bonding to peers, bonding to school, and bonding to teachers. A twenty-five item Likert-type Social Bonding Scale was administered. Eleven separate multivariate analyses (MANOVAS) were conducted in which eight showed that students in teamed schools scored higher overall on at least one of the three measures of social bonding than students in non-teamed schools The author implies that if a linear relationship exists between social bonding and dropping out of school, then, perhaps interdisciplinary teaming may be a low cost intervention for keeping at risk students in schools."

346.   Arhar, J. M. (1991). The effects of interdisciplinary teaming on the social bonding of middle level students (Doctoral dissertation, University of Cincinnati, 1990). *Dissertation Abstracts International*, *52*, 65A.

The author investigated whether interdisciplinary teaming increases the likelihood that middle level students will form stronger social bonds with their peers, their school and their teachers than students in non-teamed schools do. Organizing middle level schools into interdisciplinary teams was believed to create a sense of community for the students. A matched pairs design was used. Eleven teamed schools were compared to eleven nonteamed schools. Social bonding was measured by student responses to the Seventh Grade Student Questionnaire from the Wisconsin Youth Survey. The study found that the greatest effect of teaming is on bonding to teachers and somewhat less for bonding to school and to students. Another apparent finding was that teaming may have the potential to decrease student dropouts.

347.   Arhar, J. M. (1992). Interdisciplinary teaming and the social bonding of middle level students. In Judith L. Irvin (Ed.), *Transforming middle level education: Perspectives and possibilities* (pp. 139-161). Needham, MA: Allyn and Bacon.

Presents a theoretical rationale and a brief overview of the research base for interdisciplinary teaming. Among the topics the author addresses are a brief history of the use of interdisciplinary teaming in schools, adolescent alienation, social bonding theory, the value of interdisciplinary teaming, and recommendations for further research.

348.   Bradley, E. (1988). The effectiveness of an interdisciplinary team organization pattern compared with a departmentalized organizational pattern in a selected middle level school setting. In David B. Strahan (Ed.), *Middle school research: Selected studies 1988* (pp. 85-113). Columbus, OH: The Research Committee of the National Middle School Association.

The purpose of this study was "to determine the effectiveness of an Interdis-ciplinary Team Staff Organizational Pattern (I.T.S.O.P.) when compared with the traditional Departmentalized Staff Organizational Pattern (D.S.O.P.) in the areas of: 1) academic achievement of low, average, and high ability students;

2) student attendance; 3) student discipline problems; and, 4) parent opinion of school program.

The researcher evaluated the impact of the two designated staffing patterns by matching 78 pairs of students on previous achievement and I. Q. The students were matched from groups who had been randomly selected for the I.T.S.O.P. and D.S.O. P. programs. It was concluded theInterdisciplinary Team Staff Organizational Pattern was more effective than the Departmentalized Staff Organizational Pattern in fostering math achievement. Both the I.T.S.O.P. and D.S.O.P. programs were equally effective in fostering reading achievement.

349.   Clark, S. N., & Clark, D. C. (1992). The Pontoon Transitional Design: A missing link in the research on interdisciplinary teaming. *Research in Middle Level Education, 15*(2), 57-81.

The purpose of this study was twofold: (1) to provide information about a noted model of interdisciplinary teaming—the Pontoon Transitional Design, and (2) to discuss the significance of the Pontoon Transitional Design to current research and practices. It describes the rationale and organization of the pontoon and discusses the procedures and findings from ten studies of pontoons in grades seven, eight, and nine conducted between 1964 and 1972. Implications for current practices are also discussed.

350.   Feirsen, R. (1987). A model for assessing team meetings. *The Clearing House*, *60*(8), 360-362.

Reports the results of a study designed to assess interdisciplinary team meetings through the use of Flanders' interaction model. Concludes that the model can accurately predict and analyze classroom interaction based upon teachers' perceptions.

351.   Gatewood, T. E., Green, G., & Harris, S. E. (1992). Middle school interdisciplinary team organization and its relationship to teacher stress. *Research in Middle Level Education, 15*(2), 27-40.

"The purpose of this study was to compare stress reported by middle school teachers participating on interdisciplinary teams with stress of teachers in middle schools without these teams. Participants in the study were 111 teachers in 25 middle schools with teams and 113 teachers in 25 other middle schools without teams. All teachers are located in the mid-Atlantic regions of the United States. Data were collected using the 49 item Likert-type Teacher Stress Inventory (TSI). A regression MANOVA was conducted with several predictor variables. Univariate F tests contributed individual predictors to each of the dependent variables. The effects of teaming were found to be independent of any heightened sense of support from peers or supervisors. Interdisciplinary teaming was associated with slightly reduced teacher stress scores. Teaming was associated positively with the enhancement of the image teachers had of themselves as professionals. Teachers on teams had a stronger sense of themselves as professionals than comparable teachers without teaming experiences."

352.   Gibson, P. K. (1992). Factors present during the development of exemplary interdisciplinary teams in middle level schools (Doctoral dissertation, Virginia Polytechnic Institute and State University, 1992). *Dissertation Abstracts International, 53,* 2223A.

Conspicuously absent on exemplary teams were coordination with non-team teachers, use of uniform discipline policies and scheduling guidelines, and observing peers' teaching and proposing staff development programs. Exemplary teams concentrated on either administration, curriculum, or change to new activities, and valued training, support, and activities in their teams' development, but reported school organization and decision-making structure as less important. Team members respected individuality in the context of strong team identity and whole-school work environment.

353.   Hart, L. E., Pate, E. P., Mizelle, N. B., & Reeves, J. L. (1992). Interdisciplinary team development in the middle school: A study of the Delta Project. *Research in Middle Level Education, 16*(1), 79-98.

"The Delta Project involved one team of four middle school teachers and their approximately 100 students working together throughout grades 6-8 to make a number of changes in team organization, curriculum, and instruction. The purpose of the study was to examine the development of the four teachers as they worked together as an interdisciplinary team. The four data sources were (a) observations of team planning sessions, (b) group interviews with the teachers, (c) interviews with the school administrators, and (d) a chronicle of the Delta Project written by the teachers."

354.   Hirsch, D. (1994). *Schooling for the middle years: Developments in eight European countries.* New York, NY: Carnegie Council on Adolescent Development, Carnegie Corporation of New York. Presentation at the Frontiers in the Education of Adolescents Conference, November 3-5, 1994.

Provides a description of the educational structure developed to meet the needs of children ages 10 to 14 in "the Czech Republic, Denmark, England, France, Italy, [and] the Netherlands, ...Germany, and Switzerland" (p. 3). Frames the descriptions by posing six key questions: "Extension of elementary, preparation for a secondary, or a stage in its own right?... Together or separate: Should the middle years be a common experience, or adapted to different needs?... Equal success or equal opportunity to fail?... The organization of teaching and counseling: Qualified specialists or caring generalists?... Academic instruction or educating the whole person?... Can schools be made 'communities for learning?'" (pp. 5-11).

355.   Husband, R. E., & Short, P. M. (1994). Interdisciplinary teams lead to greater teacher empowerment. *Middle School Journal, 26*(2), 58-60.

This study revealed that interdisciplinary team teachers felt significantly more empowered than traditional teachers in all six areas examined: decision making, professional growth, status, self-efficacy, autonomy, and impact. Offers definitions of areas and possible reasons for results. Findings parallel those for self-directed or self-managed teams found in business and industry.

356.   Kruse, S., & Louis, K. S. (1995). Teacher teaming - opportunities and dilemmas. *Brief to Principals,* 11.

A report on research in four middle schools that "examines some of the potential conflicts between teacher teaming and the development of schoolwide professional community" (p. 1). Begins with a discussion of the characteristics of a professional community: "reflective dialogue... de-privatization of practice... collective focus on student learning... collaboration... shared norms and values" (p. 2). While teachers in the four schools reported support for teaming, they also reported that "schoolwide collective responsibility for student work can be undermined" (p. 4). The basic reason given was that time devoted to team planning was not available for whole faculty planning. No suggestions for how to overcome the perceived difficulties are offered.

357.   MacIver, D. J., & Epstein, J. L. (1991). Responsive practices in the middle grades: Teacher teams, advisory groups, remedial instruction, and school transition programs. *American Journal of Education, 99*(4), 587-622.

The authors surveyed nationally (Education in the Middle Grades) 1,753 principals in schools teaching grade seven. The effects of the following practices were discussed in the article: (1) interdisciplinary teacher teams; (2) group advisory periods; (3) remedial instruction programs; and (4) school transition programs.

358.   Mills, R. A., Powell, R. R., & Pollak, J. P. (1992). The influence of middle level interdisciplinary teaming on teacher isolation: A case study. *Research in Middle Level Education.* Special issue on Interdisciplinary Teaming, *15*(2), 9-25.

"This study was conducted during an entire school year in a middle school with grades six through eight and explored the influence of interdisciplinary teaming on feelings of isolation and collegiality among teachers on teams. Using methods associated with long-term field studies, researchers observed and interviewed teachers on three interdisciplinary case study teams. The personal isolation frequently experienced by teachers was nonexistent by early in the school year; however, other themes of isolation emerged. Inter-team isolation and subject matter isolation concerned teachers who were case study team members. Implications for teacher decision making, for novice teacher development, and for administrative support of teaming are discussed."

359.   Powell, R. R., & Mills, R. (1994). Five types of mentoring build knowledge on interdisciplinary teams. *Middle School Journal, 26*(2), 24-30.

Discusses aspects of the natural mentoring process that occurs almost contin-uously among team teachers. Teachers were both individually interviewed and regularly observed during their team planning meetings and during informal interactions at lunch and between classes. Five types of mentoring were identified: collaborative, clerical, professional teacher, interdisciplinary content, and social informal. Teachers engaged in their mentoring activities simultaneously.

360.   Sinclair, R., & Zigarmi, D. (1979). The effects a middle school interdisciplinary staffing pattern and a middle school departmentalized staffing pattern has on student achievement levels, perceptions of school environment, and attitudes toward teachers. *Middle school research: Selected studies 1977-1979. Volume 1* (pp. 55-64). Fairborn, OH: National Middle School Association.

Two of the key conclusions drawn from this study by the researchers are: 1. Students taught under interdisciplinary staffing organizational patterns (ISOP) will have greater gains in academic achievement than they would if taught under a departmentalized staffing organizational pattern (DSOP); and 2. A student's perception of school climate will be enhanced to a greater degree under an ISOP than under a DSOP.

361.   Stefanich, G. P., Mueller, J. C., & Wills, F. W. (1992). A longitudinal study of interdisciplinary teaming and its influence on student self-concept. *Research in Middle Level Education, 15*(2), 41-55.

"The present study was partial replication of a study done five years earlier which examined interdisciplinary teaming in middle schools and their resulting impact of interdisciplinary teaming on student self-concepts. The degree of interdisciplinary teaming was measured using the stages-of-concern instrument that is a component of the Concerns Based Adoption Model (CBAM). Student self-concept was measured by the Piers-Harris Children's Self Concept Scale. Results showed that the majority of teachers in Iowa schools are at the early stages of usage of interdisciplinary team teaching and usage over time does not lead to higher levels of implementation of the concept. In contrast to the 1987 study, which found students who attended middle schools with interdisciplinary teaming had higher self-concepts than middle schools in which teaming had not been implemented, this study did not find a significant difference between students in user and nonuse schools."

B. INTERDISCIPLINARY TEAMING - PRACTICAL

362.   Alexander, W. M. (1995). 2-teacher teams promote integrative curriculum. *Middle Ground,* 6-7.

Describes positive experiences as a member of a two-person team responsible for up to 60 students in grades 6-8. Highlights the advantages of a two-person team over larger teams in planning and implementing an integrative program.

363.   DiVirgilia, J. (1973). Guidelines for effective interdisciplinary teams. *The Clearing House, 47*(4), 209-211.

Discusses the role of interdisciplinary teams within middle level programs. Also includes suggestions for effective teaming.

364. Hendrickson, J. M., Ross, J. J., Mercer, C. D., & Walker, P. (1988). The multidisciplinary team: Training educators to serve middle school students with special needs. *The Clearing House, 62*(2), 84-86.

Discusses the role of interdisciplinary teams in providing appropriate instruction for students with special needs. Specifically discussed is a program developed at the University of Florida.

365. Kain, D. L. (1995). Teaming with a purpose: Getting to the point of middle level teaming. *Schools in the Middle 4*(4), 6-9.

Suggests that team identity and sense of purpose contributes to success. Describes an activity to accomplish this through the development of an "'advertisement' for another team member" (p. 8). The text and graphics developed help a team hone in on shared values.

366. Knight, S. (1991). Create a team handbook. *The Transescent, 16* (1), 25-33.

Includes a copy of the handbook compiled by a team at Hixson Middle School in St. Louis, Missouri. Includes the following columns: To Parents, To Student, Homework, Your Child's Behavior at School, Supplies, English Goals and Objectives, Math Goals and Objectives, Physical Science Goals and Objectives, Social Science Goals and Objectives, Classroom Rules and Expectations, Parent Communication, Discovery Period, and Conference Times. Can be adapted for use in any middle level setting.

367. Lounsbury, J. H. (Ed.), (1992). *Connecting the curriculum through interdisciplinary instruction.* Columbus, OH: National Middle School Association. 162 pp.

This collection of articles (most of which previously appeared in the *Middle School Journal*) focus on the whys and hows of interdisciplinary teaming, the benefits of interdisciplinary teaming, interdisciplinary instruction, and the development of interdisciplinary units.
　　The articles that focus specifically on interdisciplinary units are as follows: "There is No Finish Line" (the description of an interdisciplinary unit built around the Olympics); "The Interdisciplinary Unit—It's Here to Stay" (about a New Jersey faculty's use of IDUs and the positive impact it had on the teachers); "The Simulation Technique Applied in an Ancient Egypt IDU"; "Interdisciplinary Units: Keystones of Learning (three examples of interdisciplinary units used at a middle school); and, "The Roaring Twenties—An Interdisciplinary Unit."

368. Merenbloom, E. Y. (1991). *The team process: A handbook for teachers*. Columbus, OH: National Middle School Association. 168 pp.

Written by one of the foremost authorities on middle level education, this book provides an outstanding overview of the whys, how, and whats of teaming. In doing so, he provides practical examples of how to develop teams, how to build in a common planning time within the master schedule, activities that can enhance a team's effectiveness, the most effective ways to use common planning periods, how to resolve conflicts among team members, the importance of leadership within a team and how to accomplish that, staff development, and much more.

369.   Mueller, J. C. (1993). The physical education specialist on the interdisciplinary team. *New Mexico Middle School Journal*, *3*, 14-16.

Discusses the importance of including a physical education specialist on a middle level program's interdisciplinary team. Includes three different scenarios in regard to how both the physical education teacher and physical education curriculum can enhance the efforts of any middle level program.

370.   Pickler, G. (1987). The evolutionary development of interdisciplinary teams. *Middle School Journal*, *18*(2), 6-7.

Delineates the stages through which an interdisciplinary team progresses over time. Teachers are encouraged to evaluate their own teams and identify their current standing. Offers several ideas for improving team cohesiveness and effectiveness.

371.   Smith, H. W. (1991). Guide teaming development. *Middle School Journal*, *22*(5), 21-23.

Provides solid advice in regard to what educators need to do in the way of pre-planning and pre-organization work as they set about developing their interdisciplinary teams. Particularly helpful is the chart "Teaming Expectations Guide," which clearly delineates a master plan to carry out the development of a strong interdisciplinary team structure.

C. INTERDISCIPLINARY TEAMING - GENERAL

372.   Alexander, W. M., Jr. (1993). Team organization: Taking steps beyond the interdisciplinary unit. *Journal of the New England League of Middle Schools*, *6*(3), 5-7.

Questions the effectiveness of four- or five-teacher teams in developing and planning interdisciplinary units. Offers an alternative model of smaller, two-member teams. Offers evidence that smaller teams allow time for students and teachers to interact. Also addresses the need to include parents on each team.

373.   Ambrose, A., Blair, M., Brodeur, G., & Vemmer, K. (1986-1987). How we survived the first year of teaming. *KAMLE Karavan: Journal of the Kansas Association for Middle Level Education*, *1*, 16-17.

The title is misleading in that it does not really address the issue of survival, but it does do a good job of explaining the operation of a team as well as the various benefits to students, parents, teachers and the entire school.

374.   Burkhardt, R. M., & Read, J. E. (Spring 1993). Teachers on teaching: Learning from colleagues—mentors and models. *In Transition*, pp. 7-10.

Discusses the importance of developing collaborative skills, working together, and reflecting upon their experiences. The authors argue that teaming encourages reflection. This insightful article recognizes the importance of appreciating collegial relationships as a source of "wisdom if we take time to stop and reflect, and this reflection serves both us and those we serve, our students" (p. 10).

375.   Dumpert, B. S., Sturis, S. M., Winfrey, D. S., & Ennis, S. (1986-1987). Comments from an experienced team. *KAMLE Karavan: Journal of the Kansas Association for Middle Level Education, 1,* 17-18.

Discusses the many benefits of teaming as well as how the team operates.

376.   Erb, T. O., & Doda, N. M. (1989). *Team organization: Promise—practices and possibilities.* Washington, D.C.: National Education Association. 128 pp.

"Details the four basic elements of team organization and provides teaching strategies and techniques to improve instruction and decision making."

377.   Kain, D. L. (1993). Helping teams succeed: An essay review of *Groups That Work (and Those That Don't), Creating Conditions for Effective Teamwork. Middle School Journal, 24*(4), 25-31.

Overview of how it is possible to make interdisciplinary teams more effective, including "tripwires" that educators need to be aware of so they can avoid them.

378.   Knight, S. (1991). Being on two teams—Twice the support twice the satisfaction. *The Transescent, 16,* (2), 6-8.

Discusses the benefits of belonging to grade level teams and to content area teams. Includes minutes of team meeting from which results detailed lesson plans and sharing of ideas.

379.   Lank, J. (1993). Interdisciplinary learning: Teaming's natural product. *New Mexico Middle School Journal, 2,* 7-11.

Discusses the need for teams to "evolve" into a supportive, comfortable structure. Outlines the following steps in the maturation process: (1) emotional support, (2) awareness of other team members' curriculum and perception of students, (3) idea sharing, (4) project sharing, and (5) integrated instruction and interdisciplinary units.

380.   Lewis, A. C. (Ed.). (1990). Teaming [Special issue]. *High Strides*, 2 (1).

Includes five articles focusing on the following issues related to teaming: pros and cons, size and grade span of teams, role of guidance counselors, curriculum, and parental involvement.

381.   Presnell, C. D. (1980). Counselor-team collaboration in middle and junior high schools. *The Clearing House, 54*(2), 58-59.

Discusses the benefits of teaming with emphasis upon increased opportunities for collaboration among teachers and counselors. Concludes that teaming allows counselors more time for professional development and participation in parent-teacher conferences. Also includes a model for an effective parent-teacher conference.

382.   Richardong, A. (1993). School-based teams help improve school learning and environments. *Schools in the Middle, 2*(4), 26-29.

As part of a restructuring effort, Kramer Middle School in Connecticut established specialized teams as one means of meeting the unique needs of middle level students. Specifically discussed are the following teams: School Learning Climate Team, Teaching Team Model, Pupil Progress Monitoring Team, Staff Development Team, Students-at-Risk Team, Parent Involvement Collaborative, Affective Educational Team, and Cocurricular Activities Team.

383.   Williams, E. C. (1987-1988). Now you're talking, it's team time. *KAMLE Karavan: Journal of the Kansas Association for Middle Level Education, 2*, 11-12.

A principal praises the concept of interdisciplinary teaming and the benefits it has for both students and faculty.

VIII

Advisor/Advisee

A. ADVISORY - RESEARCH

384.   Cole, C. G. (1994). Teachers' attitudes before beginning a teacher advisory program. *Middle School Journal, 25*(5), 3-7.

This study explored the beliefs about teacher advisory (TA) programs from more than two hundred middle school teachers in three states. Based on survey results, Cole offers suggestions for developing a TA program.

385.   Putbrese, L. (1989). Advisory programs at the middle level - The students' response. *NASSP Bulletin: The Journal for Middle Level and High School Administrators, 73*(514), 11-115.

Discusses the findings of a national study whose goal was to "determine whether or not advisory programs were accomplishing their desired outcomes."

386.   Totten, S., & Nielsen, W. (1994). Middle level students' perceptions of their advisor/advisee program: A preliminary study. *Current Issues in Middle Level Education, 3*(2), 8-33.

This study was conducted in order to ascertain middle level students' perceptions of their advisor/advisee program (particularly in regard to whether students perceived the program as meeting their social and emotional needs). It was conducted in a school in Bentonville, Arkansas, that was acclaimed an exemplary middle school ("a middle school that has become known because of its level of excellence to researchers and practitioners on a local, state, national, or international basis") by Paul George and William Alexander.

387.   Ziegler, S., & Mulhall, L. (1994). Establishing and evaluating a successful advisory program in a middle school. *Middle School Journal, 25*(4), 42-46.

Models and discusses the development of an advisory program in the City of Toronto. Explains roles of participants and beginning-of-school activities. Gives survey results on process and outcomes from advisors, students, and parents. Concludes with a list of elements of a successful advisement program.

B. ADVISORY - PRACTICAL

388.   Ayres, L. R. (1994). Middle school advisory programs: Findings from the field. *Middle School Journal, 25*(3), 8-14.

Discusses the need for advisories and presents an outline for developing an advisory program over three years. Includes reasons cited by teachers for lack of commitment to advisories, including general fear of the unknown, lack of training as a counselor, and fear of and lack of skills for dealing with students affectively. Schools must devise their own advisory programs and teachers must feel total commitment to advisories if advisories are to be successful.

389.   Bergmann, S., & Rudman, G. J. (1985). *Decision making skills for middle school students.* Washington, D.C.: National Education Association, 64 pp.

The book provides suggestions for including a decision-making unit in the middle level curriculum.

390.   Canfield, J., & Siccone, F. (1993). *101 ways to develop student self-esteem and responsibility, Volume 1: Teacher as coach.* Needham Heights, MA: Allyn and Bacon. 276 pp.

Part one of a two part series, this volume contains activities for teachers to help improve their own self-esteem. The activities prepare the teachers as student empowerment leaders, role models, and coaches. Combined, the two volumes contain more than 100 activities, some designed specifically for teachers and others for students. (See Siccone and Canfield for Volume 2.)

391.   Churchill, E. R. (1992). *Who I am and who I want to be.* San Antonio, TX: ECS Learning Systems. 161 pp.

This self-directing activity text shows students how to form their own identities and set goals. Includes reading, writing, talking, and drawing activities to help students realize their strengths and talents.

392.   Cole, C. G. (1992). *Nurturing a teacher advisory program.* Columbus, OH: National Middle School Association. 54 pp.

In this booklet, Cole cogently and succinctly delineates the whys, whats, whos, and wheres of an advisory program. The booklet is comprised of twelve chapters: 1. Why have a teacher advisory program. 2. What happens in a teacher advisory program. 3. Who does what in an advisory program? 4. Who is an advisor? 5. How do you prepare to be an advisor? 6. What kinds of activities work best? 7. What are sources for advisory activities? 8. What are administrative considerations in establishing a program? 9. How are parents and other community members involved? 10. What pitfalls should you avoid when setting up a program? 11. How do you keep an advisory program viable? and 12. Where can you get additional help?

393.   Forte, I. (1991). *Operation orientation—Motivators, ice breakers, discussion sparkers, & get-acquainted activities.* Tampa, FL: National Resource Center for Middle Grades/High School Education. 80 pp.

Contains activities which will help build rapport between advisor and advisee.

394.   Garawski, R. A. (1982). Middle school "walking advisement": A model for successful implementation. *The Clearing House, 56*(1), 5-7.

A step-by-step outline of how to design, implement, and maintain a "walking" advisement program for middle level students.

395.   Henderson, P., & La Forge, J. (1989). The role of the middle school counselor in teacher-advisor programs. *The School Counselor, 36*(5), 348-351.

Discusses three roles of the counselor in the development, coordination, and implementation of a teacher-advisor program: (1) assessing and reporting the school's readiness for a TA program, (2) establishing a teacher advisory committee, and (3) training teachers for their role as teacher-advisors.

396.   Herbert, R. (1982). The advisory class: Foundation of a positive school climate. *Thrust, 11*(5), 22-24.

Provides a brief description of the whys and hows regarding the development of an advisory program at an "intermediate school" in California. Also discusses the impact on the students and the school as a whole.

397.   Hoversten, C., Doda, N., & Lounsbury, J. H. (1991). *Treasure chest: A teacher advisory source book.* Columbus, OH: National Middle School Association. 268 pp.

This booklet is comprised of the hows, whys and whats of developing a sound advisor/advisee program as well as over 120 activities that advisors can use over a three year period in their advisor/advisee sessions. The table of contents is as follows: Part One: Getting Ready. Chapters: 1. How to Use this Source Book. 2. Why Have a Teacher Advisory Program? 3. Widespread Advocacy for TA Programs. 4. What Are the Objectives for the Program? 5. Getting Off to a Good Start. 6. How Should a TA Program Be Organized? 7. What Comprises a TA Curriculum? 8. How to Keep an Advisory Notebook. 9. Musing About Advisory. Part Two: Activities: Chapters: 10. First Year Categories. 11. Second Year Categories. 12. Third Year Categories.

398.   Jacobs, M. (1988). *Building a positive self-concept, 113 activities for adolescents.* San Antonio, TX: ECS Learning Systems. 126 pp.

Uses drawings, poems, short stories, or role playing to teach assertiveness techniques and problem-solving strategies to students who lack self-expression.

399.   James, M. A. (1986). *Adviser-advisee programs: Why, what and how*. Columbus, OH: National Middle School Association. 70 pp.

In this booklet, James emphasizes the reasons/needs for a strong guidance and affective education strand in middle level education programs. A particularly valuable component of this booklet is the section where James highlights six successful advisor/advisee programs around the nation. He concludes by providing insights into problems problems that schools and teachers encounter as they implement an advisory program and then provides a section entitled "Guidelines for Success." The booklet also includes a list of helpful resources.

400.   James, M. A. (1993). Refocusing advisories, thematically. *Middle School Journal*, *25* (1), 44-45.

Suggests the integration of student-generated concerns/questions into advisement topics and activities. Includes a sample unit on "stereotyping," with examples in each of the following categories: theme, advisement topics and/or questions, activity outcomes or objectives, possible activities, assessment and/or evaluation, follow-up activities, and related advisement topics.

401.   Marsh, M. (1987-1988). Manhattan middle school advisor-advisee program. *KAMLE Karavan: Journal of the Kansas Association of Middle Level Education*, *2*, 7-10.

Discusses the development of an advisor/advisee program at a junior high school that was making the transition to a middle school. Addresses such issues as designing the delivery system, organizing the groups, including awards and projects in the program, using special coordinators to handle the burden of planning, etc.

402.   Monroe, J., & Sharp, W. L. (1994). 101 memorable ideas for winning advisor/advisee programs. *Ohio Middle School Journal*, *20*(3), 15-17.

The authors state that what is delineated in this article are "one hundred and one of the most unique and effective ideas we have begged, borrowed, and stolen just for you."

403.   *Operation Orientation*. (1993). National Resource Center for Middle Grades/High School Education. Tampa, FL.

Offers practical suggestions and activities for building advisor/advisee relationships. Includes activities designed to enhance vocabulary, reading, and writing competence; problem-solving skills; and productive thinking skills.

404.   Phelps, P. H. (1993). The challenge of building character. *The Clearing House*, *66*(6), 353-355.

Emphasizes the need for middle level students to gain self-respect and to display responsible behavior. Outlines strategies that teachers will find useful in encouraging students to build "respectable" character traits.

405.   Schrumpf, F., Freiburg, S., & Skadden, D. (1993). *Life lessons for young adolescents: An advisory guide for teachers*. Champaign, IL: Research Press. 212 pp.

A collection of 94 activities designed to assist students in learning life skills in the following areas: team building, contributing to whole-school success, increasing self-esteem, coping with stress, resolving conflicts, relating to others, and becoming actively involved in the community. Offers practical guidelines and suggestions for implementing advisories.

406.   Scicone, F., & Canfield, J. (1993). *101 ways to develop student self-esteem and responsibility, Volume II: The power to succeed in school and beyond*. Needham Heights, MA: Allyn and Bacon. 238 pp.

The second volume in a two volume series, the activities in this book is designed to help students set and achieve goals, participate in peer counseling groups, resolve conflicts, and expand their expertise in these areas beyond the classroom and into the community at large. Combined, the two volumes contain more than 100 activities, some designed specifically for teachers and others for students.

407.   Van Hoose, J. (1991). The ultimate goal: A/A across the day. *Midpoints*, 2(2), 1-8. (Available from the National Middle School Association, 4807 Evanswood Drive, Columbus, OH 43229-6292).

In this occasional paper published by the National Middle School Association, Van Hoose "examines the context of advisory programs, their various components, and concludes with a discussion of an exemplary model for advisor-advisee programs in middle level schools."

408.   Whisler, J. S., & McCombs, B. (1992). *Middle school advisement program*. Aurora, CO: Mid-continent Regional Educational Laboratory (McREL). No pp. listed.

This program is built in flexible modules that deal with self-awareness, personal responsibility, communication, goal setting, relationships, conflict resolution, and stress management. Activities are designed to match the varying maturity levels and interests among 6-8th graders. Includes written worksheets, art activities, role plays, discussions and problem-solving situations. Teacher guides within the program manual provide one-page descriptions of each activity explaining the the teacher's role, step by step. Extensively field tested.

C. ADVISORY - GENERAL

409.   Barnes, D. (1989). *Decision-making skillbook*. San Antonio, TX: ECS Learning Systems. 116 pp.

A sequential program of lessons, comprehension checks, activities, and problems that helps students develop essential decision-making skills.

410.   Bourman, A. (1990). *Tough decisions—50 activities in values and character education.* San Antonio, TX: ECS Learning Systems.

Presents real-life situations in which students develop integrated language skills through discussion, reading, writing, and role playing. Issues deal with parental expectations, cheating, divorce, respect, and more. 50 reproducible cards.

411.   Karns, M. (1994). *How to create positive relationships with students.* Champaign, IL: Research Press. 174 pp.

Offers an innovative approach that provides communication skills training for teachers and easy-to-do group activities for upper elementary and middle level students. The 50 activities are ideal for use during classes, homerooms, or advisory periods.

IX

Core Subjects

A. LANGUAGE ARTS - RESEARCH

412.   Gamoran, A., & Nystrand, M. (1991). Background and instructional effects on achievement in eighth-grade English and social studies. *Journal of Research on Adolescence, 1(3),* 277-300.

Reports a research study of eighth-grade students in 16 schools to see what effect types of instructional activities, instructional discourse between students and teachers, student participation, and selected sociological variables had on achievement in English and social studies. A key component in the final regression model was discussion time.

413.   Hooper, M. L., & Miller, S. D. (1991). The motivational responses of high, average, and low achievers to simple and complex language arts assignments: Classroom implications. *Research in Middle Level Education, 15*(1), 105-119.

"The influence of simple and complex language arts assignments on high, average, and low ability groups in middle school was measured by student interview. A randomly selected sample of 18 students from 3 sixth grade classrooms was interviewed using understanding, expectancy, and value questions with different types of assignments. 71 interviews were conducted to obtain 93 observations... Data were coded both quantitatively and qualitatively and analyzed for motivational focus (intrinsic, extrinsic, work-avoidant, or their combination) at both the group and individual level. Results showed that students liked or were interested in most assignments and had motivational focus that was related to the assignment's complexity and creativity levels. As assignments progressed from simple to complex, students at all achievement levels progressed towards an intrinsic-mastery focus. Further, the motivational foci formed cluster patterns by assignment type: discrepancies were on assignments that limited creativity. The implication for teaching, planning and instruction are discussed."

414.   Johnson, E. M. W. (1990). Literary interpretation and moral reasoning

patterns of transescent students in selected middle schools (Doctoral dissertation, Georgia State University, 1990). *Dissertation Abstracts International*, *51*,1938A.

This study had two purposes: (1) to assess the impact of a literary-based moral intervention program on the moral reasoning levels of eighth graders and (2) to assess the effects of the program on the students' responses to a literary work. The theoretical research of Piaget and Kohlberg on cognitive-moral development formed the basis for this study. Peer group membership was found to reflect higher levels of moral reasoning than individual status of students. Also, a literary-based moral intervention program produced significant changes in the moral reasoning of intact peer group members. Concerning literary responses, intact peer group members mainly produced responses in the personal mode, while individualists mainly produced responses in the interpretive mode.

415.   Mills, R. F., & Ohlhausen, M. M. (1992). Negotiating a workshop in middle school language arts: A case study of two team teachers. *Research in Middle Level Education*, *16*(1), 99-113.

"This study, conducted during a school year in a middle school, explored the implementation of a workshop approach for teaching language arts by two middle level teachers who shared students on an interdisciplinary team. Using methods associated with long term field studies, researchers observed and interviewed two middle level teachers and their students. Issues of procedures, assessment, and empowerment emerged as major categories in data analysis embedded within the overall theme of negotiations. Implications for interdisciplinary teaming, for teacher development, and for student decision-making are discussed."

416.   Wieland, S. J. (1989). Changes in students' perceptions of the writing process and themselves as writers in a middle school language arts classroom (Doctoral dissertation, Indiana University of Pennsylvania, 1988). *Dissertation Abstracts International*, *49*, 2136A.

The author investigated middle school students' model of the composing process and the role students perceive for themselves as participants in that process. Data, in the form of field notes, interviews, transcripts, collections of writing, and audio tapes, were collected for one school year of day-to-day observations of students. The study described the effects that audience, evaluation, writer's history, publication, and topic choice had upon middle level students' perceptions of the writing process. The students' model for the composing process was shown as it changes throughout the year. This changing model affected students' perception of themselves as writers. The author suggested a connection between the students' ownership of their writing and their perception of themselves as real authors.

B. LANGUAGE ARTS - PRACTICAL

417.   Albert, A. (1994). Drama in the classroom. *Middle School Journal*, *25*(5), 20-24.

Classroom drama is an excellent hands-on, interactive activity for middle level students. Offers several short drama activities, including story reading, storytelling, tableaux/pantomime, monologues, role playing, improvisation, creative drama, reader's theater, and performance theater for the classroom.

418. Athanases, S. Z. (1995). Fostering empathy and finding common ground in multiethnic classes. *English Journal*, *84*(3), 26-34.

Discusses several instructional strategies designed to encourage middle level and high school students to develop empathy and respect for others through the study of literature and language. Focuses upon appropriate text selection, seating arrangements, bulletin boards, wall displays, displays of student work, and role-playing.

419. Barclay, K. H., & Lane, J. (1993). Reading, writing, thinking, and change. *Middle School Journal*, *24*(5), 37-43.

Discusses the development and implementation of a fifth-grade reading/language arts program. Using a conversational format, the authors talk about the transition from a standardized program to one based on literature and writing. Includes descriptions of specific assignments and activities as well as problems and concerns that arose during the transitional period.

420. Beckman, J., & Diamond, J. (1984). Picture books in the classroom: The secret weapon for the creative teacher. *English Journal*, *73*(2), 102-104.

Presents a strong argument, including rationale and suggestions for implementation, for using colorful picture books in the classroom.

421. Breen, L. (1989). Connotations. *Journal of Reading*, *32*(5), 461.

Offers a method of extending comprehension of synonyms to include semantic shading imposed by context.

422. Burton, D. L., & Fillion, B. C. (1971). A literature program for the middle school. *The Clearing House*, *45*(9), 524-527.

Discusses the importance of incorporating the study of literature into a middle level curriculum. Analyzes a model program already in existence.

423. Denman, G. A. (1988). *When you've made it your own...Teaching poetry to young people*. Portsmouth, NH: Heinemann. 201 pp.

Denman, a former elementary and junior high teacher and now a storyteller and writer, identifies some of the common problems he has observed in poetry instruction. He shares his responses to those problems, and provides a wealth of ideas as to how teachers can incorporate poetry into a middle level language arts curriculum.

424.   Dunning, S., & Stafford, W. (1992). *Getting the knack: 20 poetry writing exercises.* Urbana, IL: National Council of Teachers of English. 203 pp.

This book, which was written by two award-winning poets, is packed with excellent exercises for beginning poets. The book is divided into twenty sections, each covering a different kind or phase of poetry writing. The authors provide thorough explanations of each exercise and numerous examples of poems drawn from the work of both students and professional writers.

425.   Edwards, A. T., & Dermott, R. A. (1989). A new way with vocabulary. *Journal of Reading, 32*(6), 559-561.

Recommends that vocabulary be taught before reading a selection via the use of quotes from the selection. Enables students to make full use of context clues and engage in quality pre-reading activities without studying words in isolation.

426.   Edwards, C. A. (1990). Mnemonics relieves homophone misuse. *Journal of Reading, 33*(7), 559-561.

"Vocabuphone" lessons involved students in their own learning as they compiled a reference book and devised mnemonic devices to correctly use homophones.

427.   Edwards, D. (1991). Try it! You might like it. *The Transescent, 16*(2), 15-16.

A brief description of a "super Highway to Writing" program that allows middle level English students to complete individualized education plans based upon pretest scores, chapter test scores, and workbook tests scores. Encourages teachers to be innovative and risk-taking when selecting teaching strategies.

428.   Ehrenberg, R. A. (1983). Clubs in English—Publish or perish. *English Journal, 72*(8), 64-65.

Practical suggestions for setting aside one day a week in English class to allow students to participate in clubs. Students work productively on self-selected "club" projects. Parent involvement is encouraged, and ESL students are easily assimilated into the groups.

429.   Flint-Ferguson, J. (1995). "And now, a word from our sponsor." *English Journal, 84*(2), 107-110.

Discusses a simulated advertising campaign designed to enhance middle-level students' sense of power over language. Although it was developed specifically for eighth-graders, the content of the unit will encourage students of all ages to see the "broad picture" of language usage.

430.   Francis, Z. (1991). Thinking about reading. *High Strides: The Bimonthly Report on Urban Middle Schools, 4*(1), 6.

Discusses a program developed at Stanford University called "Project Read," which is a set of ideas "for moving reading and writing from being very basic skills that are materials-directed to being a very meta- language" (e.g., in which students use language and structures to solve problems and to communicate).

431.   Freedman, L. (1994). Six beliefs: Literature in the middle. *English Journal, 83*(7), 95-98.

Discusses Kathy Short's philosophy of learning and its relevance for middle school literature classes. Focuses upon the way students think about literature, the role of literature in the lives of students, and selected strategies that enhance the teaching of literature.

432.   Freedman, S. C. (1993). Reflections on a visiting author program—9 years later. *Journal of Reading, 36*(4), 312-317.

Discusses the success of an on-going visiting author program and includes practical guidelines for setting up such a program.

433.   Garber, D. H. (1987). The basal speller: A sad saga—but one that can be rewritten. *Middle School Journal, 19*(1), 14-15.

Suggests a move away from basal spellers toward individual lists of spelling demons. Recommends that students be required to write, be taught spelling patterns and useful linguistical generalizations, and learn to use spelling reference books.

434.   Gauthier, L. R. (1989). Carve a text flexibly. *Journal of Reading, 32*(5), 458.

Suggests deleting words from selected text sentences to generate discussions about the flexibility of language and shades of meaning.

435.   Gilles, C. (1994). Discussing our questions and questioning our discussions: Growing into literature study. *Language Arts, 71* (7), 499-508.

Stresses the importance of peer discussion in literature classes with an emphasis upon the need for teachers and students to be persistent, to reflect upon the process, and to be flexible. Also discussed are experiences and suggestions of three teachers who, by overcoming obstacles, effectively utilized peer discussions in their own classrooms.

436.   Hesse, K. D., & Robinson, J. W. (1982). Strategies for improving spelling instruction. *Middle School Journal, 13*(2), 16-20.

Describes three types of middle school spellers. Natural spelling strategies include visual memory, recall gimmicks, choosing alternate words, and "asking for help." Spelling is a convergent skill in which students identify alternatives, locate errors and select responses. Word lists are the enemy of mastery. Nine spelling strategies are listed: use manuscript and cursive writing, use a student-teacher analytic procedure for locating errors, use mnemonic devices, provide novel and independent trials, correct each trial, restrict the use of phonics, eliminate the use of syllabication, use morphological structures, omit vocabulary instruction. Argues that word meanings should be learned in reading prior to instruction in spelling. Also suggests that reinforcing spelling standards will encourage students to learn to spell.

437.   *High Strides: The Bimonthly Report on Urban Middle Schools.* (1991). Theme Issue on "Reading, Writing, Relevancy," 4(1).

Includes the following articles: "Adapt, Not Adopt, Writing Process"; "Language is a 'Group Thing'"; "Hewing City Life: Foxfire and Urban Youth"; STR/STW: Reading, Writing and Togetherness"; "Thinking About Reading."

438.   Hubbell, E. (1991). A closer look at spelling. *Becoming, 2* (2), 23-27.

Discusses six strategies for learning how to spell: focusing, relating, practicing, testing, learning from past errors, and repeating the first five steps as necessary. Concludes with a brief discussion about the benefits of improved spelling skills.

439.   Hudson, T., & Alderman, M. K. (1988). Increasing success in the middle grades. *English Journal, 77*(1), 86-87.

Discusses mastery learning, reteaching, and giving students "second chances" without penalty to do or re-do assignments and take tests.

440.   Johnson, R. K. (1982). Homophones: An approach to teaching spelling/vocabulary. *Middle School Journal, 13*(2), 20-21, 31.

Homophones are words that have identical pronunciation but differ in orthography and meaning. Homophones focus attention on spelling and meaning differences of pairs of words. Recommends activities and games for improving spelling.

441.   Krogness, M. M. (1995). Takin' care of business. *English Journal, 84*(1), 46-49.

Written by a middle-level English teacher, the article outlines several strategies designed to encourage students to discover the power of language. Specifically discussed are experimenting with words, compiling dictionaries, and chanting poetry.

442.   Lazarski, J. (1987). Memo to student teachers. *English Journal, 76*(5), 93-94.

A humorous, yet practical list of suggestions for student teachers and new teachers.

443.   Lewis, A. C. (1991). Hewing city life: Foxfire and urban youth. *High*

Strides: The Bimonthly Report on Urban Middle Grades, 4(1), 4.

An excellent and thought-provoking article that succinctly delineates how the highly acclaimed Foxfire program (an oral history approach to learning that was developed in 1967 by Eliot Wigginton for his English classes in rural Rabun Gap, Georgia) is being used to engage middle level students in urban schools.

444.   Lewis, H. E. (1987). L'Amour on education. *The Clearing House*, *60*(6), 261-262.

Presents a rationale for asking middle level students to read books by L'Amour. Reasons cited include high interest level, allusions to classical literary works, and references to ethics and values.

445.   Lucas, J. (1991). STR/STW: Reading, writing, and togetherness. *High Strides: The Bimonthly Report on Urban Middle Grades*, 4(1), 5.

Discusses two cooperative learning strategies (Student Team Reading and Student Team Writing) and a language arts program, a comprehensive, teacher-directed, collaborative curriculum that stresses active learning and integrates all the language arts. The latter was "was designed to motivate students to read more, enjoy and understand what they are reading and hopefully reduce the escalating student dropout rate in Baltimore city schools."

446.   Madsen, A. L. (1987). Language games and language usage. *English Journal*, *76*(6), 81-83.

Includes a rationale for playing language games with middle school students and includes resources and directions for playing several simple games.

447.   Maltese, R. (1995). The game game. *English Journal*, *84* (1), 55-58.

Discusses the use of games in middle level and high school classrooms. Stresses that teachers must consider the needs of all students when selecting games and attempt to ensure that all students will benefit from participating in a gaming activity.

448.   Manning, M. M, & Manning, G. L. (1982). Spelling instruction in the middle school: An overview. *Middle School Journal, 13*(2), 14-16.

Explains the difference between informal and formal spelling instruction and provides suggestions for the implementation of both. In informational spelling instruction, students do not have formal spelling lists. Student improve their spelling by reading and writing. Decisions that must be made to implement a formal spelling program include: how much time should be designated for instruction, who provides the instruction, what materials should be used. Spelling kits may be made by placing lists of words on index cards.

449.   Manning, M. M., & Manning, G. L. (1986). *Improving spelling in the*

middle grades. Washington, D.C.: National Education Association, 48 pp. Includes more than ten specific-research-based instructional practices, twelve alternatives to traditional spelling programs with sample forms, and fifteen spelling activities.

450.   Miller, J. (1995). Battle hymn of American studies. *English Journal*, *84*(1), 88-92.

Discusses cross-curricular team teaching as an effective method for teaching literature via a whole language approach. Specifically discussed are the author's experiences as a member of an instructional team who developed and implemented an American Studies unit.

451.   Naftel, M. I., Driscoll, M., Elias, M. J., & Jerardi, J. A. (1993). Problem solving and decision making in an eighth-grade class. *The Clearing House*, *66*(3), 177-180.

Discusses the use of literature as a means of teaching critical thinking skills and problem solving skills to young adolescents. Includes sample activities.

452.   Roller, C. M. (1994), Sometimes the conversations were grand, and sometimes... *Language Arts*, *71*(7), 509-515.

Discusses several strategies for facilitating discussions about literature. Acknowledges that "less-than-perfect" discussions play an important role in the learning process. Specifically discussed are reading workshops for students ages eight through twelve, individualized reading programs, teacher-student conferences, and mini-lessons.

453.   Sheppard, R. (1985). *Enhancing learning through oral and written expression: Strategies for subject area teachers*. Columbus, OH: National Middle School Association.

Based upon the philosophy that the use of communication skills offers a natural process for planning and implementing instruction. Consists of four sections: (1) communication as a vehicle for learning in all subject areas, (2) strategies for enhancing learning in all subject areas, (3) models for instructional planning, and (4) communication and learning in perspective.

454.   Shuman, R. B. (1994). Assessing student achievement in the study of literature. *English Journal*, *83*(8), 55-58.

Discusses the impact that outcomes-based education has had upon assessment of student achievement in the study of literature. Concludes that literature teachers should assist students in developing interpretive skills and then should implement an evaluation system designed to assess their progress and achievement.

455.   Steirer, M. D. (1973). Mini-electives enliven English studies. *The Clearing House*, *47* (5), 284-286.

Discusses the role of mini-courses in middle school English programs. Lists twenty-four electives, each with an emphasis on media.

456.   Taylor, J. (1987). Creativity in spelling?: Build mnemonic devices. *Middle School Journal, 19*(1), 15-16.

Discussion of methods for helping students create their own mnemonic devices: "a word in a word," "silly sentences," "syllables, sounds, and singing." Includes rationale for using mnemonics to teach spelling.

457.   Tsujimoto, J. I. (1988). *Teaching poetry to adolescents.* Urbana, IL: National Council of Teachers of English. 105 pp.

An outstanding booklet by a 7th-8th grade English teacher on how to teach poetry to elementary, middle level, junior high and high school students. It is not only replete with ideas on different types of poems (e.g., found poem, two-word poem, circle poem, change poem, transformation poem, animal poem, memory poem, bitterness poem, paradox poem, awe poem, self-portrait poem) and how to teach them, but also such concerns as choosing sample poems to share with students, making assignments, organizing assignments, revision, evaluation, and poetry books.

458.   Vande Kopple, W. J. (1995). Pun and games. *English Journal, 84*(1), 50-54.

Discusses the use of games, specifically puns, as an effective teaching strategy in language arts classrooms. Argues that experimenting with language through games and simulations will assist students in developing an appreciation for language.

459.   Wanner, S. Y. (1994). *On with the story: Adolescents learning through narrative.* Portsmouth, NH: Boynton/Cook. 256 pp.

Discusses the various ways of using the narrative as an effective learning tool for adolescents. Includes classroom examples and student products to illustrate the usefulness of the narrative in each content area. Includes suggestions for classroom applications. Consists of fourteen chapters and covers a variety of topics, ranging from autobiographies to essays.

460.   Wiencek, J. (1994). From teacher-led to peer discussions about literature: Suggestions for making the shift. *Language Arts, 71*(7), 488-498.

Discusses the role of peer discussions in enhancing students' understanding and interpretations of literature. Focuses upon questions asked by teachers making the transition from teacher-led discussions to student-student discussions.

461.   Wilson, D. E. (1992). Teaching literature at the middle level: Capitalizing on adolescent needs. *Schools in the Middle: Theory Into Practice, 2*(2), 22-26.

Discusses ways to engage students in a meaningful way in the acts of reading and writing. Includes a list of premises for teaching writing and literature.

462.   Wood, K. D. (1993). Promoting lifelong readers across the curriculum. *Middle School Journal*, 24 (5), 63-66.

Answers questions commonly asked by middle level teachers concerned about using literature across the curriculum. Also includes a sample Reader Response Form, a list of sources for literature appropriate for middle level students, and a list of literary selections on various topics appropriate for young adolescents.

463.   Zitlow, C. S. (1995). Did Patty Bergen write this poem? Connecting poetry and young adult literature. *English Journal*, 84(1), 110-113.

Discusses story-poem connections as one strategy for integrating a study of young adult literature with that of poetry analysis. Specifically presented are teaching ideas for connecting *Summer of My German Soldier* and *Hatchett*.

C. LANGUAGE ARTS - GENERAL

464.   Buckley, M. H. (1995). Oral language: A curriculum yet to come. *English Journal*, 84(1), 41-45.

Argues that oral language instruction should be a top priority in middle level and high school language arts curricula. Specifically discusses a definition of oral language, the absence of oral language from current programs of study, and a justification for including the study of oral language in English curricula.

465.   Dunleavey, M. P. (1995). Children's writers plumb the depths of fear. *Publishers Weekly*, 242(13), 28-29.

Discusses the popularity of horror books among young adolescents. Also discusses the impact that such works have upon students' imaginations.

466.   Gallo, D. R. (Ed.). (1990). *Speaking for ourselves: Auto-biographical sketches by notable authors of books for young adults*. Urbana, IL: National Council of Teachers of English. 231 pp.

This interesting book includes an autobiographical sketch by 87 authors who write for young people in middle school, junior high, and high school. The sketches include such personal insights as when certain authors began writing and why, their formative experiences, and the joys an difficulties of writing. A short listing of the key works by each author follows his/her autobiographical sketch.

467.   Gauthier, L. R. (1990). Helping middle school students develop language facility. *Journal of Reading*, 33(4), 274-276.

Details in a step-by-step manner two strategies that develop students' language competency: "inverse close" and "building content vocabulary." Includes rationale explaining why the strategies work.

468.   Greenwood, S. C. (1995). Learning contracts and transaction: A natural marriage in the middle. *Language Arts, 72*(2), 88-96.

Discusses the effective and efficient use of learning contracts in building learning communities among middle level students while simultaneously enhancing their language skills.

469.   Manning, M., & Manning, G. (1982). Spelling instruction in the middle school: An overview. *Middle School Journal, 13*(2), 14-16.

Explains the difference between informal and formal spelling instruction and provides suggestions for the implementation of both. In informational spelling instruction, students do not have formal spelling lists. Student improve their spelling by reading and writing. Decisions that must be made to implement a formal spelling program include how much time should be designated for instruction, who provides the instruction, and what materials should be used. Spelling kits may be made by placing lists of words on index cards.

470.   Miller, T. (1994). Improving the schoolwide language arts program: A priority for all middle school teachers. *Middle School Journal, 25*(4), 26-29.

Since higher-level reading/writing/problem solving strategies have not yet been mastered by young adolescents, middle level teachers must plan and implement curricula which will help their students demonstrate language processing strategies, as well as content area knowledge outcomes. A key to a successful middle school language arts program is to keep it simple. Desired outcomes must be clearly understood by teachers, parents, and students. Discusses teachers' concern for teaching and planning time. Suggests all teachers participate in language instruction so students get modeling, practice, and feedback in all of their classes. Offers ideas for motivating students to read. Above all, schoolwide improvement in language arts requires schoolwide commitment.

471.   Nilsen, P. A. (Ed.), and the Committee on the Junior High and Middle School Booklist. (1991). *Your reading: A booklist for junior high and middle school students.* Urbana, IL: National Council of Teachers of English. 342 pp.

This massive bibliography includes annotations of quality books for young adolescents that were published between 1988 and 1990. It is divided into six sections: I. Connections (e.g., connecting with ourselves, connecting with families, connecting with friends and foes, connecting with boyfriends and girlfriends); II. Understandings (e.g., understanding ourselves, understanding the past, understanding others, understanding real people); III. Imaginings (imagining our fellow creatures, imagining excitement, imagining what if), IV. Contemporary Poetry and Short Stories; V. Books to Help with School Work, and VI. Books Just for You (e.g., managing your life, how-to books, and fun and facts).

472.   Stover, L. T., & Karr, R. (1990). Glasnost in the classroom: Likhanov's *Shadows across the Sun. English Journal, 79*(8), 47-53.

Presents a rationale for teaching literature other than American and British in the English curriculum.

473.   Taylor, S. J. (1986). Grammar curriculum—back to square one. *English Journal, 75*(1), 94-98.

Generally reviewed the literature on grammar instruction. Found that grammar should be taught, but formal grammar instruction should not begin before seventh grade and then suggested that discovery and inquiry approaches might be more effective, with direct instruction beginning in high school.

474.   Thompson, S. J. (1986). Teaching metaphoric language: An instructional strategy. *Journal of Reading, 30*(2), 105-109.

Offers an explanation of metaphor comprehension and the processes of comparison it entails, then describes a strategy for teaching metaphor that focuses on the processes of comparison. Includes a demonstration lesson.

D. MATHEMATICS - RESEARCH

475.   Bell, J. G. (1992). A history of mathematics class for middle school teachers (Doctoral dissertation, Illinois State University, 1992). *Dissertation Abstracts International, 53,* 2283A.

Course emphasized the history of material normally included in the middle level mathematics curriculum: number systems, computation, number theory, algebra, geometry, probability, and statistics. Included some trigonometry and calculus to give students a taste of the overall flavor of mathematics. Discussed how mathematicians from different eras solved problems. Middle school teachers responded favorably to the course.

476.   Blando, J. A., Kelly, A. E., Schneider, B. R., & Sleeman, D. (1989). Analyzing and modeling arithmetic errors. *Journal for Research in Mathematics Education, 20*(3), 301-308.

The authors tested thirty-nine seventh-grade students to discover errors involving misunderstandings of operations with whole numbers, grouping symbols, and order of operations. Errors were found to be closely related to the format of the test item. A small number of errors, especially order of operations, were common across students. The findings suggested that teachers should teach a mathematical rule by using many different formats. Also, teachers should test learning by varying the format of items in their tests.

477.   Byrd, D., McIntyre, D. J., Copenhaver, R., & Norris, W. (1982). A study of the engagement of middle school aged children during mathematics instruction. In Thomas Owen Erb (Ed.), *Middle school research: Selected*

studies 1982 (pp. 16-24). Columbus, OH: Research Committee of the National Middle School Association.

Focused on engaged student behaviors within various activities in math classes. "Among the findings of the study were the following: 1. The engagement rate of students varied greatly among various teachers' classes, with the least engaged classes being on-task only half of the alloted time; 2. The dominant activity during math period was seatwork, while teacher-led activities accounted for the second largest block of time. That said, in grade five seatwork was the most dominant activity while teacher led activities were most prevalent in the seventh grade; 3. Students were 'stalled' or waiting for directions or work for nearly the same percentage of time that they were verbally interacting or attempting to interact in class; and 4. As one progresses from grades five through seven, an increase in teacher led activities and decrease in seatwork is paralleled by a slight decrease in engaged student time in mathematics classrooms."

478.   Chaiklin, S., & Lesgold, S. B. (1984). Prealgebra students' knowledge of algebraic tasks with arithmetic expressions. (ERIC Document No. 247 147).

This paper reports an empirical study of six middle level students who judged the equivalence of three sets of three-term arithmetic expressions with an addition and a subtraction operator. Analyses of thinking-aloud protocols on this task reveal that the students (a) use several different methods to parse and judge the equivalence of such expressions, (b) sometimes use a different parsing of judging method with the same expression, depending on which expression it is compared against, and (c) are able to work with different conceptual interpretations of expressions. Additional results are provided about specific errors that were made and trends in the students' application of these methods. The results are briefly discussed along with three comments on their educational implications.

479.   Davidson, N., & Kroll, D. L. (1991). An overview of research on cooperative learning related to mathematics. *Journal for Research in Mathematics Education, 22*(5), 362-365.

The authors succinctly summarize the research on cooperative learning related to mathematics. This strategy has been recommended as one teaching strategy appropriate for middle level mathematics classrooms. The authors found that cooperative learning is more effective than interpersonal competition or individualistic efforts on mathematics achievement, and that production, intergroup relations, mainstreaming of students, cooperativeness, liking of school, self-esteem, increased efforts to achieve, enhanced psychological health and caring relationships, and ability to consider the perspective of another person.

480.   Dubois, D. J. (1991). The relationship between selected student team learning strategies and student achievement and attitude in middle school mathematics (Doctoral dissertation, University of Houston, 1990). *Dissertation Abstracts International, 52*, 408A.

The author investigated the relationships among cooperative learning, student achievement, and attitudes in mathematics. This eighteen-week study of 2175 middle school students focused on the combined use of two selected cooperative learning strategies, Student Teams-Achievement Divisions and Teams-Games-Tournament. Math Computational skills and concepts of students in the cooperative groups were higher than those students in non-cooperative groups. There was no difference in attitudes between the cooperative learning groups and non-cooperative learning groups. The author found that with a minimum of staff development and change in the organizational design of the lesson, selected cooperative learning strategies can have a significant impact on student achievement in mathematics.

481.   Ekstrom, R. B., & Villegas, A. M. (1991). Ability grouping in middle grade mathematics: Process and consequences. *Research in Middle Level Education*, *15*(1), 1-20.

"This paper reports the findings from a study of middle grade mathematics grouping in six urban school districts. In five of the six districts, a clear academic hierarchy was evident. Minority students were overrepresented in classes designated as low ability, suggesting that grouping practices may be resulting in segregation. Low ability students received a more limited curriculum and engaged in less favorable interactions with the teacher, as compared to their high ability counterparts. Minority students had more negative contacts with their teachers, relative to white students, especially in the less advanced groups."

482.   Fraser, L. A. (1991). Evaluation of Chapter I Take-Home Computer program. Report Number 7, Volume 25. Atlanta Public Schools, GA: Department of Research and Evaluation. (ERIC Document No. 337 531).

The Chapter I Take-Home Computer (THC) program was established in nine elementary and eight middle schools in Atlanta in the 1989-90 school year. One hundred and eighty computers were sent home with 422 students, for six-week periods, to be used by the students to help with their math homework assignments. The study found no significant statistical difference between the 307 control group members and experimental group members overall, although a significant improvement for the middle level students in mathematics was found.

483.   Garnett, K. F. (1991). Developing problem-solving heuristics in the middle school: A qualitative study. *Research in Middle Level Education*, *15*(1), 83-92.

The study primarily examined the following research question: Will students develop heuristics for mathematics problem solving through exposure to a highly structured problem-solving model? The study was conducted with 60 sixth grade children by the classroom/researcher. Qualitative data collection methods were used to evaluate teaching episodes and to investigate covert cognitive processes as children responded to imposed instruction during the noncontructivist teaching experiment. An inductive data analysis was conducted and working hypotheses were generated. In this study, consistent systematic instruction and application of the problem-solving model, over time, appeared to enhance mathematics achievement generally and problem-solving ability specifically.

484. Gay, A. S. (1991). A study of middle school students' understanding of number sense related to percent (Doctoral dissertation, Oklahoma State University, 1990). *Dissertation Abstracts International*, *52*, 454A.

The author found that middle level students performed better when interpreting a quantity expressed as a percent given a pictorial continuous region than when using a pictorial discrete set. Students had difficulty interpreting a quantity expressed as a percent of a number. Students used various correct (50% and 100% as reference points, fractional relationships, estimations, and mental computation) and incorrect (computational procedures and numerical comparisons) approaches when comparing percent quantities.

485. Glover, W. R. (1991). The effect of problem-solving instruction upon computational skills, algebra readiness and problem-solving ability of middle school students (Doctoral dissertation, University of Central Florida, 1990). *Dissertation Abstracts International*, *52*, 4006A.

The author studied the effects of replacing the traditional time spent in middle level mathematics classes on drill and practice, review and skill building problem sets with a process problem-solving component that included heuristic instruction. The author found that the problem-solving component enhanced student readiness for algebra and increased problem-solving ability for middle school students. The decreased emphasis on drill and practice did not significantly affect students' basic computational ability.

486. Goldin, G. A. (1992). Meta-analysis of problem-solving studies: A critical response. *Journal for Research in Mathematics Education*, *23*(3), 274-283.

The author criticizes Hembree's (1992) meta-analysis of studies in problem-solving because of skepticism about the use of meta-analysis to synthesize educational research findings. Four basic objections are discussed: the meta-analysis study lacked a psychological theory as to its basis; the assumptions of meta-analysis itself are not satisfied; questionable summaries were provided by the meta-analysis; and the potential for misuse of the findings exist. See also Hembree (1992a and 1992b).

487. Harrison, B., Brindley, S., & Bye, M. P. (1989). Allowing for student cognitive levels in the teaching of fractions and ratios. *Journal for Research in Mathematics Education*, *20*(3), 288-300.

The authors found in their study that seventh graders had significantly higher achievement in, and attitude toward, fractions and ratios when using a concrete, process-oriented approach versus the "traditional" textbook approach. Also, the development of general mathematical strategies was enhanced and computational skills maintained.

488.   Hart, L. C. (1985). Mathematical problem-solving processes of average-ability middle school students working in small groups (Doctoral dissertation, Georgia State University, 1984). *Dissertation Abstracts International*, *45*, 2429A.

The study investigated the processes of average ability seventh graders working in small groups solving applied mathematical problems. The students, in groups of three, met three times. At the first meeting, the students were administered the Problem Solving Sort Task and a Problem Solving Attitude Questionnaire. At the second meeting, the groups were video-taped solving an applied mathematical problem. A follow-up discussion with each group was audio-taped at the third meeting. The students showed the use of some basic heuristics which were generally not helpful in solving the problem. The following factors hindered their problem-solving process: (1) lack of problem-solving experiences; (2) lack of mathematical or situational concepts; (3) lack of metacognitive processes; and (4) influence of belief system. Some of these factors were offset by the group that frequently supplied background information individual students lacked.

489.   Hart, L. E. (1989). Classroom processes, sex of student, and confidence in learning mathematics. *Journal for Research in Mathematics Education, 20*(3), 242-260.

The purpose of this study was to compare the classroom processes or experiences of seventh grade boys and girls who differed in confidence in learning mathematics. The findings for public interaction indicate that sex of student was a more important determinant of teacher-student interactions than was confidence level of student. The findings for private interaction found that neither sex nor confidence level of student was an important determinant of teacher-student interactions. High confidence students engaged in mathematics more often than low confidence. Sex of student was not a significant factor for engaged time.

490.   Heller, P.M., Post, T.R., Behr, M., & Lesh, R. (1990). Qualitative and numerical reasoning about fractions and rates by seventh- and eighth-grade. *Journal for Research in Mathematics Education, 21*(5), 388-402.

The authors reported a study they conducted that examined the relationship between junior high school students' directional reasoning about rates and numerical reasoning on proportional-related word problems. They also studied the extent to which the ability to solve context-free fraction exercises is related to the ability to solve mathematically similar word problems. Four hundred twenty-one seventh-grade and 492 eighth-grade students were involved in the study. Analysis of the data by regressional analysis indicated that a high directional score is related to greater numerical success on proportion-related problems. Also, the study found that students are not using the structurally similar nature of fraction-equivalence and missing-value problem situations and of fraction-ordering and numerical-comparison situations.

491.   Hembree, R. (1992a). Experiments and relational studies in problem solving: A meta-analysis. *Journal for Research in Mathematics Education, 23*(3), 242-273.

The author integrated results from 487 reports (335 from grades 5-8) to study four areas of problem solving: characteristics of problem solvers, conditions for harder and easier problems, effects of different instructional methods on problem solving performance, and effects of classroom related conditions on problem solving performance. The following characteristics for middle level students were identified as having the greatest influence on problem solving ability near middle grades (5-7): being the best at basic mathematics, especially reasoning and concepts; being good readers; and having higher IQ levels. Heuristics method of problem solving strategy appeared to have the largest gain for problem solving performance in middle grades (6-8). See also Goldin (1992) and Hembree (1992) for critique and analysis of this study.

492.   Hembree, R. (1992b). Response to critique of meta-analysis study (Goldin, 1992). *Journal for Research in Mathematics Education, 23*(3), 284-289.

This article is written in direct response to Golden's (1992) critique of the author's (1992) meta-analysis study. The author does an adequate job of addressing concerns Goldin described in his critique on the use of meta-analysis. The article could be considered an informative type article about meta-analysis. See also Hembree (1992) for meta-analysis study and Goldin (1992) for critique of meta-analysis study.

493.   Leinhardt, G., Zaslavsky, O., & Stein, M. (1990). Functions, graphs, and graphing: Tasks, learning, and teaching. *Review of Educational Research, 60* (1), 1-64.

An extensive review of research on interpretation and construction tasks associated with mathematical functions. Employs intuitions and misconceptions as means of analyzing the nature of learning in middle level students.

494.   Lias, A. R. (1991). Influence of grade level and ability level on students' perceptions of their classroom experience in middle school mathematics (Doctoral dissertation, University of Pittsburg, 1990). *Dissertation Abstracts International, 51*, 2671A.

This study focused on the possible influences grade level of students and ability level of the class as a whole may have on students' perceptions of their classroom experiences. The study involved one hundred forty-one students in seventh, eighth, and ninth grade mathematics classes at three ability levels. Students grouped in the middle level ability group represented a wide range of IQ's and mathematical abilities. This study helps document the fact that by just grouping math students by their ability levels does not adequately address the diverse needs of middle level students.

495.   Malouf, D. B. (1990). Evaluation of instructional model applied to Functional Math Project on effective computer instruction for effective special education, Prince George's County Public Schools. Upper Marlboro, MD: Prince George's County Public Schools. (ERIC Document No. 337 964).

This study evaluated an instructional model which was intended to prepare middle level special education students for state functional mathematics test. The model consisted of eight major components: pretests/posttests, diagnostic evaluations, domain directories, software matrix, software summaries, skill sheets, computer software, and miscellaneous materials. The model was evaluated by comparing math performance and attitudes of middle level special education students who received instruction based on the model with those of matched control students and by conducting interviews with teachers using the model.

496.   Middleton, J. A. (1992). Teachers' vs students' beliefs regarding intrinsic motivation in the mathematics classroom: A personal constructs approach. Paper presented at the Annual Meeting of the American Educational Research Association (San Francisco, CA, April 22, 1992). (ERIC Document No. 353 154).

The author investigated the relationship between teachers' and middle level students' personal constructs regarding intrinsic motivation in the mathematics class. Results indicate that when teachers are able to predict what motivates their students, they are better able to fine tune their instruction to turn middle level students on to mathematics.

497.   Muth, K. D. (1992). Extraneous information and extra steps in arithmetic word problems. *Contemporary Educational Psychology, 17*(3), 278-285.

Students were asked to solve word problems similar to those used by the National Assessment of Educational Progress. Extraneous information and extra steps were added to the problems to increase processing demands on students. Results indicated that accuracy of student solutions was reduced. Thinking-out-loud records revealed student misconceptions about solving word problems.

498.   O'Brien, M. L. (1983). Using Prescriptive Test Theory to develop and analyze useful diagnostic math tests for middle school students. In Thomas Owen Erb (Ed.) *Middle school research: Selected studies 1983* (pp. 97-110). Columbus, OH: Research Committee of the National Middle School Association.

"The results of this study supported the feasibility of using Prescriptive Test Theory for diagnosing and remediating individual student performance for students across a wide range of schooling experiences. It was shown that a student's mastery of a multiplication skill can be estimated from using a few items that represent that skill. Inconsistencies between response patterns and curricular expectations can be used to diagnose instructional or remediational needs."

499.   Rech, J. F. (1991). The relationships between mathematics attitude, self-concept, learning styles, socioeconomic status, gender, and mathematics achievement among fourth and eighth grade black students (Doctoral dissertation, University of Nebraska-Lincoln, 1990). *Dissertation Abstracts International*, *52*, 457A.

Fourth grade students were found to have higher math achievement and more positive math attitude than their eighth grade counterparts. A predictive equation of Blacks' mathematics achievement was formulated using the Mathematics Attitude Inventory score, Group Embedded Figures Test, and gender identification. This equation accounted for only ten percent of the variance of the California Achievement Test mathematics score. This study could assist educators in determining when African-American middle level students develop negative attitudes toward math.

500.   Reynolds, A. J., & Walberg, H. J. (1992). A process model of mathematics achievement and attitude. *Journal for Research in Mathematics Education, 23*(4), 306-328.

The authors describe a process model of mathematics achievement and attitude which identified middle level students' in- and out-of-school experiences that influence achievement and related outcomes. Prior achievement and home environment influenced subsequent mathematics achievement the most.

        Motivation, exposure to extramural reading materials, peer environment, and instructional exposure also had significant influences on achievement. Previous attitudes had the most powerful influence on subsequent attitude. Previous student achievement influenced appropriate teacher use of instructional time, thorough textbook coverage, and daily introduction of new material. Also instructional practices are influenced by students' initial attitudes.

501.   Romberg, T. A., & Wilson, L. D. (1992). Alignment of tests with the standards. *Arithmetic Teacher, 40*(1), 18-22.

The authors present the results of two studies which a) investigated how six commonly used standardized tests (Science Research Associates Survey of Basic Skills, the California Achievement Test, the Stanford Achievement Test, the Iowa Test of Basic Skills, the Metropolitan Achievement Test, and the Comprehensive Test of Basic Skills) for eighth grade are aligned with the middle level NCTM standards; and b) identified several sources of test items that are more closely in alignment to the NCTM standards.

        The first study found that the six standardized mathematics achievement tests contained mainly computations based on algorithmic procedures. The tests did not address problem solving, communication, reasoning, and connections which are the four primary NCTM standards. The follow-up study found appropriate test items from newly developed state tests (California, Connecticut, South Carolina, Massachusetts, and Vermont) and foreign tests (Britain, Australia, France, Korea, the Netherlands, and Norway) for assessing the NCTM standards. Examples of appropriate and non-appropriate test items were discussed.

502.   Useem, E. L. (1992). Getting on the fast track in mathematics: School organizational influences on math track assignment. *American Journal of Education. 100*(3), 325-253.

An examination of school policies and procedures which influence students' probabilities of entering higher level math courses. Parental education levels and personal philosophies of school administrators had some effect. Tracking policies in some schools were found to hamper qualified students from enrolling in higher level math courses.

503.   Whiteman, F. C. (1989). The role of computer-based instruction in the development of strategies for computational estimation with middle school children (Doctoral dissertation, Ohio State University, 1988). *Dissertation Abstracts International, 49*, 2629A.

This study investigated the effects of computer-based instructional activities on eighth graders acquiring and using estimation strategies. These activities were designed to introduce students to three strategies for rounding both numbers in a two-factor multiplication exercise and to provide practice with a range of numbers.
     The students had widespread deficiency in their estimating abilities prior to the study. The study showed that the computer-based activities had a positive influence on students' use of estimating strategies. This influence was greater for the students with weak estimating skills than for those with strong estimating skills.

504.   Zambo, R. (1992). Word problem solving in middle grades mathematics. *Research in Middle Level Education, 16*(1),143-157.

"The purpose of this project was to synthesize a step by step problem solving plan for routine mathematical word problems and to investigate its usefulness. A review of middle grades mathematics textbooks identified nine commonly recommended steps to problem solving. Those same nine steps were supported in the literature of problem solving. Sixth and eighth grade students (n=302) solved 10 two-step, routine word problems using the step by step plan.
     The problem solving plan predicted 66% of the observed variance in the problem situations. The individual steps uniquely contributing most were Choosing the correct operations (31%), Identifying the facts (14%), Identifying the question (8%), and Computing the answer (5%). Other steps contributed lesser amounts. The eighth grade data considered separately indicated that the step of Diagramming (12%) contributed significantly compared to sixth grade Diagramming (4%)."

E. MATHEMATICS - PRACTICAL

505.   Austin, R. (1988). Mathematics teaching and teachers in the Year
2000. *The Clearing House, 62*(1), 23-25.

Examines the future of mathematics instruction and outlines a curriculum
designed to meet the needs of future middle level students as well as the needs of
society in the year 2000. Also investigates the present and future roles of
teacher preparation institutions in the training of mathematics teachers.

506.   Badger, E. (1992). More than testing. *Arithmetic Teacher, 39*(9),
7-11.

The authors explain a set of processes that teachers could use to structure their
evaluations of students' learning in accordance with the NCTM standards. The
processes include setting goals about student learning, deciding what to assess,
gathering information about student learning, and using the results. One of the
strengths of this article is how the authors clearly illustrate their processes for
evaluations. Middle level teachers should be able to incorporate into their own
classrooms the suggestions discussed in the article.

507.   Bitner, J., & Partridge, E. (1991). Stocking up on mathematics skills.
Arithmetic Teacher, 38(7), 4-7.

The authors discuss how teachers in the middle grades can use the "stock-market
game" to reinforce calculating percentages, common fractions, and decimal
fractions through a meaningful, real-life experience. Problem-solving skills are
strengthened while developing economic concepts and awareness of world
events in a motivating activity. Students are taught how to interpret newspaper
stock-market quotations, make fictitious purchases of stocks, and keep a record
of their worths. Suggestions for integrating the activity with other curriculum
areas are discussed.

508.   Bobango, J., & Milgram, J. (1993). Establishing family math. *Middle
School Journal, 24*(5), 44-47.

Discusses a program called Family Math, which was created as an outgrowth of
the Equals Program at the Lawrence Hall of Science at the University of
California at Berkeley. The basic philosophy of Family Math is "Families 'doing
math' will get the same result as families who read; the skill of the child will
increase and the enjoyment will grow." The authors discuss how to get a Family
Math program under way, the role of the instructor, the curriculum, recruitment
of parents, content of course sessions, and evaluation.

509.   Boling, A. N. (1991). They don't like math? Well, let's do something!
Arithmetic Teacher, 38(7), 17-19.

A Chapter I mathematics coordinator discusses four major factors which can
cause many middle level students to lose interest in and begin having trouble

with learning mathematics. These factors include the mathematical content becoming more difficult, a mismatching of teaching methods and learning stages, peer influences, and rapid physical growth. The author discusses numerous teaching strategies and activities which can be used to alleviate the effects of the factors.

510.   Brendel, S. (1993). *Calculators at work in daily living*. Portland, ME: J. Weston Walch, Publisher. 72 pp.

A student activity book, it includes "self-teaching lessons" which cover basic calculator use math operations, decimals and fractions, percents, measurements, and memory keys. Answers are included.

511.   Brown, N. M. (1993). Writing mathematics. *Arithmetic Teacher, 41*(1), 20-21.

The author describes how she integrated mathematics with writing to improve the interest and mathematics achievement of low mathematics achievers at the middle level (grade 7). The students wrote their own story problems. Their problems were checked for mathematical accuracy. The written work was edited in their writing class. The finished problems were bound into a class book which was distributed across their school district to be used in other mathematics classroom.

512.   Clayton, G. A. (1990). Successful mathematics teaching for middle-school grades. Research Triangle Park, NC: Southeastern Educational Improvement Lab. (ERIC Document No. 316 432).

Several competencies and instructional strategies necessary to accommodate the changing role of teachers of mathematics at middle level are described by the author. Also provided are teacher-generated and teacher-tested instructional activities that can be used to facilitate student success in learning mathematical concepts. Successful teaching strategies and typical middle level student errors with hypothetical diagnosis of and instructional strategy for each error are discussed.

513.   Crowder, W. W. (1982). Teaching about credit cards in middle and junior high schools. *The Clearing House, 55*(6), 260-262.

Presents an instructional unit designed to enhance middle level students' understanding of consumer economics. Using credit cards as a base, the author outlines activities with an emphasis on advantages and disadvantages of using credit cards, definitions of key terms, and understanding monthly statements.

514.   Cuomo, C. (1994). *In all probability (Great explorations in math and science (GEMS) series)*. Berkeley, CA: Lawrence Hall of Science. 100 pp.

The author uses a variety of activities involving flipping coins, spinning spinners, playing cards, and rolling dice to explore statistics, prediction, and probability.

515.   Curcio, F. R., Bezuk, N. S., et al. (1994). *Understanding rational numbers and proportions: Addenda series, grades 5-8*. Reston, VA: National Council of Teachers of Mathematics. 95 pp.

Provides classroom-ready activity sheets that show how rational numbers and proportions are present in many real-world situations. Includes data collection and analysis of fractions, ratios, percents and proportions, as well as rational number connections with similarity.

516.   Dodd, A. W. (1992). Insights from a math phobic. *Mathematics Teacher, 85*(4), 296-298.

The author presents several personal and process-oriented math activities designed to help solve students' math phobia. These activities address a variety of student characteristics: lack of confidence, anxiety, loneliness, attention span, and learning styles. A variety of writing activities are included to illustrate how teachers can foster students writing across the curriculum.

517.   Dolan, D. (1991). Making connections in mathematics. *Arithmetic Teacher, 38*(6), 57-60.

The author discusses how middle level students should be able to recognize relationships among different topics in mathematics and be able to apply them when needed in other disciplines. Several classroom activities (K-8) are provided to illustrate how teachers can assist the students in applying mathematical thinking in problems that occur in other areas of study, including the world around them. A sixth-grade activity integrated mathematics, social studies, English, science, library skills and the mathematical topics of measurement, ratio, proportion, large numbers, and scale drawings. An eighth-grade activity integrated science, social studies, mathematics, art history, forensic medicine, and the mathematical topics of measurement, fractions, decimals, ratio, and proportion.

518.   Education Development Center, Inc. (1994). *From the ground up: Modeling, measuring, and constructing houses*. Portsmouth, NH: Heinemann. 194 pp.

Middle level students discover the mathematics of architecture as they design and construct a model home. The concepts of scale and proportion, geometric representations, and area measurement are reinforced throughout the construction process.

519.   Education Development Center, Inc. (1994). *The language of numbers*. Portsmouth, NH: Heinemann. 170 pp.

An activity book for middle level students to use to explore and compare systems for representing numbers, resulting in deeper understanding of the nature and properties of numbers systems in general and of the base-ten place value system in particular.

520.   Education Development Center, Inc. (1995). *Chance encounters: Probability in games and simulations.* Portsmouth, NH: Heinemann. 272 pp.

Provides activities to test, revise, and design games and simulations which examine key concepts in probability and statistics, percents, fractions, decimals, and ratios. Hands-on experiences help middle level students build an understanding of the law of large numbers, randomness, and the relationship between experimental and theoretical probability.

521.   Education Development center, Inc. (1995). *Designing spaces: Visualizing, planning, and building.* Portsmouth, NH: Heinemann. 304 pp.

Middle level students use geometry to analyze buildings from around the world, design and build their own house models, create plans for their designs, and build from each other's plans. Activities throughout help students develop spatial visualization skills, understand two-dimensional shapes and three-dimensional structures.

522.   Education Development center, Inc. (1995). *What comes next? Forecasting with algebra.* Portsmouth, NH: Heinemann. 200 pp.

This book can be used to guide seventh and eighth-grade students through models of linear and exponential growth. Using calculators, middle level students investigate the relationships between numerical sequences and visual displays, applying the two growth models in a variety of situations, such as forecasting world population, predicting future numbers of women legislators, and measuring the effects of birthrate and life span changes on population growth.

523.   Garner-Gilchrist, C. (1993). Inservice training: Teaching geometry at the middle school level. *Current Issues in Middle Level Education, 2*(1), 31-38.

The author discusses a program called the Geometry Institute, a teacher training program developed at Hampton University that was designed to teach middle level teachers how to teach geometry more effectively. The Geometry Institute was comprised of fifteen middle level teachers who were interested in increasing their subject matter knowledge and improving their pedagogical skills for teaching mathematics.
        These teachers participated in a 16 week course that focused on six units of geometry. The results of the inservice suggested that the teachers' anxiety about mathematics was reduced, their conceptual understanding of geometry was increased, and their pedagogical skills were enhanced.

524.   Geddes, D., et al. (1994). *Measurement in the middle grades: Addenda series, grades 5-8.* Reston, VA: National Council of Teachers of Mathematics. 87 pp.

Activities focus on learning measurement that is used in the real world. Activities also emphasize estimation and higher-order thinking skills.

525.   Graves, B. (1995). Quasar. *High Strides, 7*(4), 8-9.

Reports on a nationwide project that used visual aids to help students understand mathematical concepts. Achievement gains have been promising. The project requires an investment in faculty development, but all six participating middle schools plan to continue using the program.

526.   Hart, L.C., Schultz, K., Najee-ullah, D., & Nash, L. (1992). The role of reflection in teaching. *Arithmetic Teacher, 40*(1), 40-42.

The authors discuss how a teacher can become a reflective practitioner. A reflective practitioner is a teacher who regularly, thoroughly, and systematically thinks about his/her teaching. Reflective teaching provides the teacher a method for self-assessment which can lead to improvement of the teaching process. What should a teacher look for in teaching? The authors answer the question by discussing the following key areas addressed in the NCTM *Professional Teaching Standards* : nature of the mathematical task, teacher's communication, students' communication, tools for enhancing discourse, and the learning environment. Appropriate times for reflecting and appropriate methods of reflection are discussed by the authors.

527.   Harvey, J. G. (1991). Using calculators in mathematics changes testing. *Arithmetic Teacher, 38*(7), 52-54.

The author discusses strategies and activities which teachers can use to effectively integrate calculators into their own instruction. The relationship between instruction and assessment with calculators is first addressed by presenting pertinent NCTM curriculum and evaluation standards (K-8) and then illustrated with appropriate activities incorporating the use of calculators. Appropriate calculators for the middle level classroom are briefly discussed.

528.   Hemmerich, H., Lim, W., & Neel, K. (1994). *Primetime: Strategies for life-long learning in mathematics and science in the middle and high school grades.* Portsmouth, NH: Heinemann. 126 pp.

The authors present innovative strategies to help middle level and high school students become autonomous, life-long learners as they discover the importance of mathematics and science in the real world. Strategies are organized around three aspects of learning: activating prior knowledge, multiple intelligence, and reflections.

529.   Hersperger, J., & Frederick, B. (1995). Flower beds and landscape consultants: Making connections in middle school mathematics. *Mathematics Teaching in the Middle School, 1*(5), 364-367.

Describes the use of spreadsheet capabilities to help students solve problems and "to think algebraically" (p. 367).

530.   Hester, J. P., & Morris, A. (1994-1995). Using cognitive levels matching to develop a gifted education and middle grades algebra program. *NCMSA Journal, 16*(1), 32-34.

Describes one setting's implementation of Cognitive Level Matching (CLM) which "refers in its broadest sense to the teacher's ability to assess students' cognitive levels, and then adapt curricular tasks in ways consistent with these levels" (p. 32). Provides a table of "Screening devices for placement in pre-algebra and algebra I classes" (p. 33). Use of the assessment materials led to the development of an algebra I class for the eighth grade that met the cognitive needs of a significant number of students.

531.   Hosticka, A. (1991). Highlights of the National Council of Math standards for the middle level student. *Becoming*, *2*(2), 16-19.

Presents an overview of the National Council of Teachers of Mathematics standards and their implications for instructional practices at the middle level. Concludes with a brief description of the impact of the standards upon the roles of teachers.

532.   Jacobson, L. (1995). Setting standards for excellence: Math goals help teachers aim higher. *High Strides, 7*(4), 1, 4-5.

Reports on the efforts of teachers to operationalize the National Council of Teachers of Math's standards in the classroom.

533.   Jamski, W. D. (1991). *Mathematical challenges for the middle grades: From the mathematics teacher calendar problems.* Reston, VA: National Council of Teachers of Mathematics.

This is an excellent resource for middle level mathematics teachers. The book is a collection of problems intended to supplement the regular middle level mathematics textbook. There are six categories of problems: Numbers, Computation, "Oldies but Goodies," Offbeat and Unusual, Geometry, and Probability. An answer section with clearly explained solutions is included.

534.   Johnston, J., & Friesner, K. (1991). Helping middle school students be successful with math word problems. *KAMLE Karavan: Journal of the Kansas Association for Middle Level Education, 5,* 20-22.

The authors discuss how the use of calculators and "cooperative learning" are used to assist students to overcome their frustration and difficulties with problem solving. What the authors call "cooperative learning" does not really constitute true "cooperative learning," and probably is more aptly defined as "small group work." That said, the suggested methods are worthy of serious consideration.

535.   Kieran, C. (1991). Helping to make the transition to algebra.

Arithmetic Teacher, 38(7), 49-51.

The author presents researched instructional approaches which develop middle level students' understanding of nonnumerical notation (prealgebraic concept) that are compatible with a constructivist position. The uses of letters to represent a range of values or to represent unknowns are the focus of the activities. These are supportive of the NCTM's curriculum and evaluation standards.

536.   Lewis, A. C. (Ed.). (1991). Mathematics [Special issue]. *High Strides*, *3*(5).

Includes six articles focusing on selected issues related to mathematics instruction for middle level students. Specifically discussed are grouping, assessment, student attitudes, cooperative learning, and writing to learn. Includes a list of twelve resources available to middle level math teachers.

537.   Lobb, N. (1993). *Using a calculator: Easy lessons and practice activities.* Portland, ME: J. Weston Walch, Publisher. 32 pp.

Comprised of 32 worksheets, this set provides exercises whose purpose is to help students build speed and accuracy with the calculator. A test and teacher guide with objectives, procedures, games, activities and answers are included.

538.   Loewen, A. C. (1991). Lima beans, paper cups, and algebra. *Arithmetic Teacher, 38*(8), 34-37.

The author presents a classroom exercise which uses inexpensive manipulatives to help middle level students learn how to solve simple algebraic equations. The three major operations used in modeling algebraic equations include adding inverses, removing opposites, and sharing equally. A rationale for the use of such materials is clearly discussed. The author also includes concerns that a classroom teacher may have about using manipulatives and addresses them in a succinct manner.

539.   *Mathematics Teaching in the Middle School* (National Council of Teachers of Mathematics, 1906 Association Dr., Reston, VA 22091-1593).

A quarterly magazine, *Mathematics Teaching in the Middle School* is touted by NCTM as a "practical journal that focuses on issues, teaching concepts, and practical ideas for teachers working with the middle grades. Articles cover how math matters in the real world, students insights, and turning technology into math teaching power."

540.   McCallum, R., & Whitlow, R. (1994). *Linking mathematics and language: Practical classroom activities.* Portsmouth, NH: Heinmann. 140 pp.

This is a must resource for middle level teachers seeking to integrate language instruction and mathematics. The authors provide both a philosophical rationale and a wide range of practical classroom activities to address all the basic strands of mathematical instruction.

541.   Meconi, L. J. (1992). Numbers, counting, and infinity in middle school. *School Science and Mathematics, 92*(7), 381-383.

Author discusses the use of middle level students' natural understanding of large numbers to introduce the concept of infinity. Activities are included which investigate infinite sets by demonstrating a one-to-one correspondence between the counting numbers and the given set. Examples include prime numbers, Fibonacci numbers, fractions, even and odd numbers, and points on a segment.

542.   Miller, L. D. (1991). Writing to learn mathematics. *Mathematics Teacher, 84*(7), 516-521.

The author discusses how writing can be a means through which students can communicate their understanding of mathematics and its applications. Writing in mathematics can improve learning because it involves many thought pro- cesses Several ways for implementing writing in mathematics classes (K-12) are discussed. These include journal writing, expository writing, and impromptu writing prompts. Suggestions for getting started were included in the article.

543.   Morrow, L. J. (1991). Geometry through the standards. *Arithmetic Teacher, 38*(8), 21-25.

The author emphasizes a variety of ways to incorporate the recommendations in the NCTM curriculum standards into the K-8 geometry curriculum. Geometry is discussed in relationship to problem solving, visualization, measurement number sense, and making connections to other subjects or the world around the middle level student. Each significant point the author addresses is clearly illustrated by appropriate models which clearly could lead to classroom activities.

544.   Muth, K. D. (1993). The thinking-out-loud procedure: A diagnostic tool for middle school mathematics teachers. *Middle School Journal, 24*(4), 5-9.

Describes the thinking-out-loud procedure, the advantages and disadvantages of using such a procedure, suggestions for classroom implementation, and six examples that illustrate how the the procedure can be used with individual students.

545.   Norman, F. A. (1991). Figurate numbers in the classroom. *Arithmetic Teacher, 38*(7), 42-45.

Several activities which involve using figurate numbers to integrate numerical, geometric, arithmetic, patterning, measuring, and problem-solving skills are described. Figurative numbers are described as those numbers which can be represented by a particular geometric configuration. Most of these activities are appropriate for fifth and sixth grades.

546.   Parker, J., & Widman, C. C. (1992). Teaching mathematics with

technology: Statistics and graphing. *Arithmetic Teacher, 39*(8), 48-52.

The NCTM curriculum standards for statistics and probability (K-8) are presented and briefly discussed. The authors discuss how students need to understand the processes used in analyzing data in addition to the skills required to construct and read graphs. These processes include: a) formulating the key problem or questions; b) collecting and organizing data; c) analyzing and interpreting data; and d) summarizing and reporting findings. Clear examples of classroom activities are presented for each. Additional problems based on real-world problems are presented for grades K-8.

547.   Piston, C. (1992). Supplementing the graphing curriculum. *Mathematics Teacher, 85*(5), 336-341.

The author, via explanations and example problems, describes three types of graphing problems which can help more fully to develop middle level and high school student graphing skills. One problem type, analysis of one parameter with respect to another, involves presenting a graph to students and asking them to read it. A second problem type involves the comparison of two quantities represented graphically. The third problem type is prediction.

548.   Porter, P. (1991). Three fantastic math ideas. *The Transescent*, *16*(1), 3-6.

Outlines three activities designed to increase the motivation and achievement of middle level students enrolled in mathematics classes. The first activity (Math Wall of Fame) focuses on basic math facts; the second (Blue Ribbon Quilt Blocks) targets geometry; and the third (Math Is Flying High) presents kite-making as an activity for teaching mathematical concepts.

549.   Rathmell, E. C., & Leutzinger, L. P. (1991). Number representations and relationships. *Arithmetic Teacher, 38*(7), 20-23.

The authors describe several activities on number relationships and representations that incorporate the first four NCTM curriculum standards for K-4 and 5-8. These standards include solving problems, reasoning, communicating, and making connections. Many of the activities are drawn from real-world examples.

550.   Rowsey, R. E., & Jones, M. L. (1993). Metrics across the curriculum. *Middle School Journal, 25* (1), 39-40.

Describes a model for integrating instruction in metrics across the curriculum. Includes examples of activities designed to teach estimating and measuring to middle level students of different academic abilities, gender, and ethnicity.

551.   Sanfioenzo, N. R. (1991). Evaluating expressions: A problem-solving approach. *Arithmetic Teacher, 38*(7), 34-35.

The author describes activities and the rationale for activities that provide middle level students experiences in altering the order of mathematical operations. The activities use a problem-solving approach to teaching grouping symbols. Challenge activities are also discussed for the gifted students.

552.   Siverman, F. L., Winograd, K., & Strohauer, D. (1992). Student-generated story problems. *Arithmetic Teacher, 39*(8), 6-12.

The authors report on their experiences with middle level (grade 5) students' writing, solving, and sharing original mathematics story problems. The authors used an immersion strategy whereby the students learned to be problem solvers by writing their own problems. This strategy is clearly described in a step-by-step format. The authors' perspective on instruction in mathematics-problem solving using student-generated stories is presented through their discussion of three beliefs about learning and cognitive behavior. A few commonsense teaching practices are also discussed which could be helpful in getting the students to become more aware of their everyday mathematics experiences.

553.   Snyder, B. B. (1994). *Partner projects for middle school math. Volume 1: Numbers, operations, patterns*. Portland, ME: J. Weston Walch.

One of two volumes of math exercises with reproducible student worksheets that are designed to be used in pairs of students. Contains a section on ways to pair students to work together. Emphasizes cooperation and the facilitative role of the teacher.

554.   Sommers, J. (1992). Statistics in the classroom. *Mathematics Teacher, 85*(4), 310-313.

The author describes math projects for middle level students which focus on the problem solving, communication, reasoning, mathematical connections, number and number relationships, number systems and number theory, computation and estimation, patterns and functions, and statistics standards of the NCTM's curriculum standards for grades 5-8. The projects were used by the author to incorporate writing across the curriculum into her middle level math program. Students learned to integrate mathematics with their writing skills via a written report investigating a topic of their choice. The author reports that the projects helped students learn math concepts and generalize them while enhancing their student self-esteem.

555.   Spangler, D. A. (1992). Assessing students' beliefs about mathematics. *Arithmetic Teacher, 40*(2), 148-152.

The author discusses how the relationship between students' beliefs about mathematics and their learning of mathematics can be used to reinforce positive attitudes towards mathematics. Assessment of student beliefs is an important component of the overall assessment of students' mathematical knowledge according to the NCTM standards. The author presents several open-ended questions, which used in conjunction with class discussions and observations of students' interactions in the mathematics classroom, can assist in providing valuable information about student beliefs that influence mathematical learning. The more knowledgeable the classroom teachers are concerning student beliefs towards mathematics, the better able they are in planning the most appropriate classroom environment for learning mathematics.

556.   Strickland, J. F. Jr., & Strickland, K. A. (1992). The NCTM standards: A new vision for middle school mathematics. *The New England League of Middle Schools Journal*, 5(2), 14-17.

The authors discuss the focus and strengths of the new National Council of Teachers of Mathematics standards and discuss several areas of emphasis (problem solving, making mathematical connections, reasoning and communications, and the use of technology) and provide concrete sample activities of each.

557.   Taylor, L. (1992). Exploring geometry with the Geometer's Sketchpad. *Arithmetic Teacher, 40*(2), 187-191.

The author clearly discusses the importance of providing middle level students with geometric activities which encourage exploration, creativity, and discovery. The activities described use a computer program, Geometric Sketchpad, to provide the student with an electronic version of a point tool, a compass, and a straightedge. The activities clearly illustrate to the teacher and students how the geometric figure, a triangle, can be conjectured about, classified, and explored. The complete article supports the NCTM standards in getting students actively involved in communicating in mathematical terms.

558.   Tooke, D. J., Hyatt, B., Leigh, M., Snyder, B., & Borda, T. (1992). Why aren't manipulatives used in every middle school mathematics classroom? *Middle School Journal*, 24(2), 61-62.

Discusses the need to make the use of manipulatives an integral part of math courses at the middle level. Also discusses the impediments to integrating the use of manipulatives at the middle level as well as ways to encourage and prod middle level math teachers to integrate the use of manipulatives in their classes.

559.   Tsuruda, G. (1994). *Putting it together: Middle school math in transition*. Portsmouth, NH: Heinemann. 120 pp.

A personal account of the author's transition from a "traditional" teacher to an innovative one. Includes excellent examples of activities designed to encourage students to have fun while learning problem solving skills. Also an invaluable resource to assist teachers in meeting the objectives of the National Council of Teachers of Mathematics Standards. Includes seven chapters: The Seeds of Change, Paradigm Shift, Problem Solving, Student Writing, Assessment Alternatives, Grouping Practices, and Putting It All Together.

560.   Vatter, T. (1992). Teaching mathematics to the at-risk secondary

school student. *Mathematics Teacher, 85*(4), 292-294.

The author describes commonly identified characteristics of at-risk students. These include "poor self concept; poor academic performance, high absenteeism, and discipline problems; low aspirations and parents or guardians with low expectations; low family socioeconomic level; nontraditional family life often with a single or foster parent or with a stepparent; and inadequate goals and lack of future orientation" (p. 292). To effectively meet the needs of these students, schoolwork should actively involve the students, nurture students' feelings of worth and accomplishment, and have connections to the real world. A sample student project is described which meets these basic needs of the at-risk student.

561.   Vochko, L. E. (Ed.) (1979). *Manipulative activities and games in the mathematics classroom.* Washington, DC: National Education Association, 112 pp.

Provides twenty-two practical, easy-to-adopt approaches for involving students in mathematical concepts that are often difficult to get across.

562.   Yarworth, J. S., Schwambach, T. L., & Nicely, Jr., R. F. (1988). Organizing for results in elementary and middle school mathematics. *Educational Leadership, 46*(2), 61-64.

Presents a diagnostic-prescriptive model to revise and improve mathematics curriculum and instruction.

F. MATHEMATICS - GENERAL

563.   Barnett, C., Goldenstein, D., & Jackson, B. (Editors). (1994). *Fractions, decimals, ratios, and percents: Hard to teach and hard to learn? (Mathematics teaching cases).* Portsmouth, NH: Heinemann. 93 pp.

Written by upper-elementary and middle level teachers about their experiences covering fractions, decimals, ratios, and percents. These cases could be used to enhance professional development of middle level math teachers by stimulating reflection and dialogue about problems encountered in the classroom.

564.   Burton, L. (1991). *Gender and mathematics: An international perspective.* Cassell Education: New York.

Collection of research and essays from around the world with regard to the role of women in mathematics. The book is divided into four sections: Gender and Classroom Practice, Gender and Curriculum, Gender and Achievement, and Women's Presence. Several middle level classroom issues are included within these sections. One issue concerns classroom interaction patterns and possible relationships to achievement.

565.   Moses, R. P., Kamii, M., Swap, S. M., & Howard, J. (1989). The Algebra Project: Organizing in the spirit of Ella. *Harvard Educational Review,*

59(4), 423-43.

An argument is presented that all children should have access to the college preparatory mathematics curriculum of high schools. The Algebra Project, a math-science program in Cambridge, Massachusetts, is described. The project makes algebra available to all seventh and eighth graders regardless of level of math or academic achievement with the intent of enabling students to participate in higher math and science courses in high school.

566.   Ohanian, S. (1995). *Math at a glance: A month-by-month celebration of the numbers around us.* Portsmouth, NH: Heinemann. 128 pp.

Provides a chronology of historical events and zany facts that generate mathematical thinking and entertaining activities across all curriculum areas: language arts, literature, geography, environment, science, art, music, and sport and physical fitness.

567.   Pardini, P. (1995). If I can do math, I can do anything. *High Strides,* 7(4), 6-7, 12.

Advocates the inclusion of algebraic concepts in middle level programs with an "emphasis on reasoning and problem-solving" (p. 7).

568.   Reys, R. E., & Nobda, N. (Editors). (1994). *Computational alternatives for the twenty-first century: Cross-cultural perspectives from Japan and the United States.* Reston, VA: National Council of Teachers of Mathematics. 211 pp.

Examines both the Japanese and American views of computational alternatives—mental, written, with calculators, and through estimation—and their implications for school mathematics at all levels.

569.   Thornton, C. A., & Bley, N. S. (Editors). (1994). *Windows of opportunity: Mathematics for students with special needs.* Reston, VA: National Council of Teachers of Mathematics. 466 pp.

A professional resource for both regular classroom and special education teachers in grades K-12 who work with students with disabilities in mathematics, or students who are gifted or talented in mathematics.

570.   Wentworth, N. M., & Monroe, E. E. (1995). What is the whole? *Mathematics Teaching in the Middle School, 1*(5), 356-360.

Provides a description of the influence of constructivism on the teaching of math and three examples of how models can confuse students studying fractions unless the whole is carefully defined. The authors recommend having students construct their own area models.

571.   Whitin, D. J., & Wilde, S. (1995). *It's the story that counts: More*

children's books for mathematical learning, K-6. Portsmouth, NH: Heinemann. 240 pp.

The authors show how stories are natural invitations for learners to explore the mathematics of their own lives and the lives of others. The authors use children's books to examine multicultural themes and images, number systems, statistics, and probability. Includes an extensive bibliography of over three hundred new books arranged by category.

G. PHYSICAL EDUCATION - RESEARCH

572.   Ferguson, K. J., Yesalsi, C. E., Pomrehn, P. R., & Kirkpatrick, M. V. (1989). Attitudes, knowledge, and beliefs as predictors of exercise intent and behavior in school children. *Journal of School Health, 59(3),* 112-115.

A pilot study that used self-report information from 603 middle school children in two different schools to examine the ability of attitudes, knowledge and beliefs about exercise to predict intent to exercise or current exercise behavior. Significant amounts of the variance in exercise intent (37%) and current exercise behavior (27%) were explained by the variables. The authors make suggestions for physical education teachers.

573.   Long, M. J. (1993). Adventure education: A curriculum designed for middle school physical education programs (Doctoral dissertation, Middle Tennessee State University, 1993). *Dissertation Abstracts International, 54,* 860A.

A manual was created consisting of six levels, each being a three-week unit including materials and lesson plans for adventure education.

H. PHYSICAL EDUCATION - PRACTICAL

574.   Bell, J. (1990). Physical education and the middle school: "Just try." *KAMLE Karavan: Journal of the Kansas Association for Middle Level Education, 4,* 19-20.

Describes a physical education program in which students start out with an "A" in class and must lose points to lower their grade. Provides a rationale for the program as well as the rules and regulations of the program.

575.   Hovland, D. (1990). Middle level activities programs: Helping achieve academic success. *NASSP Bulletin: The Journal for Middle Level and High School Administrators, 74(530),* 15-18.

Hovland, a principal of a junior high, delineates what he perceives would be a sound athletic program at the middle level. Key components, he says, would be: "total participation, no emphasis on winning, short athletic seasons that provide several choices, no community 'all star' teams, no tournaments or post-season play, organize athletic teams so that no will will dominate, train coaches in middle level philosophy, and recognition for all participants."

576.   Rikard, G. L., & Woods, A. M. (1993). Curriculum and pedagogy in middle school physical education. *Middle School Journal, 24*(4), 51-55.

Provides a set of curricular recommendations for developing quality middle school physical education programs. Discusses the issues of indepth instruction, appropriate and extended practice, teacher-augmented feedback, and the need for students to have opportunities to showcase their abilities in cooperative and competitive situations throughout the units rather than as a culminating activity.

577.   Stueck, P., Batesky, J., Carnes, M., Jacoby, T., Monti, B., Schutte, R., Tenoschok, M., & Weinberg, H. (1995). Appropriate practices for middle school physical education: Quality physical education. *Becoming, 6*(2), 10-18.

Draft of a document to be presented to the Georgia Middle School Association on appropriate practices. The document is comprehensive and contrasts appropriate and inappropriate practices so readers can have a clearer of the intent.

I. PHYSICAL EDUCATION - GENERAL

578.   Eder, D., & Parker, S. (1987). The cultural production and reproduction of gender: The effect of extracurricular activities on peer-group culture. *Sociology of Education, 60*(3), 200-213.

Examined the effects of athletic-related activities on peer group culture in a middle school. "Male athletes are encouraged to be achievement-oriented and competitive, and cheerleaders are reminded of the importance of appearance and emotion management." It is likely that extra-curricular activities in many schools may encourage gender segregation and prepare girls to enter lower-status occupations.

579.   Lueke, P. J. (1993). Middle school sports: Intramurals vs. interscholastics. *The New England League of Middle Schools Journal, 6*(1), 1-4.

A former athletic director and physical teacher (who is now an assistant principal at a high school) argues in favor of focusing on intramural sports programs over interscholastic sports programs and provides a solid rationale for his position.

580.   Wadewitz, R. A., Tuescher, K., S., Pecinovsky, V. R., & Lenhart, J. A. (1989). The impact and analysis of aerobic activities on the middle level student. In David B. Strahan (Ed.), *Middle school research: Selected studies 1989* (pp. 60-76). Columbus, OH: Research Committee of the National Middle School Association.

"This study focused on the fitness level of 122 fifth grade students. The purpose of the study was to measure the fitness level of the fifth grade students and then determine the effects of a six-week aerobic fitness exercise program. The components of fitness that were measured in the pre- and post-test included body fat composition and aerobic capacity. Physical education teachers implemented a six-week session conducted three days a week. The results were analyzed and indicated a significant difference in submaximal oxygen uptake of the experimental group as compared to the control group... Assessment of the body composition data showed no statistically significant change between the two groups."

J. READING - RESEARCH

581.   Alvermann, D. E., O'Brien, D. G., & Dillon, D. R. (1990). What teachers do when they say they're having discussions of content area reading assignments: A qualitative analysis. *Reading Research Quarterly, 25*(4), 296-322.

Analysis of teacher-conducted classroom discussions. Teachers conducted discussions in a variety of ways depending upon teaching objectives and defined discussions differently from the ways they practiced discussion strategies. Teachers appeared to be more concerned about classroom control and covering material rather than generating active participation from students.

582.   Angeletti, S. (1990). Using literature to develop critical thinking. Paper presented at the International Reading Association, Atlanta, GA, May 6-11. (ERIC Document No. 320 107).

Reports findings on testing a questioning technique for teaching critical thinking strategies in fourth-and fifth-grade classes using student-selected reading materials. The author found gains made in skill areas and in attitude toward reading. The process has been successful with high, average, and low ability readers in second, fourth, and fifth grades.

583.   Armbruster, B. B., Anderson, T. H., & Ostertag, J. (1989). Teaching text structure to improve reading and writing. *The Reading Teacher, 43*(2), 130-137.

The authors report the results of their study investigating a method of teaching text structures which proved successful in improving both reading comprehension and summary writing of fifth graders. Their study focused on the problem-solution structure in which text with a problem-solution structure conveys information about a problem that an individual or group encounters, strategies for solving the problem, and the results of the attempt to solve the problem. The authors discuss how with the use of a simple, generalizable frame and a pattern for writing summaries, middle level students (fifth graders) can learn to attend to and remember the main ideas from problem-solution passages in their history textbooks. The students also learned how to write summaries about what they had read.

584.   Baer, B. T., Kachur, D., Goodall, R., & Brown, L. (1982). Middle grade reading instruction: Preferences and grouping practices. *The Clearing House*, *55*(8), 341-344.

Reports the results of a study designed to investigate the differences between what middle level reading teachers perceive as "best practices" in grouping students for reading instruction and what they actually practice on a day-to-day basis. Concludes that teachers need additional training in making informed decisions about groups versus individualized instruction.

585.   Chang, S. Q. (1983). Differential effects of oral reading to improve comprehension with severe learning disabled and educable mentally handicapped students. *Adolescence*, *18*(71), 619-626.

The author evaluated the effectiveness of oral reading for improving reading comprehension of eleven educable mentally handicapped or severe learning disabled middle level students who answered comprehension questions from a short factual article. Oral reading appeared to improve comprehension among the poorer readers but not for readers with moderately high ability.

586.   Dana, C., & Rodriguez, M. (1992). TOAST: A system to study vocabulary. *Reading Research and Instruction*, *31*(4), 78-84.

The authors describe a vocabulary study system that guided middle level students to pretest their knowledge, organize their vocabulary words, anchor them in memory, practice them at prescribed intervals to facilitate retention, and perform an exit test (TOAST: test, organize, anchor, say, and test). The study showed that the study system was more effective than the student-selected study methods both for immediate and delayed retention. The authors discuss how teaching study procedures that students can use on their own time can improve learning and retention of vocabulary.

587.   DuPont, S. (1992). The effectiveness of creative drama as an instructional strategy to enhance the reading comprehension skills of fifth-grade remedial readers. *Reading Research and Instruction*, *31*(3), 41-52.

According to the author's study, fifth-grade remedial reading students' comprehension skills, as measured by standardized and criterion-referenced tests, are enhanced through a reading program that uses the strategy of creative drama. The author discusses how the kinesthetic-tactile learning style characteristic of remedial readers can be accommodated and attended to when the teacher uses a strategy like creative drama to teach reading.

588.   Emery, D.W., & Milhalevich, C. (1992). Directed discussion of character perspectives. *Reading Research and Instruction*, *31*(4), 51-59.

The authors found that directed discussion of character perspectives can have an effect on middle level students' understanding of characters in new stories. Sixth-grade students who were involved in character perspective discussions were more likely than those students who had not participated to consider the long-range social context rather than merely the immediate situation. The authors also discuss other strategies to use with middle level students that may encourage them to consider more than one point of view.

589.   Gambrell, L. B. & Chasen, S. P. (1991). Explicit story structure instruction and the narrative writing of fourth- and fifth-grade below average readers. *Reading Research and Instruction*, *31*(1), 54-62.

The authors found that teaching explicit story structure to below average middle level (grades 4 and 5) readers improved the quality of their narrative writing. Teacher modeling and teacher-directed application were very important elements of explicit story structure instruction. The authors also found that explicit story structure instruction could easily be incorporated into most classrooms.

590.   Gordon, C. (1990). Changes in readers' and writers' metacognitive knowledge: Some observations. *Reading Research and Instruction*, *30*(1), 1-14.

The author reports observations made to gain information on how middle level students (grade 6) change their awareness of the characteristics of text, self as reader and writer, and monitoring strategies during the reading and writing of narrative and expository text. The following trends were discovered: an increased awareness of text structure, knowledge about the importance of affect in personal decisions made on strategy use, the gradual awareness of oneself as a user of a variety of sensemaking strategies during reading and writing, and a slight shift to greater use of a number of self-monitoring strategies.

591.   Kos, R. (1991). Persistence of reading disabilities: The voices of four middle level students. *American Educational Research Journal*, *28*(4), 875-895.

"This multiple case study explored the perceptions of four reading-disabled middle school students for the purpose of uncovering factors that may have prevented these students from progressing in their reading development. Results identified a) students' lack of effective use of reading strategies, b) students' perceptions of their reading instruction, c) students' stress related to reading, and d) aspects of students' educational histories as contributing in varying degrees to their lack of reading progress."

592.   Labbo, L. D., & Teale, W. H. (1990). Cross-age reading: A strategy for helping poor readers. *The Reading Teacher*, *43*(6), 362-369.

The authors describe their study which investigated poor fifth grade readers reading to kindergartners. The fifth graders were free to match themselves with kindergarten students in reading pairs. Some students read the same storybook over a 4 or 5 day period to several kindergartners. Other fifth graders chose to read a different storybook during each visit. The cross-age reading helped improve the poor fifth grade reader's fluency and comprehension. The study used a small number of students and there was a lack of an adequate control group.

593.   Lee, N. G., & Neal, J. C. (1992). Reading rescue: Intervention for a student "at promise." *Journal of Reading, 36*(4), 276-282.

A case study in which Marie Clay's model of one-on-one intervention intended for first graders is adapted for use with a middle school student. Could be effectively used in clinical settings and reading resource classrooms. Suggests guidelines for modifications for use by regular classroom teachers.

594.   Manna, A. L., Misheff, S., & Robitaille, N. (1988). Do middle school students read for pleasure? *Middle School Journal, 19*(4), 28-30.

Study used an open-ended questionnaire to determine extent students read for pleasure. Almost 80% of students indicated that they read for pleasure (71% boys compared to 84% girls). Twelve-year olds and 14-year olds read more than 13-year olds. Six of ten age/sex categories chose adventure stories as their favorite genre. When asked the title of their favorite book, the most popular type of book represented was realistic fiction. Overall, boys liked adventure and mystery stories. Girls progressed from mystery and adventure stories to romance novels.

595.   Many, J. E., & Anderson, D. D. (1992). The effect of grade and stance on readers' intertextual and autobiographical responses to literature. *Reading Research and Instruction, 31*(4), 60-69.

The study compares responses written by middle level students to three realistic short stories. The authors found no relationship between the stance taken in a free response and the types of intertextual or autobiographical connections made by the middle level students. Students tended to make more connections to television shows than to works of literature. Implications for middle level reading teachers who would like to understand better ways to assist students as the students make sense of their world through the literature they read are discussed.

596.   Many, W. A. (1965). Is there really any difference-reading vs. listening? *The Reading Teacher, 19*(2), 110-113.

The purpose of this study was to attempt to determine whether there is any significant superiority in visual mode of presentation over the auditory mode for six graders. The study included 352 students from fourteen six grade classrooms in three Midwestern communities. Two separate tests, a listening and a reading test were administered. The listening test measured nine listening skills: 1) keeping related details in mind; 2) observing single details; 3) remembering a series of details; 4) following oral directions; 5) using contextual clues; 6) recognizing organizational elements; 7) selecting the main idea; 8) drawing inferences; and 9) recognizing subordinate ideas that support main ideas. The visual test was an adaptation of the oral test using slides. The reliability of the visual test was .90 and .82 for the oral test. There was a correlation coefficient of .68 obtained between the listening and reading test scores. The study found that the six graders comprehended better through the visual mode than the oral mode. The students may also need more effective training in listening.

597.   Miller, D. E. (1993). The Literature Project: Using literature to improve the self-concept of at-risk adolescent females. *Journal of Reading, 36*(6), 442-448.

The purpose of the Literature Project was to improve the self-concepts and perceptions of at-risk adolescent females using selections from women's literature. The study showed that through the readings and activities in the Literature Project, the at-risk adolescent females began to view themselves as capable and talented individuals.

598.   National Assessment of Educational Progress. (1985). *The Reading Report Card.* Report no. 15-R-01. Princeton, NJ: Educational Testing Service.

This is a major report on four different national reading assessments conducted by NAEP in 1971, 1975, 1980, and 1984. The sample included over 250,000 students aged 9, 13, and 17.

599.   Neville, D. D., & Searls, E. F. (1991). A meta-analytic review of the effect of sentence-combining on reading comprehension. *Reading Research and Instruction, 31*(1), 63-76.

The results of this meta-analysis of 24 studies showed that sentence-combining training in the elementary grades increased reading comprehension more than similar training given middle level students or older. The authors found steady developmental increments in children's ability to understand syntactic structures until about the age of 13.

600.   Norris, D. J. (1990). Improve quantity and quality of student writing through the implementation of telecommunications and process writing activities between fifth and sixth grade students. Educational Specialist Practicum. Fort Lauderdale, FL: Nova University. (ERIC Document No. 324 685).

The author examined the effectiveness of a writing program designed to increase the quality and quantity of written communication of three heterogeneously grouped classes of fifth graders. The international news programs of the Cable News Network was used as a stimulus for the interaction of students located at schools 25 miles apart. The study found increased levels of achievement in students' communication and writing skills.

601.   Oldfather, P. (1993). What students say about motivating experiences in a whole language classroom. *The Reading Teacher, 46*(8), 672-681.

The author presents research findings from an eight-month collaborative inquiry of student motivation which involved students from a fifth- and sixth-grade classroom as co-researchers. The students are in their fourth year as co-researchers and will continue in that role through high school. The students had many choices about what to learn and how to learn, and they became personally invested and connected to their literacy activities. Students were actively involved in an integrated, thematic curriculum. The classroom culture was described as respectful and responsive. The author discussed the key connection between motivation for literacy and students' self-expression. Through self-expression students link their learning activities with who they are, how they think, and what they care about. This article provides a good discussion of how a whole language class could be used in the middle level grades.

602.   Ollmann, H. E. (1993). Choosing literature wisely: Students speak out. *Journal of Reading, 36*(8), 648-653.

Choosing what to read is part of becoming a reader. Self-selection enables middle level students to pursue personal interests. This study investigated how middle level students (grade 7) selected the books they read. What the literature will be about was the most important consideration for middle level students. Other important reasons included subject over text difficulty, misleading titles, and interesting plots. Suggestions on how to help middle level students improve their selection of literature are included.

603.   Questad, B. A. (1992). A case study of the effects of Accelerated Learning methodology on reading gains of ten middle school students in southwest Washington (Doctoral dissertation, Oregon State University, 1992). *Dissertation Abstracts International, 53,* 3496A.

Regular classroom instruction and special education instruction using Englemann and Hanner's Direct Instruction methods showed average gains in reading of five months a year. Under Eclectic instruction, students gained nine and a half months per year and using Accelerated Learning instruction the gain was approximately 15 1/2 months a year.

604.   Reutzel, D. R., & Hollingsworth, P. M. (1990). Reading comprehension skills: Testing the distinctiveness hypothesis. *Reading Research and Instruction, 30*(2), 32-46.

The author found that the teaching of discrete comprehension skills to middle level students (grades 4 and 6) resulted in equal gains for all comprehension skills assessed regardless of the skill taught. In contrast, the distinctiveness hypothesis predicts gains in only the skill being taught. The authors make three recommendations about instruction: (1) Increase the amount of time students are encouraged to read connected texts; (2) focus teaching the student on how to comprehend a given text selection or book rather than on mastery of discrete comprehension skills; and (3) substitute in place of comprehension worksheets opportunities to read and respond to a variety of literature, tradebooks, and informational texts.

605.   Rinehart, S. D., & Welker, W. A. (1992). Effects of advance organizers on level and time of text recall. *Reading Research and Instruction, 32*(1), 77-86.

The study investigated how advance organizers may differ in effectiveness on narrative text recall when they are read silently by the middle level students (grade 7) or read aloud to the students by the teacher, they are followed or are not followed by guided discussion, recall measures are literal or interpretive, and recall tasks are immediate or delayed. The authors found that advance organizers, used by seventh-graders, enhance text recall. The most resilient effects were seen when an oral presentation was followed with guided discussion. The oral presentation with discussion was more effective than the oral presentation without discussion. Similarly, the silent reading presentation was more effective with discussion than without discussion.

606.   Risko, V. J., & Alvarez, M. C. (1986). An investigation of poor readers' use of a thematic strategy to comprehend text. *Reading Research Quarterly, 21*(3), 298-316.

Thematic organizers designed to highlight central themes and relate information to students' prior knowledge increased student recall of text ideas and aided in comprehension.

607.   Roe, M. F. (1994). Microethnography of a seventh grade social studies curriculum. *Research in Middle Level Education, 18*(1), 21-38.

Using participant observation to examine the "instructional strategies" (p. 23) related to comprehension in a middle level content classroom, Roe describes daily routines, exchanges between teacher and students, and the use of the dominant influence of the textbook in determining use of instructional time. Suggests "posing questions that require assimilating information" (p. 35) as an alternative to finding answers in the text. Discussion strategies that require involvement from all students are also detailed. The title of the article is misleading in that the focus is not on the actual content but rather the strategies used in the classroom.

608.   Stanley, P. D., & Ginther, D. W. (1991). The effects of purpose and frequency on vocabulary learning from written context of high and low ability reading comprehenders. *Reading Research and Instruction, 30*(4), 31-41.

The authors found that vocabulary learning increased for both high- and low-ability middle level (grade 6) readers as number of encounters with new words increased. The study suggests that presenting new words in a variety of written contexts is an effective vocabulary teaching tool when the passages are easily understood by readers and unknown words are held to ten percent or less of the total vocabulary included.

609.   Taylor, B. M., & Frye, B. J. (1992). Comprehension strategy instruc-tion in the intermediate grades. *Reading Research and Instruction, 32*(1), 39-48.

The study found that reciprocal teaching procedures can be used to improve fifth- and sixth-grade students' comprehension of social studies material. Reciprocal teaching makes use of four effective strategies: self-questioning, summarizing, clarifying (self-monitoring) and predicting. Using this procedure, groups of three or four students work paragraph by paragraph through expository text. Students take turns being teacher as they lead the others in the group in the activities of questioning, summarizing, clarifying, and predicting.

610.   Tregaskes, M. R. (1989). Effects of metacognitive strategies on reading comprehension. *Reading Research and Instruction, 29*(1), 52-60.

The study found that the use of metacognitive strategies (visual imagery, summary sentences, webbing, self interrogation, and self-monitoring of comprehension) can significantly improve reading comprehension in middle level students (grade 6).

611.   Wells, M. C. (1993). At the junction of reading and writing: How dialogue journals contribute to students' reading development. *Journal of Reading, 36*(4), 294-302.

The author studied her eighth-grade students' reading dialogue journals in order to understand how the journals promoted reading development. There were five categories of student responses noted: ongoing business, summaries, metacognitive responses, connections, and evaluation of text and author. The study found that students necessarily become conscious of themselves as readers when they prepare to and actually write in their journals.

K. READING - PRACTICAL

612.   Alvermann, D. E. (1984). Using textbook reading assignments to promote classroom discussion. *The Clearing House, 58*(2), 70-73.

Argues that middle level students seldom engage in meaningful classroom discussions. Includes strategies for encouraging students to become active classroom participants by responding to content-area reading assignments.

613.   Anderson, R. C., Hiebert, E. H., Scott, J. A., & Wilkinson, I. A. G. (1984). *Becoming a nation of readers: The report of the Commission on Reading.* Washington, D.C.: National Institute of Education. 147 pp.

An outstanding and fascinating book which highlights early 1980s research on reading and literacy as well as the best practices. The book is comprised of the following chapters: What is Reading? Emerging Literacy, Extending Literacy, The Teacher and the Classroom, Testing and Reading, Teacher Education and Professional Development, and Recommendations. The recommendations section is a must reading for all parents and all educators at the public school level and in teacher education programs.

614.   Barnes, D. L. (1991). *As sure as eggs is eggs: Thinking and reading skills for middle school.* San Antonio, TX: ECS Learning Systems. 152 pp.

Fifty high-interest readings with exercises for developing basic reasoning basic skills. Includes relevance of information, fact versus opinion, relationships, cause and effect, and more.

615.   Bayer, A. S. (1990). *Collaborative-apprenticeship learning: Language and thinking across the curriculum, K-12.* Mountain View, CA: Mayfield Publishing Company.

This text is an excellent starting place for middle level teachers who would like to start using whole language in their classes. The author's model of teaching, called Collaborative-Apprenticeship Learning (CAL), is based on the idea that learning is a social activity. Key features of this model include apprenticeship, zone of proximal development, scaffolding, and expressive language. There is a section in the text which describes what CAL classrooms look like and how to implement one. A third section of the text discusses how to keep CAL going.

616.   Bedsworth, B. (1991). The neurological impress method with middle school poor readers. *Journal of Reading, 34*(7), 564-565.

Explains the method of using neurological impress method and highly recommends its use for students needing individual reading instruction. In this study, students made huge gains (3.5 *years*) in silent reading with 10 minutes of daily instruction over nine weeks. Instruction could be supplied by teachers, paraprofessionals, trained student aides, and (possibly) peer tutors.

617.   Bell, L. C. (1981). Individualizing a middle school reading program. *Middle School Journal, 12*(4), 12-14.

Requires self-selection of books by students, individual teacher-student conferences, groupings according to students' needs and interests. The highlight of the program is the individual teacher-student conference. Provides questions teachers might use to assess reading comprehension in conferences. Gives instructions for initiating an individualized program, including a variety of ways to share books and record-keeping for teachers.

618.   Bell, L. C. (1987). Let them READ: Using a thematic approach to teaching reading. *Middle School Journal, 19*(2), 16-17.

Suggests using three or more novels of varying reading levels centered around a particular theme. Skill activities and supplemental activities augment the program. Students are given time to read daily. Includes suggestions for developing a thematic unit, an example of a unit, and methods for evaluating the unit.

619.   Beyersdorfer, J. M., & Schauer, D. K. (1992). Writing personality profiles: Conversations across the generation gap. *Journal of Reading, 35*(8), 612-616.

The authors discuss how middle level reading teachers can design experiences with literature that stimulates the adolescent's growth toward mature decision making. The personality profile assignment is a reading-writing-project which can strengthen the adolescent's understanding of adult motivation. Middle level students progress through eight stages of the profile. Each stage is discussed with classroom activities provided.

620.   Braught, L. R. (1992). Student operated paperback bookshops: A program to encourage middle-grade literacy. *The Reading Teacher, 45*(6), 438-444.

The author describes how school bookshops were started in various schools to assist in the development of literacy in middle-grade students. The project involved a two-year grant which funded start up costs for bookshops in sixty-one middle schools located in 53 lowest income communities of Indiana. All the bookshops were set up independently and in a self-supporting manner. The author describes how students manage the individual bookshops with adult administrative support. Excellent recommendations for setting up bookshops for as little as $500 are discussed. The author emphasizes the key ingredient in starting a bookshop has clearly been leadership.

621.   Camp, D. J. (1987). Answering middle grade teachers' questions about readability. *Middle School Journal, 19*(1), 8-10.

In addition to answering readability questions, the author also suggests strategies designed to make instructional materials more readable, including schematic maps, tape recordings, video resources, trade books, and shortened reading assignments.

622.   Carroll, P. S. (1992). "i cant read i wont read": Will's moment of success. *English Journal, 81* (3), 50-52.

Describes the successful implementation of a Directed Individual Reading (DIR) project with a reluctant student. Includes directions for setting up DIR activities.

623.   Champney, L. L. (1989). Intervention assessment in middle school. *Journal of Reading, 32*(6), 556-558.

Describes a simple model for assessing students' actual reading processes with recommendations for remediation. Suitable for use on an individual basis in remedial reading classes. May have classwide applications.

624.   Cochran, J. (1990). *Insights to literature—A complete reading guide for middle grades*. Tampa, FL: National Resource Center for Middle Grades/High School Education. 240 pp.

A complete reading program designed to accompany ten widely-acclaimed books. Each piece of literature is presented through a reproducible unit and teacher's guide. Units contain comprehension questions and activities for each book chapter along with journal-writing activities. Teacher's guides contain pre-post reading questions and activities that touch on all areas of the curriculum. Everything is correlated to Bloom's taxonomy with a symbol indicating the thinking skill level.

625.   Collins, C. (1991). Reading instruction that increases thinking abilities. *Journal of Reading, 34*(7), 510-516.

Delineates eight lessons which increased thinking abilities and scholastic achievement. Lessons positively affected self-esteem, communication with peers and teachers, and increased breadth and depth of thinking while writing.

626.   Commeyras, M. (1993). Promoting critical thinking through dialogical-thinking reading lessons. *The Reading Teacher, 46*(6), 486-493.

The author describes one instructional approach designed to engage middle level students in reasonable reflective thinking in order to decide what to believe about a story-specific issue. The student is encouraged to (a) return to the text to verify or clarify information; (b) consider multiple interpretations; (c) identify reasons to support interpretations; and (d) evaluate the acceptability and relevance of competing or alternative interpretations. This instructional approach could help prepare middle level students to engage in the kind of critical inquiry that is needed for responsible citizenship. A list of trade books and basal stories is included.

627.   Cook, S. (1990). *Story journal for middle grades.* San Antonio, TX: ECS Learning Systems.

Seventeen pieces of literature have been carefully selected to inspire creative thinking, daily journal-writing activities, and vocabulary enrichment. Reproducible activities. Keyed to Bloom's taxonomy.

628.   Criscuolo, N. P. (1975). Five creative approaches to reading in New Haven middle schools. *The Clearing House, 49* (3), 113-115.

Discusses strategies for teaching reading to young adolescents. Includes ideas that are interesting, effective, and relevant for middle level students.

629.   Criscuolo, N. P. (1985). How to develop discriminating readers. *Middle School Journal, 17*(1), 28-29.

Presents 10 classroom-tested ways of reinforcing critical reading skills: "which is accurate," "a spicy account," "check the statement," "fact or opinion," "comparing two accounts," "what's the outcome," "imagine," "making inferences," pick the right answer," and "anticipating events." Argues that to be truly commited readers, students must be discriminating.

630.   Davidson, J., & Koppenhaver, D. (1988). *Adolescent literacy: What works and why.* New York: Garland Publishing. 275 pp.

Initially the authors discuss the problem of adolescent illiteracy and the extent of the problem in the United States. The bulk of the book focuses on case studies of various literacy programs across the United States which have increased adolescents' literacy. The common elements which have contributed to the programs' success are described. The table of contents provides a solid sense of the book's breadth: Adolescent Illiteracy: A National Problem; Methodology; The Kenosha Model: Academic Improvement Through Language Experience; Star: Structured Teaching in the Areas of Reading and Writing; Hilt: High Intensity Language Training—An Effective Model of Second Language Literacy Instruction; After-School Literacy Programs for Young Adolescents; Summer Literacy Programs for Young Adolescents; Special Findings; What Works and Why; and, Policy Implications. It concludes with a short annotated resource list.

631.   Davis, S. J. (1989). Using multiple criteria to place middle school students. *Journal of Reading, 32*(8), 720-728.

Presents an alternative to test scores in placing students in reading groups. The Reading Placement Profile (RPP) was designed to measure both formal and informal data: current placement, grade in reading, teacher recommendation, an achievement test score, an IQ score, and an attitude score. Includes models of the RPP form, a self-assessment attitude scale, and a teacher recommendation form. Teachers felt this manner of placement to be fairly easy to use and provided more accurate information for student placement than simple test scores.

632.   Deaton, C. D. (1992). Idioms as a means of communication: Writing in the middle grades. *The Reading Teacher, 45*(6), 473.

The author describes idioms as commonly used language expression whose meaning cannot be predicted from the meanings of the individual words but only from context. A five day instructional plan is discussed to familiarize students with idioms by having students use them. The activities could be used as creative writing ideas also.

633.   Dever, C. T. (1992). Press conference: A strategy for integrating reading with writing. *The Reading Teacher, 46*(1), 72-73.

The author describes how her middle level students role-play press reporters at a press conference to learn how writing is a process of recursive stages (pre-writing, drafting, revising, editing, and publishing). The class first reads a selection of literature. Student volunteers role-play story characters. The remaining students conducted a literacy press conference as press reporters. The student reporters then turn their interviews into effective news stories for the student newspaper. Middle level students improved their skills in notetaking, public speaking, and listening.

634.   Dixon, D. J. (1989). Story flow charts. *Journal of Reading, 32*(5), 456-458.

Introduces a graphic story flow chart to help students organize and classify events and story elements including conditions, feelings, choices, and reactions.

635.   Flynn, L. L. (1989). Developing critical reading skills through cooperative problem solving. *The Reading Teacher, 42*(9), 664-668.

The author describes an instructional model for helping middle level students (grade 5) to analyze, synthesize, and evaluate ideas through problem solving. Problems are presented to the students by using popular mysteries in children's literature. The Ideal approach to problem solving is used to solve the mysteries and has five steps: Identifying, Defining, Exploring, Acting, and Looking. The author describes how this strategy was implemented in her middle level classroom.

636.   Forte, I. (1982). *Read about it—Activities for teaching basic reading skills.* Tampa, FL: National Resource center for Middle Grades/High School Education. 80 pp.

Interesting, fun-filled pages are designed to help students achieve reading independence. Easy-to-follow directions, fantasy-based themes, and the use of a controlled, but not limited, vocabulary encourage purposeful reading. Activities, puzzles, and games stress skills such as comprehension, word meaning, structural analysis, and the use of reference materials.

637.   Forte, I. (1987). *Kids' stuff book of reading and language arts for the middle grades.* Tampa, FL: National Resource Center for Middle Grades/High School Education. 240 pp.

Developed by the original KID'S STUFF authors, this resource is loaded with ideas, activities, lessons, teaching strategies, and reproducibles for every language arts curriculum. Illustrations enhance high-interest activities to capture and hold the attention of middle level students. Lessons and activities are indexed by skill and area.

638.   Francis, Z. (1991). Thinking about reading. *High Strides: The Bimonthly Report on Urban Middle Schools, 4*(1), 6.

Discusses a program developed at Stanford University called "Project Read," which is a set of ideas "for moving reading and writing from being very basic skills that are materials-directed to being a very meta- language" (e.g., in which students use language and structures to solve problems and to communicate).

639.   Froese, V. (1981). Middle years reading instruction: Suggested principles. *The Reading Teacher, 34*(5), 547-551.

The author describes reading in the middle school years as a process of discovering meaning from print. This meaning comes from an interaction of experience, language competence, and visual or auditory information. The following 14 principles were described to assist in developing a curriculum guide for the middle school grades: 1) teachers should de-emphasize decoding, emphasize comprehension; 2) a range of subprograms must be considered within a school; 3) three kinds of cuing systems operate within the reading process;

4) the goal of reading is to read a variety of materials; 5) teachers should use every opportunity available to capitalize on reading experiences as a means of clarifying and extending the concepts under discussion and to relate them to other concepts; 6) teachers should encourage the development of life-reading skills which help students select appropriate material, locate sources, initiate and self-direct learning through reading; 7) the teacher should model reading; 8) oral reading must be purposeful; 9) reading should be integrated with writing, listening, and speaking; 10) for instructional purposes, materials need to be matched to the reader; 11) a reader's competence and self-concept are often interdependent; 12) skills teaching should be based primarily on diagnosis; 13) a reader's purpose should determine the rate of reading; and 14) thinking is at the center of all reading.

640.   Goggin, W. F., & Ehrmantraut, A. M. (1981). Magazines in the classroom. *Middle School Journal, 12*(3), 20-21.

Discusses problems and advantages of the uses of periodical use in the classroom. Suggests magazines be used in individual learning packets. Gives five examples of magazine-centered activities. All activities are easily adaptable to a variety of periodicals.

641.   Groff, P. (1980). Phonics in the middle schools? *The Clearing House, 54* (4), 160-163.

Presents a research-based discussion on the pros and cons of phonics instruction with middle level students. Concludes that teaching phonics is appropriate for students who have not previously acquired that knowledge and skill.

642.   Hamann, L.S., Schultz, L., Smith, M. W., & White, B. (1991). Making connections: The power of autobiographical writing before reading. *Journal of Reading, 35*(1), 24-28.

Reading requires students to supply their own previously acquired background knowledge and experiences for meaning to occur. The authors describe how when middle level students write about relevant autobiographical experiences prior to reading, they are more on-task, offer more sophisticated responses to characters, and like the texts more. This strategy has been effectively used with multi-cultural middle level classes.

643.   Hancock, M. R. (1993). Exploring and extending personal response through literature journals. *The Reading Teacher, 46*(6), 466-474.

The literature response journal is described as an effective way of capturing emerging reader response while linking writing to the reading process. The author shares response options from a classroom study of sixth-grade students who responded to four books of realistic fiction in a response journal format. Categories (personal meaning making, character and plot involvement, and literary criticism) of response were explored and used to encourage students to move beyond writing summaries, but to explore and become actively involved with the book they are reading.   An excellent set of guidelines for literature response journals is discussed.

644.   Irvin, J. L.   (1990).   *Reading and the middle school student: Strategies to enhance literacy*. Boston: Allyn and Bacon.

This text is primarily written for the preservice and inservice middle level teachers interested in content reading. The first part of the text focuses on the foundations and strategies supporting content reading. This information can be helpful to middle level teachers in making instructional decisions. The final part of the text provides middle level teachers with the information to make programmatic decisions.

645.   Irwin, J. W.   (1980).   Implicit connectives and comprehension. *The Reading Teacher, 33* (5), 527-529.

The authors describe how students in grades 4-6 treat inferences necessary for linking sentences together as if they were actually stated in the material. Inferences are critically important because they connect ideas. Middle level students generally do not comprehend critical relationships when they are implicit, and their total recall of the reading material will likely be reduced because of this lack of understanding of critical connectives. The authors recommend that middle school teachers should teach students the following strategies to improve their comprehension of implicit connectives: 1) focus questioning on implicit connective relationships; 2) discuss with the students the necessity for looking for such relationships; and 3) don't assume a passage is easy to understand just because it has short sentences and easy words. The student should look for implicit relationships.

646.   Koenke, K.   (1986).   Reading instruction in the middle school: Instruction appropriate for students in transition. *Journal of Reading, 30*(2), 172-174.

A goal of middle school reading is to help students learn to read to learn. Students, not subject matter, are the focus of instruction. Includes a brief overview of suggested reading strategies appropriate for use with middle school students.

647.   Lewis, A. C.   (1993).   Juliet seeks Romeo in jail. *High Strides, 5*(3), 3.

Describes "Books Behind Bars," a program designed to link young adults with prison inmates through common interests in reading. Also discussed are collaborative efforts among college students, who serve as mentors; middle level students; and prison inmates.

648.   McWhirter, A. M.   (1990).   Whole language in the middle school. *The Reading Teacher, 43*(8), 562-565.

This is an easy to read "how to" article with an excellent research base provided.

The author describes how she was able to get her middle level students (eighth graders) interested in reading by using a whole language approach. Whole language is described as the use of natural and authentic learning situations in which language is dealt with in context. The students discover that classroom language has a function because it is related to the world around the students. The author used a dialogue journal to help provide information to the teacher and also feedback to the students about their reading comprehension. A classroom management system is discussed in the article.

649.   Muth, D. (1987). What every middle school teacher should know about the reading process. *Middle School Journal, 19*(1), 6-7.

Explains reasons for difficulties many students encounter as they progress from reading narrative books to content-area texts. Suggests content-area teachers spend time helping students develop memory management techniques and use metacognition strategies. Includes practical examples.

650.   Nehiley, J. M. (1991). Use of cartoons and drawings to improve content reading. *Journal of Reading, 34*(7), 563-564.

Humor makes learning less threatening and illustrations aid in comprehension. Both line illustrations and cartoons were more effective than photos in boosting long-term retention.

651.   Norton, D. E. (1992). Understanding plot structures. *The Reading Teacher, 46*(3), 254-258.

The author discusses how helping students develop understandings of story grammars and plot structures enhances their comprehension of literature. Strategies are presented which may help the middle level student to understand various types of plot structures and to relate those plot structures to characterization and theme. A list of suggested books for middle level students which develop strong plot structures is included.

652.   Oberlin, K. J., & Shugarman, S. L. (1989). Implementing the Reading Workshop with middle school LD readers. *Journal of Reading, 32*(8), 682-687.

Describes how one teacher used Atwell's Reading Workshop to significantly improve LD students' reading attitudes and levels of book involvement.

653.   Reyes, M. D. L., & Molner, L. A. (1991). Instructional strategies for second-language learners in the content areas. *Journal of Reading, 35*(2), 96-103.

This is an excellent resource article for middle level teachers who teach language-diverse students. The authors present several strategies that have been found to be effective in helping these students. The following three strategy characteristics are discussed as being important in teaching language minority students: (1) language learning is integrated with content instruction, (2) students are provided access to problem-solving activities in nonthreatening cooperative contexts designed to foster higher order thinking and complex processing of content information, and (3) learning activities are mediated or scaffolded so as to build background and promote learning across the subject areas.

654.   Ribovich, J. K. (1977). Developing comprehension of content material through strategies other than questioning. Paper presented at the International Reading Association Annual Convention, Miami Beach, Florida, May 1977. (ERIC Document Number ED 141 786).

The author describes four instructional strategies to help develop comprehension as the student reads: 1) have students specify content expectations in a variety of forms and then read with a focus on the expected and unexpected; 2) direct students in writing experiences to help them become more familiar with material organization and author style; 3) discuss and provide self-monitoring activities for students experiencing extreme difficulty in comprehension; and 4) stimulate concept development and thinking processes prior to reading.

655.   Richie, J. R. (1981). What's black and white and should be read all over? *Middle School Journal, 12*(2), 10-12.

Newspapers can be used in place of textbooks to provide relevancy. LAP's may be developed for use by individuals for remedial work or enrichment. Discusses the creation of individual study projects and learning about life and career education via the newspaper.

656.   Rief, L. (1992). *Seeking diversity.* Portsmouth, NH: Heinemann Educational Books.

The text provides a guide into workshop-based teaching and portfolio assessment for the middle level grades. The author discusses how she promotes diversity in her eighth-grade language arts classroom through democratic choice in writing and reading, and portfolios provide examples of this diversity. All aspects of the portfolio process are discussed.

657.   Riley, J. D. (1992). Using the proficient reader protocol to evaluate middle school reading behaviors. *The Clearing House, 66* (1), 41-43.

Discusses the role of a "Proficient Reader Protocol" (PRP) in evaluating middle school readers. Also defines and discusses the six components of proficient reading and illustrates how each component is measured by PRP. Concludes with a list of implications for the middle level classroom.

658.   Roe, M. F. (1992). Reading strategy instruction: Complexities and possibilities in middle school. *Journal of Reading, 36*(3), 190-196.

Discusses the challenges of classroom decision making during reading instruction and lists beliefs the author has about middle school reading instruction. Gives scenarios of whole-class instruction to demonstrate a framework for implementing specific reading strategies.

659.   Round table, The. (1992). Grading and evaluation in the reading/
writing workshop. *English Journal, 81*(6), 80-82.

Six brief, practical articles by practitioners explaining their own methods of
assessment in reading/writing workshops.

660.   Samway, K. D, Whang, G., Cade, C., Gamil, M., Lubandina, M. A., &
Phommachanh, K. (1991). Reading the skeleton, the heart, and the brain of a
book: Students' perspectives on literature study circles. *The Reading Teacher,
45*(3), 196-205.

Literature study circles emphasize reading and discussing unabridged,
unexcerpted children's literature. The teacher first introduces a book to her class
by talking about it to gain their interest. Students choose which book they would
like to read and discuss with other students who also read the same book. The
students work on an activity designed to extend their understanding of the
author's writing style or creation of story elements. The authors found that by
using literature study circles in their classes (elementary and middle level) the
students understood themselves and others better; students viewed themselves as
readers; students preferred reading complete books compared to abridged books;
and they enjoyed talking about books they read.

661.   Scott, K. P. (1982). Teaching about sex differences in language. *The
Clearing House*, *55*(9), 410-413.

Reports the results of a study designed to investigate the inclusion of gender-
specific references in reading materials. Includes strategies for assisting middle
level students in recognizing such references.

662.   Sheppard, R. (1985). *Enhancing learning through oral and written
expression: strategies for subject area teachers*. Columbus, OH: National
Middle School Association. 108 pp.

The author provides practical ideas on how to teach reading and writing across
the curriculum at the middle level. In doing so, Sheppard presents both
theoretical information as well as concrete suggestions vis-à-vis projects,
lessons, and instructional strategies.

663.   Singleton, B. (1986). Going once, going twice—sold—on the auction
for motivating reluctant readers. *Middle School Journal, 17*(4), 12-13.

Explains organization of a auction as a school-wide motivational strategy for
reading. For one month, students read and report on as many books as possible.
Books are rated easy ($3), average ($5), and difficult ($7). Play money is used
to bid for donated items on auction day.

664.   Sipe, L. R. (1993). Using transformations of traditional stories:

Making the reading-writing connection. *The Reading Teacher, 47*(1), 18-26.

Transformations are described as new stories which are deliberately modelled on older ones. Transformations may be parallel, deconstructed, or extended versions of the original tale, or the tale may be transformed through illustrations. The author describes how middle level (grade 6) students used transformations to develop tools of literacy understanding such as comparing and contrasting the new and old stories; being sensitive to setting, plot, and characterization; and understanding the concepts of point of view and sequel. Also, the students' skill in using the writing process was improved.

665.   Smith, L. L., & Riebock, J. (1971). A middle school tries contractual reading. *The Clearing House, 45*(7), 404-406.

Outlines a program in which each student negotiates an individualized contract with the teacher. Emphasis is upon providing the most appropriate learning opportunities for each student.

666.   Speaker, R. B., & Speaker, P. R. (1991). Sentence collecting: Authentic literacy events in the classroom. *Journal of Reading, 35*(2), 92-95.

The author discusses how sentence collecting by middle level students can help foster an appreciation of literature as well as higher level thinking skills and analysis. Students find sentences from their reading that seem interesting and important. They bring these sentences to class to discuss. Added benefits from sentence collecting include: developing communication skills among students and fostering parental involvement.

667.   Thomas, K. J. (1978). The directed inquiry activity: An instructional procedure for content reading. *Reading Improvement, 15*(2), 138-140.

Thomas' Directed Reading Inquiry (DRI) activity is a procedure for any grade level, including middle level, to help students categorize and retrieve factual information found in subject area textbooks. This activity focuses on six points of inquiry: Who? What? When? Where? How? Why? The students preview the selection to be read by making predictions to each of six inquiry questions. The teacher records student predictions on the board and helps students discover interrelationships among the ideas and categories through class discussion. This helps to establish both purposes for reading and the mind set required for the reading experience. As the students read the assigned material, they confirm their predictions or make necessary changes in them. The teacher definitely must be thoroughly familiar with the material and also introduce technical terms necessary for student understanding.

668.   Tierney, R. J., Carter, M. A., & Desai, L. E. (1991). *Portfolio assessment in the reading-writing classroom*. Norwood, MA: Christopher-Gordon Publishers.

The first part of the text answers questions about portfolios, describes a portfolio classroom and the role of the teacher, and discusses classroom-based assessment programs. The second part of the text introduces portfolios, outlines getting started, discusses how to sustain portfolios, presents the role of student self-assessment, and documents how to analyze and keep records of portfolio contents and processes. The authors emphasize throughout the text that portfolios should reflect the strengths, needs, and individuality of each student. Ideally, the portfolio process resists standardization, simplification, and formalization.

669.   Tovey, D. R. (1981). Thought, language, and reading in the content fields. *Middle School Journal, 12*(2), 3-5.

Discusses the relationships between thought and language in the reading process. "Reading appears to be mostly a non-visual process." Lists and explains six psycholinguistic understandings necessary for middle school teachers of reading in the content areas.

670.   Walker, J. E. , & Vacca, R. T. (1983). The "book an hour" strategy. *Middle School Journal, 15*(1), 12-13.

Students are assigned to read individual chapters in a simple book. Then each student briefly summarizes his or chapter to the others. Predictions are encouraged. Students are exposed to the story line of an entire novel in one hour. For use as a motivational device for further reading. The method is clearly explained and is effectively used with reluctant readers.

671.   Wigginton, E. (1985). *Sometimes a shining moment: The Foxfire experience.* Garden City, NY: Anchor Press. 438 pp.

A fascinating and inspiring book in which Wigginton describes his struggles and successes as a teacher as well as his development of the Foxfire program, one of the most touted and innovative literacy programs in the United States.

672.   Wilson, R. M. (1965). Oral reading is fun. *The Reading Teacher, 19*(1), 41-43.

The author describes a reading program designed to improve sixth grade students' oral reading skills (stress on pitch, proper pronunciation of words, and reading without regression) without the critical ears of their peers. The program is modeled from foreign language study. First, the student silently reads a story of interest to them at their independent level or other materials such as reports or plays that they will use later in class work. Second, the student reads the material orally into a tape player. The student then listens to the tape recording and evaluates his/her reading in reference to predetermined instructional goals (with teacher assistance). Finally, the student rereads the materials orally and compares the two readings. The author did measure the oral reading skills of the students before and after their language lab experience and found that accuracy improved the most with comprehension and rate also having improved. The students began looking forward to oral reading with enthusiasm. The technique definitely assisted students with class presentations of reports, plays, and stories.

673.   Wolfthal, M. (1989). Put reading back in remedial reading. *Journal of Reading, 32*(5), 460-461.

Offers a rationale for combining silent reading with individual conferences in a remedial reading class.

674.   Wood, K. D. (1987). Helping students comprehend their textbooks. *Middle School Journal, 18*(2), 20-22.

Recommends the use of textbook activity guides (TAG) for lower ability students. Includes procedures (with examples) for developing TAG's and offers suggestions for use in the classroom.

675.   Wood, K. D. (1988). A guide to reading subject area material. *Middle School Journal, 19*(3), 24-26.

Shows content area teachers how to create a "Reading Road Map," a type of reading guide for textbooks. Includes explanations for designing, implementing, and evaluating the guide.

676.   Wood, K. D. (1992). Fostering collaborative reading and writing experiences in mathematics. *Journal of Reading, 36*(2), 96-103.

The author discusses several collaborative strategies for middle level instruction which integrate reading and writing with mathematics instruction. These strategies include paired or group retellings, reaction guide, list-group-label and write, interactive guide, and capsule vocabulary. These strategies provide ways to increase students' conceptual knowledge of mathematics through the communication processes of reading, writing, listening, and speaking. Sample lessons are included.

677.   Wood, K. D. (1992). Oral reading in the middle school. *Middle School Journal, 23*(5), 56-59.

Wood briefly discusses the research on the value of oral reading, and then suggests a number of alternative approaches to oral reading (e.g., paired or assisted reading, Cloze procedure oral reading, mumble reading, whisper reading, choral reading, imitative reading, four-way oral reading, and paired reading/retelling.

678.   Wright, J. P. (1980). Practice in using location skills in a content area. *The Reading Teacher, 34*(2), 184-186.

The author describes a project used in six grade to give students meaningful and interesting practice in using location skills (using books, dictionaries, and reference books) in the content area of science. The project was seen as an intermediate step between the presentation of study skills and a research paper. The first step involved identifying basic concepts to be developed in science and placing these on task cards which required the student to locate certain information. Next the student makes a series of task cards to be used to develop vocabulary pertinent to the science concepts. The student alphabetizes the cards, looks up each word in the dictionary, and writes the pronunciation of the word and the meaning or meanings that apply to the study of the particular science concept. Finally, a set of information task cards are used to provide additional information to support the science concept. To complete these task cards, the student must use specific study skills to locate information outside their textbooks.

L. READING - GENERAL

679.   Aiex, N. K. (1990). Using literature to teach reading. *ERIC Digest,* (ERIC Document No. ED 313 687).

The article is helpful and informative for middle level teachers who are considering the use of children's literature in teaching reading. The author has provided a brief review of material in the ERIC database on literature-based reading instruction. There are sections on recent research, basic resources, assessment of literature based reading, diverse methods approaches, and practical teaching guides.

680.   Alexander, J. E., & Cobb, J. (1992). Assessing attitudes in middle and secondary schools and community colleges. *Journal for Reading, 36*(2), 146-149.

The strong relationship between attitude and reading comprehension is discussed as the main reason for assessing middle level students' attitudes toward reading. Types of attitude assessment techniques, cautions in assessment, and content area attitudes are discussed with supporting research by the authors. Examples of frequently used instruments for measuring attitudes are included.

681.   Armbruster, B. B., & Nagy, W. E. (1992). Vocabulary in content area lessons. *The Reading Teacher, 45*(7), 550-551.

Very concise and informative article concerning vocabulary in content area readings. Three important points are discussed. The first concerns how closely the meaning of the word is tied to the major purpose of the lesson. The second point involves how content vocabulary is rarely associated with familiar concepts. The third point concerns how content vocabulary within lessons are generally related in meaning. The authors discuss some important implications for instruction.

682.   Condon, M. W. F., & Hovda, R. A. (1984). Reading & writing & learning: Skill flexibility for middle school. *Middle School Journal, 16*(1), 14-21.

Discusses several parallels between composition and reading: personal reading/diary writing, skimming/outlining, scanning/summaries, study reading/final drafts. Recommends that the teaching of reading and writing be integrated to develop flexible language skills. Includes a table showing the relationship of reading and composition flexibilities.

683.   Frender, G. (1990). *Learning to learn—Strengthening study skills and brain power*. San Antonio, TX: ECS Learning Systems.

A hands-on guide filled with practical hints, methods, tips, procedures, resources, and tools that will teach students to maximize their ability to learn. Includes information on learning styles, note and test-taking advice, reading and study skills, and much more.

684.   Hall, S. (1990). *Using picture storybooks to teach literary devices: Recommended books for children and young adults*. Phoenix: Oryx Press.

The first part of this book describes the genre of picture story books and how to use them with middle level students to teach literary devices. The second part of the book categorizes 275 books under headings such as alliteration, imagery, personification, and theme. Excellent resource for the middle level writing teacher.

685.   Potter, R. L. (1989). *Using microcomputers for teaching reading in the middle school. fastback 296*. Bloomington, IN: Phi Delta Kappa Educational Foundation.

The author discusses how the use of a computer helps middle level students improve their reading. There are sections on software, managing computer-assisted instruction, word processing, and remedial reading.

686.   Rafoth, M. A., Leal, L., & DeFabo, L. (1993). *Strategies for learning and remembering: Study skills across the curriculum*. Washington, DC: National Education Association. 112 pp.

Teachers will learn where students have developed in their learning styles both as a group and as individuals. Includes curriculum-specific strategies for teaching middle school students the most effective ways to learn and remember.

687.   Shannon, D. (1985). Use of top-level structure in expository text: An open letter to a high school teacher. *Journal of Reading, 28*(5), 426-431.

Explains "top level structure" as the major points in an outline of a discourse and offers rules for helping students identify the main ideas of a selection. Reviews pertinent research.

688.   Smith, F. R., & Feathers, K. M. (1983). The role of reading in content classrooms: Assumption vs. reality. *Journal of Reading, 27*(3), 262-267. Observed the reading process in four social studies classes in order to determine

the role that reading actually plays in the content area classroom. Analysis revealed that for most students reading was neither meaningful nor necessary. Teachers placed emphasis on the acquisition of specific information rather than on the development of higher learning skills. Offers suggestions for improving the quality of reading in content area classrooms.

689.   Wood, K. D., & Muth, K. D. (1991). The case for improved instruction in the middle grades. *Journal of Reading, 35*(2), 84-90.

The authors briefly discuss the organization of middle schools and their purposes. They do an excellent job in explaining how middle level teachers can instruct middle level students in motivating, interesting, and developmentally appropriate ways. A strong knowledge base is included.

M. SCIENCE - RESEARCH

690.   Erb, T. O. (1981). Attitudes of early adolescents toward science, women in science and science careers. In Thomas Owen Erb (Ed.), *Middle school research: Selected studies 1981* (pp. 108-118). Columbus, OH: Research Committee of the National Middle School Association.

Erb's study focused on the attitudes of male and female students ages 10 to 16 toward scientists, science, women in science, careers in technical fields, and careers in science. He states that "on the sex variable three of our five hypotheses were confirmed. Early adolescent boys are more positively disposed toward science and careers in technological fields than are girls in the same age groups. Also girls are more positively disposed toward women in science than are boys."

691.   Gabel, D. (Editor). (1994). *Handbook of research on science teaching and learning.* Arlington, VA: National Science Teachers Association. 736 pp.

A comprehensive survey of current research in science education (including middle level science) which provides an assessment of the significance or research, evaluates new developments, and examines current conflicts, controversies, and issues.

692.   Hadfield, O. D., & Lillibridge, F. (1993). Can a hands-on, middle grades science workshop have staying power? *The Clearing House, 66* (4), 213-217.

Reports the results of a study designed to test the effectiveness of a hands-on workshop for middle level science teachers. Results indicate that the participants continue to use the materials and information two years after the initial workshop. Specifically discussed are the program components that appear to be responsible for the sustained, long-term effectiveness of the workshops.

693.   Hawk, P. P. (1984). Graphic organizers: Increasing the achievement

of life science students. In Hershel D. Thornburg and Stefinee E. Pinnegard (Eds.), *Middle school research: Selected studies 1984*. Columbus, OH: National Middle School Association.

The results of Hawk's study indicates that the use of graphic organizers is an effective and practical strategy and that life science teachers at the middle level should find them beneficial to their students' learning.

694.   Linn, M. C., & Songer, N. B. (1991). Cognitive and conceptual change in adolescence. *American Journal of Education, 99*(4), 379-417.

The authors present a theoretical perspective for examining conceptual change in adolescence and the social context of learning. A case study of the Computer as Lab Partner project is used to illustrate the following: (1) conceptual and cognitive changes in eighth graders' understanding of physical science concepts; (2) ways concepts are constructed; and (3) several successful intervention types.

695.   Prather, J. P. (1989). Review of the value of field trips in science instruction. *Journal of Elementary Science Education, 1*(1), 10-17.

The author provides an easy to read summary of the research on science field trips for K-12. Field trips help broaden the students' environmental experience and insight, increase their process skills, improve attitudes toward science and science education, provide direct student involvement with the subject matter, promote student self-confidence, enhance social skills, and develop leadership. Research has found that field trips can be one of the most productive instructional methods used by science teachers if used in conjunction with other methods such as lectures, laboratory activities, audio-visuals, and assigned reading to introduce the concepts and/or processes to be studied.

696.   Ramsey, J. M., & Kronholm, M. (1991). Science related social issues in the elementary school: The extended case study approach. *Journal of Elementary Science Education, 3*(2), 3-13.

The Extended Case Study (ECS) strategy uses a community-based, science-related social issue (SRSI) as an instructional context to identify and develop science concepts, as well as skills such as information processing, research methods, and decision making. The authors describe how middle level (grade 5) students used the ECS approach to understand, analyze, investigate, and act on a science-related social issue in their community.

697.   Reynolds, A. J., & Walberg, H. J. (1991). A structural model of science achievement. *Journal of Educational Psychology, 83*(1), 97-107.

Tested Walberg's nine-factor productivity model. Eight productivity factors contributed in diverse ways to science achievement. Positive direct effects resulted from prior achievement, peer environment, and the amount and quality of instruction. Discusses implications for improving educational performance.

698.   Saunders-Harris, R., & Yeany, R. H. (1981). Diagnosis, remediation, and locus of control: Effects on immediate and retained achievement and attitudes. *Journal of Experimental Education*, *49* (4), 220-224.

Reports the results of a study designed to compare the effects of "no diagnosis," "diagnosis," or "diagnosis and remediation" upon the retention level of middle level students. Findings indicated that "diagnostic" or "diagnostic and remedial" interventions are more effective than "no diagnostic" in increasing the retention levels of middle level science students.

699.   Schlegal, R. A. (1991). Identifying elements of attitude formation by middle school students toward high school science (Doctoral dissertation, Temple University, 1990). *Dissertation Abstracts International*, *51*, 2623A.

This study involved 4045 students from grades six, seven, and eight in urban, suburban, and rural districts with varied socioeconomic and ethnic populations. The following variables, listed by importance, were found to foster positive science attitudes: (a) teacher's ability to make science exciting; (b) peer-social influences; (c) parental interest, support, and involvement; (d) availability of science-related materials at home; (e) past performance in science; (f) student gender; (g) student grade level; (h) past performance in math; (i) parent occupation; and (j) parent educational levels. It should be noted that the teacher, by presenting science in an exciting manner, was the most important factor in fostering a positive attitude toward science in students.

700.   Shaw, Jr., E. L., & Doan, R.L. (1990). An investigation of the differences in attitude and achievement between male and female second and fifth grade science students. *Journal of Elementary Science Education*, *2*(1), 10-15.

The authors investigated the differences in attitudes toward and achievement in science between boys and girls in grades two and five to see if the gender differences observed in middle school and high school may apply to elementary students. The study found that no significant gender differences were observed in grades two and five. The authors conclude that the disparity of attitudes and achievement between female and male students may originate after grade five.

701.   Welborn, T., & McKenzie, D. L. (1989). Science, achievement, attitudes, and career selection of females: A review of research. *Journal of Elementary Science Education*, *1*(2), 3-9.

The authors examined research focusing on the science achievement and career selection of females and related these variables to attitudinal characteristics of female students (K-12). Females begin to show a general decline in science achievement during the middle school years (ages 12-15). Also, females begin to display negative attitudes toward science at around age 13. All of the factors contribute to the middle school female's "science self-concept."

702.   Yager, R. E. (1993). The advantages of STS approaches in science

instruction in grades four through nine. *Bulletin of Science/Technology Society*, *13*, 74-82.

Reports the results of a study designed to test the effects of implementing science/technology society in middle level classrooms. Specifically discussed are the effects of STS instruction upon the following domains: concept, process, applications and connections, creativity, and attitudinal.

703.   Yager, R. E., Mackinnu, & Blunck, S. M. (1992). Science/Technology/ Society as reform of science in the elementary school. *Journal of Elementary Education, 4*(1), 1-13.

Study of 12 middle level (grades 4-6) science classes found no advantages for middle level students in STS sections vs non-STS sections in terms of concept mastery. However, there were significant advantages for the STS approach in terms of students' growth in process skills, applications of science concepts and processes to new situations, creativity skills (including quantity and quality of questions generated, causes suggested, and consequences predicted), and development of more positive attitudes (toward science classes, teachers, and careers). STS instruction resulted in significant improvement in attitude toward science for female middle level students.

704.   Yager, R. E., Tamir, P., & Kellerman, L. (1993). Introducing STS in middle school classrooms. *Current Issues in Middle Level Education, 2*(1), 47-65.

"This is the study of the results of using STS (science/technology/society, which is primarily an approach to science teaching that utilizes constructivist practices) in 306 middle school classrooms involving 10,215 students. Pre- and posttest assessments in five goal and assessment domains were collected. The results indicate that STS instruction generally results in significant student growth in terms of concept mastery, knowledge and use of process skills, application of concepts and processes to new situations, creativity skills (i.e., questioning, hypothesizing, and predicting), and more positive attitudes toward science, science classes, science teachers and science careers."

N. SCIENCE - PRACTICAL

705.   Barba, R. H. (1989). Seize the science-math connection. *Science Scope, 12*(7), 38-39.

The author discusses the importance of integrating science and mathematics at the middle level as frequently and appropriately as possible. Science, in the real world, is described as problem solving with mathematics the language of science. The author describes a hot air balloon activity which easily integrates science and mathematics at the middle level. Additional ideas on mathematics and science integration are clearly presented in a chart.

706.   Barman, C. R. (1989). The learning cycle: Making it work. *Science*

Scope, 12(5), 28-31.

The author discusses the learning cycle as having three distinct phases: exploration, concept introduction, and concept application. The exploration phase provides students with concrete experiences to help them build mental images of the new concepts presented in the concept introduction phase. The concept application phase provides students with the opportunities to use the new concept in different situations. This cycle is to assist the middle level student to internalize new concepts. The author describes two activities (studying pond water and soil) to illustrate how the learning cycle can be used in middle level science classes

707. Beals, K., & Willard, C. (1994). *Mystery festival (Great explorations in math and science [GEMS] series)*. Berkeley, CA: Lawrence Hall of Science. 258 pp.

Students try to solve a mystery by investigating a "crime scene," observing clues, and running forensic tests. Even though the book is suitable for grades 1-8, many activities are appropriate for middle level students.

708. Bull, L. A. (1993). A publishing model for science class. *Science Scope*, 17(3), 36-39.

Middle school science students (grade seven) are able to improve their writing skills and independent thinking through lab reports. These lab reports require the students to role play scientists writing about their findings. The teacher acts as the managing editor, reading the lab reports and either accepting them for publication (student's individual collection of scientific writings) or suggesting ways for improvement. Criteria for these specialized lab reports and managing editor form are included and discussed.

709. Butzow, C. M., & Butzow, J. W. (1989). *Science through children's literature: An integrated approach*. Englewood, CO: Teacher Ideas Press. 240 pp.

Presents practical ideas for teaching elementary and middle level concepts through reading. Part I discusses an integrated approach to scientific instruction while Parts II, III, & IV provide specific classroom activities for use in life science, earth and space science, and physical science.

710. Bybee, R. W., Buchwald, C. E., Crissman, S., Heil, D. R. Kuerbis, P. J. Matsumoto, C., & McInerney, J. D. (1990). *Science and technology education for the middle years: Frameworks for curriculum and instruction*. Andover, MA: The NETWORK Inc. The Regional Laboratory for Educational Improvement of the Northeast and Islands. 142 pp.

This report delineates learning goals for science and technology in the middle grades along with the type of specific knowledge, attitudes, and skills that should be taught. It includes a curriculum and instruction framework based on the unique needs of young adolescents.

711.   Cook, N. (1994). *In the pharmacy*. Arlington, VA: National Science Teachers Association. 112 pp.

An excellent resource for middle level teachers in helping their students explore ratios, proportions, and percents in a hypothetical pharmacy.

712.   Cothron, J., Giese, R., & Rezba, R. (1989). *Students and research: Practical Strategies for science classrooms and competitions*. Washington, DC: National Science Teachers Association.

The authors present field-tested teaching strategies for developing research skills in students at all grade levels. The book is presented in four parts: (1) helping students generate ideas, (2) designing experiments, (3) constructing tables and graphs, and (4) writing simple reports.

713.   Cronin, J. (1993). Cholera and the scientific method. *Science Scope, 17*(3), 20-23.

The author describes an interesting and effective way of teaching the scientific method to middle school students (grade six) by simulating an outbreak of a real disease within the school. Students act as epidemiologists and use the scientific method to track down the source of the disease.

714.   Dempsey, A. D. (1990). Van Helmont's tree revisited. *Science and Children, 27*(6), 18-19.

The author describes an excellent activity for fifth-to seventh-graders with which to discover the concept of photosynthesis. The students will learn that many factors contribute to the growth of plants with photosynthesis being the major factor.

715.   Flick, L., & Dejmal, K. (1989). Sixth-grade aeronauts. *Science and Children, 27*(1), 51-53.

The author describes an activity in which sixth-grade students (working in small groups) constructed hot air balloons. The students learned how to determine the best design and production techniques to construct a tissue paper balloon. The dynamics of hot air, air currents, and symmetry were experienced by the students when they flew their balloons. The author uses the activity to discuss how students must manipulate a given problem mentally in order to form connections between physical events and their understanding of the problem. This process allows the science activity to become meaningful to the student.

716.   Florida Association of Science Teachers. (1994). *Planning and managing dissection laboratories*. Arlington, VA: National Science Teachers Association. 36 pp.

Presents guidelines developed by science teachers for conducting dissection labs to explain legal, safety, and ethical factors.

717.   Gates, J. M. (1989). *Consider the earth: Environmental activities for grades 4-8*. Englewood, CO: Teacher Ideas Press.

This book includes ways for middle level students to learn about their environment by working within it. Soil, plants, water, wildlife, ecosystems, weather, and environmental problems are discussed along with fun and enlightening activities. Excellent resource for environmental education.

718.   Goode, C. (1990). Putting science in action. *Science Scope, 14*(3), 37-39.

The author describes how Science in Action is a hands-on, independent process designed to demonstrate middle level students' proficiency in working through the scientific method. Students conduct science demonstrations in their class and answer questions from their classmates. Designed as an alternative to science fairs.

719.   Graika, T. (1989). Minds-on, hands-on science. *Science Scope, 12*(6), 18-20.

The author discusses the importance of middle level science teaching, especially experiences that help students develop creative and critical thinking skills. Minds-on, hands-on science stresses divergent thinking in students as compared to convergent thinking. The author describes how to change convergent thinking activities into activities requiring divergent thinking.

720.   Grand, G. L. (1994). *Student science opportunities*. NY: Wiley. 292 pp.

Profiles more than 300 national science programs, competitions, internships, and scholarships for middle and high school students.

721.   Hampton, C., Hampton, C., & Kramer, D. (1994). *Classroom creature culture: Algae to anoles (revised edition)*. Arlington, VA: National Science Teachers Association. 96 pp.

This anthology of articles from *Science and Children* provides the basics about collecting, investigating, and caring for plants and animals in middle level classroom settings. A practical resource for any middle level teacher considering the use of plants and/or animals in the classroom.

722.   Haney, R. E. (1991). The nuts and bolts of STS. *Science Scope, 14*(5), 16-18.

This is a very short and clearly written article describing theScience/Technology/ Society (STS) approach to teaching middle level science concepts. The author recommends organizing science lessons and units around such life problems as food-getting, clothing, shelter, transportation, and communication. A sample activity is included.

723.   Hassard, J. (1990). Cooperative learning: The Science Experience. *Science and Scope, 13*(7), 33-37.

The author describes Science Experiences as a middle level science program which focuses on the study of natural phenomena, everyday examples, and problem-solving activities that will help explain the real world science to students. The program consists of eight units or experiences which address a variety of science topics in a holistic manner. Each experience consists of cooperative learning activities that focus on central science concepts and processes for the lesson; interdisciplinary activities that link science with other academic subjects; and projects that involve teams of students in problem-solving activities. The author discusses some general principles that can help implement Science Experiences in the middle level science classroom.

724.   Hassard, J. (1990). *Science experiences: Cooperative learning and the teaching of science*. Washington, DC: National Science Teachers Association.

The author discusses the theory of science teaching and cooperative learning. The second part of the text has eight units that deal with life science, health science, physical science, space science and oceanography, geography, energy and ecology, environmental education, and the future. This book is appropriate for elementary/middle level teachers of science.

725.   Hein, G. (1990). *The assessment of hands-on elementary science programs*. Washington, DC: National Science Teachers Association.

The author describes how the elementary/middle level teachers can assess the results, value, and success of science activities in the classroom. Special attention is given to assessment theory, large-scale assessments, and new approaches to science teaching. The author also discusses assessment in science education research and development. New assessment approaches with specific emphasis on assessment and teaching of thinking skills are discussed in some detail by the author.

726.   Hepner, N., & Simons, G. (1993). Integrating special education students in science. *New Mexico Middle School Journal, 2*, 9-12.

Presents strategies for successful integration of special education students into regular science classes. Stresses the need for cooperation and communication among teachers, students, and parents. Offers practical suggestions for establishing classroom routine, facilitating lab work, adapting daily work and course content, and implementing appropriate assessment/evaluation procedures.

727.   Horak, W. J., & Potter, T. G. (1989). More inquiry investigations. *Science Scope, 12*(7), 14-17.

The authors describe some excellent introductory demonstrations and suggest follow-up questions which can develop middle level students' inquiry skills and lead them to further investigative activities. The demonstrations used commonplace objects related to everyday experiences that provide dramatic or unexpected results.

728.   Hosoume, K., & Barber, J. (1994). *Terrarium habitats (Great explorations in math and science [GEMS] series)*. Berkeley, CA: Lawrence Hlal of Science. 92 pp.

Several of the activities in this book could be used with middle level students to explore soil and the animals that make it their home. A culminating activity is the construction and maintenance of a class terrarium.

729.   Johnson, C. V. (1994). *Packaging the environment*. Arlington, VA: National Science Teachers Association. 90 pp.

Uses surface area and volume formulas to examine packaging and the social and environmental effects of packaging decisions.

730.   Johnson, C. V. (1995). *Investigating apples*. Arlington, VA: National Science Teachers Association. 102 pp.

An interesting resource book which can be used to guide middle level students through data and analysis methods and measurement using apples.

731.   Johnson, H. A., & Jett, P. (1993). Making the connection. *Science Scope, 16*(6), 4-6.

The authors describe how a multidisciplinary unit incorporates the methods and skills from more than one discipline to teach or examine a central theme, focus, topic, issue, or situation. The authors describe a five-step model middle level teachers can use to develop and organize interdisciplinary units. These steps are: (1) identifying a central theme, concept, or focus for students to examine; (2) brainstorming and choosing unit objectives; (3) developing lessons and activities; (4) establishing evaluation criteria; and (5) finalizing unit logistics.

732.   Lewis, A. C. (Ed.). (1992). Science [Special issue]. *High Strides*, *4*(5).

Includes five articles designed to "put curious, active, exploring youngsters together with a curriculum that allows them to use their minds, work together, and enjoy discovering on their own." Issues discussed include assessment, technology, and teacher education. Contains a list of eleven organization/ resources for middle level science teachers.

733.   Loucks-Horsley, S., Grennon-Brooks, J., Carlson, M. O., Kuerbis, P. J., Marsh, D. D., Padilla, M. J.. Pratt, H., & Smith, K. L. (1990). *Developing and supporting teachers for science education in the middle years*. Andover, MA:

The NETWORK Inc. The Regional Laboratory for Educational Improvement of the Northeast and Islands. 86 pp.

This report provides insights into the type of staff development that is needed in order to help teachers acquire the knowledge, skills, and attitudes to foster science learning in the middles grades. It also suggests the types of conditions and support needed at the school, district, and state levels to create an environment where good science teaching can flourish.

734.   Marek, E. A., & Bryant, R. J. (1991). On research. *Science Scope, 14*(4), 44-45.

The learning cycle is discussed as an alternative way of teaching science concepts in which middle level students learn science concepts from experiences, rather than through textbook-driven lessons. The three phases of the learning cycle (exploration, conceptual invention, and expansion) are described with activities included.

735.   McGrew, R. (1989). It's a liquid! It's a solid! It's oobleck! *Science Scope, 12*(4), 6-8.

The author describes how to make a harmless substance, oobleck, which can be used to reinforce student understanding of life functions and physical science concepts such as density, mixture, and solution. Four easy to do activities are explained. These activities are used by the author to foster observation and verbalization skills, measurement skills, comparison and contrasting skills, and problem solving skills within middle level students. There is an excellent description by the author concerning the use of two problem solving strategies: brainstorming and scamper.

736.   Mechling, K. (1990). See-through science. *Science Scope, 13*(6), 16-18.

The author describes how he uses science-career resource people as speakers whose occupations directly or indirectly involve science. The X-ray technologist helps the middle level science teacher present such topics as the body and its systems, health, bones, first aid, and other similar similar subjects. The middle level students can learn information necessary to better understand their bodies and make informed that affect their health as well as their lives.

737.   Mothersbaugh, E., & Walter, M. (1991). The 5 R's. *The Transescent. 16* (2), 11-14.

Outlines a seventh-grade interdisciplinary unit on Solid Waste. Includes numerous examples of hands-on activities such as scavenger hunts.

738.   Murphy, C. P. (1989). Riddle me science. *Science and Children, 27*(3), 28-30.

The author discusses how he uses riddles as a model for the scientific method. This model is used at the beginning of a semester or school year to help introduce the discipline of science and also to help students feel comfortable working together. The author discusses a sample scientific query with students and how to design an experiment. Interdisciplinary activities with writing are discussed.

739.   Nason, P. L. (1993). Freedom to learn. *Science Scope, 16*(6), 9-12.

Task Oriented Modules System (TOMS), a resource-based learning model, is designed to help middle level students learn how to process and use information in everyday problem solving. The author describes how TOMS give the student options to choose modules that best fit their learning styles and interests. The teacher's role is primarily a facilitator. A sample module is described in sufficient detail to illustrate TOMS.

740.   Nemcik, J. R. (1989). Modeling for ideas: The case of the missing volume. *Science Scope, 12*(4), 28-31.

The author describes a good model (paper dot model for the study of water/alcohol interaction) which middle level students can use to study the interaction of molecules. The author discusses how tangible models help middle level students practice the process of formulating and testing hypotheses. A good model should be simple, make sense, be supported by the data, and explain an observation.

741.   Ossont, D. (1993). How I use cooperative learning. *Science Scope, 16*(8), 28-31.

The author describes how he uses cooperative learning in his middle level science classes. Heterogeneous grouping and student selected job assignments within the groups are advocated by the author. The author explains how individual grades are primarily awarded for student work but bonus points are awarded to the entire group based on selected group criteria. The author clearly describes how he uses cooperative learning groups in developing vocabulary, reviewing notes and study guides for tests, and conducting hands-on laboratory work. The author has found that cooperative learning meets middle level students' needs for social interaction.

742.   Parker, S. (1995). *Inside dinosaurs and other prehistoric creatures*. NY: Delacorts. 48 pp.

The author uses excellent full-color, explanatory diagrams to expose the intricate organs, twisting tubes, and muscle layers inside various prehistoric animals.

743.   Pedersen, J., & Bonnestetter. (1990). S/T/S for students. *Science and Scope, 13*(4), 49.

The authors briefly describe one approach to making S/T/S (Science, Technology, and Societal issues) a useful and usable strategy for middle level science. The approach uses cooperative and disequilibrium learning.

744.   Pottle, J. L. (1993). Learning through experience: A workshop for middle school science teachers. *The Clearing House, 66*(6), 339-340.

Outlines a two-week workshop designed for teachers of middle level science students. Based upon the premise that teachers should model strategies and techniques, the workshop provides opportunities for the participants to be actively involved in all of the activities.

745.   Rakow, S. J. (1989). Middle/junior high science speaks out. *Science Scope, 12*(7), 24-30.

The author summarizes the responses from a group of middle/junior high science educators on what they considered most useful and effective in teaching science at the middle level. Most of their comments are still very relevant for teaching middle science today.

746.   Roth, W. M., & Bowen, M. (1993). Maps for more meaningful learning. *Science Scope, 16*(4), 24-25.

The authors describe how concept mapping can be designed to assist middle level students in understanding concepts and the relationships between them, to establish hierarchical relationships among concepts, and to recognize the evolving nature of scientific understanding. The authors report that concept mapping forces the middle level student to truly understand what they are investigating. Students communicate their own ideas in their own words. Also, the concept mapping process gets students to rethink their ideas and consider them in the context of the initial experiment and to try to connect new ideas to each other and to their prior knowledge.

747.   Roth, W. M., & Bowen, M. (1993). The unfolding Vee. *Science Scope, 16*(5), 28-32.

The authors discuss how Vee maps are meant to lead middle level students to discover the relationship between doing and knowing science by helping them to better organize their thinking, investigate more efficiently, and create guidelines for learning. The students start with a focus question concerning what is to be discovered. The Vee map model assists the students in describing what they already know and what information is needed. The students carry out their investigations, refining their Vee maps as information is discovered. Some examples of how to evaluate student learning is included in the article. The authors explain how Vee maps are used with concept maps.

748.   Roth, W. M., & Verechaka, G. (1993). Plotting a course with Vee Maps. *Science and Children, 30*(4), 24-27.

The authors describe Vee-Mapping as an effective teaching/learning strategy that helps students understand how to learn. The Vee-Map strategy helps students to understand how new knowledge is attained in an experimental situation. Vee Maps have two sides which are the knowing and the doing sides. These two sides are separated by the focus question and by the events, which form the link between previously learned knowledge and new knowledge. Students work together in groups to select the focus question. The students list their previously acquired knowledge on the Know side. The students collect data to help answer their focus question. Finally, the students create a concept map that integrates both prior and new knowledge. This final step allows the students to reflect on what they have learned through their investigation. Very appropriate for middle level students.

749.   Ruck, C. L. (1992). A new kind of learning community. *Science and Children, 30*(1), 29-31.

The author discusses three varieties of science study resources (appropriate for middle level classrooms) which can be found in the local community. People resources are those people knowledgeable or have been involved with the scientific concept or process being studied in the classroom. Object resources are items the students can use to better understand the scientific concept or process being studied in the classroom. Place resources are places the students can visit in order to observe and possibly interact with those concepts or processes. The author describes how the teacher and/or students can discover these resources in their local community. Searching for science resources can help middle level students become actively involved within their communities.

750.   Scharff, C. E. (1989). Smoking-Let your students make an educated decision. *Science and Children, 27*(1), 54-58.

The author does an excellent job of discussing the costs and dangers so that students will have the facts that they need to make a thoughtful decision as to whether or not to smoke. Two activities are described which shows the effects of cigarette smoke on plants and the accumulation of tar.

751.   Smith, K. R., & Bush, A. H. (1994). *Investigating science through bears.* Englewood, CO: Teachers Ideas Press. 212 pp.

Examines bears through excellent activities which look at behavior, habitats, interaction with humans, and bears in literature.

752.   Smith, P. S., & Ford, B. A. (1994). *Project earth science: Meteorology.* Arlington, VA: National Science Teachers Association. 234 pp.

Offers 19 hands-on activities, 10 supplemental readings, and a thorough meteorological resource guide for middle level teachers. Activities include such topics as reading weather maps and making forecasts; modeling the water cycle; using real data to track a hurricane; the heating of the equator vs the poles; and the formation of clouds.

753.   Smith, W.S., & Burrichter, C. (1993). Look who's teaching science

today! *Science and Children, 30*(7), 20-23.

The author describes how she prepares her middle level students to cross-age tutor in a first grade classroom. The students use the learning cycle to teach science to first graders. The single greatest reward for the middle level students is enhanced self-esteem. The most significant academic gains by middle level students are achieved by the least able.

754.   Stahl, N. N., & Stahl, R. J. (1995). *Society and science: Decision-making episodes for exploring society, science, and technology.* Arlington, VA: National Science Teachers Association. 370 pp.

Thirty-three decision-making episodes explore science as it affects and is affected by humans in the modern world. Extensive discussions of decision-making strategies are included. An excellent resource for middle level teachers considering or currently using the Science/Technology/Society (STS) approach to teaching science.

755.   Sumners, C. (1994). *Exploring science with the astronauts.* Arlington, VA: National Science Teachers Association. 142 pp.

An excellent, active exploration of physics for middle level students. Students conduct experiments and then predict the results from experiments shuttle astronauts actually performed with toys in two missions in space. Real NASA data on the results are included to check student predictions.

756.   Tolley, K. (1994). *The art and science connection for intermediate students (grades 5-10).* Redding, MA: Addison-Wesley. 206 pp.

Offers strategies to help teachers integrate art and science concepts and processes in creative art activities. Contains 30 lessons organized around three themes of science: structure, interactions, and energy. Drawings, painting, sculpture, bas-relief, printmaking, collage, graphic arts, and mixed media are included in the activities.

757.   Van Burgh, D., Lyons, E. N., & Boyington, M. (1994). *How to teach with topological maps.* Arlington, VA: National Science Teachers Association. 24 pp.

Excellent "how to" manual for teachers of middle level grades in teaching the special language of maps—quadrangles, contour lines, and mapping symbols — and apply it to develop basic map reading skills. Includes activities which explore longitude and latitude, the concepts of scale, terrain changes, and how to use topo maps for environmental studies.

758.   VanCleave, J. (1994). *Dinosaurs for every kid.* Arlington, VA: National Science Teachers Association. 232 pp.

Includes excellent activities, background sections, and a glossary which help inform middle level students about dinosaurs.

759. Yager, R. E., & Penick, J. E. (1990). Creativity and science learning. *Science Scope, 13*(4), 15.

The author discusses how to develop creativity in middle level students by having the students offer their own explanations and interpretations of what they observe and experience. One activity described by the authors has the students create cartoons that use catchy, humorous explanations for observed results.

760. Young, L. (1990). Pond-ering the possibilities. *Science and Children, 27*(8), 18-19.

The author describes how a pond can be at the center of a seventh-grade science curriculum. This is a hands-on approach to science. The students learn how to map their pond (from traditional map-or chart making techniques to creating three-dimensional models), make their own data gathering instruments, use field guides, record their observations through pictures or writings, use the microscope, present their findings orally to the class, and make connections between concepts learned at their pond and the rest of the world.

761. Young, P. (1992). Reader-friendly science. *Science Scope, 16*(1), 22-24.

The author discusses a four-step process that middle level students can use to better understand their reading of a science textbook. This process helps the student to understand the technical vocabulary; learn how to use the headings and sub-heading; and then to integrate the vocabulary and the headings and subheadings. The four steps include (1) gathering terms, (2) rephrasing headings, (3) mapping the information (creating concept maps) and (4) putting it all together. Cooperative learning groups are used extensively throughout this process.

O. SCIENCE - GENERAL

762. Anderson, H. O. (1991). Y'all can. *Science Scope, 14*(8), 28-31.
The author discusses various factors which affect the development of cognitive self-esteem (feeling good about what one knows of a subject) in middle level students. Giving the students a purpose for learning what is to be learned, practicing to master the competency, and developing pride in the accomplishment comprises the author's formula for teaching successfully middle school science.

763. Hassard, J. (1990). Cooperating classroom. *Science Scope, 13*(6), 36-39, 45.

The author discusses how cooperative learning has been shown to enhance students' social skills, learning and cognitive development, self-esteem, positive attitudes toward school, and development of higher-level thinking skills. The author describes four cooperative learning models (STAD, Jigsaw II, Co-op Co-op, and Group Investigation) which could be used in the middle level science classroom.

764.   Horizon Research. (1994). *Science and mathematics education briefing books: Volume IV*. Arlington, VA: National Science Teachers Association. 350 pp.

Includes information on middle level student course taking, attitudes, and proficiency in science and mathematics, and state-by-state information on middle level science and mathematics teachers.

765.   Koker, M. (1993). Science teaching at the middle level: Needs and problems. *Science Scope, 16*(7), 36-38.

The author reports the results of a recent survey of members of the National Middle Level Science Teachers Association (NMLSTA). Middle level science teachers are more concerned with the need for developing new teaching techniques than for acquiring additional content. Overall, there are strong needs in teaching methods, assessment, and curriculum. Effective programs are needed to address these concerns.

766.   Martinello, M. L., & Cook, G. E. (1994). *Interdisciplinary inquiry in teaching and learning*. New York: Macmillan. 232 pp.

Offers background materials, development strategies, and evaluation and implementation ideas to help create a classroom that fosters interdisciplinary inquiry by students.

767.   National Center for Improving Science Education, The. (1992). *Building scientific literacy: A blueprint for science in the middle years*. Washington, DC: Author. 64 pp.

According to the authors (some of the most noted educators and science educators in the nation), this report constitutes a blueprint for the creation of an effective, national program of science education for students in the middle grades. "It draws together the best that is now known about curriculum, instruction, assessment, and teacher development for middle-level science." The report is divided into five chapters: I. Science and Technology Education in the Middle Years; II. A Vision of Science and Technology Education at the Middle Level; III. Achieving the Vision; IV. Special Concerns; and V. Summary and Recommendations.

768.   National Science Teachers Association. (1994). *World resources 1994-1995*. Arlington, VA: National Science teachers Association. 384 pp.

An up-to-date and comprehensive reference guide which provides essential economic, environmental, population, and natural-resource data on 146 countries. More than 150 tables, charts, maps, and figures are included.

769.   National Science Teachers Association. (1994-1995). *Supplement of science education suppliers*. Arlington, VA: National Science Teachers Association. 104 pp.

This is an excellent resource directory for middle level science teachers. Includes the names, addresses, phone numbers, and product lines for more that 300 firms that manufacture or distribute products for the science classroom.

770.   Raizen, S. A., Baron, J. B., Champagne, A. B., Haertel, E., Mullis, I. V. S., & Oakes, J. (1990). *Assessment in science education*. Andover, MA: The NETWORK Inc. The Regional Laboratory for Educational Improvement of the Northeast and Islands. 123 pp.

This report discusses the purposes and nature of various forms of assessment that can be used to enhance, support, and monitor of science learning science learning in middle grade classrooms.

771.   Sanders, M. (1993). Science and technology: A new alliance. *Science Scope, 16(6)*, 56-60.

The author discusses how the Technology/Science/Math (T/S/M) Integration Project requires middle level students to apply science and math principles to solve technological problems. The Integration Project has developed activities that fit within the existing middle level structure and curriculum. A sample activity is described to illustrate Project activities. T/S/M differs from STS (see Pedersen and Bonnestetter, 1990) in that STS emphasizes the social sciences vs T/S/M emphasizes technology.

772.   Simons, G. H., & Hepner, N. (1992). The special student in science. *Science Scope, 16(1)*, 34-39, 54.

The authors discuss a range of adaptations middle level science teachers could make to their curriculum for students with special needs. The needs of a student with learning disabilities and the needs of a hearing impaired student are described. Several adaptations are described for each student. This is an appropriate article for all middle level teachers.

773.   Wilke, R. J. (Editor). (1994). *Environmental education teachers resource handbook*. Millwood, NY: Kraus International. 320 pp.

The handbook includes information on funding, state-level guidelines, sources for special projects, and listings of environmental education curriculum producers. An excellent resource for middle level science teachers.

774.   Wright, E. L. (1991). Priorities for teaching life science in the middle school: A vision of the future for Kansas middle school life science programs. *KAMLE Karavan, 5*, 11-14.

Discusses how the National Science Teacher's Association's Task Force for

Defining Excellence in K-12 Biology Curriculum and Teaching has redefined the science curriculum, the role of the middle level teacher in carrying out those goals, the importance of the goals, and how the goals fit with the goals of education in Kansas.

P. SOCIAL STUDIES - RESEARCH

775.   Alleman, J. E., & Rosaen, C. L. (1991). The cognitive, social-emotional, and moral development characteristics of students: Basis for elementary and middle school social studies. In James P. Shaver (Ed.), *Handbook of research on social studies and learning* (pp. 121-133). New York: Macmillan Publishing Co.

In this essay the authors review and critique the most recent research on the cognitive, social-emotional and moral development characteristics of students, and in doing so, construct hypotheses regarding what elementary and middle school students, "as emergent citizens, are capable of learning and doing in social studies." A sample of the titles of the various sections found in this essay provides a sense of the essay's breadth: What is Citizen Education?; A Nondeficiency View of Development; Cognitive Development Characteristics: A Basis for Becoming an Informed Person; Social-Emotional Characteristics: Self Concept and Self-Esteem.

776.   Brophy, J. (1992). Fifth-grade U.S. history: How one teacher arranged to focus on key ideas in depth. *Theory and Research in Social Education, 20*(2), 141-155.

Brophy summarizes the findings of a study of a fifth-grade teacher's approach to teaching U.S. history. A unit on the English colonies is highlighted, and what is particularly instructive about her methods is how she focused on depth vs coverage. Among the notable goals and strategies of this teacher are connecting main themes and related basic facts; using storytelling, rather than relying on the textbook, as the major source of information for the study; thoroughly integrating of history content with language arts; emphasizing significant writing assignments; and using cooperative learning rather than worksheets and traditional tests.

777.   Fouts, J. T. (1988). The middle school social studies classroom: An exploratory study. *Middle school research: Selected studies 1988* (pp. 12-22). Columbus, OH: The Research Committee of the National Middle School Association.

"This study examined middle school students' views of social studies along with the types of classroom environments found in social studies classes. In addition, classes taught by teachers with differing professional preparation were compared. Among this sample only 40% of the teachers' teaching middle school social studies were found to have that area as their area of professional preparation. Students in these teachers' classes were more likely to identify social studies as their favorite class. Analysis of the environmental data using inferential techniques did not find statistically significant differences among the class environments based on teacher preparation."

778.   Hom, K. J. (1991). The effects of an integrated social studies curriculum on inner-city middle school students' attitudes toward and achievement in social studies (Doctoral dissertation, United States International University, 1990). *Dissertation Abstracts International, 51*, 3316A.

Examined the effects of an integrated eighth grade curriculum on the attitudes of middle level students toward social studies and on student achievement scores. Included in the integrated curriculum were music, art, literature, and drama. The study showed that middle level students in the integrated curriculum had higher achievement scores than those students in the nonintegrated curriculum. No significant difference in attitudes of either group was found.

779.   Lockledge, A., Andres, K., Price, A., & Williams, M. (1994). Social lives of young adolescents. *Middle Ground*, pp. 3-5.

Results of a small survey of middle level students regarding how they use their time outside of school. Results were shared with another group of middle level students to help researchers interpret the comments.

780.   Pate, E. P., Alexander, P., & Kulikowich, J. (1989). Assessing the effects of training social studies content and analogical reasoning processes on sixth-graders' domain-specific and strategic knowledge. In David B. Strahan (Ed.), *Middle school research: Selected studies 1989* (pp. 19-29). Columbus, OH: Research Committee of the National Middle School Association.

In this study the researchers examined "the effects of training on domain-specific strategic knowledge and their interaction. A sample of 201 sixth-grade students received training in social studies content (domain only), in analogical reasoning (strategy only), in both social studies and analogical reasoning (both domain and strategy) or were assigned to control. Training was delivered by a direct instruction model. Findings showed that there was a significant overall effect for domain-specific training, strategy training, and students' utilization of such training on an interactive measure."

781.   Schug, M. C., Davis, J. E., Wentworth, D. R., Banazak, R., & Robertson, D. (1989). An evaluation of middle school economics curriculum materials: Implications for improving quality. *Theory and Research in Social Education, 17*(2), 121-135.

Among the key findings of this research are: 1. Economics education materials at the middle school differ significantly in their quality; 2. Supplemental materials are stronger in providing opportunities for improved instruction than are textbook readings; 3. Textbooks tend to present more accurate economics content and are more attractive than are supplemental materials; 4. Most of the economic materials designed for use at the middle school grades are bland, uninteresting, and do not draw on the economic experiences of young adolescents; 5. Successful use of economics materials at the middle school level depends in part on a strong inservice education program for teachers. A key problem with this research is that the researchers do not define "middle school"; as a result, readers do not know if the researchers are simply referring to grade configuration or schools that are both immersed in the middle level philosophy and have unique middle level components in place.

782.   White, R. M. (1990). Middle school students' perceptions toward social studies methodologies. In Judith L. Irvin (Ed.), *Research in middle level education: Selected studies 1990* (pp. 51-63). Columbus, OH: Research Committee of the National Middle School Association.

In this study "data were collected through an open-ended questionnaire from 140 middle schools students in a two-state area. Students in the sample were from three schools: an inner-city school, a suburban school, and a school located in a rural area. In addition to the written questionnaire, several students were randomly selected and interviewed. Students clearly identified specific teaching methodologies that they liked and disliked and favored activities which allowed them the opportunity to 'do' or be active while learning. These activities included building models, acting in skits, holding class discussions, and working on projects. Traditional social studies activities such as reading the textbook, writing answers to questions, listening to the teacher, and taking tests were viewed with disfavor by students."

Q. SOCIAL STUDIES - PRACTICAL

783.   Allen, R., & Molina, L. S. (1992). Escape geography—Developing middle school students' sense of place. *The Social Studies* , 83(2), 68-72.

Describes various methods for incorporating a study of geography into the curriculum through the theme of "escape." The authors argue that such a theme enhances the study by making it more intriguing to middle level students.

784.   Andel, M. A. (1990). Digging for the secrets of time: Artifacts, old foundations, and more. *Social Studies and the Young Learner* , *3* (2), 9-11.

Describes a five-week project in which middle level students and their mentors functioned as research teams. Specifically discussed is a two-week archaeological dig, one of the major components of the project.

785.   Chilcoat, G. W. (1991). The illustrated song slide show as a middle school history activity. *The Social Studies*, 82(5), 188-190.

Describes an innovative method (e.g., using song slide shows) to engage students in a hands-on/minds-on study of history.

786.   Cooper, R. A. (1994). From Holocaust to hope: Teaching the Holocaust in middle school. *Middle School Journal,* 25(4), 15-17.

Offers a variety of suggestions and examples for teaching students about the Holocaust. In the model presented, as a culminating activity sixth graders displayed Holocaust unit projects in a "museum" in the school's media center. A "museum opening" planned by teachers and students involved the entire school, parents, and various community members. Lists follow-up activities to reinforce concepts covered in the unit.

787. Dougherty, P. S. (1992). Reading *The Talking Earth* with middle school students: Using literature to teach about national parks, geography, and the environment. *The Social Studies*, *83*(4), 172-175.

Discusses methods for using a novel about a young Native American girl's adventures in the Everglades focusing in on issues regarding the environment.

788. Fuerst, D., & Loh, A. (1986). Creating an oral history project. *Middle School Journal, 17*(2), 10-13.

Provides a rationale for creating an oral history project. Explains the steps for developing the project including selection of narrators, preparation for interviews, conducting the interview, and what happens after the interview. The initial project led to other activities, including fundraising, workshops on the oral history process, and an increase in community involvement with the school. Students gained an appreciation of their community and their role in it while furthering their own education.

789. Harvey, K. D. (1981). Creative social studies teaching in middle and high schools. *The Clearing House, 54* (8), 359-362.

Discusses a time-efficient strategy for supplementing social studies texts with teacher-made resource units. Presents examples of effective units that can be developed with a minimal amount of time and materials.

790. Haskvitz, A. (1989). Award winning program paves way for new framework. *Thrust, 18*(4), 30, 54.

Describes an an award winning social studies program in a California middle school and argues that the program could be used as a model for assisting schools to implement California's new framework for history and social studies. The social studies program involves students in a study of social issues and community service.

791. Holub, B., & Bennett, C. B. (1988). Using political cartoons to teach junior/middle school U.S. history. *The Social Studies, 79*(5), 214-216.

Provides a number or useful ideas and suggestion for hands-on activities to engage students in the study of history through the use of political cartoons.

792. Humphrey, E., & Fee, S. (1992). Where the hawks are hams. *New Mexico Middle School Journal, 2*, 16-18.

Discusses a geography project that allows students to communicate with
people in others of the country and even overseas. Using ham radios as the
medium for communication, students have exhibited increased motivation
in locating contact areas on a map. Includes a sample Ham Radio Contact
Record that students may use to document the contact and gather interesting
information from that contact.

793.   Johnson, N. M., & Ebert, M. J. (1992). Time travel is possible:
Historical fiction and biography-passport to the past. *The Reading Teacher*,
45(7), 488-495.

The article discusses how middle level students can be motivated and gain a
wider knowledge base of the historical time period under study by using a
literature-based approach. The authors delineate an excellent teaching strategy
on how to use trade books in teaching history to middle level students. A sample
unit on the American Revolution is included.

794.   Mociun, T. (1989). Geography by cargo ship. *Educational
Leadership*, *47*(3), 33-34.

Geography project developed around an actual ship en route to Yokohama,
Japan, involved students in a high-tech learning environment.

795.   National Council for the Social Studies. (1988). Middle school class
projects. *Social Education*, *52*(2), 120-122.

Provides a brief description of seven middle school social studies projects. The
titles of the projects are: "Touring to Teach Geography," "Using Hats to Teach
Social Roles," "Acting Out History," "The Change Project," "Proving it with
Facts," "Humanities in the Middle School," and "Cultural Carts for Global
Studies."

796.   O'Brien, L., & Pulliam, W. E. (1984). Collaborative research and
development: A source of optimism for the future. *The Clearing House*, *58*(3),
101-103.

Outlines a social studies unit based upon collaboration among university faculty
members, graduate students, public school teachers, private school teachers, and
middle level students. Emphasizes the importance of modeling collaboration as
a means of teaching the concept to young adolescents.

797.   Pang, V. O. (1992). Issues-centered approaches to multicultural
education in the middle grades. *The Social Studies*, *83*(3), 108-112.

Initially the author discusses the question "How Does Issues-Centered Education
Strengthen a Multicultural Education Program?" and then provides an example
of how a multicultural issue (e.g., the rights of citizens during wartime, using the
plight of the Japanese-Americans during World II as an example) can be
incorporated in the the extant curriculum.

798.   Phelps, S, Liebler, R., & Ramos, J. (1987). Reading *and* thinking in social studies. *Middle School Journal, 18*(3), 14-16.

Advocates the use of reading guides for content-area texts, which turn into discussion guides as needed. Discusses organizing curriculum objectives around student needs. Guided reading and thinking activities alert readers to important information and ideas and allow students to make connections and draw conclusions about their reading.

799.   Simpson, M. S. (1986). Turgenev in a middle school class. *The Clearing House, 56*(5), 236-239.

Describes a unit designed to increase cultural awareness among middle level students. Outlines classroom activities that allowed students to become totally involved in Russian culture and history as a means of understanding *Mumu* by Turgenev.

800.   Smiddie, L. (1989). Geography resources for middle school and high school teachers. *Georgia Social Science Journal, 20* (2), 30-32.

Describes resources that geography teachers can obtain from the Educational Resources Information Center. Targeting economics, political and social interactions, and interdependence, the available resources include maps, sample lesson plans, and sample unit plans.

801.   Totten, S. (1994). Telling the Holocaust story to children. *Social Studies and the Young Learner: A Quarterly for Creative Teaching in Grades K-6, 7* (2), 5-7.

The author presents guidelines for teaching about the Holocaust to middle level students and highlights some key resources for doing so.

R. SOCIAL STUDIES - GENERAL

802.   Allen, M. (1991). Social studies and our future. *Becoming, 2* (2), 30-33.

Discusses the role of social studies in a middle level curriculum. Focuses on the Civics Achievement Award Program (CAAP), an invaluable resource for encouraging middle level students to become active participants in a social studies class. Answers the following questions: What is CAAP? Who can participate? What do students do in CAAP? What does CAAP cost? Why a program for fifth through eighth grade students? Who do I learn more about CAAP?

803.   Allen, M. G. (1988). Middle grades social studies: A modest proposal. *Social Education, 52*(2), 113-115.

Initially argues that social studies education for young adolescents should "reflect conscious commitment to 'three educational goals seen as dominating the curriculum of the middle school'—personal development, skills of communication and learning, and major knowledge areas." Allen then proceeds to list and discuss a set of recommendations for restructuring middle level social studies education.

804.   Diakiw, J. Y. (1990). Children's literature and global education: Understanding the developing world. *The Reading Teacher, 43*(4), 296-300.

The author describes a UNICEF project which allows the teachers of grades 3-8 to teach students about developing nations using appropriate children's literature. The author discusses the research that shows that middle level students (ages 11 to 13) are receptive to learning about people from other countries. Research also shows that after age 14, attitudes formed about people from other countries are somewhat negative. Suggested units on Africa, India, global interdependence, and Latin American city life are included.

805.   Lounsbury, J. H. (1988). Middle level social studies: Points to ponder. *Social Education, 52*(2), 116-118.

Lounsbury raises and briefly discusses a series of important issues that all social studies educators need to ponder: How valid are scope and sequence? Are all social studies objectives being met? Are we developing critical thinking? Is ability-grouping justified? He then discusses how the traditional junior high "actually inhibits the appropriate development of early adolescents in many ways." He concludes his piece with an annotated list of basic resources on middle level education.

806.   National Council for the Social Studies. (1988). "Can Middle Schools Make a Difference?" Special issue of *Social Education, 52*(2).

Includes the following articles on middle level education and/or middle level social studies education: "Making a Difference in the Middle" by Tedd Levy; "Schools in the Middle: Rhetoric and Reality" by William M. Alexander; "What to Know About Young Adolescents" by Conrad F. Toepfer, Jr.; "Middle Grades Social Studies: A Modest Proposal" by Michael G. Allen; "Middle Level Social Studies: Points to Ponder" by John H. Lounsbury; "Middle Grade Reform" by Bill Honig; and, a description of seven middle level social studies projects.

807.   Savage, R. J. (1991). A principal's perspective on social studies in the middle level school. *NASSP Bulletin: The Journal for Middle Level and High School Administrators, 75*(531), 53-60.

A fascinating article in which the author argues that "of all the disciplines history should offer the greatest flexibility, next to language arts, in facilitating interdisciplinary instruction and indepth study of issues." He goes on to argue that "if scholars really want to contribute to a curriculum that responds to the middle level, they must work to identify such a program for the '90s." He also discusses some exemplary programs currently in existence.

808.   Toepfer, C. F. Jr. (1988). What to know about young adolescents. *Social Education*, *52*(2), 110-112.

Presents a general overview of the following: needs of young adolescents, crucial need to focus on the affective concerns of young adolescents, cognitive readiness issues, and middle level social studies education issues (including but not limited to, the need for social studies educators to deal with social issues that have an impact on young adolescents as well as the need to focus on citizenship issues and young adolescents' heightened sense of altruism).

S. WRITING - RESEARCH

809.   Browning, N. F. (1995). Acting, talking, and thinking like a writer: Sixth graders become authors. *Language Arts*, *72*(2). 105-112.

Discusses a program designed to provide opportunities for middle level students to interact with a "working writer" who regularly visits their classroom. Results of the program indicated that students viewed language and writing from a more position perspective, that the quality of their writing improved, and that they learned to communicate with one another about the writing process.

810.   Brownstein, M. (1994). Sharing: When parents say yes to drugs. *Learning*, *23*(1), 100.

A brief description of a project in which young adolescents wrote stories about how they remained drug-free even when their parents and other relatives used drugs. With student permission, parents were allowed to read the works composed by their children. Also offers suggestions for incorporating similar programs in other elementary and middle school classrooms.

811.   Cosgrove, C. (1995). How to deflate writing grades: Doing unto our students what we do unto ourselves. *English Journal*, *84*(3), 15-17.

Argues that in recent years composition teachers have lowered their expectations for student progress and have adopted lenient evaluation criteria. Discusses several strategies for evaluating student writing without compromising quality.

812.   Gregory, C. (1994). Editing that engages. *Instructor*, *104*(3). 40.

A brief article that discusses peer editing as an effective strategy for motivating middle level students to improve the quality of their writing.

813.   Hough, D. L. (1991). An analysis of the middle level writing program in California. *Research in Middle Level Education*, *15*(1), 55-82.

"This study analyzes the content and instructional practices of the middle level writing program in California. Curricular and instructional components are described, classified and analyzed to assess the degree to which different writing experiences for children at the middle level vary within different school grade-span organizational types—K-8, 6-8, 7-8, and 7-9. Data were collected by surveying 771 English/language arts teachers, school counselors, and building principals from 178 California schools. Univariate and multivariate statistical procedures were used to describe the type of writing program middle level grades children experience. Differences among various writing curricula and instructional components are explained relative to school organizational type, that is, grade-span configurations. Underlying interrelationships among the variable set are conceptualized into four domains: (A) teacher characteristics, (b) the writing program, (c) philosophical commitment to middle level programs and practices, and (d) policies that impact the writing program."

814. Kingen, S. (1994). When middle school students compose: An examination of processes and products. *Research in Middle Level Education, 18*(1), 83-103.

Studied writing samples from 12 middle level students in an attempt to describe how they approached the writing assignment and the results of their efforts. Used a complex method of coding the students' work and analyzing the impact of factors found in the "writer, task, and context" (p. 86). Compared the results with previous research.

815. Kucera, C. A. (1995). Detours and destinations: One teacher's journey into an environmental writing workshop. *Language Arts, 72*(3), 179-187.

Presents the results of a qualitative research study designed to encourage systematic reflection on writing instruction. The author, a teacher-researcher, discusses the role of writing instruction in the development and successful implementation of an environmental workshop. This article provides motivation for classroom teachers interested in conducting action research within their own classes.

816. Lonberger, R., & Lonberger, W. (1995). Enhancing literacy skills with a time capsule. *Teaching PreK-8, 25*(7), 52-53.

Discusses a seventh-grade class project in which students produced a video documenting key events in their lives. The video, based upon original scripts by each student about his/her life, was placed into a time capsule to be opened during the students' senior year.

817. Manning, M. (1994). 12 guidelines for teaching writing in middle school. *Teaching PreK-8, 25*(3), 59-61.

Profiles Mark Barber, an eighth-grade English teacher, with an emphasis upon 12 suggestions for becoming a "remembered" writing teacher. Included is a discussion of the need for parental involvement and a language-oriented curriculum.

818. Martin, J. M. (1994). Curriculum of middle school: A descriptive study of the teaching of writing (Doctoral dissertation, Michigan State

University, 1994). *Dissertation Abstracts International, 53,* 2378A.

Described and explained the writing curriculum of one class of entering middle-school students during one school year. Included selection of writing components, implementation of the curriculum, student responsibilities, and relationship of the writing curriculum to other elements of the school curriculum.

819.   Mitchell, D. (1994). Scripting for involvement and understanding. *English Journal, 83*(6), 82-85.

Describes a project in which eighth-graders wrote a script for either a news show or a puppet show. Concludes that script writing is an effective strategy for involving students in language and for helping them understand the importance of language in real-world situations.

820.   Mitchell, D., & Rigby, I. (1995). The skill without the drill. *English Journal 84*(1), 101-104.

Discusses effective strategies for reviewing skills acquisitions. Focuses upon the tendency of language arts teachers to use drill strategies even though students exhibit little transfer from drill sheets to actual written products. Presents several effective strategies for reviewing skills acquisitions and for integrating skills instruction into writing activities.

821.   Olshansky, B. (1994). Making writing a work of art: Image-making within the writing process. *Language Arts, 71*(5), 350-356.

Discusses the effectiveness of integrated art and writing programs. Also discusses specific instructional strategies designed to integrate visual imagery into the writing process. Emphasis is upon "image-making within the writing process."

822.   Palmer, B. C. (1994). Improving student reading, writing with newspaper-based instruction. *Newspaper Research Journal, 15*(2), 50-55.

Discusses a program that incorporates newspapers as a tool for enhancing students' reading and writing abilities. Results of the 55-day program originally implemented in Florida revealed that both middle level and high school students improved their reading and writing skills.

823.   Smede, S. D., & Manning, G. (1995). Flyfishing, portfolios, and authentic writing. *English Journal, 84*(2), 92-94.

Discusses the effectiveness of using a writing process model with seventh-graders. Emphasis is upon writing proposals, composing first drafts, revising, editing, and publishing the finished product. Also discussed is the role of portfolios in improving student writing.

824.   Spencer. A. F. (1995). Laurel and Hardy bridge a culture gap.

English Journal, 84(3), 67-69.

Discusses the use of silent films, such as *Laurel and Hardy*, as an effective instructional strategy for teaching writing in a multicultural setting. Emphasis is upon the element of humor as a common element among diverse cultures.

825.   Sudol, D, & Sudol, P. (1995). Yet another story: Writers' workshop revisited. *Language Arts, 72*(3), 171-178.

As a follow-up to April 1991 article in *Language Arts*, this article discusses the development and implementation of a writers' workshop for fifth-graders. Includes numerous suggestions for incorporating an effective workshop format in a middle-level classroom.

T. WRITING - PRACTICAL

826.   Atwell, N. (Ed.). (1989). *Coming to know: Writing to learn in the intermediate grades*. Portsmouth, NH: Heinemann. 248 pp.

Written by teachers of grades three through six, this book clearly delineates unique and powerful ways to incorporate writing across the curriculum. The book is comprised of six parts: Introduction, Researching and Reporting, Power of Learning Logs, Reading and Writing, Teaching and Learning, and Appendices.

827.   Beachy, C. J. (1992). Enhancing writing through cooperative peer editing. In Neil Davidson and Toni Worsham (Eds.), *Enhancing thinking through cooperative learning* (pp. 209-221). New York: Teachers College Press.

The authors discuss how middle school teachers can effectively incorporate cooperative peer editing into their instructional program. In doing so, they discuss the key components of the peer editing process and the methods to use when implementing peer editing in a seventh grade classroom.

828.   Bingham, A. (1987). Using writing folders to document student progress. In Thomas Newkirk and Nancie Atwell (Eds.) *Understanding writing: Ways of observing, learning, and teaching* (pp. 129-135). Portsmouth, NH: Heinemann.

An elementary teacher discusses her use of writing folders to document student progress. In doing so, she also suggests how writing folders can serve to document the success of a writing program. Finally, she also discusses the value of such folders to students, teachers, and parents.

829.   Bourman, A. (1991). *100 writing starters for middle school*. San Antonio, TX: ECS Learning Systems. 100 pp.

Each starter has an introductory paragraph and the beginning of a second which students complete with four of their own sentences. Topics deal with relationships, self-concept, problem solving, and values education.

830.	Brown, A. H. (1993). Kids recite their writing in a coffeehouse. *The Quarterly of the National Writing Project and the Center for the Study of Writing and Literacy, 15*(Fall), 272-28.

Discusses the use of discussion groups for eighth-graders in a coffeehouse setting. Instead of coffee, students drink tea, hot chocolate, or juices with their breads. Concludes that the informal, conversational atmosphere helps relieve students' anxiety about writing and increases their willingness to discuss their writings.

831.	Calkins, L. McC. (1986). *The art of teaching writing*. Portsmouth, NH: Heinemann.

In this practical book, Calkins focuses on teaching writing at the elementary school. In doing so, she provides many practical suggestions and also delineates what teachers can expect students to do at each grade level.

832.	Connell, M. E. (1990). Click: Poets at work in the middle school. *English Journal, 79*(7), 30-32.

Discusses the use of slides taken of the "real" world of students as a basis to begin and continue a motivating poetry unit for eighth graders.

833.	Cunningham, P. M. (1988). A middle school teacher's guide to revising and editing. *The Clearing House, 61*(5), 202-204.

Discusses the importance of process writing in middle school classrooms. Specifically discussed are strategies for assisting students with revising and editing. Also focuses on the need to receive feedback from peers and to display the final product.

834.	Farnan, N., & Fearn, L. (1993). Writers' workshops: Middle school writers and readers collaborating. *Middle School Journal, 24*(4), 61-65.

Basically discusses the purposes of writers' workshops, rules that were established for conducting a writers workshop in a middle level setting, strategies for getting a writers' workshop underway, a description of a group of sixth graders' performance in writers workshops, and students comments about various aspects of their participation in writers' workshops.

835.	Forte, I. (1983). *Write about it! Activities for teaching basic writing skills*. Tampa, FL: National Resource Center for Middle Grades/High school Education. 80 pp.

Students are encouraged to stretch their minds and develop their imaginations. Activities fall into a natural skills sequence to develop vocabulary and technical writing skills, and proficiency in composition and original writing. Reproducible worksheets may be used to supplement and reinforce any adopted courses of study and are appropriate for use in individual or group settings.

836.   Forte, I. (1991). *Composition and creative writing for the middle grades*. Tampa, FL: National Resource Center for Middle Grades/High School Education. 80 pp.

A perfect companion to *Writing Survival Skills*, this resource was created to increase the fluency, flexibility, and originality in the written communication skills of students. A thorough resource to help students increase their love of language and sense of self-worth as they create and perfect written pieces.

837.   Forte, I. (1991). *Writing survival skills for the middle grades*. Tampa, FL: National Resource Center for Middle Grades/High School Education. 80 pp.

Test-taking, resumes, business letters, and job applications are only a few of the topics covered in this essential writing skills resource with its high-interest reproducible student pages and invaluable teacher-directed sections.

838.   Frank, M. (1987). *Complete writing lessons for the middle grades*. Tampa, FL: National Resource Center for Middle Grades/High School Education. 128 pp.

Contains high-interest writing lessons. The easy-to-use format allows teaching to start right away, with complete teacher-directed writing lessons.

839.   Freedman, S. W. (1995). What's involved? Setting up a writing exchange. *Language Arts, 72(3), 208-218*.

As co-director of the National Center for the Study of Writing and Literacy, the author offers suggestions for developing and implementing a writing exchange. Also discussed are the benefits that students receive as participants in a writing exchange program and the role of such an exchange in a global society.

840.   Graves, D. H. (1983). *Writing: Teachers and children at work*. Portsmouth, NH: Heinemann. 336 pp.

Widely acclaimed as *the* basic text in the movement that established writing as a central part of literacy education, this book presents real teachers in the midst of helping children learn to express themselves, conferring with children, keeping records, talking to parents, and organizing their classroom. Features of children's development in spelling, handwriting, use of concepts, revision, use of the page and process are charted through descriptions of their behaviors in writing and the classroom.

841.   Grobe, W. J. (1981). Improving writing through student-teacher interaction. *Middle School Journal, 12*(2), 20-21.

Suggests improving writing skills instruction by improving student-teacher interaction and developing student-teacher interaction through student-teacher planning and conferencing. Provides ideas for initiating interactions and guidelines for successful conferences.

842.   Howard, K. (1990). Making the writing portfolio real. *The Quarterly*, *12*(2), 1-7, 27.

Howard discusses five phases that middle level students experienced as they created and used portfolios: modeling and oral reflection, first written reflection, beginning portfolio, updating portfolio, and completing the portfolio.

843.   Hudson, T. (1987). Great, no, realistic expectations: Grammar and cognitive levels. *English Journal, 76*(7), 82-83.

Middle school students function at different cognitive levels regardless of IQ scores. Rather than spend time teaching specific grammar skills at lower cognitive levels, teachers should be concentrating on fluency, experimentation, and written expression.

844.   Hudson, T. (1988). It's only fair. *English Journal, 77*(3), 74-75.

Gives guidelines for writing a comparison and contrast paper and encourages teachers to move from a subject-centered to a student-centered approach to learning.

845.   Jackson, R. M. (1988). It's *just* a note. *Educational Leadership, 45*(6), 60-63.

Note writing is an important form of communication serving many purposes in middle school. Even students who claim to hate writing write notes.

846.   Johnston, R. E., & Gill, K. (1987). Writing to learn—Writing a basic for middle level students. *NASSP Bulletin: The Journal for Middle Level and High School Administrators, 71*(501), 70-74.

An excellent article on why and how a school implemented a writing across the curriculum program. Presents a number of excellent ideas on how teachers can incorporate writing into any curricular area.

847.   Joy, F. (1984). Homophones. *Middle School Journal, 15*(2), 22-24.

Composition lesson centers upon homophone interpretation and spelling through the creation of a set of cartoons called "Homophone Hysterics." Includes rationale and booklet preparation instruction with examples.

848.   Kirby, D., & Liner, T., with R. Vinz. (1988). *Inside out: Developmental strategies for teaching writing*. Portsmouth, NH: Boyton/Cook. 288 pp.

An outstanding book which is full of practical and fascinating ideas on how to incorporate the writing process across the curriculum.

849.   McCarthey, S. J. (1994). Students' understanding of metaphors in teachers' talk about writing. *Language Arts, 71* (8), 598-605.

Discusses the effectiveness of using metaphors in writing process instruction. Specifically discussed are metaphors as a tool for enhancing students' understanding of language, for demonstrating the complexity of students' understanding of the writing process, and for enhancing interpersonal communication within the middle level classroom.

850.   Moffett, J. (1981). *Active voice: A writing program across the curriculum.* Portsmouth, NH: Boyton/Cook. 160 pp.

An early and insightful book that is packed with ideas on how teachers can incorporate writing across the curriculum. "Within each progression, the student is asked to make increasingly sophisticated and artful decisions. Since the assignments can be done with varying maturity at different ages, the program is suitable for elementary through college students."

851.   Murphy, S., & Smith, M. A. (1991). *Writing portfolios: A bridge from teaching to assessment.* Markham, Ontario: Pippin Publishing Limited.

The text is full of insights and practical advice about portfolios in the middle and high school grades. Recommended for providing an initial knowledge base for teachers considering the use of portfolios in their classrooms.

852.   Nathan, R., Temple, F., Juntunen, K., & Temple, C. (1989). *Classroom strategies that work: An elementary teacher's guide to process writing.* Portsmouth, NH: Heinemann. 162 pp.

This useful book is comprised of five main sections: Introduction—Principles for Teaching the Writing Process; 1. Setting Up a Writing Program; 2. Focused Lessons (which illustrate ways to call out certain aspects of writing for improvement and getting students to teach each other within the process classroom); and, 3. Writing Across the Curriculum; and an Epilogue.

853.   Neubert, G. A., & McNelis, S. J. (1990). Peer response: Teaching specific revision suggestions. *English Journal, 79*(5), 52-56.

Very helpful suggestions for improving the quality of peer responses to writing assignments. After instruction, student responses improved dramatically from 28% specific responses to 60% specific responses.

854.   Noguchi, R. R. (1991). *Grammar and the teaching of writing: Limits and possibilities.* Urbana, IL: National Council of Teachers of English. 127 pp.

Research-based, this booklet provides insightful information on how and why teachers should not teach grammar in a vacuum but must incorporate it as an integral part of their writing program.

855.   O'Brien, M. C., Conroy, A., & Conroy, M. T. (1988). Writing day at Barnes Intermediate School. *The Clearing House, 61*(5), 205-207.

Discusses "Writing Day at Barnes," a program designed to incorporate writing in each content area. Includes an overview of the program, suggestions for teacher training, sample lesson plans, and guidelines for developing and implementing similar programs.

856.   O'Hare, F. (1973). *Sentence combining: Improving student writing without formal grammar*. Urbana, IL: National Council of Teachers of English. 108 pp.

While this booklet primarily focuses on research concerned with the value of sentence combining, its three appendices do provide ideas regarding the practical application of the research: Appendix A (Sample Lessons and Sentence-Combining Problems From the Experimental Group's Text), Appendix B (Sample Lessons and Problems From an Expanded Version of the Sentence-Combining System Used in this Study), and Appendix C (Composition Evaluation Assignments).

857.   Oberlin, K. J., & Shugarman, S. L. (1988). Purposeful writing activities for students in middle school. *Journal of Reading, 31*(8), 720-723.

Discusses the purpose of writing before reading and describes three instructional activities: Relating prewriting and prereading, previewing unfamiliar texts, and connecting prior knowledge to text information.

858.   Olsen, C. B. (1987). *Practical ideas for teaching writing as a process*. Sacramento, CA: California State Department of Education. 190 pp.

This outstanding and extremely practical booklet is chock full of unique and fascinating ways to incorporate various components of the writing process across the school (K-12) curriculum. All of the articles are written by practicing teachers, many of them at the elementary, middle and junior high levels. The booklet is divided into the following sections: The Process, Prewriting, Prewriting in the Elementary School, Prewriting in Different Subjects, Showing, Not Telling, Writing, Domains of Writing, Writing the Saturation Repot, Point of View in Writing, Writing the I-Search Paper, Sharing/Responding, RAGs for Sharing/Responding, Rewriting/Editing, Revising for Correctness, Building Vocabularies,, Evaluation, and Evaluation Techniques.

859.   Parsons, L. (1990). *Response journals*. Portsmouth, NH: Heinemann.

Excellent handbook for middle level teachers. This book shows how journals provide a means of evaluating progress, exploring personal responses, developing small group discussions, guiding student-teacher conferences, tracking independent reading, maintaining dialogues, and developing sourcebooks for writing. Provides excellent lists of response-provoking questions.

860.   Pottle, J. (1988). *Writing frames: 40 activities for learning the writing process*. San Antonio, TX: ECS Learning Systems, Inc. 154 pp.

Sequential, cloze-style exercises teach the process of pre-writing, writing, editing, and revising. Guided by frames, students gain confidence in their ability to express themselves.

861.   Rico, G. L. (1983). *Writing the natural way: Using right-brain techniques to release your expressive powers*. New York: St. Martin's Press. 287 pp.

This useful book focuses on various right-brain techniques such as clustering, recurrence, re-vision, image and metaphor, creative tension, webbing and language rhythm.

862.   Silberman, A. (1991). *Growing up writing: Teaching our children to write, think and learn*. Portsmouth, NH: Heinemann, Boyton/Cook. 304 pp.

"Silberman shows the vital connection that links writing, thinking, and learning, taking the reader into classrooms in every part of the country to show us how ordinary teachers are helping ordinary students become extraordinary writers."

863.   Strouf, J. (1990). *Hooked on language arts! Ready-to-use activities and worksheets for grades 4-8*. West Nyack, NY: The Center for Applied Research in Education. 243 pp.

An easy-to-use collection of 130 educational games and activities that motivate students in grades 4-8 and help them master basic language arts skills in four key areas, including writing and composition; reading and literature; words and sentences; listening, speaking, and oral presentation. Includes step-by-step directions, reproducible worksheets, informative illustrations, and answer keys.

864.   Tchudi, S. N., & Huerta, M. C. (1983). *Teaching writing in the content areas: Middle school and junior high*. Washington, DC: National Education Association. 64 pp.

Succinctly presents ideas on how to incorporate writing across the curriculum. Rather slight on depth.

865.   Tuchudi, S. N., & Huerta, M. C. (1983). *Writing in the content areas: Middle school*. Washington, DC: National Education Association. 64 pp.

Explores basic principles and procedures through model units and lessons. Includes applications and extensions to show teachers how to develop specific materials for their own classrooms. Special sections are devoted to finding topics, evaluation, and grading.

866.   Wood, K. D. (1987). Teaching vocabulary in the subject areas. *Middle School Journal, 19*(1), 11-13.

Explains the semantic mapping of vocabulary words and the use of semantic maps in each stage of the writing process. Includes clearly designed examples.

867.   Yancey, K. B. (Ed.). (1992). *Portfolios in the writing classroom: An introduction.* Urbana, IL: National Council of Teachers of English. 128 pp.

The contributors to this booklet provide practical, rich, and varied insights in regard to using portfolios in the classroom. In dong so, they address both the theoretical and the practical concerns of using portfolios. Among the various chapters in this book are the following: Writing Portfolios—Changes and Challenges; Teachers' Stories: Notes Toward a Portfolio Pedagogy; Increasing Student Autonomy Through Portfolios; Portfolio Practice in the Middle School: One Teacher's Story; Portfolios: Process for Students and Teachers; and, Portfolios Reflections in Middle and Secondary School Classrooms. It concludes with an annotated bibliography.

868.   Zemelman, S., & Daniels, H. (1988). *A community of writers: Teaching writing in the junior and senior high school.* Portsmouth, NH: Heinemann. 288 pp.

"A *Community of Writers* bridges the gap from theory to practical classroom activity, showing teachers of writing and all subject areas from grades six through twelve how to promote involvement and growth in students' written language. This book demonstrates how the much talked-about 'writing process' becomes most meaningful when used to create a community of learners whose thoughts and questions instruct one another.... Building on the experience and expertise of many teachers they've worked with, as well as the growing literature about composing, classroom dynamics, and whole language, Zemelman and Daniels offer detailed guidance for all aspects of teaching and using writing, from workshop methods to pre-writing and revising to issues of grammar and evaluation."

U. WRITING - GENERAL

869.   Davis, V. I. (1995). Working toward language-centered writing and literature courses. *English Journal, 84*(1), 35-40.

Uses vignettes to outline functions of language in real-life situations. Concludes by emphasizing the need for American schools to assume responsibility for including the study of language in writing and literature courses.

X

Integrated Curriculum

A. INTEGRATED CURRICULUM

870.   Alexander, W.M. (1995). 2-teacher teams promote integrative curriculum. *Middle Ground*, 6-7.

Argues from experience for "partnerships of teaching generalists who share small groups of students and truly team teach" (p. 7) rather than simply share students.

871.   Brazee, E., & Capelluti, J. (1995). *Dissolving boundaries: Toward an integrative curriculum.* Columbus, OH: National Middle School Association. 160 pages.

Combines theoretical and practical applications of integrative curriculum in middle level settings.

872.   Cook, G. E., & Martinello, M. L. (1994). Topics and themes in interdisciplinary curriculum. *Middle School Journal, 25*(3), 40-44.

Explains how themes can be developed from students' common interests, adolescent literature and trade books, textbook topics, current events, local sites and community resources, cultural heritage, teachers' interests or expertise, objects and artifacts, and abstract concepts. Emphasizes student opportunities for real inquiry through their consultation of varied resources to explore their own questions. Authors believe that inter-disciplinary inquiry encourages sustained and thorough study of major concepts and big ideas that can lead students to exceed grade level expectations for achievement.

873.   Cunningham, F. B. (1984). A middle school approach to peace education. *Harvard Educational Review, 54*(3), 334-336.

A description of how one middle school integrated nuclear war and peace education into the curriculum. Three activities are described: a student study group, a simulation game "Firebreaks," and an Asian history course.

874.   DelForge, C., DelForge, L., & DelForge, C. (1993). Integrating
aerospace. *Science Scope, 17*(3), 41-43.

A school-wide integrated unit is described by the authors. All teachers are
involved at their school in determining unit objectives and what topics each
teacher will focus on in their own classrooms. Ideas for science, language arts,
mathematics, social studies, foreign language, industrial arts, physical education,
and art are included in the article.

875.   Gaskins, I. W. (1988-89). Teachers as thinking coaches: Creating
strategic learners and problem solvers. *Journal of Reading, Writing, and
Learning Disabilities International, 4*(1), 35-48.

This article describes an across the curriculum program developed to teach
learning, thinking, and problem solving skills to bright middle level
underachievers. The author discusses the program's theoretical basis, axioms of
program development, guidelines for teaching metacognitive strategies, and a
framework for strategy implementation.

876.   Lounsbury, J. (1994). Review of *Watershed* by M. Springer, National
Middle School Association. In *Middle Ground* , Fall, p. 9.

An enthusiastic review of the accomplishments of two teachers who developed a
successful "full day experiential program for seventh graders" (p. 9).

877.   Pate, P. E., Homestead, E., & McGinnis, K. (1994). Middle school
students' perceptions of integrated curriculum. *Middle School Journal, 26*(2),
pp. 21-23.

Examines student responses to an open-ended questionnaire about integrated
curriculum. Breaks down responses by gender and ability. Three-fourths of
male students and over one-half of female students responded in favor of
integrated curriculum. Higher ability students generally ranked it more
favorably than lower ability students. Positive comments were similar in all
groups: "it was fun, interesting, and different, " "you do big projects and learn a
lot," it helps us understand how it all works together." High ability students
were concerned about too many group projects, staying with the same people,
preparation for high school, and assessment. Low ability students worried about
not knowing which subject they were studying and felt it was hard for them to
learn more than one subject at a time.

878.   Shams, M., & Boteler, T. (1993). Jurassic Park: Adventure in
learning. *Science Scope, 17* (1), 12-17.

The authors describe how their middle school uses a school-wide
interdisciplinary period (two-to fourteen-week block) to teach in a holistic
manner. Students spend one period each day in the interdisciplinary class.
Students have much of the responsibility for their learning, set personal goals,

cooperatively plan and carry out activities. Student input is a key component in the direction of study. A sample unit is described in the article.

879.   Smith, J. L., & Johnson, H. (1993). Bring it together: Literature in an integrative curriculum. *Middle School Journal, 25*(1), 3-7.

Based upon the premise that the curriculum of a middle school should be relevant to the concerns and questions of young adolescents. Provides a model for incorporating adolescent literature into the curriculum. Also includes examples of integrated, thematic literature units. Examples include units based upon *The Witch of Blackbird Pond, Z for Zachariah, A Family Apart,* and *Among Friends.*

880.   Springer, M. (1994). *Watershed: A successful voyage into integrative learning.* Columbus, OH: National Middle School Association. 208 pages.

The inside story of two middle level teachers implementation of an integrative curriculum.

881.   Stevenson, C., & Carr, J. F. (Eds.). (1992). *Integrated studies in the middle grades: "Dancing Through Walls."* New York: Teachers College Press. 211 pp.

This highly acclaimed volume is a compilation of stories by teachers about how they have integrated curriculum in the middle grades. The beauty of the collection is that the contributors present concrete examples as to how teachers and students, in collaboration with one another, have created units of study that are developmentally responsive to young adolescents. According to the editors, the criteria that were used to measure the success of each integrated unit were the following: students must experience feelings of efficacy and safety, they must be engaged in the production of knowledge and collaborative work, and they must develop an increasing sense of responsibility. The studies the units were designed around are studies of self, studies of the community, studies of nature, and interest studies. "The teachers spent a week together in the summer creating their teaching plans, and they gathered on fall weekends to share experiences and successes. Their insights are presented , showing ways they responded to their students' interests and dispositions.... Concrete examples, planning guidelines, and practical advice are included herein."

B. WHOLE LANGUAGE

882.   Atwell, N. (1991). *In the middle: Writing, reading and learning with adolescents.* Portsmouth, NH: Boyton-Cook. 295 pp.

A highly acclaimed book about the way a teacher and her students "learned together as collaborating writers and readers." Not only is the book full of practical ideas on teaching writing, but it is also "a book about adolescents themselves—how they learn, what they believe and value, and what we can learn from and about them." But it does not stop there either; it also presents a fascinating portrait of how one teacher's mode of instruction was transformed when she became "concerned enough to question her own assumptions about teaching." *In the Middle* was awarded the 1987 Mina P. Shaughnessy Prize of the Modern Language Association of America, and in 1990 it received the NCTE David H. Russell Award for Distinguished Research in the Teaching of English.

883.   Brady, S., & Sills, T. (Eds.) (1993). *Whole language: Philosophy, theory, and practice.* Kendall /Hunt, Nashville. 217 pp.

Practical overview and introduction to the whole language philosophy of instruction. Includes both theoretical and practical articles by leaders in the whole language movement.

884.   Cambourne, B. (1994). The rhetoric of "The rhetoric of whole language." *Reading Research Quarterly, 29*(4), 330-332.

Accuses Moorman, Blanton, and McLaughlin of unconsciously using the "rhetoric of camouflage" to present a one-sided picture of the whole language movement.

885.   Danehower, V. E. (1993). Implementing whole language: Understanding the change process. *School in the Middle, 2*(4), 45-46.

Begins with a brief description of "whole language" instruction. Presents the need for professional development prior to implementing whole language instruction, or any other innovation. Discusses the role of administration in ensuring that teachers receive adequate training and follow-up support when implementing new programs.

886.   Fuhler, C. J. (1993). The learning disabled adolescent and whole language. *The Clearing House, 67*(2), 107-111.

Discusses issues related to whole language and their role in meeting the needs of young adolescents with special needs. Specifically discussed are whole language philosophy and response theory, literary response journals, and problems with textbooks. Concludes that students with special needs benefit from a holistic approach to teaching and learning.

887.   Goodman, K. S. (1994). Deconstructing the rhetoric of Moorman, Blanton, and McLaughlin: A response. *Reading Research Quarterly, 29*(4), 340-346.

Informative rebuttal to Moorman, Blanton, and McLaughlin's article "The Rhetoric of Whole Language." Declares that he is "weary of attacks on whole language disguised as helpful hints for whole language advocates." A reading of both articles allows for a greater understanding of whole language. Other rebuttals to the Moorman, et al, article are included in this issue of *Reading Research Quarterly.*

888. Hansen, J., Newkirk, T., & Graves, D. (Eds.). (1985). *Breaking ground: Teachers relate reading and writing in the elementary school.* Portsmouth, NH: Heinemann.

In this book thirteen K-8 teachers and seven teacher educators demonstrate how process approaches to reading and writing can be successfully integrated at the elementary and middle levels.

889. Manning, G., Manning, M., & Long, R. (1990). *Reading and writing in the middle grades: A whole language view.* Washington, DC: National Education Association, 64 pp.

This book provides a step-by-step explanation of how to incorporate whole language concepts into the classroom. It includes sixteen specific methods for developing readers and twelve simultaneous strategies for developing writers in a constructive, holistic approach.

890. Moorman, G. B., Blanton, W. E., & McLaughlin, T. (1994). The rhetoric of whole language. *Reading Research Quarterly, 29*(4), 309-329.

Makes a comprehensively researched attempt to answer the following two questions: 1. What are the explicit assumptions by which the whole language movement defines itself? 2. What implicit beliefs underlying the basic assumptions are evident when the rhetoric of whole language literature is examined? Examines three recurring theoretical themes: general definitions, learning and teaching, and the reading process and reading instruction. Moorman, et al, respond to criticism by Cambroune, Willinsky, and Goodman in another article in the same issue of *Reading Research Quarterly.*

891. Sapper, L. F. (1993). Applying a whole language approach to middle grades teaching. *KAMLE Karavan: Journal of the Kansas Association for Middle Level Education, 7,* 10-15.

Provides an overview of what whole language is as well as a rationale for the set of beliefs that constitute whole language and delineates a three-phase instructional planning model. It also includes an extensive annotated bibliography of adolescent literature on the theme of courage and survival.

892. Sharp, S. J. (1989). Using content subject matter with LEA in middle school. *Journal of Reading, 33*(2), 108-112.

Explanation of the Language Experience Method (LEA) of teaching reading including a specific list of LEA goals. Using a small class of low achieving students as subjects, the author describes an LEA learning experience from implementation to evaluation.

893. Sheppard, R. L., & Moore, M. T. (1991). *Breaking traditions: A process approach to teaching reading and language arts in the middle school.* Topsfield, MA: New England League of Middle Schools.

Explores the connections of reading, writing, and middle level students.
Presents whole language strategies and models for use in middle level
classrooms. Useful resource for interdisciplinary teams and others interested in
developing an integrated curriculum.

894.   Sheppard, R. L., & Stratton, B. D. (1993). *Reflections on becoming:*
Fifteen literature-based units for the young adolescent. Columbus, OH:
National Middle School Association.

Designed to assist middle level students in understanding themselves and their
problems through the study of characters from books written for specifically for
young adolescents. Includes suggested discussion questions and journal writing
activities.

895.   Willinsky, J. (1994). Theory and meaning in whole language:
Engaging Moorman, Blanton, and McLaughlin. *Reading Research Quarterly,*
29(4), 334-339.

Tries to present an objective, scholarly analysis of the article "The Rhetoric of
Whole Language" written by Moorman, Blanton, and McLaughlin.

XI

Exploratory and Elective Subjects

A. EXPLORATORY PROGRAMS

896.   Berch, J. A. (1973). Personalized vocational courses for middle school pupils. *The Clearing House*, *47*(1), 30-33.

Emphasizes the need for middle level students to demonstrate competency in note-taking and keyboarding skills.

897.   Bergman, S. (1992). Exploratory programs in the middle level school: A responsive idea. In Judith L. Irvin (Ed.), *Transforming middle level education: Perspectives and possibilities* (pp. 179-192). Needham Heights, MA: Allyn and Bacon.

Under a section entitled "Research on Models of Exploration," Bergman briefly discusses some of the more recent research findings regarding the exploratory curriculum/offerings in middle level programs.

898.   Blanchard, F. (1986-1987). Outdoor education as a team experience. *KAMLE Karavan: Journal of the Kansas Association for Middle Level Education*, *1*, 9-12.

Discusses how an interdisciplinary team planned and implemented an outdoor classroom/exploratory experience (camping, along with rotation through 45-minute classes of canoeing, first aid, field journals, soil studies, seining, kitemaking, fossil hunting, and primitive pottery) in conjunction with a study and observation of Halley's Comet.

899.   Kueny, M. (Ed.). (1987). *Junior high school/middle school journalism curriculum*. Journalism Education Association.

A general and practical resource for middle level journalism teachers. Includes articles and suggestions from practicing journalism teachers.

900.   Toepfer, Jr., C. F. (1994). Vocational/career/occupational education at

the middle level: What is appropriate for young adolescents? *Middle School Journal, 25*(3), 59-65.

Recommends vocational exploratory experiences be provided for middle level students. Gives a brief historical perspective of the need for vocational education, but recommends that efforts at the middle level be limited to exploratory activities. Considers the goals of America 2000 and SCANS targets for the year 2000 to be unrealistic and offers alternatives.

B. ART

901.   Anglin, J. (1986). A descriptive study of middle art curriculum. In David B. Strahan (Ed.). *Middle school research: Selected studies 1986* (pp. 56-73). Columbus, OH: The Research Committee of the National Middle School Association.

"This study described both written curriculum documents and the implemented curriculum of selected middle school art programs in Northeastern Ohio. Three types of research techniques — content analysis, participant observation, and ethnographic interview — were employed to answer the questions: What are the planned, written art curricula and What are the actual implemented art curricula in selected middle schools?... Highlights of the findings include a congruence found between the written and implemented curriculum which was developed at the local level by art teachers. A higher percentage of art activities was based on media and material uses and less emphasis was placed on art appreciation activities at this age level."

902.   Beaulieu, L. (1993). Colorizing worlds: Making much with a mouse. *High Strides: The Bimonthly Report on Urban Middle Grades, 4*(6), 3.

A fascinating article that discusses how a middle level teacher in Columbus, Ohio, teaches art via a computer and has his students use video camcorders and computers to create art. Their color monitors are their canvases and the mechanical mouses serve as their brushes.

903.   Burden, B. (1993). If Michelangelo can do it... *High Strides: The Bimonthly Report on Urban Middle Grades, 4*(6), 4.

Describes the innovative program of a fifth grade teacher in Atlanta, Georgia, who uses a discipline-based arts education approach (which integrates the four disciplines of aesthetics, art criticism, art history and studio art production into the instructional content of the class) for teaching art.

904.   Erickson, M. (1995). Why stories? *School Arts, 94*(7), 38-39.

Discusses an art project based upon the story "Kag and the River People" that allows middle level students to construct and decorate three kinds of clay pots. Includes a condensed version of "A Story of Art in the World."

905.   Garcia, J. (1993). Museum offers the works. *High Strides: The Bimonthly Report on Urban Middle Grades*, 4(6), 8.

Describes the Ringling Museum of Art's efforts to establish a partnership with local school systems in Sarasota, Florida. The museum offers art instruction that uses a discipline-based arts education approach (which integrates the four disciplines of aesthetics, art criticism, art history and studio art production into the instructional content of the art class).

906.   Greene, C. (1995). Expectations in watercolor. *School Arts*, 94(7), 21-22.

Discusses a watercolor project in which middle level students explore the concepts of composition through a study of shapes and textures of fruits and vegetables.

907.   *High Strides: The Bimonthly Report on Urban Middle Grades*. (1993). Special Issue on Art Education, 4(6).

This special issue on art education includes an outstanding array of articles on various facets of teaching art to middle level students. Among the topics addressed are: the key components of a discipline-based arts education approach (a method of teaching art that integrates art history, art criticism, and the production of art); the relationship between the study of the arts and other academic disciplines; art as homework; a program entitled Teachers Involve Parents in Schoolwork (TIPS); an art program at a middle school in Columbus, Ohio, where a teacher teaches art via computers (in which the color monitor is a canvas and the brush is the "mouse" that commands the computer); an art program in Atlanta, Georgia, that is DBAE-based; the arts program called ARTS PROPEL (in which the subjects of music, writing, and the visual arts are integrated); an innovative art class in an alternative middle school in Forth Worth, Texas; and, an art museum in Sarasota, Florida, that has set up partnerships with schools.

908.   Johnson, M. G. (1993). Making brushes dearer than weapons. *High Strides: The Bimonthly Report on Urban Middle Grades*, 4(6), 7.

Describes the success of an art program at Fort Worth's Middle Level Learning Center (an alternative, "pull out" school) in reaching its students, most of whom have been expelled from school for fighting, chronic truancy or bringing guns and knives to school.

909.   Make the arts academic. (1993). *High Strides: The Bimonthly Report on Urban Middle Grades*, 4(6), 2.

Succinctly discusses research findings that indicate that "integrated with other academic subjects, [art] leads to higher performance improved attitudes, and greater self confidence." One example given states that "the study of geometric forms in sculpture, visual illusions, and architecture helped female students almost double their mean scores on spatial abilities (geometry)." It also succinctly discusses two innovative arts programs "Learning to Read Through the Arts" and "Teachers Involve Parents In Schoolwork (TIP)."

910.   Menninga, B. (1993). Getting a vision in Omaha. *High Strides: The Bimonthly Report on Urban Middle Grades*, 4(6), 10.

Discusses a summer institute in Nebraska called "Prairie Visions: The Nebraska Consortium for Discipline-based Art Education," which is geared for K-12 educators in all subject areas. The express purpose of the summer institute is to teach educators how they can integrate art in innovative and meaningful ways across the curriculum.

911.   Michael, J. A. (1983). *Art and adolescence: Teaching art at the secondary level*. New York, NY: Teachers College Press.

Presents a framework for the development and implementation of an art program designed to meet the needs of young aolescents. Includes numerous illustrations, including photographs of classroom activities and student products.

912.   Morris, B. (1991). My many hats. *Becoming*, 2(2), 28-29.

Begins with an overview of the many hats worn by art teachers in middle level schools. Includes a brief description of the four integral components of Discipline-Based Art Education (art history, art criticism, aesthetics, and artistic products), and suggestions for integrating the components into the curriculum.

913.   Negron, E. (1993). Learning to just say "no" to ads. *High Strides: The Bimonthly Report on Urban Middle Grades*, 4(6), 6.

Describes the unique three-year interdisciplinary media arts production and analysis program in grades 6-8 at the John Wilson Intermediate School's (IS 211) Magnet School of Telecommunications and Mass Media.

914.   Reynolds, N. W. (1990). *Art lessons for the middle school: A DBAE Curriculum*. Portland, Maine: J. Weston Walch, Publisher. 70 pp.

This teacher's book is comprised of 56 lesson outlines that are based on a discipline-based arts education approach, which is comprehensive and includes learning across the curriculum. DSABE's four disciplines include aesthetics, art criticism, art history, and studio art production. Each lesson includes objectives, introductory activities, a materials checklist, step-by-step instructions, optional resources, vocabulary, extension projects, and evaluation guides.

C. MUSIC

915.   Larson, B. (1992). Music programs at the middle level: Scheduling for success. *NASSP Bulletin: The Journal for Middle Level and High School Administrators*, 76(544), 27-29.

Argues that subjects such as music and the arts should not be given second-class treatment nor should the teachers of such subjects. Discusses how middle level programs can schedule music into the curriculum and speaks about the benefits of music education.

916.   Morgan, H. W., & Berg-O'Halloran, S. L. (1989). Using music as a text. *Journal of Reading, 32*(5), 458-459.

Adapts the SQ3R reading strategy to reading music in an instrumental music class.

917.   Musoleno, R. R. (1990). A model for a music curriculum suited to exemplary practices of middle school education (Doctoral dissertation, University of Kansas, 1990). *Dissertation Abstracts International, 52,* 460A.

Lists twelve essential elements of a model music program for the middle school.

918.   Nelson, B. J. P. (1988). The development of a middle school general music curriculum: A synthesis of computer-assisted instruction and music learning theory (Doctoral dissertation, University of Rochester, Eastman School of Music, 1988). *Dissertation Abstracts International, 49,* 1728A.

Using computers as an important lesson component, lesson plans were developed which would enable students to learn to perform, read, and write music within a 12-week exploratory course.

D. FOREIGN LANGUAGE

919.   Freeman, L. M., & Gregory, L. L. (1990). Language programs at the middle level: Some design considerations. *NASSP Bulletin: The Journal for Middle Level and High School Administrators*, *74*(530), 75-82.

Discusses assumptions about language programs at the middle level, describes a "language program design procedure," and provides recommendations for developing a foreign language program at the middle level.

920.   Mason, D. A., & Mason, B. C. (1993). Trini Saldana and Clement Junior High School: A choreography of second language learning. *Middle School Journal*, *24*(5), 67-71.

Describes a ESL model classroom in Redlands, California. Includes a description of the room arrangements, a typical class period, typical challenges faced by ESL and foreign language teachers in middle schools, and characteristics of effective ESL teachers as identified by students.

921.   Olson, M. L. (1976). Teaching middle school French. *The Clearing House*, *49*(4), 188-189.

Outlines a model program at Roosevelt Junior High School in West Palm Beach,

Florida. Includes strategies for assisting middle level students in developing and maintaining an interest in learning a foreign language.

XII

Social Issues, Community Service, and Service Learning

A. SOCIAL ISSUES

922.   Allen, M. (1993). Knowledge, skills, values, and practice citizenship for middle grades. *The AIMS Journal, 8* (1), 40-45.

Discusses the importance of providing young adolescents with opportunities for involvement in political and social arenas. Presents an overview of the Civic Achievement Award Program (CAAP), a supplemental program designed to promote civic literacy, citizenship competence, and citizen involvement.

923.   Arnold, J., & Vasu, E. S. (1988). Teaching about nuclear disarmament: Attitudes of middle level teachers. In David B. Strahan (Ed.), *Middle school research: selected studies 1988* (pp. 1-11). Columbus, OH: The Research Committee of the National Middle School Association.

Based on the answers to a questionnaire that was administered to 546 middle level teachers in one public school system in the southeast. The authors state that while "most" of the respondents "believed that the issue" [nuclear disarmament] was significant for humanity to ponder, only a small percentage taught their students about the issue. The authors discuss a variety of reasons as to why the teachers did not include the subject in their own curriculum.

924a.   Totten, S., & Pedersen, J. (in press). Issues-centered curricula and instruction at the middle level. *Handbook on Teaching Social Issues*.

The authors provide and discuss the rationale for incorporating the study of social issues at the middle level, examine recent developments in middle school curriculum and instruction in regard to the study of an issues-focused education, discuss ways to create developmentally appropriate studies of social issues as well as opportunities for infusing social issues into the middle level curriculum, and conclude by examining implications of issue-focused middle level curriculum for literature, drama, art, oral history and other areas.

924b.   Totten, S., & Pedersen, J. (Eds.). (in press). *Social issues and service at the middle level*. Needham, MA: Allyn and Bacon.

This volume is comprised of fifteen essays on incorporating social issues and/or service (community service and service learning) into the middle level curriculum. The essays have been written by middle level teachers, middle level teachers and administrators, middle level teachers and professors, and individuals in private and public organizations.

B.   COMMUNITY SERVICE AND SERVICE LEARNING - RESEARCH

925.   Beane, J., Turner, J., Jones, D., & Lipka, R. (1981). Long-term effects of community service programs. *Action in Teacher Education, 11*(2), 143-155.

Discusses a research project that was conducted in order to "explore methodological considerations and to gather data that might suggest directions for further research on the strength of community service projects effects considered over time. Within this context, a study was conducted which attempted to examine the attitudes and experiences of adults who had participated in a particular community service project program during the years 1945 to 1949 and to compare these to attitudes and experiences of same-year graduates who had not participated in such a program." Discusses both the difficulties of such a study, the drawbacks, suggestions for future studies, and implications.

926.   Goodman, J., Baron, D., Belcher, M., Hastings-Heinz, U., & James, J. (1994). Toward a comprehensive understanding of service education: Reflections from an exploratory action research project. *Research in middle level education, 18*(1), 39-63.

A case study conducted by teachers to examine the nature and impact of service learning projects developed and implemented in a private middle school. Sug- gests that "comprehensive service education might likely include several aspects... within a social context...both community service and service learning projects... fully integrated into the academic curriculum...contain both social service and social action projects...initiated by both teachers and students" (p. 61).

927.   Kinsley, L. C. (1992). A case study: The integration of community service learning into the curriculum by an interdisciplinary team of teachers at an urban middle school. (Doctoral dissertation, University of Massachusetts, 1992). *Dissertation Abstracts International, 53*, 3435A.

Documents a positive experience with integrating school with community to extend learning experiences for students. Involving all curriculum areas, subjects created a model and process for implementation suitable for adaptation throughout a school district.

C.   COMMUNITY SERVICE AND SERVICE LEARNING - PRACTICAL

928.   Adams, L. B. (1993). How one school builds self-esteem in students

and serves its community. *Middle School Journal*, 24(5), 53-55.

Discusses the benefits of participating in community service projects. Presents the philosophy underlying the need to involve students in community service projects. Outlines a model program developed and implemented in Pennsylvania. Also includes suggestions for service activities.

929.   Arth, Alfred A. (1992). The middle level education civic service project. *Current Issues in Middle Level Education*, 1(1), 40-48.

This piece discusses possible ways to incorporate a civic service project into the middle level grades as well as some possible outcomes.

930.   Burkhead, M. (1994-1995). Community service at Charlotte Country Day Middle School. *NCMSA Journal*, 16(1), 20-21.

The story of successful service learning project involving multiple grade levels in a variety of ways. The authors reflect on how the projects support the philosophy of the setting.

931.   Community Service Learning Center (1993). *Whole learning through service: A guide for integrating service into the curriculum, kindergarten through eighth grade*. Amherst, MA: Author.

"This guide, which provides models for incorporating community service components into school's program, is based on five themes: intergenerational, homeless/hungry, citizenship, community health awareness, and environmental."

932.   Far West Laboratory for Educational Research and Development. (1992). *Toward a Community of Learners: A Regional Newsletter on Authentic Instruction for the Middle Grades, Volume II.*

The authors delineate how student social action projects constitute an example of authentic curriculum and instruction. They discuss various programs across the nation in which students engage in various social action projects, list ten tips for taking social action, and discuss a popular social action model that schools have adopted.

933.   Gill, J. (1992). Community service: A basic in middle level education. *KAMLE Karavan: Journal of the Kansas Association for Middle Level Education*, 6(3), 5.

Gill, the principal of Leawood Middle School in Kansas, discusses the value of community service at the middle level, the various types of community service that the students at Leawood engage in, the school's school/business partnership program, and how community service is an integral component of the advisor/advisee program at Leawood.

934.   Kiner, R. W. (1993). Community service: A middle school success

story. *The Clearing House*, *66* (3), 139-140.

Discusses a successful community service project at Whittier Middle School in Sioux Falls, South Dakota. Presents a brief rationale for community service projects, components of a successful program, and examples of successful projects.

935.   National Center for Service Learning (Ed.). (1991). *Connections: Service learning in the middle grades.* New York: Author. 51 pp.

"Connections is a collection of case studies and brief descriptions of youth community service." In addition to program profiles, the text includes chapters on the rationale for community service involving young adolescents, suggestions and caveats from practitioners and young people based upon "hands on" experience, recommendations for policy related to youth service, and a resource list.

936.   National Center for Service Learning in Early Adolescence. (1990). *Connections: Service learning in the middle grades.* New York: Author. 57 pp.

This report presents the rationale for service learning during early adolescence, case studies of fifteen programs, the criteria and process used to identify the models highlighted herein, analysis of the common elements and obstacles in these programs, and recommendations for both policy-makers and program administrators. It concludes with a short list of organizations around the nation that can provide information on community service programs and related policies.

937.   National Women's Law Center and American Youth Policy Forum. (1993). *Visions of service: The future of the National and Community Service Act.* Washington, DC: Authors. 61 pp.

This fascinating and thought-provoking booklet is comprised of six sections: Introduction; 1. Why Service?; II. What is Service?; III. Who Shall Serve?; IV. Where Are We Headed?; and V. How Shall We Get There? Each section contains short essays that address various facets and provide different perspectives vis-à-vis the chapter's focus. The contributors constitute a "who's who" in the field of national and community service (e.g., Benjamin Barber, Amitai Etzioni, Theodore M. Hesburgh, Cynthia Parsons, Joan Schine, Kathleen Kennedy Townsend).

938.   Rolzinski, C. A. (1990). *The adventure of adolescence: Middle school students and community service.* Washington, DC: Youth Service America. 139 pp.

This is an outstanding book that not only provides a solid rationale for incorporating community service projects into middle level programs, but it also provides case studies of how seven schools across the nation (e.g., San Antonio, Baltimore, Minneapolis; Pittsburgh, Los Angeles, Springfield, Massachusetts, and Colorado Springs, Colorado) have implemented successful community service programs. It concludes with a chapter that provides ideas in regard to the core components needed to design a strong community service program for middle school students.

939.   Sherraden, M. (1992). *Community-based youth services in international perspective*. Washington, DC: The Carnegie Council on Adolescent Development and William T. Grant Foundation Commission on Work, Family and Citizenship. 46 pp.

This fascinating volume examines youth service programs in other countries (The United Kingdom, Australia, Germany, Sweden, and Norway), the various dimensions of youth services (purposes and goals, policies and programs, structure and finance, youth workers and training, research and information), and concludes with suggestions that the United States should consider when developing its own youth services program.

940.   Totten, S., & Pedersen, J. E. (1993). Strengthening community service projects in schools by undergirding them with the study of pertinent social issues. *Current Issues in Middle Level Education*, 2(1), 16-30.

The authors suggest ways to strengthen community service projects in the schools through a continuous focus on the search for real-world solutions to real-world social problems. In addition to stating their case, they also provide a list of resources to assist classroom teachers.

941.   Zaferakis, M. L. (1993). CARE: Concerned adolescents reaching everywhere. *In Transition*, p. 27.

Discusses a community service project involving seventh-grade students. Called CARE: Concerned Adolescents Reading Everywhere, the organization has experienced great success in helping people in need. A good model for other schools to use when considering community service projects.

D.   COMMUNITY SERVICE AND SERVICE LEARNING - GENERAL

942.   Arnold, J., & Beal, C. (1994-1995). The value of service learning. *NCMSA Journal*, 16(1), 15-19.

Overview of the rationale for service learning, benefits to students and communities, selected research on effectiveness, and possible barriers. The authors provide a lsit of criteria to use to evaluate service learning programs as well as a strong list of organizations that support the concept.

943.   Obert, D. L. (1995). "Give and you shall receive:" School-based service learning. *Middle School Journal*, 26(4), 30-33.

School-based service learning is the implementation of service projects by the school. Organized groups of students participate in community improvement projects under the supervision of at least one faculty member. Discusses types of service learning and benefits to students and community. Lists and gives telephone numbers of national youth service organizations.

944.   Schine, J. (1989). *Young adolescents and community service.* New York: National Center for Service Learning. 22 pp.

"One of a series of Working Papers prepared for the Carnegie Council on Adolescent Development. This paper provides an overview of the rationale for and the basic elements of quality community service programs appropriate for the early adolescent."

XIII

Pedagogical Issues and Strategies

A. GROUPING - RESEARCH

945.   Hallinan, M. T. (1991). School differences in tracking structures and track assignments. *Journal of Research on Adolescence, 1(3)*, 251-175.

Describes the results of a longitudinal study of 2,050 students in middle and secondary schools to develop a model of the factors related to placement in different tracks in math and English in the eighth grade. Found significant differences in tracking placement decisions. Concludes that such variation in placement can have a strong impact on student learning experiences.

946.   Hallinan, M. T. (1992). The organization of students for instruction in the middle school. *Sociology of Education, 65(2)*, 114-127.

Comprehensively examines the structure of a tracking system and the process of assigning students to various tracks. Argues that tracking is a valuable method of organization, but offers suggestions for improvements including the need for flexibility among tracks and concern for a better fit between students' learning needs and a track structure.

947.   Silvernail, D. L., & Capelluti, J. H. (1991). An examination of the relationship between middle level school teachers' grouping preferences and their sense of responsibility for student outcomes. *Research in Middle Level Education, 15(1)*, 21-29.

This study examined the relationship between the grouping preferences of middle level teachers and their sense of responsibility for student outcomes. A sample of 151 teachers completed a modified version of the Responsibility for Student Achievement Questionnaire. Approximately two-thirds of the sample indicated they preferred to teach heterogeneously grouped classes. An analysis of the survey results indicated those teachers who preferred heterogeneously grouped classes assumed greater self-responsibility for student academic outcomes than their counterparts who preferred homogeneously grouped classes. In addition, teachers who preferred heterogeneous groups tended to attribute academic failure to weaknesses in instruction while teachers who preferred homogeneous groups tended to attribute them to student ability.

948.   Slavin, R. E. (1986). *Ability grouping and student achievement in elementary schools: A best evidence synthesis.* (Report #1) Baltimore, MD: Center for Research on Elementary and Middle Schools.

A synthesis of research on ability grouping of elementary students and young adolescents. Identifies grouping practices that promote student achievement.

949.   Spear, R. C. (1994). Teacher perceptions of ability grouping practices in middle level schools. *Research in Middle Level Education, 18*(1), 117-130.

Used a qualitative approach to understand teacher perceptions related to ability grouping. Interviewed 31 teachers in a variety of middle schools.

B. GROUPING - PRACTICAL

950.   Canady, R. L., & Rettig, M. D. (1992). Restructuring middle level schedules to promote equal access. *Schools in the middle: Theory Into practice, 1*(4), 20-2.

The authors discuss how scheduling can be used to "move away from tracking and toward a practical method of working with heterogeneous group of students." In doing so, it describes in detail (with charts) a middle school parallel block schedule and discusses the advantages of the parallel block schedule.

951.   Willis, S. (1993). 'Untracking' in the middle. *ASCD Curriculum Update*, pp. 4-5.

Highlights and discusses how three middle schools (in Massachusetts, Maryland, and Vermont) dismantled their "tracking system" and have gone with "mixed-ability grouping."

C. GROUPING - GENERAL

952.   George, P. S. (1993). Tracking and ability grouping in the middle school: Ten tentative truths. *Middle School Journal, 24*(4), 17-24.

George lists and then discusses his ten tentative truths, using research to substantiate his points. The tentative truths that George presents are: (1) "Identification and placement of middle school students into ability groups is far more difficult to accomplish fairly and accurately than often thought to be the case"; (2) "Once placed in a group it appears that students are increasingly unlikely to be moved to a supposedly faster group. It is a 'locked in/locked out' situation."; (3) Ability grouping unnecessarily downplays the importance of student, teacher, and parent effort and unjustifiably emphasizes the centrality of individual student ability"; (4) Ability grouping seems to be related to substantial differences in student self-esteem"; (5)

"Academic achievement does not appear to improve with the use of ability grouping"; (6) "Ability grouping may lead to racial, ethnic, and income isolation"; (7) "Ability grouping contributes to the destruction of a sense of community in school and out"; (8) "Grouping delivers the middle school's learning resources in fundamentally unfair and inequitable ways"; (9) "Some middle school ability grouping practices may be illegal"; and (10) "All middle school students, including gifted and talented students, deserve to receive effective instruction in a challenging curriculum." Also included is a list of 48 resources (books, research pieces, and general pieces) on ability grouping.

953.   Lewis, A. C. (Ed.). (1990). Tracking [Special Issue]. *High Strides*, 2(2).

Includes seven articles focusing on the pros and cons of tracking: "Tracking Exposed," "More Exposure," "Immoral in Boston," "De-Tracking in Phoenix: High Tracking in San Diego," "Behind NAEP Reading Scores, "As Students See Tracking."

954.   Oakes, J. (1985). *Keeping track: How schools structure inequality.* New Haven, CT: Yale University Press. 231 pp.

Oakes argues tracking and exclusive placement of students in homogeneous groups are detrimental to students vis-à-vis both achievement and self-esteem.

955.   Spear, R. (1992). Appropriate grouping practices for middle level students. In Judith L. Irvin (Ed.), *Transforming middle level education: Perspectives and possibilities* (pp. 244-274). Needham, MA: Allyn and Bacon.

Addresses definitions of tracking and ability grouping, assumptions about ability grouping, history of ability grouping, what research says about student selection and student ability, impact of abilty grouping on the development of young adolescents, and appropriate grouping practices as well as ways to move to more appropriate grouping practices.

956.   Wheelock, A. (1992). *Crossing the tracks: How untracking can save America's schools.* New York: The New Press. 352 pp.

Crossing the Tracks is an analysis and write up of a survey of schools across the United States that have successfully "crossed the tracks" by reducing or totally eliminating ability grouping within their schools as they strive to offer outstanding learning situations for all of their students. The book, which includes a foreword by Jeannie Oakes, is comprised of three parts and seven chapters: Part I: Introduction; Part II: Conditions for Untracking; and Part III. Strategies and Tools for Reform: Chapters I. Involving Parents and the Community; 2. Expecting the Best, 3. Organizing and Grouping for Diversity; 4. High-Level Curriculum for Heterogeneous Groups; 5. Instruction and Assessment for Heterogeneous Classrooms; 6. What About Math?, and 7. Student Aspirations and Untracking. It also includes a section on resources.

D. LEARNING STYLES

957.   Brooks, C. K. (1995). Learning their way. *English Journal, 84*(1),
98-99.

Discusses the importance of developing lessons designed to accommodate the
learning styles of all students. Reminds the reader that multi-ethnic classrooms
represent different learning modalities and multiple intelligences that must be
considered in curriculum development and delivery.

958.   Bryant, J. A. R. (1982). Activities that use both hemispheres of the
brain. *Middle School Journal, 13*(2), 26-27.

Identifies ways by which concepts normally considered "left-brained" may be
approached through both hemispheres. "File Folder Puzzle," "Puzzle Packet,"
and "Split Pea" activities are explained.

959.   Guild, P. B., & Garger, S. (1985). *Marching to different drummers.*
Alexandria, VA: Association for Supervision and Curriculum Development.
109 pp.

The authors discuss a variety of approaches to the issue of learning styles and
suggest practical applications. The volume is divided into three main parts: 1.
Defining Style, 2. Examples of Style, and 3. Using Style. It concludes with a
short annotated bibliography.

960.   Messer, P. (1979). The relationship of sex, age and sensory modality
learning style of ten to fourteen years old students. *Middle School Research:
Selected Studies 1977-1979* (pp. 23-30). Fairborn, OH: National Middle School
Association.

The findings of this study were as follows: 1. "The direction of the significant
differences for sex indicated that males, upon hearing a word given, had a visual
image of an object or an activity significantly more times than females, and that
females, upon hearing a given word, had a fleeting kinesthetic reaction, either
emotional or physical, significantly more times than males; 2. The age of young
adolescent students is not significantly related to their sensory modality learning
style, as measured by the ELSIE (Edmonds Learning Style Identification
Exercise), and 3. The age and sex of young adolescent students are not
significantly related to their sensory modality learning style, as measured by the
ELSIE."

961.   Sykes, S., Jones, B., & Phillips, J. (1990). Partners in learning styles at
a private school. *Educational Leadership, 48*(2), 24-26.

Describes a learning style approach to education as implemented in a private
school. Minor adaptations to accommodate varied learning style needs of
students both at home and at school resulted in improved performance and
satisfaction of students, teachers, and parents.

E. INSTRUCTION - RESEARCH

962.   Brady, M. P. (1989). Differential measures of teachers' questioning in mainstreamed classes: Individual and classwide patterns. *Journal of Research and Development in Education, 23*(1), 10-17.

The author reports the study of 42 middle school social studies teachers which compared two approaches to measuring teachers' questions. The approaches focused on either teacher-to-group interactions or teacher-to-individual student interactions. Teacher questioning patterns were identified, and implications of these patterns on mainstreamed and general education students were discussed.

963.   Brown, D. S. (1988). Twelve middle-school teachers' planning. *The Elementary School Journal, 89*(1), 69-87.

Used questionnaires, interview protocols, an analysis of written plans, and think-aloud typescripts to analyze 12 middle-school teachers' instructional yearly, unit, weekly, and daily planning. Teachers focused on activities rather than objectives and based planning decisions on "what had worked for them in the past, the school schedule, the availability of instructional materials, and the interests and abilities of students."

964.   Cave, L. M. (1992). The relationship of teacher behaviors and characteristics to critical thinking skills among middle-level students (Doctoral dissertation, Oregon State University, 1992). *Dissertation Abstracts International, 54*, 450A.

Five top-ranked teachers differed from the five bottom-ranked teachers (based on their respective classes' mean gain scores on the assessment tool) in the following ways: greater use of small group instruction, math manipulatives, and warm-up activities; provision for teaching higher-order thinking skills; frequency of transitions between classroom activities; and use of activities requiring the application of concepts. Lowest ranked teachers showed greater frequency of teacher-directed instruction, higher amounts of computer usage, assignment of individual student work, highly structured classes, and reliance on textbooks as the primary source of instructional materials.

965.   Conley, M. W. (1986). The influence of training on three teachers' comprehension questions during content area lessons. *Elementary School Journal, 87*(1), 17-28.

Results showed that highly trained teachers "tended to shift and adapt the distribution of questions" they asked students about three levels of comprehension during content area lessons. Found that establishment of routines freed teachers to concentrate on higher levels of instruction.

966.   Fenigsohn, G. I. (1982). Examining the effects of three methods of study skill group intervention with middle school underachievers. (Doctoral dissertation, The College of William and Mary in Virginia, 1982) *Dissertation*

Abstracts International, 43, 2892A.

Thirty-six students were divided into four study groups based on different theories and techniques: (1) control group receiving no treatment, (2) Rational-Emotive Therapy group, (3) Structural-Study Skills, and (4) Affective Education. All groups except the control group showed significant improvement in study habits, but not in GPA. Between groups, no one group showed significant improvement over any other.

967.   Hester, J. P., & Hester, P. J. (1983). Brain research and middle school curriculum. *Middle School Journal, 15*(1), 4-7, 30.

Part I reviews the history of brain-laterality research and discusses instructional implications. Part II reviews brain growth periodization. Growth spurts appear to occur between 3-10 months, 2-4 years, 6-9 years, 10-12 years and 14-16 years. A table coordinates growth spurts with Piagetian stages. Suggestions for middle level instruction include determining cognitive style and level of each learner and gearing instruction to identified levels. Teaching beyond developmental levels may actually be detrimental for middle school students.

968.   Kain, D. L. (1995). Teaming with a purpose: Getting to the point of middle level teaming. *Inside Schools in the Middle, 4*(4), 6-9.

Provides an "advertising" activity for developing a shared sense of purpose among team members. Highlights a model of team purpose developed by the author.

969.   Nolan, T. E. (1991). Self-questioning and prediction: Combining metacognitive strategies. *Journal of Reading, 35*(2), 132-138.

Found that metacognitive strategies should be integrated into instruction for students at various ability levels and may be effective across both content and skills areas.

970.   Polite, M. (1994). Team negotiation and decision-making: Linking leadership to curricular and instructional innovation. *Research in Middle Level Education, 18*(1), 65-81.

Using a qualitative research methodology, the authors offer a look at the change process in curricular decision-making within core and encore teams in a middle school. The article offers a typology of leadership styles and comments on the impact of selected styles evident within the teams. Also includes a typology of how the teams made decisions.

971.   Ritter, S., & Idol-Maestas, L. (1986). Teaching middle school students to use a test-taking strategy. *The Journal of Educational Research, 79*(6), 350-357.

"A learning-strategies approach was used to teach 28 students how to take tests.

Ten of these students were among the poorest reading comprehenders in a social studies section of a middle school; the remaining 18 students were above-average comprehenders. Benefit of instruction was measured in terms of near and far generalization. For a near-generalization measure, three pretest and posttest social studies mini-tests were administered to the experimental and control groups; the test format was tightly controlled. A second set of pretest and posttest measures, used as the far-generalization indicator, was also obtained; these were test scores from the students' science class. The far-generalization measure was typical of tests administered in the classroom.

The experimental students, including the poor comprehenders, used test-taking strategies on both near- and far-generalization measures significantly better than control students. Average and good comprehenders in the experimental group showed significant improvement on near- but not far-generalization. Overall, these results provide empirical support for teaching heterogeneous groups to use a learning-strategies approach."

972.   Sadowski, C. J., & Woodward, H. R. (1983). Teacher locus of control and classroom climate: A cross-lagged correlational study. *Psychology in the Schools, 20*(4), 506-509.

Teacher scores on the Locus of Control Scale for Teachers were compared with student scores on the Origin-Climate Questionnaire. Results indicate that teachers' locus of control have a "moderate causal impact on students' perceptions of classroom climates." Students thought that teachers with an internal locus of control (those who believed their own actions controlled learning conditions in the classroom) designed more motivating learning activities.

973.   Smith, J. A. (1992). Effective middle school teaching: Factors that promote and maintain it (Doctoral dissertation, Portland State University, 1992). *Dissertation Abstracts International, 53*, 3768A.

Identified factors included: teacher sense of commitment to early adolescents and belief he/she plays a crucial role in student lives, ability to maintain a balance between academic and affective concerns, competency in using multiple teaching strategies, pro-active and attentive principals, compatible and committed team membership, support for the "advisory" concept and ability to build student trust, participation in staff-development planning and decisions, thorough understanding of early adolescent characteristics, extensive experiences with early adolescents pre-professionally and in student teaching.

974.   Stofflett, R. T., & Baker, D. R. (1992). The effects of training in combinatorial reasoning and propositional logic on formal reasoning ability in junior high school students. *Research in Middle Level Education, 16*(1), 159-177.

"This study sought to determine three things: Can combinatorial and propositional reasoning be taught to junior high school students? Does moving from the familiar to nonfamiliar facilitate nonspecific transfer? Does gender influence the learning of reasoning skills? Subjects were concrete operational reasoners at pretest. With 20 ten minute instructional episodes, students were able to learn and use combinatorial reasoning and propositional logic, with specific transfer only. There were no significant effects for gender. Students who had received the treatments experienced less frustration and better achievement in their science classes as compared to their nontreatment counterparts. The results suggested that reasoning instruction can be effective and should be included in junior high school science through the use of daily problems."

975.   Strahan, D. B. (1979). Competencies for middle school teaching: A review of empirical studies of teacher effects. *Middle school research: Selected studies 1977-1979 . Volume I* (pp. 1-8). Fairborn, OH: National Middle School Association.

Strahan reviewed the literature on teacher effects and found eighteen different clusters of teaching behaviors that reportedly had proven significant in experimental studies involving students of middle school age. The clusters were broken down into three categories: personal characteristics (e.g., has a positive self concept, demonstrates "warmth," is optimistic, is enthusiastic, demonstrates flexibility, demonstrates spontaneity); understanding adolescent needs (e.g., demonstrates acceptance of students, demonstrates awareness of developmental levels); and, instructional skills (e.g., demonstrates knowledge of subject matter, uses a variety of instructional strategies, monitors learning, uses concrete materials and focuses on learning strategies).

976.   Strahan, D. B. (1986). Guided thinking: A research-based approach to effective middle grades instruction. *The Clearing House, 60* (4), 149-155.

A comprehensive analysis of research findings related to reasoning development and critical thinking skills of young adolescents. Includes suggestions for instruction in these areas.

977.   Swank, P. R., Taylor, R. D., Brady, M., & Freiberg, H. J. (1989). Sensitivity of classroom observation systems: Measuring teacher effectiveness. *Journal of Experimental Education, 57* (2), 171-186.

Reports the results of a study designed to examine effective strategies for determining the effectiveness of middle level teachers. Involving 43 middle school teachers, the study compared teacher-to-group (macro) and teacher-to-student (micro) measures of teaching effectiveness. Concluded that teacher-to-group measures accurately identified more effective teachers, while teacher-to-student measures were more accurate in identifying less effective teachers.

978.   Tompkins, R. S., & Divine, J. H. (1992). Using a matrix technique to help middle level students develop thinking skills. *Research in Middle Level Education, 16*(1), 131-141.

"The authors of this study evaluated the effectiveness of training practicum teachers to give direct instruction to middle level students in the use of a matrix technique to develop the thinking skills of comparing and contrasting. Both the delivery of instruction by the practicum teachers after training and the performance of their middle school students in forming comparisons and contrasts after instruction were evaluated and analyzed. Practicum teachers were able to deliver instruction effectively in the matrix technique to their middle level students.

Analysis of covariance indicated that the matrix technique did produce a significant effect upon the ability of the middle level students in the treatment group to use those thinking skills effectively. Comparison of the ratings of the teachers' delivery of instruction and their students adjusted mean scores indicated the effectiveness of teacher modeling of thinking skills process for middle level students."

979.　　Whitley, T. (1979). The effects of individualized instruction on the attitudes of middle school pupils. *The Journal of Educational Research*, 72(4), 188-193.

"This study examined the effects of a locally developed program of individualized instruction on the attitudes of middle school students toward teachers, learning processes, language arts, and arithmetic/mathematics. Instruments designed to assess these four attitudes were administered to a treatment group and a comparison group of fifth, sixth, and seventh grade pupils at the beginning and end of the school year in which the pupils in the treatment group were exposed to a program of individualized instruction in language arts and mathematics. Analyses revealed that exposure to individualized instruction had a favorable impact on pupil attitudes at each of the three grade levels studied."

F. INSTRUCTION - PRACTICAL

980.　　Beale, A. V. (1982). Getting the most from classroom discussions. *Middle School Journal*, 14(1), 16-19.

Discussions can be divided into two categories: content-centered and student-centered. Necessary conditions for group discussions include a proper setting and a facilitative teacher. Suggestions are given for improving skills as a discussion leader: clarifying, reflecting feelings, and improving questioning skills. Provides answers to commonly asked questions about holding discussions.

981.　　Bell, L. C. (1983). Learning centers in the classroom. *Middle School Journal*, 14(2), 17-19.

Students work individually or in small groups in special places in the classroom that contain materials and activities to expand learning. Scheduling, center design, record keeping, room environment, and parental contacts are discussed.

982.　　Canter, L. (1993). *Teaching responsible homework habits*. Santa Monica, CA: Lee Canter & Associates. 64 pp.

Interactive lessons give students guidelines, tips, hints and cues to help them set up a study area, create a homework survival kit, schedule daily homework time, remember to bring homework back to school, and plan long-range assignments. Parent Tip Sheets keep parents involved and informed. Available for grades 1-3, 4-6, and 6-8.

983.   Comber, G., Zeiderman, H., & Maistrellis, N. (1989). The Touchstones Project: Discussion classes for students of all abilities. *Educational Leadership, 46*(6), 39-42.

Recommends instruction in discussion be provided to all levels of students. Explains origin of the concept and offers a model for implementing a program to encourage all students to begin to listen to and speak to each other.

984.   Connors, N. A. (1991). *Homework: A new direction.* Columbus, OH: National Middle School Association. 92 pp.

Based on insights from students and responses from a national survey of teachers and administrators, Connors provides educators with a set of guidelines for developing both system-wide and school-based homework programs. In doing so, she provides practical suggestions vis-à-vis implemention within current programs and also offers ways in regard to how teachers can develop innovative homework assignments (all of which take into account the developmental characteristics of young adolescents).

985.   Dougherty, A. M. (1983). Study skills in the middle school. *Middle School Journal, 14*(4), 26-27, 31.

Presents a study skills unit adapted from Study Orientation Skills by Florey & Scroggins, 1978. Uses a group guidance format, fosters active student involvement through group interaction and personalization. Covers primary motivators, realistic goal setting, time management, listening and taking notes, effective reading of textbooks, concentration skills, and preparing for and taking exams.

986.   Ewing, J. (1985). Are you a caring teacher? *Middle School Journal, 16*(4), 30.

Self-evaluation instrument designed to assist middle level teachers in evaluating themselves in terms of characteristics of excellent middle grades teachers.

987.   Far West Laboratory for Educational Research and Development. (1992). *Toward a community of learners: A regional newsletter on authentic instruction for the middle grades*, Volume II. San Francisco: Author.

Through their discussion of social action projects, the authors delineate how teachers can implement authentic curriculum and instruction across the curriculum.

988.   Far West Laboratory for Educational Research and Development. (1993). *Toward a community of learners: A regional newsletter on authentic instruction for the middle grades*, Volume III. San Francisco: Author.

A succinct but outstanding discussion of classroom discussions, including characteristics of high-quality instructional discourse, asking the right questions, questioning procedures, and teaching with cases. Exemplary examples of each are briefly presented.

989.   Farnan, M., & Kelly, P. R. (1993). Response-based instruction at the middle level: When student engagement is the goal. *Middle School Journal*, 25(1), 46-49.

Discusses response-based instruction as a way of encouraging middle level students "to discuss and analyze issues, to express and receive opinions, and to think critically and see relationships among ideas." Includes three underlying principles that emphasize the importance of response-based instruction in engaging middle level students in the learning process.

990.   *Focus on the children: Middle school resource guide.* (1994). Available from Howard Hardin, 3332 Newburg Road, P. O. Box 34020, Louisville, KY 40232-4020.

Materials for middle level settings compiled by classroom teachers.

991.   Freedman, R. L. H. (1994). *Open-ended questioning.* Redding, MA: Addison-Wesley. 82 pp.

Provides a method for writing and using open-ended questions and for assessing student responses.

992.   Gardner, H. (1983). *Frames of mind: The theory of multiple intelligences*. New York: Basic Books. 440 pp.

A fascinating and increasingly influential book, Gardner provides a detailed discussion of the concept of multiple intelligences (including, but not limited to, body-kinesthetic intelligence, musical intelligence, personal intelligence, spatial intelligence) and provides insights into how and why educators need to take into consideration, appreciate, and nurture these various intelligences in different individuals.

993.   Grennon, J. (1984). Making sense of student thinking. *Educational Leadership, 42*(3), 11-16.

Uses a lesson in graphing to illustrate the complexity of applying developmental theory to classroom practice.

994.   Irvin, J. L. (1992). Developmentally appropriate instruction: The heart of the middle school. In Judith L. Irvin (Ed.), *Transforming middle level*

education: Perspectives and possibilities (pp. 295-313). Needham Heights, MA: Allyn and Bacon.

Includes a brief discussion of relevant research and provides numerous practical ideas. Among the issues discussed are developmentally appropriate instructional methods for middle level students, enhanced instruction with middle school organization, and components of a successful middle level instructional program.

995.   Jackson, R. M. (1986). Thumbs up for direct teaching of thinking skills. *Educational Leadership, 43*(8), pp. 32-36.

Presents a model with examples for developing lessons for directly teaching specific thinking skills.

996.   Joyce, B., Weil, M., & Showers, B. (1992). *Models of teaching (4th Edition)*. Needham Heights, MA: Allyn and Bacon. 492 pp.

A classic in the field. This outstanding book not only provides a detailed overview of different types of teaching strategies, but also includes a scenario of how each can be used, discusses the theoretical underpinnings of each strategy, and outlines methods for implementing the strategy. Among the strategies highlighted in this book are the following: cooperative learning, role playing, the jurisprudential inquiry model, concept formation, concept attainment, memorization, advance organizers, inquiry, synectics, mastery learning, and simulations. It concludes with useful chapters on learning styles and models of teaching and peer coaching guides.

997.   Kieran, E. (1992). *Imagination in teaching and learning: The middle school years*. Chicago: University of Chicago Press. 283 pp.

"Award-winning scholar Kieran Egan explains the imaginative life of the typical eight- to fifteen-year-old and offers practical advice on how it can be engaged in learning. Contains a wealth of concrete examples of curriculum design and teaching techniques structured to appeal specifically to children in their middle school years." [From an announcement of the book.]

998.   Kratzner, R., & Mannies, N. (1973). Individualized learning for middle school pupils. *The Clearing House, 47*(5), 280-283.

Discusses an individualized program for middle level students in Burris Laboratory School in Muncie, Indiana. Focuses upon students' need for meaningful interaction with one another.

999.   Mitman, A., & Lambert, V. (1992). *Instructional challenge: A casebook for middle grade educators*. San Francisco and Irvine, California: Far West Laboratory for Educational Research ad Development, and California League of Middle Schools. 134 pp.

This book presents cases of classroom instruction, all of which are based on classroom observations and interviews with principal and key teachers at seventeen California middle schools. The cases provide an examination of four areas of curriculum and instruction: heterogeneous grouping, cooperative learning, active learning, and interdisciplinary instruction. A well written and highly useful book.

1000. Nielsen, L. (1983). Teaching adolescents self-management. *The Clearing House*, *57*(2), 76-81.

Discusses the importance of teaching self-management skills to young adolescents. Includes practical suggestions for assisting students in developing and maintaining those skills.

1001. Raforth, M. A., & Leal, L. (1993). Improving the study skills of middle school students. *Middle School Journal*, *25*(1), 51-54.

Discusses the need for middle level students to improve their study skills by learning more about memory processes. Includes examples of numerous strategies that assist middle level students in remembering key concepts. Included in the discussion are mnemonics, active listening and notetaking, and self-testing.

1002. Reinhartz, J., & Beach, D. M. (1983). *Improving middle school instruction: A research-based self-assessment system*. Washington, DC: National Educational Association. 64 pp.

This booklet presents a system of case studies and instruments for the purpose of assisting middle level teachers to improve their teaching. The case studies present information on the middle school environment, the student, the teacher, the instructional process, and the results of using such a self-assessment.

1003. Ridge, A. A. (1982). The force: Middle school style. *The Clearing House*, *55*(7), 293-296.

Describes a collaborative tutorial program in Howard County, Maryland, involving senior adults and middle level students. Concludes that the students have experienced significant cognitive and affective growth as a result of the tutoring and companionship of the adults.

1004. Schilling, F. C. (1984). Teaching study skills in the intermediate grades—we can do more. *Journal of Reading*, *27*(7), 620-623.

Not reading problems, but lack of study skills may be causing low test scores in content-area classes. Offers suggestions for teaching the following study skills: thinking, organization of time, difference between studying and reading, note taking, outlining, and preparing for and taking tests.

1005. Schurr, S. L. (1995). *Prescriptions for success in heterogeneous classrooms*. Columbus, OH: National Middle School Association. 208 pages.

Offers suggestions for how to meet the needs of diverse students in the same classroom.

1006.   Seif, E. (1993). Integrating skill development across the curriculum. *Schools in the Middle*, 2 (4), 15-19.

Discusses the Integrated Skill Development (ISD) project implemented in Pennsylvania. The ISD project emphasizes basic skills instruction across content areas and grade levels. Stresses the need for middle level students to learn comprehension, writing, interpretation, learning to learn, thinking, and conflict resolution skills through a clearly articulated and integrated program.

1007.   Shockley, R. (1986). Honed from the effective school research...A few instructional practices you can trust. *Middle School Journal, 17*(4), 18-20.

Discusses the appropriate application of several instructional strategies. Time on task, classroom disruptions, and accommodation of developmental levels are examined. Active student involvement is encouraged over passive, non-interactive activities.

1008.   Stevenson, C. (1986). *Teachers as inquirers: Strategies for learning with and about early adolescents*. Columbus, OH: National Middle School Association. 52 pp.

Provides theoretical foundations and background, detailed guidelines, and numerous examples of teacher and student inquiries. Emphasis is upon student-centered learning.

1009.   Strahan, D. B. (1986). Guided thinking: A strategy for encouraging excellence at the middle level. *NASSP Bulletin: The Journal for High School and Middle School Administrators*, 70 (487), 75-80.

Strahan discusses a strategy that he says is capable of moving students from passive to active and also of assisting young adolescents to develop more sophisticated thinking and reasoning skills. In doing so, he provides the "essential elements for guided thinking" as well as ideas on how to implement a guided thinking approach.

1010.   Theobald, M. A. (1995). What students say about common teaching practices. *Middle School Journal, 26*(4), pp. 18-22.

Seventh graders were asked to rate, then explain the reasons for their ratings, each of seven basic instructional strategies: Games and Simulations, Media, Discussion, Skill Practice, Problem Solving, Questioning, and Lectures. Most students (60.6%) "really liked" Games and Simulations compared to 2.6% who "really liked" lectures. Students also offered suggestions to teachers for improving each strategy.

1011.   Tomlinson, C. A. (1993). Independent study: A flexible tool for encouraging academic and personal growth. *Middle School Journal*, 25 (1), 55-59.

Characterizes independent study projects as a "ready-made" strategy for encouraging independence and enhancing self-esteem of middle level students. Includes a chart that traces the progression from basic skills of independence to self-guided learning. Discusses appropriate uses of independent study for middle level classrooms and offers suggestions for successfully implementating independent study projects.

1012.   Tompkins, R. S., & Divine, J. H. (1992). Using a matrix technique to help middle level students develop thinking skills. *Research in Middle Level Education*, *16*(1), 131-141.

"The authors of this study evaluated the effectiveness of training practicum teachers to give direct instruction to middle level students in the use of a matrix technique to develop the thinking skills of comparing and contrasting. Both the delivery of instruction by the practicum teachers after training and the performance of their middle school students in forming comparisons and contrasts after instruction were evaluated and analyzed. Practicum teachers were able to deliver instruction effectively in the matrix technique to their middle level students. Analysis of covariance indicated that the matrix technique did produce a significant effect upon the ability of the middle level students in the treatment group to use those thinking skills effectively. Comparison of the ratings of the teachers' delivery of instruction and their students adjusted mean scores indicated the effectiveness of teacher modeling of thinking skills process for middle level students."

1013.   Vaupel, C. F., Jr., & Cobbs, C. R. (1983). A scholarship/conduct recognition plan for the middle schools. *The Clearing House*, *57*(3), 114-115.

Emphasizes the need for middle level students to receive acknowledgments and rewards for their accomplishment. Presents examples of successful programs implemented in Arkansas middle schools.

G. INSTRUCTION - GENERAL

1014.   Arth, A. A. (1984). Selecting appropriate instructional strategies. In John H. Lounsbury (Ed.), *Perspectives: Middle school education* (pp. 79-86). Columbus, OH: National Middle School Association.

Discusses the following concerns manipulating the time factor, the social factor, the mental factor, and the learning modality factor.

1015.   Blosser, P. E. (1991). *How to ask the right questions*. Washington, D.C.: National Science Teachers Association.

A sixteen-page booklet which will help middle level teachers (for all grade levels) analyze their questioning techniques, classify their questions, and improve their questioning behavior. The author discusses how to ask the most appropriate questions which will assist the students in developing the skills they need to learn for themselves.

1016.   Bosch, K. A., & Kersey, K. (1993). Teaching problem-solving strategies. *The Clearing House, 66*(4), 228-230.

Stresses the need for middle level students to learn problem solving behaviors. Includes examples of two lessons with an emphasis upon problem solving skills.

1017.   Bybee, R., & Sund, R. B. (1982). *Piaget for educators.* Columbus, OH: Charles E. Merrill.

Especially written for educators, the authors present a sound overview of Piaget's theories of cognitive development.

1018.   Derrico, P. J. (1988). Learning to think with philosophy for children. *Educational Leadership, 45*(7), 34.

Teachers and students use reasoning strategies to contemplate perennial questions and improve critical thinking skills.

1019.   Dungey, J. M. (1989). *Interactive bulletin boards as teaching tools.* Washington, DC: National Education Association. 80 pp.

Offers a new concept in bulletin boards. Shows teachers how to use bulletin boards (created by students as hands-on learning) to serve as outlines for class discussions, provide active learning tools, and enhance teaching by involving students in meaningful, critical thinking activities.

1020.   Hawthorne, R. K. (1986). The professional teacher's dilemma: Balancing autonomy and obligation. *Educational Leadership, 44*(2), 34-35.

Uses a case-study approach to explain curricular choices facing a teacher. Personal values and experience were deemed most important in selection of content, texts, methods, activities, and evaluation.

1021.   Ollmann, H. E. (1992). Team teaching with a student teacher. *Journal of Reading, 35*(8), 656-657.

Experiences of a veteran middle school reading and writing teacher as she works with her first student teacher. Found that team teaching and modeling teaching points and strategies worked effectively.

1022.   Sklarz, D. P. (1984). Making a good one into a great one. *Principal, 64*(1), 38-40.

Briefly lists and explains several student-centered programs for improving middle school education: rewards for success, working toward positive behavior, welcome wagon for kids, license to learn, homework hot line, USSR (*u*ninterrupted *s*ustained *s*ilent *r*eading) means reading, and flip-flop your schedule.

1023.   Worsham, A. (1988). A "grow as you go" thinking skills model. *Educational Leadership, 45*(7), 56-57.

Teachers replace traditional instruction with the student-centered Inclusion Process, a process model for teaching thinking in all content areas.

H. CRITICAL THINKING

1024.   Bellanca, J. (1990). *Cooperative think tank II: Graphic organizers to teach thinking in the cooperative classroom.* Palantine, II.: IRI/Skylight Publishing, Inc. 96 pp.

Teachers will increase students' critical and creative thinking by having them use twelve versatile graphic organizers.

1025.   Bellanca, J. (1992). *Cooperative think tank: Graphic organizers to teach thinking in the cooperative classroom.* Palantine, IL: IRI/Skylight Publishing, Inc. 144 pp.

The *Cooperative Think Tank* books are collections of powerful techniques to increase student achievement. They feature complete cooperative lessons for immediate use and focus on the most versatile graphic organizers—including the ranking ladder, the Venn diagram, the spectrum, and the web. Designed with all the elements of effective instruction, each lesson includes specific review and transfer activities that reinforce students' use of the skills in other subjects.

1026.   Bellanca, J. (1993). *Catch them thinking: A handbook of classroom strategies.* Palantine, IL: IRI/Skylight Publishing, Inc. 304 pp.

"If you could buy only one book on teaching thinking, this is the one you want." Offering fifty easily adaptable strategies, including model lessons demonstrating cooperative learning strategies to promote thinking, this practical resource meets the classroom needs of novices as well as experts in the teaching of thinking.

1027.   Brown, L. (1990). *Think book—Reproducible problem solving activities.* Tampa, FL: National Resource Center for Middle Grades/High School Education. 240 pp.

A comprehensive collection of visually-oriented thinking skills activities. Critical and creative problem-solving activities promote active thinking from basic visual discrimination and grouping to the logical thinking patterns of inductive and deductive reasoning. Each group of activities has clearly-stated objectives and a process/skills chart for easy implementation.

1028.   Fogarty, R. (1986). *Teach them thinking—Mental menus for 24 thinking skills*. Palantine, IL: IRI/Skylight Publishing, Inc. 128 pp.

An inventory of 24 essential thinking skills to help students become effective analyzers, evaluators, and synthesizers of facts and information. Focuses on thinking skills and cooperative group lessons that use prediction, inference, and classification to teach thinking skills.

1029.   Forte, I. (1981). *Think about it!—Activities for teaching basic thinking skills*. Tampa, FL: National Resource Center for Middle Grades/High School Education. 86 pp.

Reproducible pages in this resource were designed to develop listening, questioning, brainstorming, interpreting, predicting, and estimating thinking skills.
        Features activities for "on-your-own" participation experiences, each designed to develop at least one reasoning skill and to generate excitement for additional creative thinking.

1030.   Heiman, M., & Slomianki, J. (1986). *Critical thinking skills*. Washington, DC: National Education Association. 48 pp.

Filled with exercises and activities for use in developing critical thinking skills in students. Includes a variety of approaches from which teachers can select the most appropriate methods.

1031.   Matthews, D. B. (1989). The effect of a thinking-skills program on the cognitive abilities of middle school students. *The Clearing House*, *62* (5), 202-204.

Reports the results of a study designed to test the effects of a course in critical thinking upon students' cognitive abilities. Concludes that such a course can significantly raise intelligence levels.

I. PROBLEM SOLVING

1032.   Broda, H. W., & Burkholder, B. (1987). Problem solving in action. *Middle School Journal*, *18*(4), 26-28.

Discusses "initiative tasks," which basically constitute a variety of activities designed to help students develop group problem solving skills. All activities can be done on school grounds with a minimum of equipment. Explains use and appropriateness.

1033.   Brown, J. L. (1983). On teaching thinking skills in the elementary and middle school. *Phi Delta Kappan*, *64*(10), 709-714.

Describes ThinkAbout, a problem-solving approach to teaching students to think. Uses sixty 15-minute televisions programs as a basis for the program. Resource list provided.

1034.   Neal, P. (1994). *Problem-solving: A heterogeneous approach for integrating middle school math activities*. Columbus, OH: National Middle School Association. 62 pages.

Offers ideas for how to move math into an integrated format.

J. COOPERATIVE LEARNING - RESEARCH

1035.   Phelps, J. D. (1991). A study of the interrelationships between cooperative team learning, learning preference, friendship patterns, gender, and achievement of middle school students (Doctoral dissertation, Indiana University, 1990). *Dissertation Abstracts International*, *52*, 1633A.

The study involved 107 eighth grade students in four intact social studies classrooms. Jigsaw II, a cooperative team learning strategy, was used for nine weeks in two of the classrooms. Non-cooperative learning techniques were used in the other two classrooms. Identical subject matter was covered in all of the classrooms. Results revealed no significant difference in achievement gains between the students in the cooperative and non-cooperative classrooms. However, interview data, learning preference data, and friendship data indicated that cooperative team learning techniques may be more appropriate instructional strategies than non-cooperative methods for middle level students.

1036.   Wheeler, R. (1986). Effects of classroom goal structure on cooperative and competitive predisposition: Transescent students' attitudes and achievement in problem solving. In David B. Strahan (Ed.), *Middle school research: Selected studies 1986* (pp. 42-55). Columbus, OH: Research Committee of the National Middle School Association.

In this study, "forty fifth-grade and sixth-grade students identified as either cooperative predisposition or competitive predisposition were randomly assigned to either cooperative or competitive goal structure classroom treatments. The two groups were exposed to the same problem solving content for 10 days and worked on problems in small interdependent learning groups (cooperative goal structure) or individually (competitive goal structure). As hypothesized, it was found that competitive goal structure had a greater negative effect on cooperative-predisposition subjects' attitudes and achievement than on competitive-predisposition subjects. The implications for the utilization of cooperative and competitive goal structures in the middle school classroom are discussed."

1037.   Williams, D. R., Meyer, L. H., & Harootunian, B. (1992). Introduction and implementation of cooperative learning in the heterogeneous classroom: Middle school teachers' perspectives. *Research in Middle Level Education*, *16*(1), 115-130.

"This qualitative study identifies and describes six middle school teachers' perspectives on the introduction and implementation of cooperative learning instructional adaptations in their classrooms. The teacher voices provide insight into the evolution of cooperative behavior among young adolescents, strategies that teachers used to encourage students to support one another, and the kinds of activities that facilitated the attainment of both academic and social goals to meet young adolescent needs."

K. COOPERATIVE LEARNING - PRACTICAL

1038.   Bellanca, J. (1991). *Blueprints for thinking in the cooperative classroom.* Palantine, IL: IRI/Skylight Publishing, Inc. 368 pp.

To effectively apply cooperative learning, teachers must learn to handle issues that do not come up in traditional classrooms, such as "How do I build teams and trust?" "How do I get my students to think in groups?" Designed for cooperative learning beginners as well as experienced practitioners, *Blueprints* helps teachers know exactly what to do in their classrooms and when to do it.

1039.   Bellanca, J. (1991). *Building a caring, cooperative classroom: Integrating social skills through language curriculum.* Palantine, IL: IRI/Skylight Publishing, Inc. 128 pp.

Contains thirty easy-to-follow lessons to help students learn critical social skills. Sections include "Friendship," "Responsibility," "Working Together," "Problem Solving," and "Conflict Resolution," with valuable, ready-to-use visuals and worksheets.

1040.   Bellanca, J. (1993). *Blueprints for thinking: Team study guide.* IRI/Skylight Publishing, Inc. 160 pp.

Helps teachers learn to use cooperative learning in non-traditional classrooms. Designed for beginners as well as experienced practitioners.

1041.   Bourman, A. (1989) *61 cooperative learning activities: Thinking, writing, and speaking skills.* San Antonio, TX: ECS Learning Systems. 137 pp.

Group activities use a whole language approach through combined thinking, writing, reading, listening, research, or speaking skills. Clear, thorough guidance helps foster cooperative attitudes.

1042.   Breeden, T. (1992). *Cooperative learning companion: Ideas, activities & aids for middle grades.* San Antonio, TX: ECS Learning Systems. 96 pp.

A collection of teaching aids, bulletin board ideas, reproducible forms and guides, quick and easy lesson ideas, and techniques for teaching cooperative skills. A practical, helpful, teacher-friendly guide.

1043.   Breeden, T. (1992). *Middle grade teacher's handbook for cooperative learning.* San Antonio, TX: ECS Learning Systems. 160 pp.

A comprehensive handbook answers vital questions about cooperative learning.

The "how to" section is simply written and well-organized. The second section is filled with cooperative learning units using high-interest, real-life themes.

1044. Casion, M., Duquin, R., & Morgan, J. (1993). Student teaching cooperatively. *In Transition*, 24-25.

Applies the principles of cooperative learning to supervision of student teachers. Discusses the following activities designed to assist and support student teachers: (1) student teacher planning sessions, (2) cooperating teacher seminars, (3) weekly meetings with student and cooperating teacher, and (4) whole-day observations. Includes practical, useful suggestions for working with student teachers. Although the article targets student teachers in the middle level grades, the activities can be used in any grade level.

1045. Holt, L. (1993). *Cooperative learning in action*. Columbus, OH: National Middle School Association.

Discusses the what, why, and how of cooperative learning. Includes 53 lesson plans for use within major content areas, including mathematics, art, music, reading/language arts, science, and social studies.

1046. Rottier, J., & Ogan, B. J. (1991). *Cooperative learning in middle level school*. Washington, DC: National Education Association. 112 pp.

Helps middle level teachers center on the successful implementation of cooperative learning techniques and the teaching of social skills.

1047. Schniedewind, N., & Salend, S. J. (1987). Cooperative learning works. *Teaching Exceptional Children*, *19*, 22-25.

"This article presents special educators with practical guidelines for designing and implementing cooperative learning strategies in their classroom, along with examples of how these guidelines are used by teachers in mainstreamed, resource rooms, and self contained settings." Topics discussed are selecting a cooperative learning format, establishing guidelines for cooperative activities, forming cooperative groups, arranging the classroom, developing cooperative skills, and confronting problems.

1048. Slavin, R. E. (1990). *Cooperative learning: Theory, research, and practice*. Englewood Cliffs, NJ: Prentice Hall. 173 pp.

An outstanding handbook for elementary, middle school and secondary school teachers, it includes up-to-date research findings, a host of practical ideas (including step-by-step advice for implementing various cooperative learning strategies), and resources (including sample worksheets, quizzes, and award certificates). The most unique and valuable components of the book are the sections entitled "Teachers on Teaching," where practicing teachers comment on their experiences vis-à-vis various aspects of cooperative learning. The seven chapters are entitled as follows: An Introduction to Cooperative Learning,

Cooperative Learning and Student Achievement, Cooperative Learning and Outcomes Other Than Achievement, STAD and TGT, TAI and CIRC, Task Specialization Methods, and Other Cooperative Learning Methods and Resources. It also includes a lengthy bibliography.

L. COOPERATIVE LEARNING - GENERAL

1049.   Bosch, K. A. (1991). Cooperative learning: Instruction and procedures to assist middle school teachers. *Middle School Journal, 22*(3), 34-35.

Presents some helpful step-by-step "housekeeping" procedures to follow in order to make the use of cooperative learning a more successful strategy.

1050.   Brandt, R. (Ed.). (1989/1990). Educational leadership: Cooperative learning [Special Issue]. *Educational Leadership, 47*(4), 3-66.

Contains informative articles by researchers (e.g., Roger and David Johnson, Spencer Kagan, Shlomo and Yael Sharan, Robert Slavin, etc.) as well as elementary and secondary school teachers on such topics as group investigation, successful methods for incorporating social skills into cooperative learning lesson, the latest research on various facets of cooperative learning, a model staff development program for implementing cooperative learning into a district's schools, and a lengthy annotated bibliography.

1051.   Clarke, J., Wideman, R., & Eadie, S. (1990). *Together we learn*. Scarborough, Ontario, Canada: Prentice-Hall Canada, Inc. 216 pp.

Developed by a team of Canadian educators, this volume is designed as a "practical 'how-to' handbook to help teachers implement cooperative learning strategies in all subject areas and at all grade levels across [Canada]." It addresses a host of interesting and valuable topics, including but not limited to designing beginning group activities, incorporating five kinds of groups (informal, base, combined, reconstituted, representative), teaching cooperative skills, and evaluating group work.

1052.   Davidson, N. (Ed.). (1990). *Cooperative learning in mathematics: Handbook for teachers*. New York, NY: Addison-Wesley Publishing Co. 399 pp.

Major resource on cooperative learning in mathematics. Some of the many essays included in this book are: "The Math Solution: Using Groups of Four" by Marilyn Burns; "Student Team Learning and Mathematics" by Robert E. Slavin," "Using Cooperative Learning in Math" by David and Roger Johnson," "Cooperative Learning and Computers in the Elementary and Middle School Math Classroom" by Mary Male; and, "Implementing Group Work: Issues for Teachers and Administrators" by Laurel Robertson, Nancy Graves, and Patricia Tuck.

1053.   Gartin, B. C., & A. Digby. (1993). Staff development on cooperative learning strategies: Concerns and solutions. *Middle School Journal, 24*(3), 8-14.

Describes a fifteen-hour staff development training program on the use of cooperative learning strategies in the middle level classroom. Also discusses the results of subsequent implementation of cooperative learning strategies within the middle level classroom. Specifically discussed difficulties encountered by teachers in the implementation of cooperative learning strategies, tactics to overcome these difficulties, and benefits of using cooperative learning strategies.

1054.   Gartin, B. C., Digby, A. D., & Pedersen, J. E. (1994). Empowering teachers to empower transescent students through cooperative learning activities. *Current Issues in Middle Level Education, 3*(1), 103-111.

Reports the results of a study designed to answer the following questions: 1. Were cooperative learning practices encouraging student empowerment evident in the classroom? 2. Were cooperative learning best practice procedures used in the implementation of cooperative learning activities in the classroom? Results indicated that students should receive training in cooperative learning skills prior to participating in cooperative groups and that teacher preparation programs should emphasize pre-training activities designed to allow students the opportunity to develop skills necessary for developing and implementing cooperative learning activities.

1055.   Hannigan, M. R. (1989/1990). Cooperative learning in elementary science. *Educational Leadership, 47*(4), 25.

Discusses "Science for Life and Living: Integrating Science, Technology, and Health," a new science program for elementary students that emphasizes concrete experiences and one in which cooperative learning is a central strategy.

1056.   Harvard Educational Letter Staff. (1986). Cooperative learning. *The Harvard Educational Letter, 2*(5), 1-3.

Provides a solid overview of cooperative learning. In doing so, it addresses the following: "What Is Cooperative Learning?" "What Do Students Learn?" "Current Practice," and "In Practice: Cooperation in Colorado." Cites the work and research of Robert Slavin, Roger and David Johnson, and Nel Noddings.

1057.   Johnson, D.W., & Johnson, R. T. (1987). *Learning together & alone: Cooperative, competitive, & individualistic learning.* Englewood Cliffs, NJ: Prentice-Hall. 193 pp.

Discusses methods for systematically using cooperative, competitive, and individualistic learning in the classroom. Chapter one compares the use of the three types of instruction with an emphasis on developing interdependence among students. Chapter two discusses the importance of peer relationships, student interaction patterns, and instructional outcomes of cooperative, competitive, and individualistic learning. Chapters three, four and five explain the structure of each of the three types of learning. Additional chapters discuss "student acquisition of collaborative skills," ways to create positive interdependence, and group processing. Chapter nine is devoted exclusively to teacher concerns such as classroom management, high and low achievers, and cooperation among teachers. An epilogue stresses the importance of cooperative learning to the future of education.

1058.   Madden, N. A., Slavin, R. E., & Stevens, R. J. (1986). *Cooperative integrated reading and composition: Teachers' manual.* Baltimore, MD: Johns Hopkins University Center for Research on Elementary and Middle Schools.

Teacher's manual for a teaching strategy that uses a combination of mixed-ability cooperative groups and skill-based reading groups to teach reading, language arts, and writing in the upper elementary/middle grades.

1059.   Male, M., Johnson, R., Johnson, D., & Anderson, M. (1985). *Cooperative learning and computers: An activity guide for teachers.* Minneapolis, MN: Cooperative Learning Project. 171 pp.

Includes the following chapters: An Introduction to Cooperative Learning and Computers; Essential Ingredients of Cooperative Computer Lessons; General Design Principles for Three Cooperative Learning Strategies (Learning Together, Jigsaw, and Teams-Games-Tournaments; Software Description and Simplified Reference Cards; and Suggestions for Dividing Students into Teams. The appendices include a lesson plan guide, sample team recognition certificates, sample observation forms, and sample scoring systems.

1060.   National Middle School Association. (1993). Special Focus Section on "Cooperation in the Classroom." *Middle School Journal, 24*(3), 3-29.

Includes the following articles: "Cooperation in the Classroom," "Cooperative Learning: Passing Fad or Long-Term Promise?" "Staff Development on Cooperative Learning Strategies: Concerns and Solutions," "Improving Mathematics Evaluation Through Cooperative Learning Strategies" "Cooperative Literacy in the Middle School: An Example of a Learning-Strategy Based Approach" and "A Step Beyond Cooperative Learning."

1061.   Stahl, R. J., & Van Sickle, R. L. (Eds.). (1992). *Cooperative learning in the social studies classroom: An introduction to social study.* Washington, DC: National Council for the Social Studies. 62 pp.

This volume presents a detailed and solid view of why and how social studies educators can incorporate cooperative learning into their social studies program. Among the articles included in this booklet are "Cooperative Learning in the Social Studies: Balancing the *Social* and the *Studies*" by Robert Slavin; "Theory into Practice: A Cooperative Learning Success Story in Middle Level Classrooms" by Eric F. Luce, et al.; "Approaches to Implementing Cooperative Learning in the Social Studies Classroom" by David W. Johnson and Roger T. Johnson, and "Complex Instruction in the Untracked Social Studies Classroom" by Elizabeth G. Cohen, et al.

M. INTERDISCIPLINARY INSTRUCTION

1062.   Fogarty, R. (1991). *The mindful school: How to integrate the curricula.* Palantine, IL: IRI/Skylight Publishing, Inc. 128 pp.

A practical tool for educators interested in helping students see the connections between the things they learn. A handbook of strategies that bridge ideas for lessons and for learners. Ten models are presented, ranging from the traditional fragmented model to those that connect, sequence, nest, share, web, thread, integrate, network, and immerse teachers in curricular integration.

1063.   Fogarty, R. (1994). Thinking about themes: Hundreds of themes. *Middle School Journal, 25*(4), 30-31.

Uses the acronym T-H-E-M-E-S to demonstrate a process for brainstorming and selecting an appropriate theme for an interdisciplinary thematic unit.

1064.   Vars, G. F. (1993). *Interdisciplinary teaching in the middle grades: Why and how.* Columbus, OH: National Middle School Association.

Presents a rationale for interdisciplinary teaching and provides an overview of various organizational structures and issues. Also includes practical suggestions for planning, methods, and placement of skills development.

N. INTERDISCIPLINARY UNITS

1065.   Bannerman, K. (1993). Interdisciplinary what . . .? *In Transition*, pp. 31-32.

Presents an interdisciplinary unit entitled "Animals, Animals, Everywhere." Designed for use in a seventh-grade classroom, the unit integrates English, science, math, language, home and careers, art, and technology. Includes examples of activities in each of the content areas.

1066.   Brodsky, M. A. (1987). The Roaring Twenties—an interdisciplinary unit—or how to make use of that old raccoon coat in the attic. *Middle School Journal, 18*(4), 7-9.

Overview of an end-of-school interdisciplinary unit which involves an entire grade. One floor of the school is sealed off and transformed back in time. The intercom becomes radio station KDKA. Students participate in activities which include stock market demonstrations, character day (students dress up), portfolio of activities, Olympic Games, Bijou showings, Gazette newspaper, cabaret, Scopes Trial, and science fair, among others. Explanations are limited, but enough information is given to allow teachers to begin brainstorming their own units.

1067.   Bumstead, R. A. (1983). The bank that failed. *Principal, 63*(1), 40-42.

A successful learning experience was halted by state bank examiners for
violating banking laws. Students and school administrators then worked to
change the law and operate a legal bank.

1068.   Cason, N., & Belveal, A. (1991). The biomic connection: A middle
school interdisciplinary approach to the reading/writing connection. *The
Transescent, 16* (1), 35-42.

Discusses the philosophy and objectives of a middle level team at Hixon Middle
School in Webster, Missouri. Outlines an interdisciplinary unit on biomes.
Includes examples of student activities and evaluation forms.

1069.   Cooter, Jr., R. B., & Griffith, R. (1989). Thematic units for middle
school: An honorable seduction. *Journal of Reading, 32*(8), 676-681.

Includes a brief history of thematic units and an explanation of the
Dublin Model emphasizing reading skills as implemented in a middle
school setting.

1070.   DC Heath Publishers. (1995). I-witness interdisciplinary
investigations. (Available from author at 1-800-235-3565).

Topics addressed in units include the human body, World War II, other cultures,
environment and business.

1071.   DeAnda, L. L. (1991). Newspapers in the special education classroom:
An interdisciplinary unit. *The Transescent, 16* (2), 9-10.

Presents suggestions for using newspapers in special education classrooms.
Includes a sample unit with activities in mathematics, social studies, English,
science, and reading.

1072.   Dunham, D. (1995). Mini-courses: Promoting interdisciplinary
relationships, creative expression, and social skill development. *Inside Schools
in the Middle, 4*(4), 20-22.

Describes a mini-course on silver for middle level students that combines
concepts from chemistry, geology, geography, history, language arts, creative
arts, and vocational/career education.

1073.   Forte, I. (1992). *Cooperative learning guide and planning pack for
middle grades thematic projects & activities.* San Antonio, TX: ECS Learning
Systems. 144 pp.

Contains complete thematic units and projects for the entire year. Contains a
bonus section with quick and easy cooperative activities and planning, record
keeping, and study guide worksheets.

1074.   Keogh, J. (1993). An interdisciplinary unit. *In Transition*, p. 30.

Describes a unit designed for seventh graders. Based upon the 1992 presidential elections, the unit includes activities in social studies, English, mathematics, science, foreign language, and art.

1075.   Kerekes, J. (1987). The interdisciplinary unit...it's here to stay! *Middle School Journal, 18*(4), 12-14.

Defines and explains interdisciplinary units (I.D.U.). Discusses the scheduling and development of an I.D.U. Lists guidelines to keep in mind when working on I.D.U.'s, including newsletters to parents, staff training, selection of topics of interest to students and staff, ways to keep costs down, common team planning and block scheduling, selection of a coordinator to oversee the entire unit, publicity for the I.D.U., and appropriate documentation.

1076.   Lasley, M. E. (1993). Dealing with a tough economy is made easy for Wantagh home and career skill students. *In Transition*, p. 15.

Presents a unit from a home and career skills class designed to assist middle level students in incorporating business skills and knowledge to everyday "real-life" experiences. Includes examples of activities that engage students in successful business practices.

1077.   Smith, F. M., & Hausafus, C. O. (1993). An academic/vocational curriculum partnership: Home economics and science. *Middle School Journal, 24* (5), 48-51.

Discusses an interdisciplinary unit designed to apply the theoretical concepts of science to practical life experiences of home economics. Includes an overview of the unit with sample questions, activities, and course content.

1078.   Stromberg, R. B., & Smith, J. M. (1987). The simulation technique—applied in an Ancient Egypt I.D.U. *Middle School Journal, 18*(4), 9-11.

The teacher acts as a facilitator in this student-centered and interactive model. For six weeks, a double classroom was transformed into a life-sized replica of the inside of the "Great Pyramid." Sixth grade students were assigned to write term papers on Ancient Egypt with an understanding of the interrelationships among the five major disciplines: social studies, math, English, science, reading. On Egyptian Day, students turned in their papers and wore carefully thought out costumes to class. Tours of the completed pyramid were given. Parents responded enthusiastically at Parent Night. The authors suggest that the success of the simulation technique at Galvin Middle School indicates that its use should be encouraged at the middle level.

1079.   Troisi, A. (1993). An interdisciplinary unit on Native American heritage. *In Transition*, pp. 20-21.

Outlines a seventh-grade unit that integrates concepts from social studies, language arts, art, science, technology, and library skills. The overall objective was to allow middle level students an opportunity to use content area reading skills to explore the Native American culture. Includes examples of activities from each of the content areas.

1080.   Vars, G. F. (1987). *Interdisciplinary teaching in the middle grades: Why and how.* Columbus, OH: National Middle School Association. 50 pp.

In addition to providing a concrete example of why and how one school went about developing and implementing an interdisciplinary exploration of a theme, Var provides a solid overview of the the the rationale for interdisciplinary teaching, various approaches, practical ideas on planning, methods, and the place of skill development. Concludes with a outline of key resources for teachers and schools that are interested in moving towards interdisciplinary teaching.

1081.   Zeferakis, M. L. (1993). Seventh graders send letters to principal using keyskills training. *In Transition*, p. 21.

Details an interdisciplinary unit that combines keyskills and communication skills. The final product is a letter to the principal in which the seventh-graders talk about their experiences and offer suggestions for improvement. The principal responds to each letter, thus assuring each student that his/her input is important.

O. PORTFOLIOS

1082.   Rief, L. (1990). Finding the value in evaluation: Self-assessment in a middle school classroom. *Educational Leadership, 47*(6), 24-29.

Classroom teacher explains her use of portfolios. Includes rationale, practical examples, and conditions for success.

1083.   Simmons, J. (1990). Adapting portfolios for large-scale use. *Educational Leadership, 47*(6), 28.

Brief explanation of a pilot program using portfolios as an alternative to holistically-scored, timed writing samples.

XIV

Educational Technology

A. EDUCATIONAL TECHNOLOGY - RESEARCH

1084.   Bosch, K. A. (1993). What are the "computer realities" in the class-rooms of the nineties." *Current Issues in Middle Level Education*, *2*(1), 9-15.

A sample of 66 preservice teachers was surveyed as to their perceptions of computer use in the middle school classrooms to which they were assigned for a 40-hour field experience. Based on the data collected, Bosch identifies five "realities" of computer use in today's schools (among them being "classroom teachers are physically and instructionally removed from computer technology, computers are not integrated into subject matter instruction, computers are not integrated into the purpose and activities of the classroom, and classroom teachers are not taking advantage of the computer's potential"). She concludes by urging teacher educators to acknowledge these "realities" in preparing preservice teachers.

1085.   Cavanna, A. P. (1990). Encouraging student computer use at the middle level. *NASSP Bulletin: The Journal for Middle Level and High School Administrators*, *74*(524), 99-104.

The purpose of this study was to answer the question "What are the administrative factors that facilitate the use of computers by students in schools?" The study included the analysis of six intermediate and junior high schools in an urban district. The article includes a description of the problem and procedures of the study, data analysis, and recommendations.

1086.   Chagas, I. (1993). Teachers as innovators: A case study of implementing the interactive videodisc in a middle school science program (Doctoral Dissertation, Boston University, 1993). *Dissertation Abstracts International*, *53*, 4268A.

Conclusions organized according to three themes: teachers as innovators, peer collaboration, and interactive videodisc in the science classroom. Discusses implementation problems, generalizability of the study's results, and recommendations for teacher training programs.

1087.   Edyburn, D. L. (1990). Examining the successful retrieval of information by students with and without learning handicaps using print and electronic databases. In Judith L. Irvin (Ed.), *Research in middle level education: Selected studies 1990* (pp. 23-38). Columbus, OH: National Middle School Association.

"This study investigated the natural information retrieval skills of thirteen learning handicapped students and fifteen nonlearning handicapped peers in grades 6-8 when using print and on-line electronic encyclopedias. Significant differences were found between the two groups' level of success on twelve retrieval tasks....No significant difference was found in retrieval success when students used electronic encyclopedias versus the print encyclopedia, students were more successful in retrieving information from the menu driven electronic encyclopedia than when using the command driven electronic encyclopedia." He also found that students were significantly more successful at simple retrieval tasks than complex ones and at assigned retrieval tasks than those that were self directed.

1088.   Freitag, P. K. (1991). Learning in the middle school earth science classroom: Students conceptually integrate new knowledge using intelligent laserdiscs (Doctoral dissertation, Boston University, 1991). *Dissertation Abstracts International, 52,* 790A.

Groups of students used a laser videodisc in conjunction with a computer to create interactive multimedia projects about "weather." Results indicate students stayed on task and effectively used laser videodisc technology to extend their learning.

1089.   Howard, C. (1987). Computers and the humanities: Project work in the middle school. *Educational Review, 39*(2), 127-136.

The author reports on a case study of a large middle school's response to using educational technology over a three-year period. The study focuses on the simulation program "Mary Rose," a shipwreck salvaging operation. The author also discusses the uses of computer simulations for instruction at the middle level, especially in history and geography.

1090.   Linn, M. C. (1985). The cognitive consequences of programming instruction in classrooms. *Educational Researcher, 14*(5), 14-16, 25-29.

Reports on a set of studies of middle school programming instruction conducted by the Assessing the Cognitive Consequences of Computer Environments for Learning project funded by the National Institute of Education. Examines both the effects of programming instruction and the relations between student characteristics and outcomes from such instruction. The study found that many students can solve computer programming problems and some may learn to generalize problem-solving skills from introductory programming courses.

Efforts need to be made to provide adequate equipment, improved curriculum, and well-trained computer teachers.

1091. McCarthy, I. D. (1988). The effect of technology on the teaching of writing in the middle school and its impact on achievement in reading and language arts (Doctoral dissertation, Boston University, 1988). *Dissertation Abstracts International, 49,* 1775A.

Results showed technology to have a positive effect on achievement of students in reading and language arts, but that the teacher and methodologies employed have a greater impact on performance than the tools used for instruction.

1092. Rocheleau, B. (1995). Computer use by school-age children: Trends, patterns, and predictors. *Journal of Educational Computing Research, 12*(1), 1-17.

Analyzed patterns of computer use based on data obtained from the Longitudinal Study of American Youth. Heavier use of computers is associated with high SES as well as higher grades. Use of computers declined from seventh grade to high school despite increasing access to computers at home. The gap between male and female use began to narrow in 1992. Computer ownership and parental interest in their children using computers exerted the biggest impacts on the possibility of being a heavier computer user.

1093. Steelman, J. D. (1994). Revision strategies employed by middle level students using computers. *Journal of Educational Computing Research, 11*(2), 141-152.

Used a pretest-posttest non-equivalent control group design with two experimental groups and one control group to study revision strategies used by middle level students in writing with computers. Study results indicated that the complexity of revision strategies applied by students may be expanded through explicit instruction and the use of the computer.

1094. Trimer-Hartley, M. (1995). Transforming technology in schools: New project pairs teachers with math & science mentors. *High Strides, 7*(3), 6-7.

Brief report of selected sites participating in the Transformations Project. "The goal is to foster long-term relationships...to develop lessons with exciting real-world applications of math, science and technology" (p. 6).

B. EDUCATIONAL TECHNOLOGY - PRACTICAL

1095. Bosch, K. A. (1993). Is there a computer crisis in the classroom? *Schools in the Middle*, 2 (4), 7-9.

Discusses the need for integration of technology, specifically computers, across the curriculum. Focuses upon the need for more efficient use of existing computers in classrooms as well as upon the need for preservice teachers to receive training in the appropriate selection and application of technology.

1096.   Dowd, C. A., & Sinatra, R. (1990). Computer programs and the learning of text structure. *Journal of Reading, 34*(2), 104-112.

Presents a variety of interactive software programs which encourage students to become better readers and writers. Helpful reading for teachers as they investigate programs suitable for the teaching of text structure to their students.

1097.   Hart, L. C. (1987). Implementing Logo in middle level classrooms. *The Clearing House*, *60*(6), 258-260.

Includes examples of five lesson plans designed to introduce the Logo language to young adolescents. Also includes practical advice on planning and implementing an effective computer language unit.

1098.   Hativa, N., & Meidav, M. (1991). Middle school science teachers' instructional support through simulation software. *Journal of Computers in Mathematics and Science Teaching, 10*(2), 49-58.

The authors describe the use of computer software, with and without guiding text, for a simulation that presents processes related to electric charges and electric forces underlying the electric-pendulum phenomenon. Included are methods for integrating this simulation with actual middle level science class demonstration.

1099.   Hunter, B., Bagley, C., & Bagley, R. (1993). Technology in the classroom. *Schools in the Middle*, *2* (4), 3-6.

Discusses the need for middle level students to be familiar with today's technology. Presents examples of activities that encourage students to utilize technology. Also discusses the role of electronic portfolio assessment.

1100.   Maley, D. (1993). Technology education: A natural for middle level students. *Schools in the Middle*, *2* (4), 10-14.

Outlines a unit that explores the evolution of technology by involving students in a variety of activities, including problem solving, writing, evaluating, and researching. Based upon the premise that students can become familiar with modern technology by learning about the technology of the past through hands-on activities. Lists fourteen steps involved in implementing an effective historical unit in technology education.

1101.   Perry, M. (1986). Developing thinking skills in middle school students using computers. *NASSP Bulletin: The Journal for Middle Level and High School Administrators, 70*(493), 97-100.

A middle school teacher in Florida describes a program based on reading, creativity and computer usage for sixth and seventh grade gifted students. Perry describes the objectives of the program, process-product evaluation, program ming activities in which the students are engaged, the use of computers for testing, and software applications.

1102. Schauer, N. M. (1993). Indian River Middle School Library. *In Transition*, 29-39.

Discusses the key role that media centers play in the day-to-day operation of a middle school. Includes examples of services offered to both faculty and students. Also includes suggestions for incorporating in media centers.

1103. Tibbs, P. (1989). Video creation for junior high language arts. *Journal of Reading, 32*(6), 558-559.

Briefly explains the non-technical components of creating a video with students. Includes several suggestions for lessons.

1104. Wangberg, E. G. (1985). Directions and developments in microcomputer applications in the schools. *The Clearing House, 58*(9), 384-386.

Analyzes the use of computers in schools. Describes a project designed to develop software to teach reading and writing skills to young adolescents and adults.

C. EDUCATIONAL TECHNOLOGY - GENERAL

1105. Boser, R. A., & Gallo, D. (1995). Pyramids to space stations: Interdisciplinary connections through technology education. *Middle School Journal, 26*(3), pp. 41-46.

Hands-on activities using thematic or interdisciplinary approaches is a key recommendation for matching instruction to the learning characteristics of middle level students. Technology learning activities, such as "Interactive Community" or "Thinking like Bucky Fuller," that emphasize problem solving and decision making provide opportunities for critical thinking in an atmosphere of diversity and choice. Group simulations encourage interaction with peers and allow students to work together on a common project. Includes a brief annotated bibliography of print materials and software-related materials.

1106. Dewitt, H. (1991). Stimulation with computer simulations. *Science Scope, 14*(6), S5-S7.

Simulations are software activities that present a problem or phenomenon and then ask students to make choices and decisions that affect the situations on screen. Computer simulations allow middle level students to interact with phenomenon previously inaccessible to the curriculum due to expense, space restrictions, or safety considerations. Dewitt describes how simulations can be used effectively in class. Criteria for selecting the software are also discussed.

1107.   Kirkman, J. L. (1986). Hey, Ms. Smith, the computer's doing something funny again! *The Clearing House*, *60*(1), 30-36.

Discusses the reluctance of classroom teachers to use computers. Emphasizes the lack of quality software in all content areas.

1108.   Lewis, A. C. (Ed.). (1990). Technology [Special issue]. *High Strides*, *2* (3).

Discusses availability and level of computer usage in urban middle schools. Includes examples of projects utilizing technology as a tool for learning among young adolescents. Includes the results of a study conducted by the National Center for Education Statistics. Also profiles model programs in Massachusetts, Florida, Georgia, and Washington, D. C.

XV

Special Needs

A. AT RISK - RESEARCH

1109.   Bishop, J. L. (1993). A qualitative study of retention in the middle grades (Doctoral dissertation, University of North Carolina at Chapel Hill, 1993). *Dissertation Abstracts International, 54,* 1237A.

Five categories of retained students were identified: (1) gifted but bored students, (2) learning impaired students, (3) disinvited/alienated students, (4) academic "acrobats," and (5) traumatized students. Each subgroup responded uniquely to retention.

1110.   Blake, Y. M. (1992). Self-esteem and academic achievement among high-risk African American middle school students: A directed vs. a non-directed counseling model (Doctoral dissertation, Texas Southern University, 1992). *Dissertation Abstracts International, 53,* 4484A.

Significant differences in test scores in the Math and Reading sections of the Texas Assessment of Academic Skills instrument were found among students who participated in the directed counseling model.

1111.   Chance, D. C. (1992). A study of five diverse middle schools and their efforts to bring about positive changes with at-risk students through invitational education (Doctoral dissertation, University of North Carolina at Greensboro, 1992). *Dissertation Abstracts International, 53,* 3415A.

Teachers learned to work with their at-risk students using the Five P's of Invitation Education (a project funded by the A. Smith Reynold Foundation): people, policies, places, programs, and processes. All five "Connection Teams" reported increased "family-type" atmosphere in their schools, increased teamwork and collaboration, and modifications in discipline policies that included clear consequences and more positive reinforcement.

1112.   Cooper, M. A. (1989). Factors associated with middle school "at risk" students in the regular classroom (Doctoral dissertation, Temple University,

1988). *Dissertation Abstracts International*, *49*, 1763A.

At risk students' aberrant performances are often attributed to willful misbehavior, stupidity or lack of interest. The author believes that a large number of middle level at risk students' problems are caused by environmental variables out of their control. This study investigated the following variables: (1) academic achievement; (2) socio-economic status; (3) self-image; (4) attitudes about school; and (5) teacher attitudes about teaching them. The at risk students were compared to an equal number of their "regular" peers from the same classrooms and taught by the same regular teacher. The study found that teacher beliefs and expectations of student performance influenced student achievement and that teacher expectations of students' performance varied as a function of students' race or social class.

1113.   Flynn, T. M. (1989). The effects of grade retention on middle school students' academic achievement, school adjustment, and school attendance. In David B. Strahan (Ed.), *Middle school research: Selected studies 1989* (pp. 1-6). Columbus, OH: Research Committee of the National Middle School Association.

"This study compared a group of 74 retained in-grade students with 74 matched, promoted students in the middle school grades. Comparisons of retained and promoted students a year later indicated that the promoted students significantly out performed retained students on measures of academic achievement, social behavior, and school attendance. Implications of the results for middle school students are discussed and alternatives to grade retention are presented."

1114.   Maxfield, R. M. (1991). The relationship of school connectedness and student learning behaviors to the reduction of "at risk" factors at the middle school level (Doctoral dissertation, Oklahoma State University, 1990). *Dissertation Abstracts International*, *52*, 412A.

The author surveyed students from three middle schools to discover the use of cognitive and metacognitive learning behaviors and the degree to which the students felt connected to their schools. Grade point averages were used to set baseline achievement standards. Parents were surveyed with respect to the assistance they provided their children with school work. An experimental group was instructed in the use of cognitive and metacognitive learning strategies. The primary recommendation which came from this study was that teachers and students use a variety of strategies related to the learning process.

1115.   Presseisen, B. Z. (Ed.). (1988). *At-risk students and thinking*. Washington, DC: National Education Association. 161 pp.

This book is comprised of essays on both research and practice in regard to the types of strategies that teachers can use to meet the individual needs of students.

1116.   Sills, T. (1991). An analysis of teacher perceptions of at-risk middle school students. *Research in Middle Level Education, 15*(1), 45-54.

Teachers first rated themselves as successful or unsuccessful instructors of at-risk students, then rated their attitudes toward selected student behaviors. Several attitudes were found to be held in common by successful teachers. Unsuccessful teachers were more structured, less flexible, and less creative in the classroom.

1117.	Simon, D. J., Reed, D. F., & Clark, M. L. (1990). The effect of cross-age mentoring on the achievement and self-esteem of at-risk students in middle school. In Judith L. Irvin (Ed.), *Research in middle level education: Selected studies 1990* (pp. 11-22). Columbus, OH: National Middle School Association.

"The purpose of this study was to examine the impact of a dropout prevention program which utilizes minority college students to improve the basic skills and self-esteem of urban middle school students at risk of dropping out. The study is based on a collaborative program entitled Project BEST (Basic Educational Skills and Training) which was developed by a university and an urban middle school... Project BEST incorporates a mentoring program which emphasizes the development of academic skills with participation in programming to encourage affective growh and positive self-esteem in both the minority middle school student and minority college student populations. Colleges students who serve as Mentor/Tutors are role models who help students cope with and overcome some of their academic and school or home-related personal problems. Subjects were 55 students considered 'at risk' of dropping out of an urban middle school in the Southeast. Results indicate that students in the control groups were absent from school more often than those in Project BEST. Further, the cross-age mentoring program had more impact on the students' self-esteem and achievement attitudes than on their academic performance during the initial year of the program."

B. AT RISK - PRACTICAL

1118.	Berger, R., & Shechter, Y. (1989). Adolescent girls in distress: A high-risk intersection. *Adolescence, 24(94),* 357-374.

Girls in distress are those with risk factors in the areas of sociodemographics, interpersonal relations, education, and culture. The authors include a very interesting table that compares the developmental characteristics of adolescent boys, adolescent girls, and adolescent girls in distress.
	The authors argue that girls in distress suffer from inconsistent social messages about their proper development and that these experiences underlie their at-risk behavior. A useful theoretical piece on the unique needs of adolescent girls in distress.

1119.	Bratina, M. B. (1986). Helping teenagers wrestle with life and death. *The Clearing House, 59(9),* 413-415.

Focuses on strategies for counseling middle level students who appear to be suicidal. Outlines a professional development institute focusing on pressures and stressful situations typically experienced by young adolescents.

1120.   Compton, B., Hughes, J., & Smith, J. C. (1990). *Adolescents in need: An approach for helping rural at-risk youth*. Chapel Hill, NC: Center for Early Adolescence, University of North Carolina at Chapel Hill.

Describes a program designed to "improve the health and human services to adolescents in rural sections of Orange County, North Carolina" (p. iii) since 1981. The program addressed the developmental needs of early and older adolescents identified as at-risk for such reasons as substance abuse, pregnancy and abuse. Their stategies included "(1) completion of education, (2) prevention of untimely pregnancy, (3) involvement of the father of the child, (4) obtaining child care, (5) procuring adequate living arrangements, (6) involving the community in adolescent pregnancy, and (7) raising adolescents' self-esteem" (p. iv). Provides clear sections on the steps needed to establish such a program with an emphasis on coordinating the services of already existing agencies. Useful resource for other communities that want to establish a similar program.

1121.   Curtis, S. (1992). Promoting health through a developmental analysis of adolescent risk behavior. *Journal of School Health, 62*(9), 417-420.

Makes a case for the delivery of health services to middle and high school students in school settings because of the behavioral and social nature of many of the causes of mortality and morbidity in this age group (accidents, suicide, homicide, sexually transmitted diseases, pregnancy, and substance abuse). Briefly highlights the developmental characteristics of adolescents and their risk taking behaviors. Makes recommendations for cognitive and psychosocial interventions that promote wellness for both early and late adolescence.
        These include such things as focusing on immediate consequences of high risk behavior and developing community groups to encourage healthy autonomy in middle level students. Also comments on the power of environmental interventions such as bans on tobacco use as a means of reinforcing health promotion concepts.

1122.   Dawson, J. (1987). Helping at-risk students in middle schools. *NASSP Bulletin: The Journal for Middle Level and High School Administrators, 71*(501), 84-88.

Dawson describes how his middle school developed a broad-based, comprehensive program to meet the needs of at-risk students. In doing so, he delineates the highlights of the program; explains how students are identified; develops a schoolwide discipline program as well as unique classes/experiences for at-risk students; and stresses the importance of establishing realistic, positive and obtainable goals.

1123.   Dorman, G., & Wheelock, A. (1988). *Before it's too late: Dropout prevention in the middle grades*. Carrboro, NC: Center for Early Adolescence. 87 pp.

"This report explores how middle-grades schools can strengthen their holding power on dropout-prone adolescents and creates a new framework for thinking about dropout prevention in the middle-grades before it's too late. Outlines a comprehensive middle grades dropout prevention strategy at the local level with a timetable for implementation."

1124.   Dryfoos, J. (1990). *Adolescents at risk: Prevalence and prevention.* New York, NY: Oxford University Press.

A strong review of four interrelated problem areas faced by at least a quarter of today's adolescents: delinquency, substance abuse, teen pregnancy, and school failure. This volume is another of the many supported by the Carnegie Corporation of New York. The main emphasis of the book is identifying successful programs and using what works to develop more comprehensive approaches to meeting the needs of high risk adolescents.

The prevalence of the four categories of at-risk behaviors is addressed in part I. An especially useful chapter, "The Overlap in High-Risk Behaviors," supports the need for interventions that "focus more on the predictors of the behavior" (p. 110) and which are comprehensive in approach. The characteristics of high risk adolescents were identified as follows: "Starting any of the behaviors early, doing poorly in school, acting out, going around with friends who act out in the same ways, having inattentive parents, and living in a disadvantaged neighborhood" (p. 100). Part II highlights successful models and comments on what hasn't worked in preventing each of the four risk behaviors.

Part III provides a useful summary of successful prevention programs. The two most powerful factors that these programs have in common appear to be "the importance of providing individual attention to high-risk children and the necessity for developing broad communitywide interventions" (p. 228). Successful programs in school settings were characterized by active support from the principal. The authors summarize expert opinion regarding what is known about successful programs and suggest strategies for new programs. Among their ideas are the need to intervene early (preschool and middle school years) and to concentrate preventive efforts in school settings because "early school failure is the signal event that predicts almost insurmountable barriers to life's opportunities" (p. 251).

1125.   Elias, M. J., & Tobias, S. (1990). *Problem solving/decision making: For social and academic success—A school-based approach.* Washington, DC: National Educational Association. 128 pp.

The authors provide strategies to assist at-risk students to increase both their confidence and competence in regard to problem solving and decision making. Specific action plans are included to promote self-control, social awareness, and group participation. This booklet would be useful for teachers who are engaged in leading advisor/advisee classes.

1126.   Elkind, D. (1984). *All grown-up and no place to go: Teenagers in crisis.* Reading, MA: Addison-Wesley Publishing Co.

Based on the author's 25 years of working with teenagers. Recommends that schools reduce class size to 18 or fewer students because of the benefits of individual attention. Offers ideas on improved television programming and strategies for stress management to help students during adolescence.

1127.   Furby, L., & Beyth-Marom, R. (1990). *Risk taking in adolescence: A decision-making perspective.* (Working paper available from the Carnegie Council on Adolescent Development, 2400 N Street, NW, Washington, DC 20037).

Provides a theoretical model for decision-making in general and risk-taking in particular. Contrasts the differences between adult and adolescent perception of risk. Discusses implications of the decision-making research for developing health promotion and health protection interventions.

1128.   Gray-Shoffner, C. (1986). A rescue program for potential dropouts. *Principal, 66*(2), 53-54.

A brief description of a successful in-school alternative to suspension for problem students. The study-center program stresses student responsibility in a non-punitive, supportive manner.

1129.   Johnston, J. H., Markle, G. C., & Coey, P. (1987). About suicide. *Middle School Journal, 18*(2), 8-10.

Suicide is second behind accidents as the leading cause of death of individuals between the ages of 10 and 20. Figures could be underreported by as much as 50 percent. Males are four times more likely to commit suicide than females, but females attempt suicide four to seven times more than males. Discusses reasons for suicide and includes a profile of suicide-prone adolescents. Lists specific strategies for responding to potential suicides.

1130.   Knight, D., & Wadsworth, D. (1994). Accommodating the at-risk student in the middle school classroom. *Middle School Journal, 25*(5), 25-30.

Offers a variety of strategies for meeting the individual needs of a diverse population of students. Three skill areas addressed are information acquisition (listening skills), information organization (note taking skills), and information utilization (test taking skills). The checklist of instructional modifications could prove helpful as a quick reminder to teachers in the classroom.

1131.   Lehr, J. B. & Harris, H. W. (1988). *At-risk, low achieving students in the classroom.* Washington, DC: National Education Association. 104 pp.

"Practical, field-tested, success-proven strategies for helping students in the middle grades not only stay in school, but succeed in school." Addresses such issues as grouping, organization and planning, teacher expectations, effective teaching, positive discipline, and collegial learning.

1132.   Levitt, M. Z., Selman, R. L., & Richmond, J. B. (1991). The psychosocial foundations of early adolescents' high-risk behavior: Implications for research and practice. *Journal of Research on Adolescence, 1*(4), 349-378.

Presents a conceptual model of risk-taking behavior of adolescents that includes "knowledge about the risk, management skills to deal with the risk, and the personal meaning of the risk" (p. 357) evolving within the context of a physical and social environment. Two categories of risk behaviors, health (substance abuse, sexual activity) and educational (class cutting, failing), are addressed. The authors contend that "there is a risk factor for children in developmental transition to adolescence, whose psychosocial maturation may not necessarily occur uniformly across components at a rate commensurate with the increasing challenges being posed by the environment" (p. 368). The conceptual model is diagrammed with path analysis arrows to provide direction for future research. The authors offer possible hypotheses to be considered. Concludes with implications for health promotion that can be enhanced by general strategies to "promote higher levels of knowledge, management skills, and personal meaning" (p. 371).

1133. Lipsitz, J. (1991). Public policy and early adolescents: A 1990's context for researchers. *Journal of Early Adolescence, 11*(1), 20-37.

Offers an impassioned plea for more work on the different contexts in which adolescents develop in our country and the need to design policies and programs that recognize these differences. Highlights the proposed approach of the Chapin Hill researchers in Chicago who recommend the development of community-based youth services for all adolescents.

1134. Martino, L. R. (1993). A goal-setting model for young adolescents at risk students. *Middle School Journal, 24* (5), 19-22.

Discusses a model program designed to help students develop an internal sense of control and responsibility through a structured goal-setting program. Based upon the premise that young adolescents need opportunities to develop an internal locus of control to accept responsibility, and to take pride in their accomplishments.

1135. Massachusetts Advocacy Center and the Center for Early Adolescence. (1988). *Before it's too late: Dropout prevention in the middle grades*. Boston, MA: Massachusetts Advocacy Center.

Reviews research findings and current trends relative to school reform, dropouts, effective schools, and successful practices for middle level students. Includes recommendations for preventing attrition among middle level students.

1136. Mathes, P., & Davis, B. (1987). Individualized instruction for pregnant adolescents. *The Clearing House, 60*(8), 375-380.

Discusses the special needs of young adolescents who choose to remain in school while pregnant. Includes suggestions for adapting curriculum and instructional strategies to meet their needs, thus encouraging them to remain in school.

1137.   Morrison, J. R., & Jensen, S. (1982). Teenage pregnancy: Special counseling considerations. *The Clearing House*, 56(2), 74-77.

Focuses on the special needs of pregnant students. Discusses issues related to health, social, and economics. Includes a listing of practical suggestions to assist middle level educators in meet the needs of these students.

1138.   Morrison, J. R., & Storey, B. (1986). Adolescent insomnia. *The Clearing House*, 60(3), 110-114.

Examines potential causes of insomnia in young adolescents. Specifically discussed are alcohol abuse, drug addiction, and behavioral and attitudinal changes. Includes strategies for detecting potential problems and for alleviating them.

1139.   Nevetsky, J. (1991). At-risk program links middle school, high school programs. *NASSP Bulletin: The Journal for Middle Level and High School Administrators*, 75(538), 45-59.

The author explains how a districtwide effort to meet the needs of at-risk students included not only a discipline program, but close cooperation among parents, students, teachers, administrators and counselors at both the middle school and the high school.

1140.   Petersen, A. C. (1993). Presidential address: Creating adolescents: The role of context and process in developmental trajectories. *Journal of Research on Adolescence*, 3(1), 1-18.

Provides support for the current lines of research on adolescence emphasizing the need for more complex models to explain behavior. Highlights the influence of cultural context on risk behavior. Recommends research on interventions delivered early enough to prevent or delay experimentation in risk behavior.

1141.   Presseisen, B. Z. (Ed.). (1988). *At-risk students and thinking*: Washington, DC: National Education Association. 161 pp.

This book is comprised of essays on both research and practice in regard to the types of strategies that teachers can use to meet the individual needs of students.

1142.   Ruff, T. P. (1993). Middle school students at risk: What do we do with the most vulnerable children in American education. *Middle School Journal*, 24 (5), 10-12.

Stresses the importance of providing specific individualized assistance to at-risk middle level students. Areas of need include providing assistance with academic skills; providing a nurturing, supportive environment; and implementing a relevant curriculum.

1143.   Scales, P. C. (1992). From risks to resources: Disadvantaged learners and middle grades teaching. *Middle School Journal*, *23*(5), 3-9.

Scales, who is the author of *A Portrait of young Adolescents in the 1990s: Implications for Promoting Healthy Growth and Development*, persuasively argues that "If we are to meet the challenge of effective middle-grades teaching, then I believe we must first wean ourselves from dependence on the concepts of youth 'at-risk" or 'disadvantaged' youth." He goes on to address the issues of adult attitudes as they relate to academic success and development needs of young adolescents. In doing so, he delineates seven key developmental needs of young adolescents.

1144.   Taylor, R., & Reeves, J. (1993). More is better: Raising expectations for students at risk. *Middle School Journal*, *24* (5), 13-18.

Outlines the procedures involved in selecting teams to provide support to at-risk students at the Meadowbrook Middle School in Orlando, Florida. Describes the desirable characteristics of team members, selection of team members, training and professional development of team members, and evaluation results.

1145.   Youth and America's Future. (1988). *Forgotten half: Pathways to success for America's youth and young families*. Washington, D.C.: William T. Grant Foundation, Commission on Work, Family and Citizenship.

Addresses the needs of young people who will not go to college. Emphasizes the need for family support services and policies as well as the expansion of community supports and opportunities for service.

C. AT RISK - GENERAL

1146.   Lewis, A. C. (Ed.). (1990). Retention [Special issue]. *High Strides*, *3* (1).

Includes six articles focusing on issues related to grade retention of urban eighth graders. Questions the benefits of retention. Also discusses the role of portfolios in assessing progress of young adolescents.

1147.   Metz, M. W. (1983). Sources of constructive social relationships in an urban magnet school. *American Journal of Education*, *91*(2), 202-45.

Discusses unusually successful teacher and student interactions in an inner city magnet school. Teachers were socialized to both give and expect respectful behavior from students. Curricular and activity reward structure and classroom activity structure are examined.

D. GIFTED AND TALENTED

1148.   Bireley, M., & Genshaft, J. (Eds.). (1991). *Understanding the gifted adolescent*. New York, NY: Teachers College Press.

Focuses on the educational and psychological issues that impact gifted adolescents as they make the transition from childhood to adulthood. A seminal work that discusses the interrelatedness between "giftedness" and developmental problems of young adolescents.

1149.   Coleman, M. R., & Gallagher, J. J. (1995). Middle schools and their impact on talent development. *Middle School Journal, 26*(3), pp. 47-56.

Compared the attitudes of middle school and gifted educators about the appropriate education for gifted middle-level students. Many items showed respondents agreed on items, but varied in intensity. The polarizing clusters were those relating to ability grouping and social and emotional and social difficulties experienced as a result of the label "gifted." Educators of gifted students strongly agreed that gifted students benefit from being grouped together, for at least part of the day, while middle school respondents disagreed. A second study looked at current best practices in meeting the needs of gifted students within the middle school framework. "Pull out" variations, separate classes, and cluster grouping systems for gifted students were examined.

1150.   Erb, T. O. (1992). Encouraging gifted performance in middle schools. *Midpoints*, 3(1), 1-24. (Available from the National Middle School Association, 4807 Evanswood Dr., Columbus, OH 43229-6292).

In this occasional paper published by the National Middle School Association, Erb discusses the issue of how to best go about meeting the needs of gifted learners in middle level programs. Among the topics he addresses are the current state of affairs in middle grades teaching, middle grades curriculum and methodological considerations, interdisciplinary curriculum, authentic outcomes, how the exemplary middle school is a radical departure from the more traditional types of schools, what is giftedness, identifying the gifted, a curriculum for gifted learners, differentiated curriculum, cooperative grouping/ability grouping, and accommodating giftedness.

1151.   Kramer, L. R. (1985). Perceptions of ability in one middle school: A study of gifted adolescent females. In David Strahan (Ed.), *Middle school research: Selected studies 1985* (pp. 11-33). Columbus, OH: Research Committee of the National Middle School Association.

Based on a qualitative study which utilized participant-observation, interviewing and artifact collection in a single middle school, the author found that "gifted girls use social interaction to determine the quality and acceptability of their achievements and to determine, through social comparison, the extent of their abilities."

1152.   O'Brien, M. (1979). Teacher response to gifted middle school students. *Middle school research: Selected studies 1977-1979* (pp. 1-7). Fairborn, OH: National Middle School Association.

The purpose of this study was to develop and pilot written and observational instruments as well as to investigate the relationships between attitudes and behaviors toward gifted children among teachers of the gifted and teachers of regular classes.

1153.   Perry, M. (1986). Developing thinking skills in middle school students using computers. *NASSP Bulletin: The Journal for Middle Level and High School Administrators, 70*(493), 97-100.

A middle school teacher in Florida describes a program based on reading, creativity and computer usage for sixth and seventh grade gifted students. Perry describes the objectives of the program, process-product evaluation, programming activities in which the students are engaged, the use of computers for testing, and software applications.

1154.   Peterman, F. P. (1990). Successful middle level schools and the development of programs for the gifted. *NASSP Bulletin: The Journal for Middle Level and High School Administrators*, 74(526),   62-65.

Peterman argues that effective middle schools and effective programs for gifted students have many of the same characteristics, especially those of meeting the unique needs of the students. It concludes by describing models of gifted education.

1155.   Peters, C. (1991). Attitude profiles of gifted achieving, gifted underachieving and nongifted middle school students (Doctoral dissertation, University of Houston, 1991). *Dissertation Abstracts International, 52*, 1631A.

Attempted to create and validate a diagnostic instrument able to identify gifted underachievers through a profile of attitudes which keeps them in an underachieving cycle. Results indicated successful completion of additional refinements and validation should create a useful tool.

1156.   Sherwood, L. A., & Strahan, D. B. (1985). Developmental patterns of logical and creative thinking among gifted learners in the middle school. In David Strahan (Ed.), *Middle school research: Selected studies 1985* (pp. 68-82). Columbus, OH: Research Committee of the National Middle School Association.

Among the findings were: "The gifted population scored consistently higher at each grade level than did the normative population; scores of the gifted population exceeded the scores of the normative group at each grade level in a dramatic fashion; the most important insights to emerge from the results are that creative thinking as measured by the TTCT [Torrance Test of Creative Thinking] and formal reasoning as measured by the ATFR [Arlin Test of Formal Reasoning] are discrete variables and that chronological age is the most significant factor in differences in performance on formal reasoning tasks; and, results also document an essential linkage between IQ scores and scores on other assessments."

1157.   Wright, J. D. (1983). *Teaching the gifted and talented in the middle school.* Washington, DC: National Education Association. 64 pp.

In addition to providing ideas on how to address individual content areas, Wright also provides insights on interdisciplinary activities, counseling, problem solving, and teaching strategies.

E. SPECIAL NEEDS - RESEARCH

1158.   Brady, M. P., Swank, P. R., Taylor, R. D., & Freiberg, H. J. (1988). Teacher-student interactions in middle school mainstreamed classes: Differences with special and regular education students. *The Journal of Educational Research*, *81*(6), 332-340.

"This paper reports the results of an investigation designed to change teacher-student interactions with mainstreamed students in middle school social studies classes. Fourteen of 40 teacher volunteers received a six-session intervention emphasizing key variables from the teacher effectiveness and special education literature. Results indicate significant differences between experimental and control teachers on a pre- and post-contrast as well as on a follow-up (maintenance) contrast. Homogeneous and heterogeneous grouping effects, independent of the intervention, also are seen. Implications of the findings are presented in terms of future training and research efforts."

1159.   Hamilton, R. K. (1983). Effects of self-evaluation on the academic behavior of emotionally handicapped middle school students (Doctoral dissertation, Florida State University, 1983). *Dissertation Abstracts International*, *44*, 460A.

Findings indicate that for the subjects in this study, a self-evaluation session had weak implications for positive academic gain within the emotionally handicapped classroom. The majority of subjects were not able to accurately depict their own academic success or failure.

1160.   Kistner, J. (1987). Perceived competence and self-worth of LD and normally achieving students. *Learning Disability Quarterly*, *10*(1), 37-44.

The author compared the responses of forty-eight elementary and middle level learning disabled and forty-eight normally achieving students to the Perceived Competence Scale for Children. LD children rated their cognitive and physical abilities more negatively than nondisabled peers. They were not more likely to express general dissatisfaction with self or their relationships with peers.

1161.   Merrell, K. W. (1990). Differentiating low achieving students and students with learning disabilities: An examination of performances on the Woodcock-Johnson Psycho-Educational Battery. *Journal of Special Education*, *24*(3), 296-305.

Significant differences between LP and LA children were found on all but one

Woodcock-Johnson subtest. Identified critical variables for use in differentiating between the two groups of students. Includes implications for special education teachers and administrators.

1162.   Rhein, B. A. (1990). A comparison of the academic achievement of elementary and middle school emotionally disturbed and learning-disabled children (Doctoral dissertation, University of Connecticut, 1990). *Dissertation Abstracts International, 51*, 3386A.

Both elementary and middle-school learning-disabled students performed significantly better than emotionally-disturbed students on the Mathematics, Reading Recognition, and Reading Comprehension subtests of the Peabody Individual Achievement Test.

1163.   Robinson, E. L., & Nagle, R. J. (1992). The comparability of the test of cognitive skills with the Wechsler Intelligence Scale for Children-Revised and the Stanford-Binet: Fourth Edition with Gifted Children. *Psychology in the Schools, 29*(2), 107-112.

Found differences between tests to range from 6 to 10 points, indicating limited comparability between the Test of Cognitive Skills and WISC-R and Stanford-Binet Fourth Edition.

1164.   Tindal, G., & Parker, R. (1989). Assessment of written expression for students in compensatory and special education programs. *Journal of Special Education, 23*(2), 169-183.

Examines several scoring methods of grading written work of special students. Compares direct and indirect assessment methods.

1165.   Tindal, G., & Parker, R. (1989). Direct observation in special education classrooms: Concurrent use of two instruments and their validation. *Journal of Special Education, 23*(2), 169-183.

Describes the validity of two instruments used to measure special education student classroom behaviors: a momentary time sample of task engagement and an event record of discrete students responses.

1166.   Vatterott, C., & Yard, G. J. (1993). Accommodating individual difference through instructional adaptations. *Middle School Journal, 24* (5), 23-28.

Based upon the belief that the majority of students needing special services can be successful in an inclusive setting. Specifically discussed are characteristics of the dissimilar learner, philosophy of the Interventions with Dissimilar Learning Model (IDL), and an overview of the IDL.

1167.   Watkinson, J. T., & Lee, S. W. (1992). Curriculum-based measures of written expression for learning-disabled and nondisabled students. *Psychology in the Schools, 29*(2), 184-192.

Uses eight measures to compare samples of written work done by learning-disabled and nondisabled students. LD students had more trouble producing syntactically and grammatically correct word sequences than they did producing legible and correctly spelled words. Non-LD students had significantly higher scores than LD students in all area of written expression.

F. SPECIAL NEEDS - PRACTICAL

1168.   Gordon, S. B., & Asher, M. J. (1994). *Meeting the ADD challenge.* Champaign, IL: Research Press. 196 pp.

Provides teachers with practical information about the needs and treatment of children and adolescents with ADD. Includes a variety of reproducible assessment and recording forms.

1169.   Johnson, A. B., & Ward, M. E. (1982). An alternative approach to educating the learning-disabled adolescent. *The Clearing House, 56*(1), 23-25.

Outlines a program for special needs students. Includes suggestions for collaboration among special education teachers and regular education teachers.

1170.   Lewis, A. C. (Ed.). (1993). Special education [Special issue]. *High Strides, 5*(2).

A collection of four articles with an emphasis on middle level students with special needs. Included are "Flocking Together," "Special Education Students Should Be 'Regular Guys,'" "Changes Coming to Special Education," "Making Us All More Human," "Oasis for Special Students," "Giving Special Students a Future," and "It's Student Achievement, Stupid!" Also includes a list of nine resources available to middle level teachers.

1171.   Mancini, G. H. (1995). *Special like everyone: Including special needs students in Indiana school communities.* Middle Grades Improvement Program NETWORK. (Available from The Middle Grades Improvement Program NETWORK, 8301 East 46th Street, Indianapolis, IN 46226).

A monograph that highlights the efforts of Indiana middle schools to make inclusion a positive experience for everyone. Begins with an historical overview of the development of inclusion from mainstreaming and discussion of the use of collaborative teaching (pairing special education teachers with regular education teachers). Profiles five middle schools that use such strategies as peer tutoring and collaborative teaching. Contact information is included for all middle schools that participated in the mini-grant program.

1172.   Margolis, H., & McCabe, P. P. (1988). Overcoming resistance to a new remedial program. *The Clearing House, 62*(3), 131-134.

Analyzes reasons often cited for resisting remedial programs. Also discusses the role of the special education teacher in promoting the benefits of remedial programs. Includes practical suggestions for communicating with colleagues, thus eliminating much of the resistance to new programs.

1173.   Morrill, L. T. (1979). S. C. A. P. E. from stigma: Will your middle school be ready for P. L. 94-142? *The Clearing House*, *52*(9), 456-457.

Describes the SCAPE program, a program for special needs students at Central Middle School in Newark, Delaware. Program components include heterogeneous grouping, team teaching, and individualized instruction.

1174.   Post, L. M. (1984). Individualizing instruction in the middle school: Modifications and adaptations in curriculum for the mainstreamed student. *The Clearing House*, *58*(2), 73-76.

Discusses the need to adapt curriculum and teaching strategies to accommodate students with special needs. Includes suggestions that regular education teachers will find useful when adapting and modifying curriculum.

G. SPECIAL NEEDS - GENERAL

1175.   Archibald, D. (1981). Rethinking mainstreaming—positively. *Middle School Journal*, *12*(4), 23-24.

"Mainstreaming should be placing students into regular classes when they have demonstrated that they have the academic and social skills to profit from a regular class placement." Discusses the attitude of teachers toward mainstreaming. The author claims that success of mainstreaming seems to be more dependent on the classroom teacher's attitude than in-service training. Argues that unless properly implemented, mainstreaming can fail to serve children and can be a major detriment to teacher morale.

1176.   Bradley, D. F., & Fisher, J. F. (1995). The inclusion process: Role changes at the middle level. *Middle School Journal*, *26*(3), 13-19.

An introductory article listing the advantages of including special education students into regular classrooms. Discusses models for system changes and role changes for teachers and parents. Emphasizes that teachers must go beyond simply allowing special education students into their classrooms; teachers must also be willing and ready to take responsibility as the key educator.

1177.   Brobeck, J. K. (1990). Teachers do make a difference. *Journal of Learning Disabilities*, *23*(1), 11.

A teacher of middle level students with learning disabilities summarizes interviews with two learning-disabled young men in which they remember the humiliation suffered because of their disability and the difference a knowledgeable and understanding teacher can make.

1178.   Sills, T. (1992). *Study guide for the Arkansas Driver's Manual*. Little

Rock, AR: Rose Publishing Company, Inc. 62 pp.

High interest workbook suitable for use with students who need help passing
state driver's tests for their learner's permit. While some material is specific to
the Arkansas driver's test, most "rules of the road" information is basic to all
state driver's tests. The book was field-tested and proved to be the basis for a
motivating reading unit for under-achievers. Includes practice tests.

1179.   Sills, T., Harvey, R., Scott, M., Walker, M., Rogers, R., Anderson, A.,
Moore, C., & Graham, C. (1988-1992). Subject area review books for the
Arkansas Minimum Performance Test. Little Rock, AR: Rose Publishing
Company, Inc.

Simple, yet comprehensive, review manuals for the basic skills in Science, Math,
Reading, Social Studies, and Language Arts. Suitable for use with special
education, remedial, or low ability students. Teacher's manuals available
for the series.

1180.   Walther-Thomas, C. S., & Carter, K. L. (1993). Cooperative teaching:
Helping students with disabilities succeed in mainstream classrooms. *Middle
School Journal*, *25* (1), 33-38.

Describes efforts by a Virginia middle school to implement a co-teaching model.
Addresses the following actions: planning for co-teaching; involving special
education students in regular classroom activities; notifying parents; co-teaching
in civics, exploratory foreign language, and science; and evaluating the program,
students, and teachers.

XVI

Multicultural Issues/ Concerns

1181.   Cooledge, N. J., Barrons, M. F., Cline, L. N., Geller, P., Keeney, V., Meier, R. D., & Paul, D. M. (1995). Rural adolescents: Are their worlds and worries different? *Schools in the Middle, 4*(4), 34-38.

Profiles student responses to the following questions: "What do you think about?; How do you spend your time?; and What do you worry about?" (p. 35). The authors compared their results with studies that used national samples.

1182.   Damico, S. B., & Sparks, C. (1986). Cross-group contact opportunities: Impact on interpersonal relationships in desegregated middle schools. *Sociology of Education, 59*(2), 113-123.

Examines the "effects of school organizational structure on students' interracial and cross-sex communication patterns." Results show that schools can create curricula that will improve minority-majority interactions.

1183.   Gould, S. C. (1991). Strategic planning in a multicultural education staff development program. *Journal of Staff Development, 12*(1), 18-21.

Describes a multicultural project which seeks to develop self-esteem, raise achievement levels, promote positive community and school relations, and increase appreciation of diversity in schools with large Hispanic and African-American populations.

1184.   Hambrick, A. (1993). Biographies of black female scientists and inventors. An interdisciplinary middle school curriculum guide: "What Shall I Tell My Children Who Are Black?" (Doctoral dissertation, University of Massachusetts, 1993). *Dissertation Abstracts International, 54,* 2039A. Developed to provide material for role models for black female students. Includes a sample interdisciplinary curriculum guide using the biographical profile of one woman for use as an example in appropriate curriculum development.

1185.   Manning, M. L. (1994). *Celebrating diversity: Multicultural education in middle level schools.* Columbus, OH: National Middle School Association. 156 pp.

Comprehensive and well-documented. Solid background information and rationale are combined with chapters presenting specific methods of implementing multicultural education in the middle school curriculum and the school itself. Includes annotated list of related resources.

1186.   Pickering, J. W. (1993). *Comparing cultures: A cooperative approach to a multicultural world.* San Antonio, TX: ECS Learning Systems. 95 pp.

Cultural diversity is discovered through cooperative learning. In Part One, students explore different cultures through case studies. In Part Two, student groups create their own cultures involving writing, history, the arts, media, politics.

1187.   Webb, C. A. (1995). Diversity and the mainstream curriculum. *English Journal, 84*(1), 120.

Briefly discusses the need for assessing the effectiveness of multicultural education programs. Specifically discussed as evaluation criteria are the following five dimensions of multicultural education: content integration, knowledge construction, prejudice reduction, equitable pedagogy, and empowerment of school culture and social structure.

XVII

Assessment

A. ASSESSMENT - RESEARCH

1188.   Winfield, L. F. (1991). Characteristics of middle grades schools implementing minimum competency testing programs. *Research in Middle Level Education*, *15*(1), 31-44.

Describes the relationship between school-level minimum competency testing (MCT) programs in middle grade schools as identified in the National Assessment of Educational Progress (1983-84) and organizational variables related to instruction. Schools with MCT programs tended to be in urban areas and had higher teacher-student ratios and more paraprofessionals, more students receiving remedial reading, and a higher number of teachers responsible for teaching reading. Unexpectedly, MCT schools had a higher percentage of students in gifted and talented programs compared to the non-MCT schools.

B. ASSESSMENT - PRACTICAL

1189.   Davies, A. (1992). *Together is better—collaborative assessment evaluation & reporting*. Palantine, IL: IRI/Skylight Publishing, Inc. 128 pp.

Based on current research about learners and learning, this book provides practical strategies for teachers concerning assessment, evaluation, and reporting. Offers ways to set learning goals and evaluation criteria with students and parents. Strategies are provided for helping students' self-evaluation. Includes models for informal reports and communications.

1190.   Hart, D. (1994). *Authentic assessment*. Redding, MA: Addison-Wesley. 120 pp.

A basic primer which provides a clear overview of assessment, including making time for assessment, tailoring assessment to desired outcomes, and scoring and evaluating student performance.

1191.   Schurr, S. L. (1992). *The ABC's of evaluation: 26 alternative ways to assess student progress*. Columbus, OH: National Middle School Association. 248 pp.

This booklet, which is designed along the lines of a programmed textbook, provides teachers with a host of alternative approaches to traditional evaluation. It provides ideas on how to evaluate student work and student progress in all curricular areas. The book is divided into two parts: Part One is comprised of five chapters: 1. Pretest on Evaluation, 2. The ABC's of Belief Statements About the Evaluation Process in the Middle Grades Classroom, 3. Ten Commandments of Testing in Middle Grades, 4. The ABC's of Research: What Experts Say to the Practitioner About Testing, 5. The ABC's of Early Adolescent Characteristics That Can Be Addressed Through Creative/Critical Thinking Questions and Tasks. Part Two is subtitled "26 Alternative Ways to Assess Student Progress."

C. ASSESSMENT - GENERAL

1192.   Archbald, D. A. (1991). *Authentic assessment: What it means and how it can help schools*. Madison, WI: National Center for Effective Schools Research and Development.

Provides a rationale for authentic assessment by first giving a brief history of standardized testing and by discussing ways that authentic instruction measures more effectively student knowledge. Also discusses the impact that authentic assessment has upon instruction.

1193.   Burke, K. (1994). *Authentic assessment: A collection*. Palantine, IL: IRI/Skylight Publishing, Inc. 176 pp.

Authentic assessment requires a shift from traditional paper-and-pencil, fill-in-the-blank, short-term memory tests to tasks that require students to demonstrate skills like speaking, writing, performing, and problem solving. How do teachers design criteria to measure those skills? How do teachers strive for significant outcomes? This book includes thoughtful discussions about these questions and more.

1194.   Burkhardt, R. (1993). *The inquiry process: Student-centered learning*. Columbus, OH: National Middle School Association. 52 pages.

The author describes the inquiry process: selecting, exploring, and sharing a topic as well as assessment.

1195.   Lewis, A. C. (Ed.) (1993). Reaching for new standards [Special issue]. *High Strides*, 5 (4).

An issue devoted to a discussion of the roles of content standards, performance standards, and assessment in educational reform. Describes important elements of the changes and includes examples of how these changes may affect urban middle schools. Includes an annotated list of fourteen characteristics of the middle grades language arts standards.

1196. Lewis, A. C. (Ed.). (1993). PACE: Performance Assessment Collaborative for Educators. *High Strides, 5* (3), 7.

A project funded by the Rockefeller Foundation, PACE includes standards; diversified approaches; and supports for learning, debate, and constructive response. Includes a discussion of portfolio assessment and parental involvement, an integral part of the PACE philosophy.

1197. Lines, C. (1994). Authentic assessment at the middle level. *Middle School Journal, 25*(4), 39-41.

A succinct overview of the purposes, attributes, and modes of assessment required by middle level educators. In the future, teachers will need to develop assessment measures which are meaningful to their students and valid for assessing real-world performances. States that authentic performances and self-evaluation are more effective in promoting students understanding than are traditional paper and pencil evaluations.

1198. Michel, P. A. (1990). Test review: Secondary & College Reading Inventory. *Journal of Reading, 33*(4), 308-310.

This informal reading inventory was developed as an assessment tool for students at and above the middle school level. Can be given to an entire class. Yields independent, instructional, and frustration reading levels as well as reading rate. Individual administration will give an in-depth review of a student's reading ability. No listening component. Should be a useful resource in reading clinics, resource rooms, and general classrooms.

1199. Paulis, C. (1985). Holistic scoring: A revision strategy. *The Clearing House, 59* (2), 57-60.

Discusses the benefits of using holistic grading in middle level classrooms. Includes examples of classroom activities to illustrate the effectiveness of allowing students to evaluate their peer's papers.

1200. Perrone, V. (Ed.) (1991). *Expanding student assessment.* Alexandria, VA: Association for Supervision and Curriculum Development. 167 pp.

This collection of essays presents a detailed overview of the issue of authentic assessment (the whys, whens, hows, wherefores). Both middle level administrators and teachers as well as teacher educators should find plenty of food for thought herein. A sample of the titles of the various chapters provides a sense of the richness found in this collection: "Authentic Assessment, Evaluation, and Documentation of Student Performance"; "Authentic Assessment: Beyond the Buzzword and into the Classroom"; "The Rhetoric of Writing Assessment"; and "Active Assessment for Active Science."

1201.   Powell, W. (1981). Middle schools without failure. *The Clearing House*, *55* (1), 5-8.

Argues that assigning grades to middle level students can be detrimental to the students' development and self-esteem. Presents an alternative grading system based upon awarding an A, B, C, or Incomplete.

1202.   Sills, T. (1985). First measure the sparkle. *English Journal*, *74*(4), 87-89.

A teacher describes personal experiences in learning and discusses problems with current methods of evaluation.

1203.   Stevenson, C. (1992). Understanding learning: Portfolios in the middle grades. *The New England League of Middle Schools Journal*, *5*(2), 8-13. A succinct discussion of the purpose and value of using portfolios at the middle level as well as practical suggestions in regard to how one can develop and use portfolios with young adolescents.

1204.   Vars, G. F. (1970). Student evaluation: A design for the middle school. *The Clearing House*, *45* (1), 18-21.

Discusses methods of assessment that have proven to be effective in evaluating the performance of middle school students. Reiterates that effective, reliable assessment measures match desired tasks and outcomes.

1205.   Vars, G. F. (1976). Student evaluation in the middle schools: A second report. *The Clearing House*, *49* (6), 244-245.

Discusses the role that evaluation plays in the lives of young adolescents. Discusses alternative assessment measures and processes that do not rely heavily upon assigning grades, thus alleviating one key source of stress for middle level students.

1206.   Vars, G. F. (1992). Humanizing student evaluation and reporting. In Judith L. Irvin (Ed.) *Transforming middle level education: Perspectives and possibilities* (pp. 336-365). Needham Heights, MA: Allyn and Bacon.

Discusses and provides critiques of conventional marking and reporting, discusses issues regarding marking and reporting at the middle level (including criterion-referenced marking, norm-referenced marking, individual-referenced marking, other alternatives), and suggests ideas for improving the system of marking and reporting.

1207.   White-Hood, M. (1993). Window with a view. *Schools in the Middle*, 2 (4), 47-48.

Discusses the need for year-end program and process evaluations. Includes suggestions for assessment that provide an objective look at the previous year's activities and that form a basis for planning programs for the coming year. Also discusses the principal's role as process evaluator.

1208.   Wood, K. (1994). *Practical strategies for improving instruction.* Columbus, OH: National Middle School Association. 118 pages.

Offers strategies in assessment, cooperative learning, using media and field trips, reading and writing.

XVIII

Achievement

1209.   Aiello, H. S. (1989). Assessment of a mentor program on self-concept and achievement variables of middle school underachievers (Doctoral dissertation, Virginia Polytechnical Institute and State University, 1988). *Dissertation Abstracts International*, *49*, 1699A.

The study investigated the impact of a mentor model on self-concept and achievement variables of middle school underachievers. The experimental group consisted of 55 underachievers matched with a mentor. A control group of underachievers functioned without mentors. The study was of a quasi-experimental, non-equivalent control group design. The author reported that even though the mentor program produced more positive gains than the nonmentored group, the gains were not significant. The value of this study is to aid in the improvement of program evaluation and assessment of mentor programs.

1210.   Atman, K. S., & Hanna, J. W. (1987). Cognitive, goal accomplishment style, and academic achievement at the middle school. In David B. Strahan (Ed.) *Middle school research Selected studies 1987* (pp. 19-35). Columbus, OH: Research Committee of the National Middle School Association.

"The Cognitive Domain, a domain of behaviors associated with striving, provides a framework for examining goal-oriented behaviors of academic achieving (GAP of 3.25 and above) and non-achieving (GPA of 1.99 and below) students at the middle school level. All sixth, seventh, and eight grade students at the Washington Park Middle School, Washington, PA, set school-related goals during the 1986-87 school year within the context of a structured study skills/guidance program.
        At the close of the year, students were administered the Goal Orientation Index. Significant goal-oriented behaviors were identified across the three grades that distinguish academic achieving students from the non-achieving students. Case study data provide additional support for the premise that students who set academic goals for themselves achieve them."

1211.   Blai, B., Jr. (1986). Educational reform, it's about "time." *The Clearing House*, *60* (1), 38-40.

Discusses issues related to extended instructional time. Investigates pros and cons of an extended school day and year. Concludes that student achievement depends more heavily upon efficient use of time than upon quantity of time spent in a classroom.

1212.   Eccles, J. S. (1991). What are we doing to early adolescents? The impact of educational contexts on early adolescents. *American Journal of Education*, *99*(4), 521-542.

The author explores the hypothesis that declines in achievement demonstrated in early adolescence result from educational context through a review of studies and analyses using National Education Longitudinal Study data (sample of 24,599 eighth graders). Evidence of a mismatch between school environment and student needs is discussed.

1213.   Flynn, T. M. (1989). The effects of grade retention on middle school students' academic achievement, school adjustment, and school attendance. In David B. Strahan (Ed.) *Middle school research: Selected studies 1989* (pp. 1-6). Columbus, OH: Research Committee of the National Middle School Association.

"This study compared a group of 74 retained in-grade students with 74 matched, promoted students in the middle school grades. Comparisons of retained and promoted students a year later indicated that the promoted students significantly out performed retained students on measures of academic achievement, social behavior, and school attendance. Implications of the results for middle school students are discussed and alternatives to grade retention are presented."

1214.   Ford, D. Y. (1992). Self-perceptions of underachievement and support for the achievement ideology among early adolescent African-Americans. *The Journal of Early Adolescence*, *12*(3), 228-252.

This "study explores the perceptions that early adolescent African-American students hold regarding the American achievement ideology and the ramifications of such support on their academic achievement or under-achievement. It also assessed social, cultural, and psychological determinants of underachievement as perceived by 148 fifth and sixth graders in an urban school district. The perceived determinants of underachievement are discussed relative to a paradox of underachievement. Descriptive, comparative, and discriminant analyses were used to examine differences in students' perceptions. Responses were compared by gender and academic program. Results were not significantly statistically different by gender. Gifted students, however, expressed the greatest support for the achievement ideology, and they perceived determinants of achievement and underachievement differently than did average students who, along with males, were more likely to personify a paradox of underachievement. Implications and recommendations are discussed for urban educators working with early adolescent African-American youth."

1215.   Gerler, E. R., & Herndon, E. Y. (1986). Learning how to succeed academically in middle school. *School Counselor*, *33*(3), 186-197.

Report of research on the "effects of the multimodal program Succeeding in School with students in grades 6 through 8" (p. 187). The program was conducted by school counselors and involved ten 50 minute sessions on the following topics: successful people, being comfortable in school, being responsible in school, listening in school, asking for help in school, how to improve at school, cooperating with peers at school, cooperating with teachers at school, the bright side of school, and the bright side of me. Dependent variables were two self-report instruments on student awareness of how to succeed in school, an attitude toward school scale, classroom behavior ratings, conduct ratings, and grades in language arts. Only increased awareness was significantly higher in the experimental groups.

1216.   Levine, D. U., & Sherk, J. K. (1989). Implementation of reforms to improve comprehension skills at an unusually effective inner city intermediate school. *Peabody Journal of Education*, *66*(4), 87-106.

Article describes changes at a Bronx middle level school which registered large gains in middle level students' comprehension performance. The success was attributed to active, engaged learning; intensive assistance for low achievers; personal development of students; coordination of instruction; availability of instructional support personnel; outstanding leadership; and focus on key skills and higher-order learning.

1217.   Lynch, S. J., & Mills, C. J. (1993). Identifying and preparing disadvantaged and minority youth for high-level academic achievement. *Contemporary Educational Psychology*, *18*(1), 66-76.

The authors report the results of the Skills Reinforcement Project, which was designed to increase basic mathematics and language arts skills of disadvantaged and minority middle level (grade six) students. Students made significantly greater gains in mathematics than comparison students and nonsignificant gains on verbal measures.

1218.   Scott, R. D. (1989). A comparative study of eighth grade students enrolled in a school employing traditional and middle school concepts (Doctoral dissertation, Pepperdine University, 1988). *Dissertation Abstracts International*, *50*, 1267A.

This six-year longitudinal study of a school investigated the relationships among student academic achievement, attendance, and discipline when the school was a traditional junior high school for three years and when it was a middle school for three years. Student academic achievement in math and science was measured by the Comprehensive Test of Basic Skills. Attendance was measured by the average daily attendance. The effectiveness of disciplinary programs was measured by the number of student suspensions and expulsions. The data dealt only with eighth graders. The study found a relationship between a middle school concept and student academic achievement in the areas of reading and math, attendance, and discipline.

1219.   Shuman, R. B. (1989). *Classroom encounters: Problems, case studies, solutions.* Washington, DC: National Education Association. 256 pp.

Includes more than 70 case studies, with alternative solutions, covering the gamut: grades/assessment, discipline, values/morals, relationships, and evaluation.

XIX

Behavior and Classroom Management

A. BEHAVIOR /CLASSROOM MANAGEMENT - RESEARCH

1220.   Correll, J. H. (1984). Characteristics of middle school students with discipline problems (Doctoral dissertation, Northern Illinois University, 1984). *Dissertation Abstracts International, 45,* 3582A.

Students with discipline problems differed from students without problems in a variety of ways. Current semester grade point average was the single strongest discriminator. Five and six-tenths percent of middle school students were identified as discipline problems with a ratio of boys to girls being five to one. Group intelligence test scores were significantly higher for sixth graders, but nonsignificant for seventh and eighth graders.

1221.   Duncan, N. G. (1990). Discipline strategies for pupil control at the middle school level in an urban setting (Doctoral dissertation, Columbia University Teachers College, 1990). *Dissertation Abstracts International, 51,* 2317A.

Identified, described, and documented appropriate discipline strategies for successful pupil control in six effective middle schools. All six schools established discipline practices that equated balance between the schools' need for order and their students' need for self-discipline and self-control.

1222.   Eisenman, J. M. (1992). An anger management intervention with middle school adolescents (Doctoral dissertation, University of Wisconsin, 1992). *Dissertation Abstracts International, 53,* 1097A.

The author discussed how increased numbers of interpersonal disputes among middle school level students and between students and teachers often result in aggravated assault and the use of weapons. Because anger was usually the cause of this aggressive behavior in middle school students, the author investigated the effects of a six-session cognitive-behavioral anger management intervention with seventh-grade African-American female students with histories of aggressive behaviors. The students were able to produce self-guiding verbalizations to anger-provoking situations for a while, but revealed no long term ability to use such techniques. This study and similar ones help middle school professionals design effective interventions with students that are most at risk for engaging in aggressive behavior.

1223.   Howard, R. A. (1980). Middle school discipline: What do teachers prefer? *The Clearing House, 54* (4), 155-157.

Reports the results of a study designed to identify effective management techniques for use with fifteen specified classroom management problems. The study involved194 teachers representing 21 middle level schools in Kentucky. Findings indicated that "individual attention" was the preferred method for dealing with minor problems and that "agreement on preferred technique" was the method of choice for dealing with serious management problems.

1224.   Jones, P., & Garner, A. E. (1978). A comparison of middle school teachers' pupil control ideology. *Clearing House, 51*(6), 292-294.

Reports the results of a study designed to compare the ideology of middle level teachers with "best practices" in the area of classroom management. Describes the type of classroom climate that provides optimum learning conditions for middle level students.

1225.   Lindholm, B. W., & Touliatos, J. (1982). Checklist agreement among observers of children. *Psychology in the Schools, 19*(4), 548-551.

Parents', teachers', and counselors' perceptions of the behavior problems of elementary and middle school children were compared using the Behavior Problem Checklist. School counselors observed more personality problems than teachers or parents did. Other behavior comparisons did not significantly differ among the three groups.

1226.   Lyon, J. M. (1991). Conflict resolution in an inner-city middle school: An alternative approach. *The School Counselor, 39*(2), 127-130.

Results of a six-week pilot program indicate that on-going conflict resolution counseling does work with some students, but must be extensive and long-term to make lasting changes in behavior. Less than a major commitment may be worse than no counseling at all.

1227.   Matthews, D. B. (1983). The effects of relaxation training on discipline in middle school. In Thomas Owen Erb (Ed.) *Middle school research: Selected studies 1983* (pp. 53-61). Columbus, OH: Research Committee of the National Middle School Association.

Reports on a study that found relaxation tapes were useful in teaching students how to relax and that evidence shows that such training had a positive effect on students' behavior.

1228.   McClellan, T. S. (1992). A study of the practice of discipline strategies in the middle school setting (Doctoral dissertation, Michigan State University, 1992). *Dissertation Abstracts International, 53,* 2227A.

Compared a subjective with an objective approach to discipline. While differences existed between the different discipline systems, no one system appeared to be better than any other. Students experienced the same level of suspensions between schools, and administrators agreed the system used made no difference.

1229.   O'Reilly, D. M. (1989). Middle school teachers' pupil control ideology, pupil control behavior, and student discipline (Doctoral dissertation, University of Missouri-Columbia, 1988). *Dissertation Abstracts International, 49,* 3226A.

This study investigated the relationship between Pupil Control Ideology, Pupil Control Behavior, and the act of referring students to the administrative office for disciplinary actions. Teachers who thought of themselves as holding a custodial parent control orientation were also thought of that way by their students. These teachers, associated with a rigid, orderly, and highly controlled classroom setting, relied more upon moderate to severe discipline techniques. Both gender and teaching assignment (subject area taught) were strong indicators of control orientation held by teachers.

1230.   Ralph, E. G. (1993). Beginning teachers and classroom management: Questions from practice, answers from research. *Middle School Journal, 25*(1), 60-64.

Answers the following five questions often asked by novice middle level teachers: (1) How are classroom management and effective teaching related? (2) What is an effective classroom climate? (3) How may effective classroom management be analyzed? (4) How do teachers establish effective management? (5) How is effective classroom management sustained?

1231.   Wollan, D. N. (1983). Alternates to suspension: Middle, intermediate, and junior high school principals' perceptions of administrative procedures and programs with the highest potential for success (Doctoral dissertation, University of Southern California, 1983). *Dissertation Abstracts International, 43,* 3483A.

Principals of elementary, middle, intermediate, and junior high schools in districts with enrollments under 50,000 in Los Angeles County responded to a questionnaire containing demographic, alternative-to-suspension, and management practice items. Results found principals do support alternative-to-suspension programs but see suspension as a necessary procedure for protecting other students. Principals in different circumstances emphasized varying strategies. Recommended that schools with seventh and eighth grade students utilize preventive and rehabilitative programs more frequently than punitive programs.

1232.   Yonek, M. M. (1992). Attributions of tracked, at-risk, middle school students: Isolation of alienated and marginal students and implications for school organization (Doctoral dissertation, University of Florida, 1992). *Dissertation Abstracts International, 53,* 3424A.

Case study involving four students tracked into two alternative schools, one urban and one rural. All four students attributed negative events to unstable or uncontrollable causes, allowing them to maintain a positive self-concept. Successes were viewed as the result of increased effort, rather than innate ability. Findings suggest that tracked programs for at-risk students need to provide individualized attention, qualified instructors, opportunities for student success, and appropriate behavioral and academic training.

B.   BEHAVIOR/CLASSROOM MANAGEMENT - PRACTICAL

1233.   Bergmann, S. (1989). *Discipline and guidance: A thin line in the middle level school.* National Association of Secondary School Principals. 24 pp.

Subtitled "What At-Risk Students Say About Middle Level School Discipline and Teaching," the pamphlet examines at-risk students' perceptions about their schools and teachers and offers suggestions for developing middle level programs to help meet these students' needs.

1234.   Bray, P., & Ousley, M. J. (1990). *Urchins and angels: Managing the middle school classroom.* Portland, ME: J. Weston Walch Publisher. 150 pp.

The authors provide tips and techniques for managing the middle school classroom. The ideas include the adoption of a student centered philosophy, the dynamics of day-to-day discipline, how to deal with stress on the students and teacher, etc.

1235.   Burke, K. (1992). *What to do with the kid who...developing cooperation, self-discipline, and responsibility in the classroom.* Palantine, IL: IRI/Skylight Publishing, Inc. 336 pp.

Addresses the common problems that occur in cooperative groups of students. Using humorous scenarios, Burke presents practical solutions for the kid who never comes to school, the kid no one wants in the group, the kid who wants to work alone, and other problems. Over 200 strategies help teachers solve behavior problems and make decisions about appropriate management strategies. Administrators will also find useful suggestions for assisting teachers with management challenges in their cooperative learning classroom.

1236.   Canter, L. (1992). *Assertive discipline-new and revised: Positive behavior management for today's classroom.* Santa Monica, CA: Lee Canter & Associates.

Emphasizing a more positive approach than the earlier edition, this book reviews the Assertive Discipline model and builds the skills and confidence teachers need to take charge in their classrooms. The new model helps teachers set firm, consistent limits for students without embarrassing them by writing names on chalkboards.

1237.   Canter, L. (1993). *Succeeding with difficult students: New strategies for reaching your most challenging students.* Santa Monica, CA: Lee Canter & Associates. 255 pp.

Offers methods to help the handful of students with whom nothing seems to work—those students who constantly disrupt, are unmotivated, demand attention, openly confront your authority, and do not complete any assigned work.

1238.   Charles, C. M. (1989). *Building classroom discipline: From models to practice. Third edition.* White Plains, NY: Longman. 202 pp.

Part One describes eight models of discipline developed by Redl and, Wattenberg, Kounin, Ginott, Dreikurs, Jones, Canter, Glasser, and Skinner (Neo-Skinnerian Model). Part Two offers examples of the models in action and aids to building a personal system of discipline.

1239.   Childress, N. W. (1982). Group consultation with middle school teachers. *The School Counselor, 30*(2), 127-132.

Describes the format and consultation techniques used in a program designed to assist teachers in developing effective classroom management strategies and skills for communicating with parents.

1240.   de Vise, D. (1995). Great expectation. *High Strides, 7*(4), 10-11.

A brief description of a "Student Court" (p. 10) designed to address the areas of "attendance problems' disruptive classroom behavior; defiance of authority; malicious mischief, including graffiti and other minor property damage; sexual harassment; and obscene or vulgar acts" (p. 10). Includes two examples of deliberations and decisions rendered.

1241.   Goldstein, A. P., Sprafkin, R. P., Gershaw, N. J., & Klein, P. (1980). *Skillstreaming the adolescent.* Champaign, IL: Research Press. 232 pp.

A valuable book which presents a prosocial skills group training program for adolescents, especially those who display aggression, immaturity, withdrawal, or other problem behaviors. Designed to help teens increase self-esteem and develop competence in dealing with peers, family, and authority figures. The training approach uses teacher modeling, student role playing, group performance feedback, and transfer training.

1242.   Gordon, T. (1991). *Discipline that works.* New York: Penguin Books USA Inc. 258 pp.

Gordon, founder of P.E.T. (Parent Effectiveness Training) provides evidence that punitive discipline is harmful to young people and promotes self-destructive behavior, as well as anti-social, aggressive acts. Presents a strategy to help adults empower children to become self-reliant, make positive decisions, and control their own behavior.

1243.   Hindle, D. R. (1994). Coping proactively with middle years students. *Middle School Journal, 25*(3), 31-34.

Provides teachers with proactive strategies for dealing with middle level students. Discusses four areas critical in dealing effectively with students: development of an effective home-school team, guidance and counseling for students, classroom management and discipline, and considerations for student learning and instruction. Strategies or suggestions based on research and practical classroom experience are offered to teachers.

1244.   Huff, J. A. (1988). Personalized behavior modification: An in-school suspension program that teaches students how to change. *The School Counselor, 35*(3), 210-214.

Describes an intervention system for troubled teenagers based on a concept called Personalized Behavior Modification (PBM). Includes a discussion of entry criteria, orientation and procedure, and an overview of the entire program. Results appear to be positive for both students and teachers.

1245.   Johnson, S. O. (1979). Better discipline for middle school students. *The Clearing House, 53* (2), 86-89.

Discusses four major causes of classroom management problems: lack of administrative leadership, inadequate teacher organization and preparation, inadequate guidelines and principles for desired behavior, and failure to identify characteristics of potentially disruptive students. Includes suggestions for alleviating or diminishing the effects of each of the four major causes.

1246.   Katz, N. H. (1994). *Resolving conflict successfully.* Thousand Oaks, CA: Corwin Press. 65 pp.

Teaches core skills essential for managing conflict and negotiating differences. Model and process provide an effective framework for managing conflicts. Topics include: Communication and Rapport, Listening and Pacing, Chunking and Problem Solving, and Using the Resolution Model.

1247.   Murphy, C. (1995). Managing students: Building positive attitudes in the classroom. *Schools in the Middle, 4*(4), 31-33.

A concise article on elements of a "successful discipline management program" that could be used as a discussion starter for students in a teacher preparation program. Includes a "conflict clarification form" that asks the student to reflect on behavior that needs changing. A list of rewards appropriate to middle level students is also included.

1248.   Nelsen, J. (1987). *Positive discipline.* New York, NY: Ballantine
Books. 242 pp.

Emphasizes the key to discipline is not punishment but mutual respect.
Discusses positive approaches to discipline from both the teacher and parent
viewpoint. Delineates formats for class meetings and family meetings to resolve
problems. Talks about the significance of birth order on behavior and explains
four mistaken goals of behavior: attention, power, revenge, assumed
inadequacy. Nelsen says the true primary goal of all behavior is to find a sense
of belonging and significance.

1249.   Purkey, W. W., & Strahan, D. B. (1986). *Positive discipline: A
pocketful of ideas.* Columbus, OH: National Middle School Association. 50 pp.
In this booklet, Purkey and Strahan describe a developmentally responsive
approach to classroom and school discipline. In doing so, they ground the
practical ideas they suggest in principles of "invitational learning." In
delineating the invitational process of good discipline, they discuss the five "p's"
that influence the total school environment: people, places, policies, programs,
and processes.

1250.   Schrumpf, F., Crawford, D. K., & Usadel, H. C. (1991). *Peer
mediation: Conflict resolution in schools.* Champaign, IL: Research Press.

A comprehensive training program which provides information needed to
organize and implement a successful peer mediation program with students in
grades 6-12. During a mediation session, disputing students are given a chance
to sit face to face and tell their sides of the story without being interrupted. After
defining the problem, solutions are discussed and then evaluated. When an
agreement is reached, a contract is written and signed. Two volumes: Program
guide (160 pp.) and student manual (64 pp.)

1251.   St. Clair, R. (1986). Human rights: A vehicle for cultural intervention.
The Clearing House, 60 (1), 27-29.

Discusses issues resulting from cultural differences of middle level students.
Specifically analyzed are the problems and solutions experienced by one middle
school in Minnesota.

1252.   Tauber, R. T. (1990). *Classroom management from A to Z.* Orlando,
FL: Holt, Rinehart and Winston, Inc. 158 pp.

Brings accepted practices and ideas on classroom management together in one
easily accessible resource. Has application for student teachers and students
involved in early clinical experiences and veteran teachers who are having
problems with maintaining good discipline.

1253.   Tierno, M. J. (1991). Responding to the socially motivated behaviors of early adolescents: Recommendations for classroom management. *Adolescence, 26*(103), 569-577.

An excellent article with clear examples on how to effectively use proximity, task-focused verbal interactions, one-to-one discussions and socially-based sanctions to control disruptive behaviors. Bases the approaches on the unique developmental needs of early adolescents.

C. BEHAVIOR/CLASSROOM MANAGEMENT - GENERAL

1254.   Bodine, R. J., & Crawford, D. K. (1994). *Creating the peaceable school*. Champaign, IL: Research Press. Program Guide, 376 pp. Student Manual, 144 pp.

Presents a comprehensive plan where learners manage and resolve conflicts, both with and without adult assistance—a place where adults and children work together and respect, trust, help, and share with one another—where students express feelings in ways that are neither aggressive nor destructive. Central to the plan is the creation of a cooperative school context, achieved through the institution of a rights and responsibilities approach to discipline and the liberal use of mediation, negotiation, and group problem solving. Students learn to recognize, manage, and resolve conflict in peaceful, noncoercive ways.

1255.   Farnette, C. (1989). *People need each other—Social awareness activity book*. Tampa, FL: National Resource Center for Middle Grades/High School Education. 80 pp.

The reproducible activity pages in this social-awareness resource will help students acquire an understanding of family, peers, and the community as they become aware of the skills and attitudes necessary for satisfying interpersonal relationships. A high interest/low vocabulary format encourages the use of basic communication skills in a positive and meaningful way. Includes an excellent section on group dynamics.

1256.   Frith, G. H., & Lindsey, J. D. (1983). Behaviors affecting the instructional process. *The Clearing House, 56* (6), 273-274.

Identifies the following behaviors as detrimental to the learning environment in middle schools: resistance to discipline, lack of interest in school, lack of motivation to learn, and inability to follow directions.

1257.   Glasser, W. (1969). *Schools without failure*. New York, NY: Harper & Row, Publishers, Inc. 235 pp.

A classic book in the field of reducing failure in the schools. Appropriate to any age level. Discusses class meetings and the role of discipline and the building administrator.

1258.   Glasser, W. (1986). *Control theory in the classroom.* New York, NY: Harper & Row, Publisher, Inc. 144 pp.

A landmark book in which Glasser translates his concept of control theory into a classroom model of team learning (teacher and students). Provides the basis for developing or restructuring a supportive and positive system of classroom management.

1259.   Goldstein, A. P. (1988). *The prepare curriculum: Teaching prosocial competencies.* Champaign, IL: Research Press. 700 pp.

This well-researched manual provides a comprehensive prosocial skills training program for use with junior high and high school students—especially those who are chronically aggressive, withdrawn, or otherwise weak in prosocial competencies.

1260.   Goldstein, A. P., & Huff, C. R. (1993). *The gang intervention handbook.* Champaign, IL: Research Press. 532 pp.

Excellent presentation of gang intervention strategies. Provides a comprehensive study of strategies and specific tactics ranging from individual-level interventions to macrolevel socioeconomic policy reform. It focuses on both preventive and rehabilitative approaches that balance the needs of gang youth with the needs of society. Chapters contributed by authorities in the fields of psychology, criminology, public policy, sociology, criminal justice, counseling and human development, special education, and law enforcement.

1261.   Katz, N. H., & Lawyer, J. W. (1993). *Conflict resolution.* Thousand Oaks, CA: Corwin Press. 59 pp.

The nature of conflict, its principle sources, and how to handle it are creatively explored. Authors suggest helpful attitudes for framing conflict and offer a process for defusing conflict at an interpersonal or small group level. Topics include: The Nature of Conflict, Positive Attitudes toward Conflict, Conflict Resolution Model, and Conflict Resolution Process.

1262.   Katz, N. H., & Lawyer, J. W. (1994). *Preventing and managing conflict in schools.* Thousand Oaks, CA: Corwin Press. 76 pp.

Teachers learn to turn negative interaction into constructive action by following steps that help prevent conflict through effective human interaction. Real-life scenarios help define teacher roles. Topics include: Agreement Management, Facilitation, Immediacy, Consensus Decision Making, Mediation.

D. MOTIVATION

1263.   Hoff, J. W., III. (1981). Encounters in excellence: An analysis and projection of an enrichment assembly approach for middle school learners (Doctoral dissertation, State University of New York at Buffalo, 1981).

Dissertation Abstracts International, 42, 72A.

Internationally renowned personalities were invited to visit Carlton Webster Junior High School in Henrietta, New York, to spend at least one day of intensive instruction with students and community. Encounters in Excellence positively impacted on adolescent self development and exposed adolescent learners to credible, positive and significant models who were emulated by students.

1264.   Horton, L., Johnson, B., & Horst, B. (1982). How to win a middle schooler's heart. *Instructor, 102*(4), 33.

Three teachers give advice on relating to middle school students. Horton says enjoy them, use humor, question your curriculum, let students talk to you, be trustworthy, do not embarrass them, and do not give up on them. Johnson and Horst say give students more attention, do subjects—don't just discuss them, develop thick skin, be enthusiastic, and be wary of inconsistency. Change and turbulence are the only constants in middle level education.

1265.   Johnston, J. H., & Markle, G. C. (1982). What research says to the practitioner—About motivating students. *Middle School Journal, 13*(4), 22-24.

Examines Maslow's theory of motivation, the motivation to achieve, rewards and motivation, and implications for teachers. Students must believe that they can learn, need a clear idea of how to achieve instructional goals, and must recognize how instruction relates to their everyday lives. Optimal motivation can be achieved when students establish their own goals and then are graded accordingly. Extrinsic rewards need to be carefully monitored to be effective. Teachers can influence student motivation.

1266.   Larson, R. W., & Richards, M. H. (1991). Boredom in the middle school years: Blaming schools versus blaming students. *American Journal of Education, 99*(4), 418-443.

Fifth to ninth graders' experiences of boredom were evaluated. Results showed that boredom is frequently reported both in school and out of school with the same people showing boredom in both circumstances. High rates of boredom correlated with high ability. Individual dispositions appeared to be an important factor in boredom, but some data suggested that restructuring of some school tasks may reduce, though not eliminate, boredom in the classroom.

1267.   Thomason, J., & Thompson, M. (1992). Motivation: Moving, learning, mastering, and sharing. In Judith L. Irvin (Ed.) *Transforming middle level education: Perspectives and possibilities* (pp. 275-294). Needham Heights, MA: Allyn and Bacon.

Among the issues the authors discuss in this chapter are theoretical principles for motivation, motivational issues affecting young adolescents, and desired practices for increasing student motivation.

XX

Counseling

A. COUNSELING - RESEARCH

1268. Davis, T. (1995). Elementary and middle level counselors courtroom hearing experiences. *NASSP Bulletin, 79*(570), 10-15.

Reports results of a survey of school counselors in elementary and middle level schools concerning their experience in testifying. Reasons most often given for testifying included child custody, sexual abuse, and child abuse.

1269. Gerler, E. R., & Herndon, E. Y. (1986). Learning how to succeed academically in middle school. *School Counselor, 33*(3), 186-197.

Report of research on the "effects of the multimodal program Succeeding in School with students in grades 6 through 8" (p. 187). The program was conducted by school counselors and involved ten 50 minute sessions on the following topics: becoming successful people, being comfortable in school, being responsible in school, listening in school, asking for help in school, improving at school, cooperating with peers at school, cooperating with teachers at school, seeing the bright side of school, and recognizing the bright side of me. Dependent variables were two self-report instruments on student awareness of how to succeed in school, an attitude toward school scale, classroom behavior ratings, conduct ratings, and grades in language arts. Only increased awareness was significantly higher in the experimental groups.

1270. Gilbert, V. W. (1992). The development of a Career Planning Readiness Inventory for middle school students (Doctoral dissertation, University of Florida, 1992). *Dissertation Abstracts International, 54,* 90A.

Concluded that the CPRI is a reliable, valid, and useful inventory that can be used to assess students' readiness for career planning, aid career guidance, and evaluate the effectiveness of career development interventions.

1271. Grainer, M. S. (1986). An investigation of the efficacy of group counseling with emotionally disturbed middle school students (Doctoral dissertation, The College of William and Mary in Virginia, 1986). *Dissertation Abstracts International, 47*, 3703A.

Examined and compared the efficacy of non-directive group counseling and structured group counseling with emotionally disturbed students. While not statistically significant, results suggested that group counseling in general and structured group counseling in particular may have some potential to effect changes with ED students.

1272.   Hagborg, W. J. (1990). Enhancing middle-school-age students' knowledge of school counseling services. *Psychology in the Schools, 27*(3), 238-243.

Found that one-session classroom presentations about school counseling services significantly increased students' awareness of those services. Grades 5-8 students were able to list four reasons for seeking out counseling, give a definition of counselling and give two methods of making an appointment with the school psychologist.

1273.   Harrison, A. S. (1993). An evaluation model for middle school counseling and guidance (Doctoral dissertation, Old Dominion University, 1993). *Dissertation Abstracts International, 54*, 1677A.

Using the framework of Daniel Stufflebeam's CIPP model, an evaluation program was developed to provide information to be used in planning a comprehensive and developmentally-appropriate counseling and guidance program for early adolescence.

1274.   Mohr, P. H., Sprinthall, N. A., & Gerler, Jr., E. R. (1987). Moral reasoning in early adolescence: Implications for drug abuse prevention. *The School Counselor, 35*(2), 120-127.

The study involving eighth graders found "that adolescents may reason at lower levels about drug use than they do about other issues and thus may be unable to make responsible decisions in drug-related matters." Suggested that drug prevention programs should focus on issues rather than matters of judgment. Sex differences in reasoning need to be taken into consideration when designing programs.

1275.   Remley, Jr., T. P., & Albright, P. L. (1988). Expectations for middle school counselors: Views of students, teachers, principals, and parents. *The School Counselor, 35*(4), 290-296.

Structured interviews were used to determine perceptions of the role of middle school counselors held by students, teachers, principals, and parents. Suggested that counselors either meet the expectations of the populations they serve or, through education, change those expectations. Recommends that counselors do more counseling with students and fewer administrative tasks.

1276.   Tilghman, W. S. (1989). The effect of peer counseling on lowering the rate of middle school suspensions (Doctoral dissertation, Florida Atlantic University, 1988). *Dissertation Abstracts International*, *49*, 2118A.

The author investigated the effect of an in-place middle level peer counseling program on the rate of suspensions. The study involved ninety-one students randomly selected from sixth, seventh, and eighth grade students suspended during one academic year. A change of student attitude was measured using the Piers-Harris Children's Self-Concept Scale to determine the effect of attitude change on the decrease of disruptive behavior. The disruptive behavior was measured by computing the change in the rate of suspensions over a predeter-mined period of time. The in-place middle level peer counseling program lowered the suspension rate within the middle school by seventy-six percent.

1277.   Wilson, J., Thomas, D., & Schuette, L. (1983). Survey of counselors on identifying and reporting cases of child abuse. *The School Counselor*, *30*(4), 299-305.

Results of survey indicated that 62% of respondents strongly agreed or agreed (33%) that child abuse was a serious problem in the United States, but felt it was more serious in the rest of the country than in their own communities and stated that they encountered few cases personally. Questions about counselor performance levels were raised.

B. COUNSELING - PRACTICAL

1278.   Badgley, M. (1992). Peer counselors—AWESOME helpers. *New Mexico Middle School Journal*, *2*, 3-5.

Discusses a model peer counseling program. Includes "six secrets for successful peer-counseling programs." Presents case studies of situations in which peer counselors have assisted students with problems.

1279.   Baharoglu, B. J. (1989). Developing and upgrading an elementary and middle school guidance program: A case study. *The School Counselor*, *37*(1), 23-30.

Describes the personal experiences of a counselor who set up a K-7 counseling program. Four stages of the program were discussed: (1) gathering information and establishing rapport, (2) setting goals and addressing needs, (3) developing and implementing the plan, and (d) planning for continued program development.

1280.   Beale, A. V. (1984). Exploring careers through volunteerism. *The School Counselor*, *32*(1), 68-71.

Explains how middle school students can use volunteerism for career exploration and skills development. Describes a workshop designed to familiarize students with the rewards of volunteerism, assist students in locating and applying for volunteer positions, and acquaint students with ways of making the most of their experiences.

1281.   Berkson, J., & Griggs, S. A. (1986). An intergenerational program at a middle school. *The School Counselor, 34*(2), 140-143.

Describes a program called "Between the Generations," which seeks to counteract the lack of knowledge and understanding between older adults in the community and school children.

1282.   Bowman, R. P. (1986). Peer facilitator programs for middle graders: Students helping each other grow up. *School Counselor, 33*(3), 221-229.

Describes the selection, training, and use of peer facilitators by school counselors. Projects for peer facilitators include providing student assistance, acting as special friends, and leading small group discussions. The author supports these activities by citing key developmental tasks of middle school children.

1283.   Brough, J. A. (1985). The teacher as counselor: Some practical considerations. *Middle School Journal, 16*(4), 4, 8-9.

The guidance job of the teacher is to assist students in daily decision-making and in their relationships. Lists considerations and activities to be used by the effective teacher-counselor. An excellent article for use in pre-teaching methods classes to help pre-teachers understand the guidance role of teaching. A good review for experienced teachers.

1284.   Bunnell, S. (1993). *Handling relationships: 50 problem solving activities*. ESC Learning Systems.

50 reproducible black-line masters. Case studies with questions help teens develop the empathy, analysis, and problem-solving skills that enable them to maintain good relationships.

1285.   Cole, C. G. (1988). *Guidance in middle level schools: Everyone's responsibility*. Columbus, OH: National Middle School Association. 29 pp.

As the title suggests, the author of this booklet delineates how it is virtually everyone's job in the middle school to act in a "guidance" role in the middle school. In the booklet Cole describes what she means by "guidance," provides a rationale for a middle level program and the guidance role, discusses the roles of specific personnel (e.g., counselors, teachers, administrators, paraprofessional and clerical assistants, parents and the community at large, students, etc.), and provides a listing of sample activities and resources. Teachers and administrators will find the two latter set of materials particularly helpful.

1286.   Crowder, W. W. (1983). Teaching about stress. *The Clearing House, 57*(1), 36-38.

Focuses on the emotional and social situations that often cause stress in young adolescents. Includes helpful suggestions for understanding and addressing those concerns.

1287.   Elkind, D. (1986). Stress and the middle grader. *The School Counselor*, *33*(3), 196-206.

Describes three types of stress experienced by middle school children: foreseeable and avoidable (drug and alcohol use), unforeseeable and unavoidable (parental divorce), and foreseeable and unavoidable (tests). Describes typical responses to such stress including anxiety, depression, and anger. Provides "guidance strategies" (p. 205) such as decision-making skills, reliance on a value system, and good work habits.

1288.   Fehr, D. E. (1993). When faculty and staff mentor students in inner-city schools. *Middle School Journal*, *25*(1), 65-68.

Case study of a mentoring program at Fonville Middle School in Houston, Texas. Focuses on mentoring activities, roles and responsibilities of mentors, and characteristics of effective mentors.

1289.   George, P. S. (1986). The counselor and modern middle-level schools: New roles in new schools. *The School Counselor*, *33*(3), 178-188.

Explores the results of effectiveness research in corporate and school settings and suggest new roles for school counselors, including nurturing the school mission, guiding program development, facilitating instruction and group involvement, and belonging to a leadership team.

1290.   Gumaer, J. (1986). Working in groups with middle graders. *The School Counselor*, *33*(3), 230-238.

Describes four types of groups that can be used by school counselors to provide support for developmental issues in middle school settings. These include: "(a) classroom group guidance, (b) discussion groups, (c) growth-centered group counseling, and (d) problem-centered group counseling" (p. 230). Provides recommendations for goals and objectives, topics, group size, and duration for each type.

1291.   Mauk, G. W., & Taylor, M. J. (1993). Counselors in middle schools: Issues of recognition, reclaiming, redefinition, and rededication. *Middle School Journal*, *24* (5), 3-9.

Discusses the importance of middle level counselors to effective middle level programs. Recognizes the need for counselors to have both the prerequisite skills and time to respond to the needs of young adolescents. Distinguishes between an advisor and a counselor and urges administrators to allow counselors to concentrate on the relevant roles and responsibilities, not on non-guidance activities.

1292.   Maultsby, Jr., M. C. (1986). Teaching rational self-counseling to middle graders. *The School Counselor, 33*(3), 207-219.

Presents a research-based, self-help method for helping middle schoolers deal with their emotions. Includes rationale, specific instructions, and a case study.

1293.   Medis, N. A., & Wilson, N. S. (1985). Teachers as partners: Extending guidance services. *Middle School Journal, 16*(4), 5-7.

Five school guidance projects are reviewed which demonstrate that a "wide variety of approaches can be utilized to involved the entire staff in developmental guidance activities." Benefits to students, teachers, and counselors are listed. Nine suggestions are provided for starting a program of staff involvement in guidance. The authors found that teachers, with "their extensive knowledge of and daily contact with students, can become valuable members of the guidance team."

1294.   Mitchum, N. T. (1983). Introducing TIP, the Total Involvement Program for peer facilitators. *The School Counselor, 31*(2), 146-149.

Describes a program for training middle school students to be counselors for elementary school students. TIP proved to be beneficial for both age levels of children.

1295.   Nelson, R. C. (1991). The counselor as reinforcer. *The School Counselor, 39*(2), 68-76.

Offers a variety of concrete and useful suggestions for offering support to students, at-risk students, teachers, parents, administrators, and staff.

1296.   Ostrower, E. G. (1987). A counseling approach to alcohol education in middle schools. *The School Counselor, 34*(3), 209-218.

Describes a program "What We Need to Know about Alcohol," which was developed to provide correct information on the subject and to help students develop decision-making skills to enable them to make better choices about the use of alcohol in their own lives.

1297.   Roberts, H. C. (1984). Uncloseting the cumulative record: A parent-student-counselor conferences project. *The School Counselor, 32*(1), 54-60.

Describes how a conference based on a child's cumulative record was conducted and provides the results of the evaluation data gathered.

1298.   Rosa, A., & Vowels, M. (1986). Helping 8th graders make a "smooth move." *Educational Leadership, 44*(1), 58.

Lists a series of rituals developed to help eighth graders make the transition to high school.

1299.   Sabatini, L. (1989). Preparing eighth graders for the social pressures of high school. *The School Counselor, 35*(3), 203-207.

Describes a program designed to prepare eighth graders for the social pressures of high school by improving leadership skills. Informal evaluations indicate positive responses to the program.

1300.   Sharp, J. V. (1984). Career education in the middle school: A teaching unit (Doctoral dissertation, Columbia University teachers College, 1984). *Dissertation Abstracts International, 45,* 2346A.

Includes rationale for and an actual teaching unit focused on a work experience program designed to provide middle school teachers and administrators with sufficient information to meet a school's obligation regarding career education.

1301.   Smith, R. M., & Mauceri, P. K. (1982). Suicide—The ultimate middle school trauma. *Middle School Journal, 14*(1), 21-24.

Reviews events that occurred in a school after learning of a student's suicide. Gives a set of recommended steps in rendering psychological first aid to potential suicides.

1302.   Steward, W. J. (1993). Optimizing classroom guidance in the middle school. *Middle School Journal, 25* (1), 41-43.

Discusses key components of an effective classroom guidance program for middle level students. Stresses that such programs must be designed to address personal, social, and emotional concerns of adolescents through guidance-integrated curriculum, home-base advisement, guidance-related units, interdisciplinary team teaching, and counseling.

1303.   Thornburg, H. D. (1986). The counselor's impact on middle grade students. *School Counselor, 33*(3), 170-177.

Reviews the developmental tasks of children in middle school (physical, intellectual, and social) and describes characteristics of effective counselors for working with this age group.

1304.   Wilson, N. S. (1986). Preparing for examinations: A classroom guidance unit. *The School Counselor, 33*(4), 297-305.

Describes a classroom guidance unit designed to assist students in exploring their skills, habits, and attitudes related to taking examinations. Includes a format for a study and test-taking student profile.

C. COUNSELING - GENERAL

1305.   McGee, L., & Fauble-Erickson, T. (1995). Multifaceted role of guidance and counseling in the middle level school. *NASSP Bulletin, 79*(570), 16-19.

Delineates the responsibilities of the school counselor as provider, consultant and coordinator. Suggests helpful roles for both teachers and administrators to meet the developmental needs of middle level students.

1306.   Sears, S. J. (1995). Career and educational planning in the middle level school. *NASSP Bulletin, 79*(570), 36-43.

Advocates inclusion of career planning involving parents and students during the middle school years. The need to explore options is emphasized with an understanding that career plans begin to take shape in high school. Cites research on gender differences in career planning with a need to improve the options perceived by girls. Outlines five goals for career counseling at the middle level.

1307.   Vaught, C. C. (1995). Letter from a middle school counselor to her principal. *NASSP Bulletin, 79*(570), 20-23.

Offers an appreciative review of the characteristics of a principal that made the work of one counselor more effective. These include several communication skills and supportive behaviors.

1308.   Wilson, N. S. (1983). "What can school do for me?": A guidance play. *The School Counselor, 30*(5), 374-380.

Brief introduction and script for a fantasy in which a middle school student and a superhero companion take a tour of the world of careers. The play lasts 15 minutes and uses a cast of twelve characters.

D. SELF CONCEPT

1309.   Beane, J. A. (1986). The self-enhancing middle-grade school. *The School Counselor, 33*(3), 189-195.

Provides arguments for the role of school personnel in "enhancing the self-perceptions of middle graders" (p. 190). Factors influencing self-esteem include "the character of the teachers, the nature of the learning activities, and the social nature of middle graders" (p. 191). Concludes with recommendations for the changing role of counselors in raising awareness of self-esteem issues, providing staff development, contributing to curriculum planning, and developing support networks.

1310.   Clayton, G. A., Horns, V., & Brown, T. (1986). Self-concept and anxiety in middle school students living in intact, single partner, and blended families. In David B. Strahan (Ed.), *Middle school research: Selected studies 1986* (pp. 2-15). Columbus, OH: Research Committee of the National Middle School Association.

"The purpose of this study was to examine the concepts of self and parents and the anxiety levels of middle school children living in intact, blended or single parent families. The sample was comprised of 219 students in grades 6 through 8. The instruments used were the Personal Attribute Inventory for Children (self-concept), and the State-Trait Anxiety Inventory for Children (anxiety) results indicated no significant differences in concepts of self or parents or in levels of anxiety related to family type."

1311.   Community Service Learning Center. (1990). *Community service elective course for high school students.* Springfield, MA: Community Service Learning Center.

A curriculum guide for students as they explore their self-worth and civic responsibilities. Designed for use in Springfield, Massachusetts, school systems but can be adapted for use in other settings.

1312.   Haynes, N. M. (1990). Influence of self-concept on school adjustment among middle-school students. *Journal of Social Psychology, 130*(2), 199-207.

The author explores the relationship between specific self-concept dimensions and school adjustment in three areas: (1) general classroom behavior; (2) group participation; and (3) attitude toward authority. There was significant bivariate correlations between each self-concept dimension. The study involved urban, inner-city, African-American, and middle level students.

1313.   Ray, N. G. (1990). The effects of participation in the Lion's Quest-Skills for Adolescence Program on student self-concept at the middle school level (Doctoral dissertation, University of La Verne, 1990). *Dissertation Abstracts International, 52*, 82A.

Results indicated significant growth in self-concept when measured by the Piers-Harris Children's Self-Concept Scale. Recommends that self-concept programs be included in middle schools and that proper training for parents and teachers be provided.

1314.   Wolfle, J. (1995). Helping middle level and high school students develop trust, respect, and self-confidence. *NASSP Practitioner, 21*(4), 1-4.

Suggests that gathering resources, assuming competency of students, expecting success, providing a safe environment, moral reflection, volunteering, and conflict mediation can all contribute to improving the confidence of students. Three middle schools with successful programs are highlighted.

E. SUICIDE

1315.   Coy, D. R. (1995). Need for a school suicide prevention policy. *NASSP Bulletin, 79*(570), 1-9.

Identifies the range of stressors that can lead to suicide as a response from young people. Includes a sample of Elkind Stress Scale (p. 4) that could be used to identify students at high risk for suicide. Outlines components of a suicide prevention program.

1316.   Kirk, W. G. (1993). *Adolescent suicide*. Champaign, IL: Research Press. 190 pp.

Provides information required to accurately identify potentially suicidal adolescents and the skills necessary for appropriate and effective intervention. Contains numerous case examples provided by parents, mental health professionals, and educators, as well as adolescents who have considered suicide or survived suicide attempts.

1317.   Toepfer, C. F. (1986). Suicide in middle level schools: Implications for principals. *NASSP Bulletin: The Journal for High School and Middle School Administrators*, *70* (487), 55-60.

Toepfer discusses the need to address young adolescents' social-emotional needs, the realities of youth suicide, problems in pubescence, the principal's responsibilities, and suicide danger signals.

1318.   Vidal, J. A. (1989). *Student suicide: A guide for intervention*. Washington, DC: National Education Association. 59 pp.

Provides a "field-tested plan" for becoming "response ready" to a crisis of this nature. Provides information on prevention techniques as well as in regard to a crisis team approach following a "completed suicide."

XXI

Health

A. EARLY ADOLESCENT AND ADOLESCENT HEALTH - RESEARCH

1319.   Davies, J. (1993). The impact of the mass media upon the health of early adolescents. *Journal of Health Education, 24*(Suppl. 6), 28-35.

Presents statistics on the popularity of media such as television, movie, and radio among young adolescents. Highlights the messages surrounding the issues of "nutrition, sexuality, alcohol and tobacco use, violence, and stress" (p. 29). Advocates the development of "media literacy" for both parents, teachers and students.

1320.   Doherty, D., Eden, J., Kemp, K. B., Metcalf, K., Rowe, K., Ruby, G., Strobel, P., & Solarz, A. (1992). Adolescent health: A report to the U.S. Congress. *Journal of School Health, 62*(5), 167-174.

A report by the Office of Technology Assessment that provides evidence on the "extent of health problems among adolescents...barriers to health services...and three major strategies...to improve adolescents' health" (p. 167). Defining adolescence as the period from 10-18 years the authors identify the major health problems of adolescents in the areas of acute and chronic illness, sexually transmitted diseases, pregnancy, mental health disorders, substance abuse and social problems involving the family and the school. Factors in the lives of adolescents who do well are identified and include "developmentally appropriate social support" (p. 168) and features of the school environment that are currently advocated in the design of middle schools: "small, comfortable, safe, and intellectually engaging and emotionally intimate communities" (p. 168). Services needed to improve the health of adolescents are "health promotion, problem prevention, and treatment" (p. 168). Financial, legal, family, cognitive, provider, and cultural barriers to access are examined. "School-linked or community based health services" (p. 170) emerge as the most effective way of providing comprehensive services. Such services need to be "responsive to the specific needs of adolescents" (p. 170). The OTA recommends three possible approaches to improve adolescent health: increased access to services; increased federal involvement in program development, research, and data collection; and support to improve the social environment.

1321.   Farrand, L. L., & Cox, C. L. (1993). Determinants of positive health behavior in middle childhood. *Nursing Research, 42*(4), 208-213.

The authors used self-report data from 260 children ages 9 - 10 years and their mothers to test the Interaction Model of Client Health Behavior. Major factors in the model are client singularity (such as demographics, environmental resources, motivation, cognitive appraisal and affective response), client-profes-sional interaction (affective support, health information, decisional control, and professional/technical competence), and health outcomes. Measures for elements of client singularity and health outcomes were examined in the study. Girls scored significantly higher on the health outcomes measure and therefore two models based on gender were tested. Fifty-three percent of the variance in health behaviors for girls was explained by the model and 43% of the variance for boys. "The modifiable variables of motivation, self-esteem, and personal perception of health influenced each other" (p. 212). The authors offer sugges-tions for providers who work with children regarding influencing health behaviors.

1322.   Forney, M. A., Forney, P. D., & Van Hoose, J. (1985). The causes of alcohol abuse by young adolescents. In David Strahan (Ed.), *Middle school research: Selected studies 1985* (pp. 1-10). Columbus, OH: Research Committee of the National Middle School Association.

Concludes that knowledge about alcohol and its detrimental effects do not appear to make a statistically significant different in regard to behavior and that middle level students (at least in this study) seem to follow the drinking patterns of their parents. The researchers make the recommendation that the basic "alcohol education program" in the middle level setting should be supplemented with special activities for potential problem drinkers.

1323.   Furby, L., & Beyth-Marom, R. (1990). *Risk taking in adolescence: A decision-making perspective.* (Working paper available from Carnegie Council on Adolescent Development, 2400 N Street, NW, Washington, DC 20037).

Provides a theoretical model for decision-making in general and risk-taking in particular. Contrasts the differences between adult and adolescent perception of risk. Discusses implications of the decision-making research for developing health promotion and health protection interventions.

1324.   Gittler, J., Quigley-Rick, M., & Saks, M. J. (1990). *Adolescent health care decision making: The law and public policy.* (Working paper available from Carnegie Council on Adolescent Development, 2400 N Street, NW, Washington, DC 20037).

Reviews laws related to requirements for, limitations of, and impact of parental consent and notification for adolescent health care. Reviews research on competency of minor's to make decisions related to health. Recommends that the Federal government consider developing policies that balance the interests of parents, adolescents, and state governments.

1325.   Hechinger, F. M. (Ed.). (1992). Adolescent health: A generation at risk. *Carnegie Quarterly, 37*(4), 2-16.

An entire issue devoted to a review of the 1992 conference "Crossroads: Critical Choices for the Development of Healthy Adolescents" sponsored by the Carnegie Council on Adolescent Development. Identifies trends in at risk behavior (early sexual activity and alcohol use). Cites the lack of training of health professionals for assessing and meeting the needs of adolescents. School-based health services are highlighted as a way to deliver developmentally-based care. Such centers need to provide comprehensive care and to be available beyond the hours of the traditional school day. Effective programs for preventing substance abuse were highlighted.

1326.   Hechinger, F. (1992). *Fateful choices: Healthy youth for the 21st Century.* New York: Carnegie Council on Adolescent Development. 255 pp.

A persuasive report supported by the Carnegie Foundation on the health risks facing today's young people. This highly readable book presents statistics on the problems of adolescent sex, sustance abuse, violence and nutrition, supplemented by stories of model programs designed to prevent or ameliorate the damaging effects of such problems. Information on the potential for youth organizations to decrease the negative impact of these problems is highlighted. *Fateful Choices* concludes with specific recommendations in the areas of education, health services, media, work, continuity of services, violence and safety, and funding. It is an essential resource for all people who work with young adolescents.

1327.   Lynch, D. O. (1988). Tobacco use behavior in grades 5-12. In David B. Strahan (Ed.), *Middle school research: Selected studies 1988* (pp. 114-131). Columbus, OH: The Research Committee of the National Middle School Association.

"In March 1987, the National Cancer Institute's standard form of common questions for school-based intervention was administered in grades 5-12 of the Oshkosh Public Schools to start a multi-year research program. Also, a pilot questionnaire of knowledge, beliefs, and attitudes concerning tobacco use was administered to a sample of grades 6, 7, 8, 10, and 12. Results indicate an important tobacco use problem beginning approximately in sixth grade and peaking at eleventh. Smoking is a significant problem among both males and females. Chewing tobacco and snuff use are significant among males (peaking at about 20%), but not among females (never over 1%). The pilot questionnaire was found useful for measuring attitudes and knowledge and predicting tobacco usage. Survey results are being used in health curricula construction and to measure the impact of curricular and other environmental changes on tobacco use behavior."

1328.   Males, M. (1992). The code blue report: Call to action, or unwarranted "dirism"? *Adolescence, 27*(106), 273-282.

A critical analysis of the recommendations of the 1990 report on adolescent health. Offers statistical evidence to dispute many of the conclusions of the report.

1329.   Massachusetts Department of Education. (1990). *Educating the whole student: The school's role in the physical, intellectual, social and emotional development of children.* (Available from Massachusetts Department of Education, Bureau of Student Development and Health, 1385 Hancock St., Quincy, MA 02169).

A position paper with information for schools to use in determining how well they are providing for the growth and development needs of their students. Makes a case for the position that all segments of society must claim responsibility for caring for children. Emphasizes the need for comprehensive planning. Strategies suggested include parent involvement, flexible curricular planning, fostering positive relationships with at least one adult, student decision-making, staff support, integrated special educational services, clarification of leadership roles of key school personnel, and the development of partnerships with other service providers. The paper includes the names and telephone numbers of numerous contact persons for each strategy.

1330.   Meeting the health needs of young adolescents. (1993). *Turning Points: State Network News,* Carnegie Corporation of New York Middle Grade School State Policy Initiative.

An entire issue devoted to efforts to meet the health needs of adolescents. Offers highlights from publications supported by Carnegie. Summarizes risk behaviors of sexuality, substance abuse, violence, safety, and nutrition and physical activity. Cites findings from a survey of 500 elementary teachers done by the American Academy of Pediatrics that indicates psychological, emotional, lifestyle, abuse and poor nutrition as the most common health problems of students in their schools. Low income children and those who have academic failure are more likely to have health risks. Comprehensive school health programs are identified as the best approach. Components of such programs (instruction, services, and environment) are discussed in the newsletter.

1331.   Millstein, S. G., Nightingale, E. O., Petersen, A. C., Mortimer, A. M., & Hamburg, D. A. (1993). Promoting the healthy development of adolescents. *Journal of the American Medical Association, 269*(11), 1413-1424.

Summarizes the "major themes and recommendations" (p. 1413) from several recent reports on the health status of adolescents. Based on a review of evaluation studies, the authors identify the following principles of successful health promotion programs: population specific approaches, recognition of cultural and social contexts, and broad-based participation by different provider groups. The authors set forth a research agenda that emphasizes the need to understand the factors that promote healthy development, the environmental context in which health behaviors are practiced, the cultural variations of health in adolescence and the view of health from the perspective of the adolescent. They recommend enhancing the role of teachers and schools in promoting health through better understanding of the developmental needs of adolescents and the ability of practitioners to collaborate across settings. Examples of policy recommendations to support health are included.

1332.   National Commission on the Role of the School and the Community in Improving Adolescent Health. (1992). *Code blue: Uniting for healthier youth.* Alexandria, VA: National Association of State Boards of Education.

Report of the American Medical Association to the National Association of State Boards of Education recommending that we "guarantee all adolescents access to health services regardless of ability to pay...make communities the front line in the battle for adolescent health...organize services around people...[and] urge schools to play a stronger role in improving adolescent health" (preface). The report describes methods for implementing the recommendations, many of which are community based. Calls for schools that are more personal, more positive, and that provide healthier environments.

1333.   Petersen, A. C., Compas, B. E., & Brooks-Gunn, J. (1992). *Depression in adolescence: Current knowledge, research directions, and implications for programs and policy.* (Working paper available from Carnegie Council on Adolescent Development, 2400 N Street, NW, Washington, DC 20037).

A synthesis of the research on adolescent depression. Provides recommendations for research particularly on the etiology and long-term consequences of adolescent depression. Calls for a preventive approach with children whose parents are depressed.

1334.   Smolak, L., Levine, M.P., & Gralen, S. (1993). The impact of puberty and dating on eating problems among middle school girls. *Journal of Youth and Adolescence*, 22(4), 355-368.

Report of a portion of a longitudinal study of middle school girls. Instruments included "pubertal and dating status, body dissatisfaction, weight management, and eating disordered attitudes" (p. 355). The results indicate that girls who experience the events of early menarche and dating have greater body dissatisfaction and may be at greater risk for developing eating disorders.

1335.   Staff. (1993). Meeting the health needs of young adolescents. *Turning Points: State Network News.* Carnegie Corporation of New York Middle Grade School State Policy Initiate.

An entire issue devoted to efforts to meet the health needs of adolescents. Offers highlights from publications supported by Carnegie. Summarizes risk behaviors of sexuality, substance abuse, violence, safety, and nutrition and physical activity. Cites findings from a survey of 500 elementary teachers done by the American Academy of Pediatrics that indicates psychological, emotional, lifestyle, abuse and poor nutrition as the most common health problems of students in their schools. Low income children and those who have academic failure are more likely to have health risks. Comprehensive school health programs are identified as the best approach. Components of such programs (instruction, services, and environment) are discussed in the newsletter.

1336.   Starfield, B., Bergner, M., Ensminger, M., Riley, A., Ryan, S., Green, B., McGauhey, P., Skinner, A., & Kim, S. (1993). Adolescent health status measurement: Development of the Child Health and Illness Profile. *Pediatrics, 91*(2), 430-435.

Describes the psychometric properties of a newly developed self-report instrument for estimating the health status of children aged 11-17 years. The instrument covers the domains of activity, comfort, satisfaction, disorders, achievement of developmental expectations, and resilience. Future research is planned to shorten the form so it could be used in settings to evaluate interventions targeted to this age group.

1337.   United States Congress, Office of Technology Assessment. (1991). *Adolescent health - Volume I: Summary and policy options*, OTA-H-468. Washington, DC: U. S. Government Printing Office.

Profiles the health needs of adolescents 10-18 years old with suggestions for improving access to health services, increasing Federal support for such services, and improving environments.

1338.   Van Hoose, J., & Cohen, S. M. (1980). Substance abuse during the middle school years: A national profile. *Middle school research: Selected studies 1980* (pp. 105-112). Fairborn, OH: Research Committee and Publications Committee of the National Middle School Association.

An interesting review of the research concerning the use of drugs by middle level students. Among the chemical substances focused on were alcohol, cigarettes, marijuana, amphetamines, barbiturates, and other drugs such as inhalants, hallucinogens, cocaine, heroin, and other opiates. The authors report that "the data indicate a relatively steady increase in substance abuse over the last several years. If one combines this fact with the findings that reflect the shift from non-usage to usage between the 6th and 8th grades, a strong research base merges, lending support to the development and implementation of a comprehensive substance abuse program no later than the 6th grade (and preferably by the fourth grade).

B.   EARLY ADOLESCENT AND ADOLESCENT HEALTH - PRACTICAL

1339.   Flora, J. A. (1990). *Strategies for enhancing adolescents' health through music media.* (Working paper available from Carnegie Council on Adolescent Development, 2400 N Street, NW, Washington, DC 20037).

Presents eight strategies for influencing adolescent health: media campaigns, dissemination of critical viewing materials, communication among participants, consultation with medial industry, media advocacy, curriculum development and federal regulation. Includes research agenda on effectiveness of interventions and studies to gain a better understanding of adolescent use of media.

1340.   Giordano, B. P., & Igoe, J. B. (1991). Health promotion: The new frontier. *Pediatric Nursing, 17(5),* 490-492.

Briefly describes several health promotion programs including the Pawtucket Heart Health Program and Teenage Health Teaching Modules which are appropriate for adolescents.

1341.   Hamburg, B. A. (1990). *Life skills training: Preventive interventions for young adolescents.* (Working paper available from Carnegie Council on Adolescent Development, 2400 N Street, NW, Washington, DC 20037).

Presents detail on several life skills training programs. Bases recommendations for widespread dissemination of life skills programs on the extensive evaluation of effectiveness of the School Health Curriculum Project (SHCP) developed by the Public Health Service. Builds on the recommendations of *Turning Points* that middle schools are an appropriate setting for life skills development.

1342.   Igoe, J. B. (1990). Beyond green beans and oat bran: A health agenda for the 1990s for school-age youth. *Pediatric Nursing, 16(3),* 289-292.

A summary of the work of the American School Health Association School Nurse Study Committee, Task Force on Health Promotion related to the role of the school nurse. Highlights efforts in disease prevention, health promotion, and health protection to reach the health objectives for the nation in the year 2000. Recommends development of interdisciplinary school task forces, expanded assessments by nurses, development of annual health promotion plans, leadership in safety programs, provision of health education, nutrition guidance, communicable disease prevention, and continuing education for staff and teachers.

1343.   Igoe, J. B. (1990). Healthy people 2000. *Pediatric Nursing, 16(6),* 584-586.

Includes the suggested health screening and promotion activities for children ages 7 to 12 years recommended by the U.S. Preventive Services Task Force. Useful for school nurses and health officials.

1344.   Igoe, J. B. (1991). Health behavior surveys for youth. *Pediatric Nursing, 17(4),* 391-392.

Highlights the characteristics of the Wellness Check Teen Health Appraisal, Adolescent Health Survey, and Youth Risk Behavior Survey. Includes time needed for administration. Recommends nurse involvement in using such tools for program planning and evaluation.

1345.   National School Boards Association. (1991). *School health: Helping children learn*. Alexandria, VA: National School Boards Association.

An outstanding guide for school leaders which describes a comprehensive approach to health in school settings through education, services, and environmental interventions. Provides detailed steps for district planning. Several exemplary programs in districts of various sizes are profiled. Includes a list of supporting organizations, literature, and funding sources.

1346.   Resnicow, K., Cherry, J., & Cross, D. (1992). Ten unanswered questions regarding comprehensive school health promotion. *Journal of School Health, 63*(4), 171-175.

Examines the research on the effectiveness of comprehensive school health education. Suggests several areas needing further research and consideration including 1) duration of effects, 2) timing of intervention, 3) isolated versus comprehensive approach, 4) key subcomponents, 5) effects on academic performance versus school attendance, 6) funding policies, 7) use of specialists in primary grades, 8) current status of such programs in the U. S., 9) feasibility, and 10) cost-effectiveness. Useful in setting a research agenda.

1347.   Smith, D. W., Stechler, A., McLeroy, K. R., Bennett, J., & Frye, R. (1991). Promoting comprehensive school health programs through summer health promotion conferences. *Journal of School Health, 61(2)*, 69-74.

Describes efforts to create effective teams to promote Kolbe's comprehensive school health model (school health services, school health education, school health environment, integrated school and community health promotion efforts, school physical education, school food services, school counseling, and health promotion services for faculty and staff) through week long conferences. Uses Rogers' diffusion of innovation model to identify participants and develop strategies to increase awareness and promote adoption of the programs.

1348.   Stone, E. J., & Perry, C. L. (1990). United States: Perspectives in school health. *Journal of School Health, 60*(7), 363-369.

A broad overview of child mortality, health care system, education system, school health, research in school settings, and federal support for health promotion.

1349.   Wilder, P. (1984). No one profits from candy in the schools. *Middle School Journal, 15*(4), 18-19, 31.

Explains the physical problems generated by too much sugar in the bloodstream, then discusses behavioral problems caused by too much sugar. Suggests alternatives to candy in schools, including better nutritional education, changes in lunch programs, and T-shirt and craft sales rather than candy sales.

C. EARLY ADOLESCENT AND ADOLESCENT HEALTH - GENERAL

1350.   Dryfoos, J. (1994). *Full-service schools: A revolution in health and social services for children, youth and families*. San Francisco, CA: Jossey-Bass, Publishers. 336 pages.

Offers a broad view of the future of service delivery where children are to better meet their needs and improve academic performance. Includes a chapter on successful school-based clinics.

1351.   Hamburg, D. A. (1989). *Early adolescence: A critical time for interventions in education and health*. New York, NY: Carnegie Corportation of New York. (ERIC Document Reproduction Service No. ED 323 453).

An opinion piece urging implementation of the recommendation related to health promotion outlined in Turning Points.

D. HEALTH EDUCATION - RESEARCH

1352.   Brindis, C. (1993). Health policy reform and comprehensive school health education: The need for an effective partnership. *Journal of School Health, 63(1)*, 33-37.

Outlines the major causes of mortality and morbidity for children. Presents the need to develop outcomes-based arguments for support of comprehensive school health education. Emphasizes the need for coalitions among decision-makers in education and health. Provides an example from the state of Michigan.

1353.   Davies, J. (1993). The impact of the mass media upon the health of early adolescents. *Journal of Health Education, 24*(Suppl. 6), 28-35.

Presents statistics on the popularity of media such as television, movie, and radio among young adolescents. Highlights the messages surrounding the issues of "nutrition, sexuality, alcohol and tobacco use, violence, and stress" (p. 29). Advocates the development of "media literacy" for both parents, teachers and students.

1354.   Errecart, M. T., Walberg, H. J., Ross, J. G., Gold, R. S., Fiedler, J. L., & Kolbe, L. J. (1991). Effectiveness of teenage health teaching modules. *Journal of School Health, 61(1)*, 26-30.

Describes the results of an evaluation of a health education curriculum for middle level, junior and senior high school students using a quasi-experimental pre-test post-test design. The final sample consisted of 4,806 students from schools in Maryland, Vermont, and California assigned to either experimental and control sections. Significant differences in gain scores were found in knowledge, attitudes, practices and priority health behaviors for some groups. Findings were confirmed through the use of linear modeling.

1355.   Gold, R. S., Parcel, G. S., Walberg, H. J., Luepker, R. V., Portnoy, B., & Stone, E. J. (1991). Summary and conclusions of the THTM evaluation: The expert work group perspective. *Journal of School Health, 61(1),* 39-42.

In addition to summarizing the significant results of the research from a quasi-experimental pre-test post-test design used to evaluate a health education curriculum for middle level, junior and senior high school students, the authors offer recommendations in the area of state level educational policy and future research strategies with emphasis on the junior high/middle level population.

1356.   Hill, H., Piper, D., & King, M. (1993). The nature of school-based prevention experiences for middle school students. *Journal of Health Education, 24*(Suppl. 6), 15-23.

Describes health education in those elementary and middle schools that participated in a study of a specific health education program, Healthy for Life, using data obtained from interviewing telected school personnel. Information was collected on how much time was devoted to "tobacco use, alcohol use, other drug abuse, sexuality, nutrition, and what were defined as 'traditional' health education issues" (p. 16); teaching strategies used; extracurricular events sponsored by the school that related to health education; support for health education; and, what topics were prioritized. Researchers found that the most time was spent on traditional topics and the least time spent on controversial topics such as sexuality. Knowledge level teaching strategies were most frequently used although they are the least effective in changing behavior. Perceived support for health education was mixed. Suggestions for dealing with the barriers to health education are provided.

1357.   Kingery, P. M., Pruitt, B. E., & Hurley, R. S. (1993). Adolescent exposure to school health education: Factors and consequences. *Journal of Health Education, 24*(Suppl. 6), 42-46.

Secondary analysis of data from the National Adolescent Student Health Survey was done to examine the "factors affecting exposure to school health education programs, and the consequences of school-based health education" (p. 42). Discriminant analysis was used to see if variables such as knowledge, behavior, and demographics could differentiate between students who received health instruction and those who did not receive instruction. A recommendation is made for providing health education before behaviors begin to surface.

1358.   Lavin, A. T., Shapiro, G. R., & Weill, K. S. (1992). Creating an agenda for school-based health promotion: A review of 25 selected reports. *Journal of School Health, 62* (6), 212-228.

A synthesis of reports by members of the Harvard School Health Education Project whose purpose is to "raise public and professional awareness of school health promotion issues, to contribute to comprehensive school health education theory, practice, and evaluation; and to examine the role of the nations colleges and universities in working with state and local departments of education, departments of health; and with other agencies and organizations to implement and improve comprehensive health education programs" (p. 214). The authors identify five themes: 1) the interrelationship of education and health; 2) threat to health from the social environment and behavior (unintentional injuries, homicide, suicide, abuse and neglect, alcohol and tobacco use); 3) need for a comprehensive, integrated approach to adolescent health promotion; 4) role of the school in health promotion; and 5) cost-effectiveness of prevention efforts. The three state level reports included in the review provide models for implementing comprehensive school health programs for others to use. Concise summaries of the 25 reports and contact information are provided in the article.

1359.   Parcel, G. S., Ross, J. G., Lavin, A. T., Portnoy, B., Nelson, G. D., & Winters, F. (1991). Enhancing implementation of the Teenage Health Teaching Modules. *Journal of School Health, 61(1),* 35-38.

Continues a report on the evaluation study of the Teenage Health Teaching Modules. Compares the predictor variables for the fidelity and proficiency factors related to use of the Teenage Health Teaching Modules by teachers who did or did not receive specific training on implementation.

1360.   Ross, J. G., Gold, R. S., Lavin, A. T., Errecart, M. T., & Nelson, G. D. (1991). Design of Teenage Health Teaching Modules evaluation. *Journal of School Health, 61(1),* 21-25.

Describes a quasi-experimental pre-test post-test design used to evaluate a health education curriculum for middle level, junior and senior high school students. The final sample consisted of 4,806 students from schools in Maryland, Vermont, and California assigned to either experimental and control sections. Specific information on the theoretical basis for the evaluation design are included. Related articles in the journal describe the evaluation results.

1361.   Ross, J. G., Luepker, R. V., Nelson, G. D., Saavedra, P., & Hubbard, B. M. (1991). Teenage Health Teaching Modules: Impact of teacher training on implementation and student outcomes. *Journal of School Health, 61(1),* 31-34.

Describes the results of an evaluation of teacher training that was done concurrently with the evaluation of a health education curriculum for middle level, junior and senior high school students. A post-test only design was used to compare teachers who received training with those who did not receive training. Significantly more program activities were implemented by the trained teachers than those who did not receive training. As far as student outcomes, there were significant differences in knowledge and attitude of students based on training.

1362.   Smith, D. W., Howell, K. A., & McCann, K. M. (1990). Evaluation of the Coalition Index: A guide to school health education materials. *Journal of School Health, 60(2),* 49-52.

Describes research using the application of Hall's Levels of Use model of the

Diffusion Process among health coordinators in relation to their use of the Coalition Index.

1363.   Smith, D. W., McCormick, L. K., Steckler, A. B., & McLeroy, K. R. (1993). Teachers' use of health curricula: Implementation of Growing Healthy, Project SMART, and the Teenage Health Teaching Modules. *Journal of School Health*, *63*(8), 349-354.

A report on the results of a diffusion study of health curricula in sixth and seventh grade classes with a focus on the implementation phase. Researchers were interested in the effect of supportive strategies to influence dissemination of curricula. School districts were assigned to experimental and control groups. After selecting one of three possible health curricula, those districts in the experimental group received extensive training in the use of the curriculum and a follow-up session to boost use. Data were collected at two time periods (initial and subsequent school years). Independent variables with significant influence on whether the curriculum was taught and/or the percent of activities taught included teacher training, presence of a school health coordinator, context of health instruction, type of curricula taught, school format, size of district, and experimental or control condition.

E. HEALTH EDUCATION - PRACTICAL

1364.   Dickerson, T., Osness, D., Scales, P., Nickerson, C., & Tanaka, G. (Eds.). (1993). Addressing the health education needs of young adolescents. *Journal of Health Education, 24*(Suppl. 6).

An entire issue devoted to the needs of children in the middle level. Includes the following articles "What's real in health education," "The centrality of health education to developing young adolescents' critical thinking," "The nature of school-based prevention experiences for middle school students," "'Turning Points' revisited: How effective middle-grades schools address developmental needs of young adolescent students," "The impact of the mass media upon the health of early adolescents," "An interdisciplinary English/health connection: Promoting health awareness and healthy behaviors," "Adolescent exposure to school health education: Factors and consequences," and five teaching ideas. Several of the articles are abstracted separately in this bibliography.

1365.   Elders, M. J. (1993). Schools and health: A natural partnership. *Journal of School Health*, *63*(7), 312-314.

Although not directed specifically to middle level settings, Elders outlines the need for and process of establishing school-based health services basing her reflections on her experience in Arkansas. Especially useful are her comments on the role of school leadership and the components of a comprehensive program.

1366.   Elias, M. J., & Kress, J. S. (1994). Social decision-making and life skills development: A critical thinking approach to health promotion in the middle school. *Journal of School Health, 64*(2), 62-66.

Makes the case for teaching and using a decision model with particular utility at the middle level when applied to risk-taking behavior. References several research studies that have used the model as the treatment variable.

1367.   Flora, J. A. (1990). *Strategies for enhancing adolescents' health through music media.* (Working paper available from Carnegie Council on Adolescent Development, 2400 N Street, NW, Washington, DC 20037).

Presents eight strategies for influencing adolescent health: media campaigns, dissemination of critical viewing materials, communication among participants, consultation with medial industry, media advocacy, curriculum development and Federal regulation. Includes research agenda on effectiveness of interventions and studies to gain a better understanding of adolescent use of media.

1368.   Holcomb, J. D., & Denk, J. P. (1993). An interdisciplinary English/health connection: Promoting health awareness and healthy behaviors. *Journal of Health Education, 24*(Suppl. 6), 36-41.

Report on the development of materials for use in eighth and ninth grade English classes that focused on health topics. Teachers were provided supportive materials and asked to design and pilot test lessons that focused on selected health topics. Evaluation results of the project are included. Lesson guides are available from the authors.

1369.   Ireland, D. F. (1990). New attitude/new look: An African-American adolescent health education program. *Pediatric Nursing, 16*(2), 175-178.

Describes the content of a program whose purpose "included helping ethnic adolescents to integrate into middle class mainstream society with an appreciation for their own culture" (p. 177). Classes were held during the summer at a school-based clinic which serves 12-18 year old females. Topics included self-esteem, nutrition and exercise, hair care and styling, greetings and introductions, self-breast exam, clothing selection, communication skills, and preparation for employment. Family and religious leaders acted in support roles.

1370.   Seffrin, J. R. (1990). The comprehensive school health curriculum: Closing the gap between state-of-the-art and state-of-the-practice. *Journal of School Health, 60*(4), 151-156.

An opinion piece that outlines the mission and purpose of a comprehensive school health curriculum. It addresses specific criteria, content, and instructional methodology. Specific recommendations for increasing broad scale implementation of such a curriculum are outlined including federal and state leadership, professional preparation and curriculum guidelines. The author recommends that "Each secondary teacher (middle school, junior high, and/or high school) should have separate certification in school health education" (p. 154). He also notes that "certain risk behaviors are especially effective at specific stages of development, for example, smoking prevention at grades six-eight" (p. 155).

1371.   Tanaka, G., Warren, J., & Tritsch, L. (1993). What's real in health education. *Journal of Health Education, 24*(Suppl. 6), 6-9.

A description of the use of focus groups to assess learning needs of middle school students related to health education. "Students identified sex, drugs, and violence as their main concerns" (p. 6). The process could be used by other groups planning to provide educational interventions for middle level.

1372.   Williams, P., & Kubik, J. (1990). Battle Creek (Michigan) schools' healthy lifestyles program. *Journal of School Health, 60(4)*, 142-146.

Describes implementation of a health promotion project in the areas of nutrition, physical fitness, substance abuse and stress management in Battle Creek area public and private school districts. Objectives related to risk, knowledge, attitudes, and behavior are addressed. School staff were targeted as role models and parents as reinforcers of health promoting behavior. Program outcomes reported include increased parent participation, support for related health initiatives such as AIDS education, and decreased staff absenteeism. Some of the problems identified include increased use of alcohol and cocaine among adolescents despite the program.

1373.   Wisconsin Clearinghouse. (1989). *BARN: The Body Awareness Resource Network*. Madison, WI: Wisconsin Clearinghouse.

A computer-assisted learning resource that allows students to explore information on the following topics: body management, stress management, alcohol and other drugs, smoking, human sexuality, and AIDS.

F. HEALTH EDUCATION - GENERAL

1374.   Brindis, C. (1993). Health policy reform and comprehensive school health education: The need for an effective partnership. *Journal of School Health, 63*(1), 33-37.

Outlined the major causes of mortality and morbidity for children. Presented the need to develop outcomes-based arguments for support of comprehensive school health education. Emphasized the need for coalitions among decision-makers in education and health. Provided an example from the state of Michigan.

1375.   Michigan Departments of Education, Mental Health, Public Health, Social Services, and State Police; Office of Highway Safety Planning; Office of Substance Abuse Services. (1990). *Michigan model for comprehensive school health education: Implementation plan for year 1991*. Lansing, MI: Center for Health Promotion.

Provides data on the impact of Michigan's comprehensive model of health education with an emphasis on substance abuse efforts. Evaluation of outcomes for 6th and 7th graders are included. An appendix with specific concepts of the program by grade level is very helpful. Would be helpful for states considering a similar model.

1376.   Millstein, S. G. (1988). *The potential of school-linked centers to promote adolescent health and development.* (Working paper available from Carnegie Council on Adolescent Development, 2400 N Street, NW, Washington, DC 20037).

Presents historical development of school-linked centers (defined more broadly than school-based center) and a review of the effectiveness research. Suggestions are made in the area of policy development to increase the number of health providers who are sensitive to the needs of adolescents and to mount a public awareness campaign to increase support for such services.

1377.   Price, R. H., Cioci, M., Penner, W., & Trautlein, B. (1990). *School and community support programs that enhance adolescent health and education.* (Working paper available from Carnegie Council on Adolescent Development, 2400 N Street, NW, Washington, DC 20037).

A review of programs designed to provide social support to adolescents. Social support is defined as "the provision of supportive aid...personal affirmation...and suppportive affect" (p. 1). Research issues needing attention include the role of ethnicity and gender on effective programs, systematic evaluation, and consideration of the adolsecent's point of view regarding needed support.

1378.   Reynolds, J. C., Jr., & Wootton, L. R.   (1973). Health education: Golden opportunity for the middle school. *The Clearing House, 47*(4), 219-222.

Discusses the importance of school-based health education programs in addressing many of the health-related societal concerns.

1379.   Scales, P. C. (1993). The centrality of health education to developing young adolescents' critical thinking. *Journal of Health Education, 24*(Suppl. 6), 10-14.

Outlines the characteristics of critical thinking. Highlights the need for young adolescents to learn to use critical thinking in relation to health issues that affect them personally. Scales describes the opposition some groups have toward including health issues in the curriculum.

1380.   Williams, P., & Kubik, J. (1990). Battle Creek (Michigan) schools' healthy lifestyles program. *Journal of School Health, 60*(4), 142-146.

Describes implementation of a health promotion project in the areas of nutrition, physical fitness, substance abuse and stress management in Battle Creek area public and private school districts. Objectives related to risk, knowledge, attitudes, and behavior are addressed. School staff were targeted as role models and parents as reinforcers of health promoting behavior. Program outcomes reported include increased parent participation, support for related health initiatives such as AIDS education, and decreased staff absenteeism. Some of the problems identified include increased use of alcohol and cocaine among adolescents despite the program.

G. AIDS

1381.   Allensworth, D. D., & Symons, C. W. (1989). A theoretical approach to school-based HIV prevention. *Journal of School Health, 59(2),* 59-65.

Application of Walberg's factors for increasing learning to the issue of AIDS prevention. Reviews the literature on instructional effectiveness. Makes reference to the influence of developmental needs on learning effectiveness. Identifies the transition from parental to peer influence that occurs during early adolescence. Offers specific ideas on how different individuals (school administrators, teachers, nurses, coaches, counselors, staff, parents, peers, and community members) can contribute to learning enhancement in various settings. Advocates comprehensive approach for meeting affective, behavioral, and cognitive learning needs.

1382.   Alteneder, R. R., Price, J. H., Telljohann, S. K., Didion, J., & Locher, A. (1992). Using the PRECEDE model to determine junior high school students' knowledge, attitudes, and beliefs about AIDS. *Journal of School Health, 62(10),* 464-470.

Used a quasi-experimental design to test the effectiveness of a one-time educational intervention related to AIDS. A pre-test/post-test was used. Five hundred and eighty-five students from the seventh and eight grade classes of six schools participated in both testing periods. The researchers designed their instrument based on the PRECEDE model which consisted of statements related to predisposing factors (knowledge, attitudes, perceptions, values, beliefs), enabling factors, and reinforcing factors. Significant differences were found for students in the experimental group for knowledge. Subgroups of students had significant differences for attitude and belief scores. Offers several questions for future research.

1383.   Bingham, C. R. (1989). AIDS and adolescents: Threat of infection and approaches to prevention. *Journal of Early Adolescence, 9 (1-2),* 50-66.

Presents a theoretical model of AIDS transmission in adolescents. Gives suggestions for prevention strategies that include "public education, anonymous testing, the provision of emotional supports, and empowerment" (p. 59).

1384.   Brown, L. K., Nassau, J. H., & Barone, V. J. (1990). Differences in AIDS knowledge and attitudes by grade level. *Journal of School Health, 60(6),* 270-275.

Uses researcher-constructed self-report instruments to examine differences in knowledge and attitudes about AIDS in 441 students in grades five, seven and ten. Significant differences were reported for knowledge by grade level. Significant differences were also reported for attitude. The authors give suggestions for designing health education strategies for children.

1385.   Centers for Disease Control, Center for Health Promotion and Education. (1988). Guidelines for effective school health education to prevent the spread of AIDS. *Journal of School Health, 58(4),* 142-148.

Offers guidelines in the following areas: planning and implementation; preparation of educational personnel; who should teach; purpose of effective education about AIDS; specific concepts and content to be included during early elementary, late elementary/middle school, or junior/senior high; curriculum time and resources; and, program assessment. The emphasis is on abstinence for those who have not engaged in high risk activities and on stopping high risk activities or taking preventive measures if already engaged in high risk activities. The program assessment questions provide a framework for evaluation that is often missing from content specific programs. Includes two appendices on policy principles and the extent of AIDS and indicators of adolescent risk.

1386.   Davidson, J., & Grant, C. (1988). Growing up is hard to do...in the AIDS era. *MCN: The American Journal of Maternal/Child Nursing, 13(5),* 352-356.

Commentary on the challenges facing today's adolescents in the areas of sexuality. Offers specific guidelines for parents, teens, and health care providers related to sexuality education.

1387.   Montauk, S. L., & Scroggin, D. M. (1989). AIDS: Questions from fifth and sixth grade students. *Journal of School Health, 59(7),* 291-295.

Report of a pilot project involving 11 medical residents who delivered a presentation to 492 fifth and sixth graders on AIDS. Outlined the content presented and categorized the questions asked by students in the discussion period. The most frequently asked questions by both fifth and sixth graders were related to transmission. Other categories included: clinical, treatment, origin, epidemiology, prevention, animals, testing, diagnosis, clinical pediatrics, doctors, ethics, and miscellaneous. Recommendations for future presentations were made.

1388.   Siegel, D., Lazarus, N., Krasnovsky, F., Durbin, M., & Chesney, M. (1991). AIDS knowledge, attitudes, and behavior among inner city, junior high school students. *Journal of School Health, 61(4),* 160-165.

Used self-report data from 1,967 students ages 11-16 years to examine the level of knowledge and attitudes about AIDS and the frequency of at-risk behavior related to sexual activity. The authors found significant associations between the use of condoms and beliefs about their effectiveness among sexually active subjects, gender differences in attitudes about condoms, and gender differences in sexual activity and drug use. Twenty eight percent of the subjects reported that they had sex at least once. The authors suggest customizing educational programs by gender.

1389.   Starn, J., & Paperny, D. M. (1990). Computer games to enhance adolescent sex education. *MCN: The American Journal of Maternal/Child Nursing, 15*(4), 250-253.

The authors describe highlights of two computer-assisted games that address issues of sexuality and dating: "Baby Game" and "Romance" which are available for $59 each and work on IBM or compatible machines. Supportive research on effectiveness in improving knowledge and changing attitudes is included.

H. NUTRITION/EATING DISORDERS

1390.   Allen, K. M., Thombs, D. L., Mahoney, C. A., & Daniel, E. L. (1993). Relationships between expectancies and adolescent dieting behaviors. *Journal of School Health, 63*(4), 176-181.

Used self-report data from students ages 10-18 in middle schools and high schools in New York to ascertain if adolescent beliefs about dieting differen-tiated dieting behaviors such as frequency, use of pills, and use of vomiting to control weight. The information is useful for teachers and school health profes-sionals who may be able to identify adolescents at risk for eating disorders.

1391.   Carruth, B. R., & Goldberg, D. L. (1990). Nutritional issues of adolescents: Athletics and the body image mania. *Journal of Early Adolescence, 10*(2), 122-140.

Reviews research on adolescent athletes related to their dieting behavior. Discusses the risks for inadequate nutrition with emphasis on female athletes. Recommends early identification of risk factors for eating disorders, implementation of nutrition education, and measurement of body weight/body fat during adolescence.

1392.   Devine, C. M., Olson, C. M., & Frongillo, E. A. (1992). Impact of the Nutrition for Life program on junior high student in New York state. *Journal of School Health, 62*(8), 381-385.

Describes the results of an evaluation study of the effects of a brief teaching program in nutrition on the knowledge, attitude and behavior of 1,863 students in 7th and 8th grade. All students received nutrition education either traditional or the Nutrition for Life program. Significant differences in the dependent variables were found. Provides a model for other evaluation studies of the impact of nutrition curriculum.

1393.   Shannon, B. K. J. (1995). Our diets may be killing us. *Mathematics Teaching in the Middle School, 1*(5), 376-382.

Details a "Food-Choice Unit" (p. 376) on dietary fat and heart disease that emphasizes development of math skills in reading graphs, working with fractions and percents. Ties the problems to meals children would likely select at area restaurants. Includes suggestions for several "expansion activities" (p. 380) including team field trips, food logs, cultural comparisons and guest speakers.

I. PREGNANCY

1394.   Barr, L., & Monserrat, C. (1992). *Working with pregnant and parenting teens*. Albuquerque, NM: New Futures, Inc.

Resource guide based on the experience of staff at the New Futures School devoted to the needs of pregnant teens. Includes articles on adolescent development, pregnancy, and adoption. Lesson plans for 17 topics include objectives, and suggestions for learning activities and helpful resource material. While not specifically related to middle level, content may be useful to settings where teen pregnancy is a problem.

1395.   Caldas, S. J. (1993). Current theoretical perspectives on adolescent pregnancy and childbearing in the United States. *Journal of Adolescent Research, 8*(1), 4-20.

Examines the research support for the following hypotheses related to adolescent pregnancy: reproductive-ignorance, psychological needs, welfare, parental-role-model/supervision, social-norms, and physiological hypotheses. Calls for the use of more sophisticated techniques to examine the complexity of influences. Recommends an examination of a combination of factors such as the sociological and biological influences.

1396.   Heller, R. G. (1988). School-based clinics: Impact on teenage pregnancy prevention. *Pediatric Nursing, 14*(2), 103-106.

Presents statistics on the pregnancy rate for adolescents. Describes selected successful school-based clinics. Advocates expansion of such services.

1397.   Palmore, S. U., & Shannon, M. D. (1988). Risk factors for adolescent pregnancy in students. *Pediatric Nursing, 14*(3), 241-245.

Describes a field research study using a convenience sample of 57 pregnant adolescents to "identify common risk factors" (p. 242) for adolescent pregnancy. The school nurse/researcher used open-ended questions to collect data. Patterns emerged in the areas of school failure, teenage pregnancy of the subjects' mothers, family violence, and substance abuse. Includes suggestions for prevention, intervention, and future research.

J. SAFETY

1398.   Coben, J. H., Weiss, H. B., Mulvey, E. P., & Dearwater, S. R. (1994). A primer on school violence prevention. *Journal of School Health, 64*(8), 309-313.

Offers recommendations for a violence prevention curriculum that includes students, teachers, members of the community and health professionals. Other components are program evaluation, early identification of and interventions with high risk children including a focus on resisting involvement in gangs at the middle level, conflict resolution, and environmental controls.

1399.   Jones, N. E. (1992). Prevention of childhood injuries part I: Motor vehicle injuries. *Pediatric Nursing, 18*(4), 380-382.

Offers suggestions on how the nurse can influence efforts to reduce the staggering rates of death and injury in children ages 1 to 14 years due to motor vehicle accidents. Suggestions include supporting enforcement of seatbelt laws, roadway improvements for pedestrians, and construction of bikepaths; encouraging air bag installation; providing parent and child safety education; and encouraging the use of reflective clothing and bicycle helmets.

1400.   Jones, N. E. (1992). Prevention of childhood injuries part II: Recreational injuries. *Pediatric Nursing, 18*(6), 619-621.

Offers suggestions for how nurses can help reduce the rates of injuries related to recreational activities including supporting regulations for swimming pools, playground equipment, firearms, and ATVs.

1401.   Moore, E. R., Strickland, R. R., Melcke, M. J., & Wilker, J. A. (1988). Protecting our children through Kid Safe. *Pediatric Nursing, 14*(1), 32-36.

Describes one hospital's use of a commercially designed program to educate parents and children ages 4 to 14 years on safety issues. Classes were held at the local hospital and covered the following topics: cardiopulmonary resuscitation, babysitting, personal safety, first aid, emergency telephone techniques, and fire safety. Approximately 2000 children were served in three sessions. Includes outlines of other program activities such as fingerprinting and hospital tours. Lists responsibilities of key planning staff. Would be useful for school nurses and health coordinators.

K. SCHOOL HEALTH SERVICES

1402.   Council on Scientific Affairs, American Medical Association. (1990). Providing medical services through school-based health programs. *Journal of School Health, 60*(3), 87-91.

Outlines the problems in delivering health care to adolescents related to parental consent, confidentiality, cost, accessibility, and lack of follow-through with treatment plans. Describes successful school-based health services as comprehensive in approach to meeting the needs of a specific group of adolescents in medically-underserved areas. Most are staffed by nurse practitioners and are sensitive to the needs of parents. Initially serving older adolescents such programs are also available to students in middle schools. Recommendations include more research into the effectiveness of school-based clinics, minimum standards for existing services (physician supervision; use of professional nurses and other health professionals; written policies on services, curricula and confidentiality), evaluation, hours of operation, referral sources, and parent involvement.

1403.   Hadley, E. M., Lovick, S. R., & Kirby, D. (1986). *School-based health clinics: A guide to implementing programs*. Center for Population Options, Washington, DC. (ERIC Document Reproduction Service No. ED 326 937).

A comprehensive manual for planning and implementing a school-based clinic for adolescents. The resource provides a timeline of critical tasks for implementation. Key assessment questions for each stage of the planning process help program planners design individualized programs. Areas addressed in the manual include formulating the planning group, documentation of the need, selecting sites, building community support, working with the media and the school, clinic design, fiscal planning and management, personnel qualifications, selection, and role, evaluation, and maintaining community support. The appendices provide sample documents for surveys and job descriptions. Ninety-four references are provided.

1404.   Klein, J. D., & Sadowski, L. S. (1990). Personal health services as a component of comprehensive health programs. *Journal of School Health, 60*(4), 164-169.

An opinion piece on the need to provide "screening or case finding, service de-livery such as preventive services, treatment, counseling, referrals, and follow-up, and health education through in-classrooms, individual one-on-one, groups, and teacher training" (p. 165). Describes the needs of at risk teens and recommends increased access to health services through such things as school-based clinics.

1405.   Klein, J. D., Starnes, S. A., Kotelchuck, M., Earp, J. A., DeFriese, G. H., & Loda, F. A. (1992). *Comprehensive adolescent health services in the United States, 1990*. Cecil G. Sheps Center for Health Services Research, the Center for Early Adolescence, and the Center for Health Promotion and Disease Prevention, The University of North Carolina at Chapel Hill.

This monograph examines the scope of services provided by 435 of 664 comprehensive health programs for adolescents in the U.S. Provides a brief overview of adolescent health status, a definition of comprehensive adolescent health services, research methodology used and a summary of the results. Several maps and tables illustrate key research findings on program config-uration, distribution, and services provided. Five percent of the programs were located in middle schools, and another five percent were shared by middle schools and high schools. The authors note that only five percent of the adolescent population is served by such programs. The information will be useful as a baseline for future studies on the growth of such programs. Current programs can see how they compare with other programs.

1406.   Kornguth, M. L. (1990). School illness: Who's absent and why?

Pediatric Nursing, 16(1), 95-99.

Reports on secondary data analysis of the 1979-1982 National School Health
Services Program data using chi square and multiple classification analysis.
Absence rates for younger (5-11 years) and older (12-17 years) students were
similar. Found that "as mother's level of education increased, the likelihood of
their children being absent decreased" (p. 96). those students who received care
from a school clinic were "least likely to be absent from school" (p. 96). Offers
suggestions on how school nurses can educate parents and teachers on
appropriate symptoms to report.

1407.   Lordi, S. (1987). School-based clinics [Special issue]. *School Nurse*,
March/April.

Includes articles on the development of school based-clinics since 1984, the
role of the school nurse, advice on starting a school-based clinic, personal
experiences of school nurses with school-based clinics, a focus on the
controversy surrounding family planning services and future challenges facing
the expansion of such services. Possible funding sources for school-based
clinics are also identified.

1408.   Pacheco, M. Powell, W. Cole, C., Kalishman, N., Benon, R., &
Kaufman, A. (1991). School-based clinics: The politics of change. *Journal of
School Health, 61*(2), 92-94.

Describes the experience of school-based clinics in Albuquerque, New Mexico,
in responding to the local opposition to school-based clinics that arose following
national media attention to services provided by New York school-based clinics.
The recommendations of the local task force resulted in better coordination
among provider groups and expansion of services to additional students.

1409. Department of Health and Human Services, Public Health Service, Office
of Disease Prevention and Health Promotion. (1993). *School health: Findings
from evaluated programs*. Washington, DC: Author.

Offers a collection of resources based on the components of a comprehensive
school health program: health education, clinical services, counseling and
mental health services, school environment, school food programs, physical
education and physical fitness, faculty and staff health promotion, and
community coordination. A major feature of the publication is the inclusion of
results from evaluations done on the individual components. Health education
resources predominate.

1410.   United States General Accounting Office. (1994). *Health care:
School-based health centers can expand access for children.* Washington, DC:
Author.

Details the results of case study profiles of eight school-based health centers
including one at a shared high school/middle school campus. Concludes that

such centers 1) do meet the needs of children who would otherwise not have access to health services, 2) face financial concerns related to third party payers including Medicaid, and 3) have trouble recruiting primary care providers and providing the full range of health services needed by adolescents.

L. SEX EDUCATION

1411.   Coker, A. L., Richter, D. L., Valois, R. F., McKeown, R. E., Garrison, C. Z., & Vincent, M. L. (1994). Correlates and consequences of early initiation of sexual intercourse. *Journal of School Health, 64*(9), 372-377.

Using a sample of high school students, self-reported data related to age at first intercourse and other risk behaviors were collected. Regression analysis was done on the data from students who reported being sexually active. Correlations were done by race and gender. "The finding of marked differences in the proportion of adolescents who begin sexually [sic] activity early by race and gender groups suggests the need to target sexuality education messages earlier..." (p. 376). Their recommendations for earlier intervention mean that such education should occur during the middle level years.

1412.   Ellenwood, S., & McLaren, N. (1994). Literature-based character education. *Middle School Journal, 26*(2), pp. 42-47.

Describes the Loving Well Project begun in 1987 at Boston University. Four years of field testing with 10,000 students in urban, suburban, and rural schools confirm the project's success. The use of engaging stories, poems, essays, folktales, and myths provides a vicarious experience that encourage students' thinking about relationships. When control group attitudes toward issues of sexuality were compared to attitudes of the experimental groups, students involved in Loving Well developed a clearer understanding of both the short term and long term consequences of premature sexual activity. Another finding showed that 8th graders involved in the program who had never had sexual relations were three times more likely to continue to abstain throughout the course of the eighth grade than were their control group peers.

1413.   Gingiss, P. L., & Basen-Engquist, K. (1994). HIV education practices and training needs of middle school and high school teachers. *Journal of School Health, 64*(7), 290-295.

Reports the results of a survey of teachers using self-report instruments developed by the researchers. Middle level teachers involved in teaching content related to HIV reported receiving less preparation than high school teachers. They also reported less time spent on the topic and more difficulty fitting the content into current classes.

1414.   Hilton, J. L. (1984). Sex education in the Middle School. *Middle School Journal, 16*(1), 4-5, 31.

With only 15% percent of mothers and 8% of fathers talking to children about sexual matters, a great need for sex education exists. As the middle school years are a time of exploration and interest in sex naturally increases, these are optimum years to provide such education. Data show that children first learn about most sexual concepts between 9 and 13 years old. Suggestions are made for implementing implementing a sex education program. Adverse reactions to programs are discussed.

1415.   McGrory, A. (1990). Menarche: Responses of early adolescent females. *Adolescence, 25(*98), 265-270.

Reports on research with 95 girls (11-15 years) conducted through a telephone interview using the Menstrual Attitude Questionnaire, Piers-Harris Children's Self-Concept Scale and a demographic form. Interestingly the authors report that several parents declined to have their daughters participate because of the personal nature of the research. The only significant finding was that premenarcheal girls perceived menses as more debilitating.

1416.   Nelson, C., & Keith, J. (1990). Comparisons of female and male early adolescent sex role attitude and behavior development. *Adolescence, 25(*97), 184-204.

Examines Bronfenbrenner's theory of environmental influences on human development applied to sex role development in early adolescents using multiple regression. The sample included 146 males and 154 females in Grades 5 through 8. For females, maternal employment, age, and level of traditionalism of father's sex role attitudes significantly predicted female sex role attitudes. For males, the level of traditionalism of the mother's sex role attitudes, level of closeness, and perception of pubertal age predicted male sex role attitudes. The authors identify the need for stronger measures of sex role attitudes and behaviors.

1417.   Schultz, J. (1994). Review of *Sex Can Wait: An abstinence-based sexuality curriculum for middle school* by P. Core-Gebhardt, S. J. Hart, and M. Young, ETR Associates. *In Middle Ground*, Fall, pp. 8-9.

Reports that the abstinence curriculum offers a "limited platform" for sexuality because it lacks information on other methods of protection from pregnancy and sexually transmitted diseases.

1418.   Scott-Jones, D., & White, A. B. (1990). Correlates of sexual activity in early adolescents. *Journal of Early Adolescence, 10*(2), 221-238.

Used a researcher-developed interview schedule to obtain data on a convenience sample of 114 adolescents aged 12.5 to 15.5 years old. Dependent variables of interest were sexual activity and contraceptive use. The sexual activity rate for the sample was 28% with a mean age of first intercourse of around 12 years. "Variables significantly related to sexual activity were mother's education, having a boyfriend/girlfriend, educational expectations, and age" (p. 231). Lower educational expectations were related to sexual activity. The author suggests that this finding provides new avenues for interventions to delay sexual activity. Sexually active subjects reported that contraceptives were not used regularly. Even though most early adolescents are not sexually active, the risks for those that are demand more creative and effective interventions.

1419. Smith, P. B., Chacko, M. R., & Bermudez, A. (1989). Contraceptive and sexuality knowledge among inner-city middle school students from minority groups. *The School Counselor, 37*(2), 103-108.

Reports results of a survey using open-ended questions seeking information about the level of sexuality and contraceptive knowledge, source, type and location of sexual knowledge of inner-city middle school students who participated in a free physical examination program. Discusses differences by sex, race, and ethnicity. Highlights trends and potential implementation of findings for use by school counselors.

1420. Sullivan, N. (1988). Successfully developing human sex-uality curricula in the middle school. *KAMLE Karavan (Journal of the Kansas Association for Middle Level Education), 3,* 23-25.

Describes the process one school district used to develop human sexuality curricula specifically for middle level children. After completing a broad-based assessment, the planning group representing parents, faculty and staff selected materials and developed a scope and sequence outline. The content outline included "1) the physiology of human growth and development, 2) the development of positive self-esteem, 3) the skills for making responsible decisions, 4) the understanding of what leads to good relationships, and 5) knowledge about AIDS and other sexually transmitted diseased" (p. 24). Sample classroom exercises are briefly described but not in sufficient details for readers to implement.

M. SUBSTANCE ABUSE - RESEARCH

1421. Castiglia, P. R., Glenister, A. M., Haughey, B. P., & Kanski, G. W. (1989). Influences on children's attitudes toward alcohol consumption. *Pediatric Nursing, 15(3),* 263-266.

Used a researcher-developed self report instrument to collect data from 500 children ages 8-15 years. The purpose of the study was to describe children's attitudes toward alcohol and the influence of peers on alcohol consumption. Subjects responded to four written situations that related to alcohol. The researchers found that "older children, ages 14 to 15, were significantly more likely to indicate that they would take a drink then younger children" (p. 265). Their data also "suggest[ed] that parents are more influential than either they or their children might think in developing decision-making attitudes" (p. 265). Suggestions for nursing interventions are offered.

1422. Ellickson, P. L., Bell, R., & Harrison, E. R. (1993). Changing adolescent propensities to use drugs: Results from Project ALERT. *Health*

Education Quarterly, 20(2), 227-242.

Examines the influence of implementation of one health program on cognitive factors thought to reduce drug use. Data were collected pre and post implementation during the seventh grade and once again in the eighth grade. The cognitive factors examined included beliefs about drug use consequence, beliefs about how many other kids used drugs, resistance, self-efficacy, and expectations for future use. The program evaluated had the most effect on beliefs related to marijuana and cigarettes and the least effect on beliefs about alcohol use.

1423.   Falco, M. (1988). *Preventing abuse of drugs, alcohol, and tobacco by adolescents.* (Working paper available from Carnegie Council on Adolescent Development, 2400 N Street, NW, Washington, DC 20037).

Outlines the current trends in adolescent drug, alcohol, and tobacco use. Reviews efforts at controlling demand for such substances through treatment and prevention programs. Calls for research on "why young people move from first use of dangerous substances to continuing use and dependence" (p. 49) and the "effect of social policy changes on adolescent behavior" (p. 50).

1424.   Kreutter, K. J., Gewirtz, H., Davenny, J. E., & Love, C. (1991). Drug and alcohol prevention project for sixth graders: First-year findings. *Adolescence, 26(102),* 287-293.

Using a quasi-experimental pre-test/post-test design the authors examined the impact of a life skills training program on knowledge, attitudes, self-concept, passivity, and locus of control of 6th graders. The training program developed by Botvin was used as the treatment variable. Significant differences in passivity, knowledge and self-concept were found.

1425.   Long, K. A., & Boik, R. J. (1993). Predicting alcohol use in rural children: A longitudinal study. *Nursing Research, 42*(2), 79-86.

Report of the final phase of research done with children in grades 6 and 7 in an attempt to predict users from nonusers of alcohol based on selected sociodemographic (age, gender, ethnicity, religious practices, family configuration, and perception of adult alcohol use) and psychometric (self-concept, school attitude, beliefs about alcohol) variables. A predictive model for alcohol use was not found. However, negative self-concept and negative school attitude were associated with alcohol use.

1426.   Shope, J. T. (1994). Longitudinal evaluation of an enhanced Alcohol Misuse Prevention Study (AMPS) curriculum for grades six-eight. *Journal of School Health, 64*(4), 160-166.

Describes the results of longitudinal experimental study of an alcohol prevention curriculum based on social learning theory at the middle level. The method section details the curriculum and instruments used. Significant treatment effects were demonstrated for increasing knowledge and for decreasing the rate of alcohol misuse.

1427.   Tajiki, M. (1989). A study of attitudinal, behavioral, and social factors related to adolescent substance abuse (Doctoral dissertation, University of San Francisco, 1988). *Dissertation Abstracts International*, *49*, 3314A.

This study investigated the predictive effects of the following factors related to adolescent substance abuse: (1) the adolescent's own attitude toward usage; (2) peer attitude toward usage; (3) parental attitudes toward usage; (4) the adolescent's sense of well-being; and (5) the adolescent's sense of life-satisfaction and well-being. Data were collected from seventh, ninth, and eleventh graders of both sexes. The strongest predictor of substance usage was peer attitudes towards usage, while the weakest were well-being and life satisfaction. The pattern of findings best supported the Domain Model of substance use based upon the belief that the degree to which any one of these factors influences substance use can significantly differ depending upon particular aspects of the substance use. This information can be very helpful in setting up middle level substance abuse programs.

1428.   Thompson, K. M. (1989). Effects of early alcohol use on adolescents' relations with peers and self-esteem: Patterns over time. *Adolescence, 24(96)*, 837-849.

Secondary analysis of data from the 1978 survey by the Research Triangle Institute. Used a panel sample of children who had participated in a 1974 survey as 7th and 8th graders. Measures of drinking behavior, peer relations, and self-esteem were selected from the survey items. One finding of interest to middle level educators is that youngsters who begin drinking in 7th and 8th grade are likely to continue to be drinking four years later.

1429.   Webb, J. A., Baer, P. E., Caid, C. D., McLaughlin, R. J., & McKelvey, R. S. (1991). Concurrent and longitudinal assessment of risk for alcohol use among seventh graders. *Journal of Early Adolescence, 11(4)*, 450-465.

Used self report data from 265 seventh graders who were in a control group for a substance abuse prevention program to examine factors related to the dependent variable of alcohol use. Significant predictors of level of use were deviant behavior, tolerance for deviance, sensation-seeking, peer use, peer approval of use, parental use and rejection of parental authority.

1430.   Werch, C. E., Young, M., Clark, M., Garrett, C., Hooks, S., & Kersten, C. (1991). Effects of a take home drug prevention program on drug related communication and beliefs of parents and children. *Journal of School Health, 61(8)*, 346-350.

Report of the effect of a take home print drug prevention program for fourth, fifth, and sixth graders and their parents. Significant differences between experimental and control groups were found in the areas of parent/child communication but not in children's intention to use drugs.

1431.   Young, M., Werch, C. E., & Bakema, D. (1989). Area specific self-esteem scales and substance use among elementary and middle school children. *Journal of School Health, 59*(6), 251-254.

Examined the relationship between self-esteem related to peers, family, and school and the use or expected use of legal and illegal drugs of 2,032 students in grades four through nine. Drugs included coffee, cigarettes, alcohol, and illegal drugs. Both school and home measures of self-esteem related significantly to lower use or expected use.

N. SUBSTANCE ABUSE - PRACTICAL

1432.   Bosworth, K., & Sailes, J. (1993). Content and teaching strategies in 10 selected drug abuse prevention curricula. *Journal of School Health, 63*(6), 24-253.

An extremely helpful review that examines aspects of curricula such as content themes (risk and consequences, decision-making, interpersonal skills, intrapersonal skills, and external nonpersonal pressure); interactive strategies (brainstorm, small groups, games, and role plays); teaching strategies (brainstorming, discussion, games, homework, lecture, media, role play, seatwork, and cooperative learning); and amount of teacher training required. The authors recommend more attention to teacher training in the use of interactive strategies if such curricula are to be effective as designed.

1433.   Evans, D.W. & Giarratano, S. (1990). *Into adolescence: Avoiding drugs*. Santa Cruz: ETK Associates / Network Publications.

Valuable resource for middle level teachers. This book provides information on the substances most commonly used during early adolescence: tobacco, alcohol, marijuana, and over-the-counter and prescription drugs. The book includes activities to build critical-thinking decision making, and refusal skills, with an emphasis on helping students identify and articulate personal alternatives to drug use.

1434.   National Commission for Drug-Free Schools. (1990). *Toward a drug-free generation: A nation's responsibility*. Rockville, MD: National Clearinghouse for Alcohol and Drug Information.

Presents the "goals for achieving drug-free schools by the year 2000; an overview of drug problems among young people; a summary of students' views on alcohol, tobacco, and other drugs; and an outline of the roles and responsibilities of community groups and organizations" (p. v) prepared by the 26-member commission appointed in 1989. Statistics from the National Adolescent Student Health Survey, 1987, are used to examine the scope of the problem. The commission noted that alcohol and tobacco use far exceeds other types of substance abuse among young people. Middle school students show increased experimentation and peer influence. Therefore, the commission recommends early intervention. Goals are directed to individual school settings and include a focus on assessment of need, and the development and evaluation of policies and programs. Several tools for assessing the scope of the problem are discussed; however, a bibliography is not included.

1435. Prevention and Intervention Center for Alcohol and Drug Abuse. (1993 revision). *PICADA 1-8*. Madison, WI: Wisconsin Clearinghouse.

An eight part curriculum designed for grades 1 to 8. Covers the following topics: alcohol and drug risks, personal awareness, interpersonal skills, and life skills. Latest revisions focus on cultural perspectives. Has specially developed materials for middle school settings covering knowledge of substance abuse, personal awareness, interpersonal skill and life skill development. Evaluation studies are available. Available from distributor at P. O. Box 1468, Madison, WI 53701-1468.

1436. Robinson, D. P., & Green, J. W. (1988). The adolescent alcohol and drug problem: A practical approach. *Pediatric Nursing, 14*(4), 305-309.

Offers suggestions on how school nurses can use an understanding of the stages of adolescent substance abuse to evaluate risk potential of clients. Includes assessment questions in the areas of home, school, peers, self, and legal and chemical history. Emphasizes primary and secondary prevention.

1437. Washburn, P. (1991). Identification, assessment, and referral of adolescent drug abusers. *Pediatric Nursing, 17*(2), 137-140.

Offers a model, Stages of Involvement, to help nurses match appropriate interventions for working with substance abusing adolescents. Identifies several referral sources.

O. TOBACCO-RELATED ISSUES - RESEARCH

1438. Bertrand, L. D., & Abernathy, T. J. (1993). Predicting cigarette smoking among adolescents using cross-sectional and longitudinal approaches. *Journal of School Health, 63*(2), 100-105.

Used multivariate analysis to examine the potential of interpersonal and intrapersonal factors for identifying future smoking behavior in adolescents in grades 6 through 9. The interpersonal factors of Peer Influences and Parent/Child Relationship were best able to predict smoking behavior. The authors suggest that health promotion interventions may be more effective if strategies for helping adolescents cope with these interpersonal or environmental influences are developed.

1439. Best, J. A., Thomson, S. J., Santi, S. M., Smith, E. A., & Brown, K. S. (1988). Preventing cigarette smoking among school children. *Annual Review Public Health, 9*, 161-201.

The authors present a "model for program development research" (p. 161) and summarize the research on smoking prevention programs. The conceptual model offers a way to build a research base regarding health promotion that moves from basic research, and program evaluation to diffusion of effective strategies. Once high risk behaviors are understood, interventions can be designed and tested for effectiveness. The best interventions can then be disseminated for wider impact. The following elements of prevention programs were examined: program content, participant, provider, setting, and methodology. Offers several ideas for research especially on the participant, provider, and setting.

1440.   Cella, D. F., Tulsky, D. S., Sarafian, B., Thomas, C. R. Jr., & Thomas, C. R. Sr. (1992). Culturally relevant smoking prevention for minority youth. *Journal of School Health, 62*(8), 377-380.

Examined the effects of participating in a rap contest after hearing anti-smoking rap messages on attitudes toward smoking. The sample consisted of 268 sixth and seventh grade students. The authors suggest that such an intervention was well received by minority participants.

1441.   Clayton, S. (1991). Gender differences in psychosocial determinants of adolescent smoking. *Journal of School Health, 61*(3), 115-120.

Reviews the research on the influence of psychosocial variables on smoking behavior of adolescents. Provides recommendations for future research on the effect of gender-based strategies for smoking prevention.

1442.   Eckhardt, L., Woodruff, S. I., & Elder, J. P. (1994). Longitudinal analysis of adolescent smoking and its correlates. *Journal of School Health, 64*(2), 67-72.

Describes variables used to predict smoking behavior at two different measure-ment points. "Results showed intentions to smoke was the strongest predictor of smoking during both early adolescence and during late adolescence" (p. 67). The authors suggest that future interventions target this factor.

1443.   Elder, J. P., Molgaard, C. A., & Gresham, L. (1988). Predictors of chewing tobacco and cigarette use in a multiethnic public school population. *Adolescence, 23*(91), 689-702.

Used stepwise multiple regression analysis of self-reported tobacco use and selected socioeconomic and interpersonal variables. The culturally diverse sample included 433 sixth and seventh grade students in San Diego. Norm perception, best friend's tobacco use, parental marital status, and ethnicity were significant predictors. The authors provide suggestions for future research, health promotion, and stricter regulation of the sale of tobacco products.

1444.   Gerber, R. W., Newman, I. M., & Martin, G. L. (1988). Applying the theory of reasoned action to early adolescent tobacco chewing. *Journal of School Health, 58*(10), 410-413.

Used a sample of 1,138 eighth and ninth grade to examine the difference between belief, motivations, and expectations of intenders and nonintenders of using chewing tobacco. Only 13% of the variance in chewing behavior was explained by the model with this sample.

1445.   Glynn, T. J. (1989). Essential elements of school smoking prevention programs. *Journal of School Health, 59*(5), 181-188.

Reviews the research and expert panel opinion on the effectiveness of programs sponsored by the National Cancer Institute to prevent smoking among adolescents. Includes descriptions of current clinical trials. Regarding the most important elements of effective programs, the authors conclude that positive effects have been seen in delaying the onset of smoking which should have an overall impact on the smoking rate of adults. Smoking prevention content was most effective when provided in at least five sessions for two years starting at the transition from elementary school. Effective program content included short-term effects (physiological and social) and refusal skills. The use of peer leaders on the teaching team was also effective. Teacher training in the use of effective programs was viewed as essential. Local community constraints should be considered when selecting a smoking prevention program to implement. Additional research recommendations included a focus on reaching high-risk groups and special populations with customized intervention programs, longitudinal studies of effectiveness, development of programs for elementary and high school students, effect of parent involvement, and the introduction of smoking cessation programs to older adolescents.

1446.   Harris, M. B., & Ford, V. L. (1988). Tobacco use in a fifth-grade Southwestern sample. *Journal of Early Adolescence, 8*(1), 83-96.

Collected self-report data from 204 subjects ages 8 to 14 years regarding their use of tobacco products and their attitudes toward smokers using a researcher developed instrument. The results support previous research on the incidence of tobacco experimentation by middle level students.

1447.   Lavengood, T. D. W. (1988). Involuntary smoking - children in crisis. *Pediatric Nursing, 14*(2), 93-95.

Reviews the risks of sidestream smoke. Calls for active involvement of nurses in positive role-modeling, support for policies regulating smoking, educating families and communities about the risks, and conducting more research on the health effects of sidestream smoke on children.

1448.   Pentz, M. A., Brannon, B. R., Charlin, V. L., Barrett, E. J., MacKinnon, D. P., & Flay, B. R. (1989). The power of policy: The relationship of smoking policy to adolescent smoking. *American Journal of Public Health, 79*(7), 857-862.

Results of a study using self-report data from students and staff, archival records and carbon dioxide of expired air to examine the effects of numbers of smoking policy components, and level of emphasis on prevention, cessation and punishment on smoking behavior of adolescents in the seventh grade. The authors used multiple regression for the analysis and concluded that "smoking policy can have an effect on reducing the amount of smoking by adolescents and, to a lesser extent, on smoking prevalence rates" (p. 860).

1449.   Polcyn, M. M., Price, J. H., Jurs, S. G., & Roberts, S. M. (1991). Utility of the PRECEDE model in differentiating users and nonusers of smokeless tobacco. *Journal of School Health, 61*(4), 166-171.

Describes the development of a questionnaire to reflect the several factors of the PRECEDE model (predisposing, reinforcing, and enabling) health education related to smokeless tobacco use. The authors used the self-report instrument to collect data from a sample of 578 seventh and eighth grade male students from 8 schools in the midwest. The model was successful in predicting smokeless tobacco use. Suggestions for developers of health promotion courses are offered.

1450.   Pomrehn, P. R., Jones, M. P., Ferguson, K. J., & Becker, S. L. (1995). Tobacco use initiation in middle school children in three Iowa communities: Results of the Iowa Program Against Smoking (I-PAS). *Journal of Health Education, 25*(2), 92-100.

Indicates that despite the inclusion of a "proven smoking prevention curriculum" (p. 99) rates of tobacco experimentation continue to rise during high school. Predictors of future tobacco use included "prior smoking experience, grade, school, sex, and best friend, sibling, and parental smoking status" (p. 92). The authors recommended "the need for booster sessions" (p. 100) to supplement earlier educational efforts.

1451.   Torabi, M. R., Bailey, W. J., & Majd-Jabbari, M. (1993). Cigarette smoking as a predictor of alcohol and other drug use by children and adolescents: Evidence of the "Gateway drug effect." *Journal of School Health, 63*(7), 302-306.

The researchers analyzed self-report data regarding substance use, perceived risk, and perceived peer approval/disapproval from 20,629 students in grades 5 through 12 in Indiana. They also provided comparison data when available from national surveys. They found a significant relationship between cigarette use and the use of other substances. The multiple regression analyses showed that 25% of the "variance in student cigarette use can be explained by age at first use, perceived peer approval/disapproval, and perceived risk" (p. 305). Perceived risk also contributed most to predicting frequency of adverse effects of drug use. Because age at first use is related to the amount of cigarette use, students should be supported in delaying their experimentation as long as possible.

1452.   van Roosmalen, E. H., & McDaniel, S. A. (1989). Peer group influence as a factor in smoking behavior of adolescents. *Adolescence, 24* (96), 801-816.

Uses data from the Waterloo Smoking Prevention Project, Study II to examine the relationship between smoking behaviors and peer group patterns of 1,689 eighth grade students.

The authors suggest that the influence of the peer group is not direct pressure to smoke but rather the formulation of positive attitudes toward smoking that is most influential in adolescent smoking behavior. They offer suggestions for improving health promotion efforts.

1453. van Roosmalen, E. H., & McDaniel, S. A. (1992). Adolescent smoking intentions: Gender differences in peer context. *Adolescence, 27*(105), 87-105.

Secondary analysis of data from the Waterloo Smoking Prevention Project, Study II on the smoking behavior and social influences on smoking behavior of 1,689 eighth grade students from 42 schools in southern Ontario, Canada. Self-report of smoking behavior was strengthened by the use of saliva studies to verify recent smoking behavior. The authors conclude that adolescent girls may be at higher risk for beginning and continuing smoking. Suggestions for targeting health promotion programs to the factors that influence adolescent girls' smoking behavior are provided.

1454. Werch, C. E., McNab, W. L., Defreitas, B., & Bertschy, M. L. (1988). Motivations and strategies for quitting and preventing tobacco and alcohol use. *Journal of School Health, 58*(4), 156-158.

Describes two classroom activities that encourage students to examine motivations for quitting or not using tobacco and alcohol. Specific directions for implementation are provided. Appropriate for middle level students.

1455. Young, R. L., Elder, J. P., Green, M., De Moor, C., & Wildey, M. B. (1988). Tobacco use prevention and health facilitator effectiveness. *Journal of School Health, 58*(9), 370-373.

Describes an experimental study of the effectiveness a semester-long tobacco prevention program presented by college students to sixth and seventh graders in reducing tobacco use. Pre- and post-treatment measures of tobacco use were obtained through student self-report. Evaluators rated the college student presenters on classroom effectiveness. Researchers correlated aspects of the evaluation with post-treatment tobacco use. Correlations from those presenters who "worked well in team, related well with students, and were well-prepared" (p. 372) were strongest.

P. TOBACCO-RELATED ISSUES - PRACTICAL

1456. Brink, S. G., Simons-Morton, D. G., Harvey, C. M., Parcel, G. S., & Tiernan, K. M. (1988). Developing comprehensive smoking control programs in schools. *Journal of School Health, 58*(5), 177-180.

Advocates a three-level intervention for smoking control in school settings involving students, schools and school districts, and governments. Outlines "components of effective smoking prevention programs" (p. 178) and smoking cessation programs based on research. Lists several resources for implementing smoking prevention and cessation programs.

1457.   DiFranza, J. R. (1989). School tobacco policy: A medical perspective. *Journal of School Health, 59*(9), 398-400.

Presents arguments for a total ban on tobacco use in school settings. Identifies two resources for implementing such a ban.

1458.   Guidelines for school health programs to prevent tobacco use and addiction. (1994). *Journal of School Health, 64*(9), 353-360.

A summary of the guidelines developed by the Centers for Disease Control. The guidelines address issues of policy, education, teaching training, community involvement, cessation, and program evaluation. The article includes a table of the essential concepts (knowledge, attitudes, and skills) to be included by grade level. There is a section for middle school/junior high school.

1459.   Olds, R. S. (1988). Promoting child health in a smoke-free school: Suggestions for school health personnel. *Journal of School Health, 58*(7), 269-272.

Explores arguments for smoke-free schools based on the risk of addiction, individual rights, role modeling, learning, and smoking as a gateway drug. Lists resources for implementing such policies in school settings.

1460.   Peck, D. D., ACott, C., Richard, P., Hill, S., & Schuster, C. (1993). The Colorado Tobacco-Free Schools and Communities Project. *Journal of School Health, 63*(5), 214-217.

Presents arguments for a total ban on tobacco use in school settings as a way to enhance health promotion efforts. Describes the Colorado experience and offers suggestions for successful implementation. Describes available resources developed in the project. Documents the effect of the project after four years.

1461.   Winkelstein, M. L. (1992). Adolescent smoking: Influential factors, past preventive efforts, and future nursing implications. *Journal of Pediatric Nursing, 7*(2), 120-127.

Reviews the biological, social, and psychological factors that contribute to adolescent smoking behavior. Highlights social learning and life skills approaches to prevention. Delineates how nurses can use this information to discourage smoking and other tobacco use among adolescents under their care.

Q. TOBACCO-RELATED ISSUES - GENERAL

1462. Boyd, G. M., & Glover, E. D. (1989). Smokeless tobacco use by youth in the U.S. *Journal of School Health, 59*(5), 189-194.

Discusses the health risk of smokeless tobacco (snuff and chewing tobacco) use and the prevalence among adolescents. Reviews the status of tobacco prevention trials sponsored by the National Cancer Institute. Urges selective inclusion of information on the health consequences of smokeless tobacco in health promotion curricula.

1463. Clubb, R. L. (1991). Promoting non-tobacco use in childhood. *Pediatric Nursing, 17*(6), 566-570.

Emphasizes the influence of social learning theory on understanding adolescent smoking behavior. Critiques selected research on smoking prevention programs. Calls for research on enforcement of restrictions on tobacco sales to minors. Outlines the role of the nurse in program delivery, policy development, and research.

1464. Totten, S. (1993). Total tobacco bans at the middle level: A major step toward developing a safe and healthy school environment. *Current Issues in Middle Level Education, 3*(1), 36-47.

The author makes a case for a total tobacco ban in middle level schools. In doing so, he talks about the dangers of second-hand smoke, middle level literature on tobacco use, the issue of adults (teachers, administrators, counselors, staff) as role models, and the current status of tobacco bans in schools across the nation.

XXII

Family and Community

A. COMMUNITY

1465.   Dornbusch, S. M. (1991). Community influences on the relation of family status to adolescent school performance: Differences between African Americans and non-Hispanic whites. *American Journal of Education, 99*(4), 543-567.

Census and student questionnaire data for 382 African-American and 3,467 white high school (7-12) students from suburban San Francisco indicate consistent positive relationships among grades and family status, level of parental education, and a two-parent home only for the white majority. The author discusses how the community context is important in understanding these ethnic differences.

1466.   Handy, G. B. (1986). The development of a volunteer handbook for the middle schools of Dorchester County (Doctoral dissertation, University of Maryland College Park, 1986). *Dissertation Abstracts International, 48,* 36A.

Section I of the handbook assists administrators and teachers who plan to utilize volunteers, and Section II is for all who volunteer to assist in the middle schools. Includes a review of current literature with an emphasis on ways to recruit, train, and use volunteers in schools.

1467.   McPartland, J. M., & Nettles, S. M. (1991). Using community adults as advocates or mentors for at-risk middle school students: A two-year evaluation of Project RAISE. *American Journal of Education, 99*(4), 568-586.

Outside adults participating in Project Raise are used as school-based advocates and one-on-one mentors for at-risk students. An evaluation of the program showed improved school attendance and report card grades in English. Promotion rates and standardized test scores were not affected. One-on-one mentoring was found to be particularly valuable. Roles and responsibilities of mentors are discussed.

1468.   Scott, P. (1994-1995). Community support: Collaboration at work.

NCMSA Journal, 16(1), 22-23.

The story of one community's response to tragedy. The development of Community Support Team (CST) to "provide a positive community support for the middle grade students, their families, and the school staff" (p. 22).

1469.   Tobman, S. (1992/93). An innovative program to sensitize fifth graders to the elderly. *The Reading Teacher, 46*(4), 353-354.

The author describes a cooperative unit planned and implemented by a fifth grade teacher and a librarian designed to develop an awareness in fifth graders about the life experiences of the elderly. The students discussed selected texts and materials about issues important to the elderly. Experts in the field of gerontology participated in class discussions. Finally, the students went into their community and visited with the elderly and participated in a panel discussion with a select group of residents.

B. FAMILY ISSUES - RESEARCH

1470.   Brandon, M. Y. (1992). The single-parent familial arrangement of urban middle school students and its effects on academic achievement in the public school enterprise (Doctoral dissertation, Texas Southern University, 1992). *Dissertation Abstracts International, 53,* 3165A.

On the whole, students from two-parent familial arrangements preformed better than students from single-parent family homes on most indicators. When family income was controlled, however, many students from single-parent families performed similar to students of two-parent families.

1471.   Featherstone, D. R., Cundick, B. P., & Jensen, L. C. (1992). Differences in school behavior and achievement between children from intact, reconstituted, and single-parent families. *Adolescence, 27(105),* 1-12.

Provides a comparative review of the literature on the effects of family type on children. Presents findings of analysis of school records of 530 students from grades 6 through 9. Used analysis of covariance and *t* test and Chi-square to examine the effect of type of family on the dependent variables of grade point average, absences, tardies, disruptive attitude, social competence and citizenship. Results supported the positive effect of intact families on children.

1472.   Horn, L., & West, J. (1992). *A profile of parents of eighth graders.* Washington, DC: U.S. Department of Education. 106 pp.

Conducted by the National Center for Education Statistics under the auspices of the U.S. Department of Education, this report had two main goals: to provide a profile of the characteristics of the eight graders' families, focusing on the sociodemographic characteristics of the students and their families and the relationship between selected family background and parental involvement in their children's education; and to provide a closer look at the influences that specific types of parental involvement have on academic achievement and on whether or not American eighth graders drop out of school between the 9th and 10th grades. In addition to the introduction (which delineates the goals and limitations of the study), the report is comprised of the following chapters: 1. The Families of Eighth Graders, 2. How Parents Participate, 3. Parents' Expectations and Beliefs, 4. School Type and Parental Involvement; 5. Parent Involvement and Student Outcomes, and 6. Summary and Conclusions.

1473. Levitan, S. A., Belous, R. S., & Gallo, F. (1988). *What's happening to the American family?* (rev. ed.). Baltimore: Johns Hopkins University Press.

Examines the changes in the American family during the 1980's. Trends in the divorce rate, out-of-wedlock births, single parent families, and poverty levels are provided. Recommends government involvement in providing support to strengthen families in the areas of birth control, enforcement of child support laws, minimum wage increases, childcare, health insurance, and shelter needs.

1474. Matthews, D., & Quinn, J. L. (1981). Congruence of parental behavior as perceived by parents and their middle school children, . In Thomas Owen Erb (Ed.), *Middle school research: Selected studies 1981* (pp. 58-74). Columbus, OH: Research Committee of the National Middle School Association.

An interesting study in which the researchers ascertained the congruence or lack thereof between the perceptions of children and their parents regarding a variety of issues/items, e.g., "I consider my child's opinion before making a family decision," "I am critical of my child's behavior," "I discuss my dissatisfaction with the school in the presence of my child."

1475. Myers, J., & Monson, L. (1992). *Involving families in middle level education.* Columbus, OH: National Middle School Association. 48 pp.

One section of this primer on family involvement at the middle level addresses some of the research findings on family involvement in schools.

1476. Newman, B. M. (1989). Changing nature of the parent-adolescent relationship from early to late adolescence. *Adolescence, 24(96),* 915-924.

Descriptive research study examining the tension between individuation and cohesion during adolescence. Used a questionnaire and interview of 110 families with an oldest child of either 11, 14, or 17. Provides evidence supporting the influence of parenting style and ego development during adolescence.

1477. Newman, I. M., & Ward, J. M. (1989). The influence of parental attitude and behavior on early adolescent cigarette smoking. *Journal of School Health, 59(4),* 150-152.

A replication of an earlier studied that used self-report data from adolescents to examine the impact of parental objection and parental smoking behavior on the smoking behavior of subjects. In the replication seven hundred and eighty-five 13- and 14-year olds completed self-report questionnaires regarding their own smoking behavior and parental attitudes and behavior. Students whose parents expressed concern about smoking were less likely to report smoking behavior. The authors suggest including parents in health promotion programs for adolescents.

1478.   Riesch, S. K., Tosi, C. B., Thurston, C. A., Forsyth, D. M., Kuenning, T. S., & Kestly. (1993). Effects of communication training on parents and young adolescents. *Nursing Research, 42(1),* 10-16.

Reports outcomes of a short-term intervention in communication skills based on a family systems model using quasi-experimental design with a sample of 258 middle school children and their parents. Significant results were observed in the treatment groups for the following outcomes: satisfaction with the family system, perception of more open communication between mothers and adolescents, and decreased antisocial content between fathers and adolescents.

1479.   Smetana, J. G., Yau, J., & Hanson, S. (1991). Conflict resolution in families with adolescents. *Journal of Research on Adolescence, 1(2),* 189-206.

Describes research involving 93 families (47 with 5th through 8th graders) and their styles of resolving conflicts (parent concession, adolescent concession, compromise, or no resolution). "Conflict resolution was found to differ as a function of adolescents' age, sex and topic of conflict" (p. 201). Findings indicate that younger adolescents were most likely to use concession. Families with girls were more often able to resolve their conflicts. The most difficult to resolve topics related to chores and interpersonal relationships. The authors called for the use of naturalistic studies to confirm their findings. The study is helpful in not restricting itself to at-risk families.

1480.   Turner, R. A., Irwin, C. E., & Millstein, S. G. (1991). Family structure, family processes, and experimenting with substances during adolescence. *Journal of Research on Adolescence, 1(1),* 93-106.

Used self-report information from 149 adolescents ages 12 - 17-years old to see what effect family structure (single parent versus intact family), parental limit-setting, and adolescent emotional detachment had on experimentation with substances (alcohol, cigarettes, marijuana, chewing tobacco, cocaine, psychedelics, or other drugs) using hierarchical multiple regression. Results indicated that "...adolescents of single parents were still more likely to engage n experimentation with substances than were those from intact families" (p. 102) after controlling for confounding factors. Of interest to health providers of adolescents in understanding the contextual influences of high-risk behavior.

C. FAMILY ISSUES - PRACTICAL

1481.   Connolly, M. R. (1993). Shouldn't every middle school offer effective parenting training? *The New England League of Middle Schools*

Journal, 6(1), 5-7.

Discusses the rationale as to why schools should offer parent training courses. In doing so, Connolly briefly discusses the kinds of programs that schools can offer to parents.

1482.   Farel, A. M. (1982). *Early adolescence: What parents need to know*. Carrboro, NC: Center for Early Adolescence at the University of North Carolina at Chapel Hill. 37 pp.

This handbook addresses many questions parents have regarding the intellectual, physical, and social development of young adolescents. In doing so, it includes a discussion of issues relating to religion, discipline, communication, and early warning signs of a variety of problems.

1483.   Johnston, J. H. (1990). *The new American family and the school*. Columbus, OH: National Middle School Association. 42 pp.

In this booklet Johnston provides an analysis of "the new American family" and its relationship to the school. In doing so, he discusses how the two institutions often have differing expectations and then goes on to provide a blueprint for involving families in the education of their children.

1484.   Kane, T. (1992). The parents' institute: Helping parents understand their early adolescent. *Schools in the Middle: Theory Into Practice, 1*(4), 12-14.

Discusses a series of school-based workshops that are carried out over a two-year period which is specifically designed to assist parents to understand the dynamics of adolescent growth as well as strategies for establishing true communication with their children.

1485.   Kochan, F. (1992). A new paradigm of schooling: Connecting school, home and community. In Judith L. Irvin (Ed.), *Transforming middle level education: Perspectives and possibilities* (pp. 63-72). Boston, MA: Allyn and Bacon.

Among the issues Kochan discusses are a "new view of the family," how the concept of family and community could be incorporated into the school curriculum, methods for uniting parents with the school, and ways to network with the community.

1486.   Manning, M. L. (1992). Parent education programs at the middle level. *NASSP Bulletin: The Journal for Middle Level and High School Administrators, 76*(543), 24-29.

Manning argues that there is a need to develop and implement effective parent education programs ("organized activities that have been developed in order to further parents' abilities to raise their children successfully") at the middle level. He states that such a program would assist parents to gain a better understanding

of the developmental aspects and needs of 10-14 year olds, to "become active
participants in their children's education, and to interact with professional
adolescent specialists." In doing so, he discusses the importance of parent
education and delineates a parent education program format.

1487.   Myers, J., & Monson, L. (1992). *Involving families in middle level
education.* Columbus, OH: National Middle School Association. 48 pp.

An outstanding primer on why the involvement of families in middle level
education is so crucial as well how educators can to begin to effectively
work with families in order to meet the unique and complex needs of young
adolescents. Among the many topics the authors address are benefits of
family involvement, research findings in regard to family involvement in
schools, ways that families can become involved in middle level education,
methods for communicating with families, how to implement family
involvement programs, and a brief overview of four programs that have
successful family involvement.

1488.   Pulver, R. (Ed.). (1992). *Living with 10- to 15- year olds: A parent
education Curriculum.* Carrboro, NC: Center for Early Adolescence at the
University of North Carolina at Chapel Hill. 247 pp.

The express purpose of this curriculum package is to assist schools and other
community groups to provide families with in-depth information and guidance in
regard to (1) understanding early adolescence, (2) communicating with young
adolescents, (3) recognizing risk-taking behavior and young adolescents, and (4)
speaking to young adolescents about issues of sexuality. The curriculum
includes planning suggestions, possible agendas, workshop designs for 20 hours
of group activities, handout materials, resource lists, and a publicity kit.

1489.   Rich, D. (1987). *Schools and families: Issues and actions.*
Washington, DC: National Education Association. 129 pp.

Provides insights and ideas on how to develop and implement a systematic,
long-range approach to strengthening school-family ties.

D. FAMILY ISSUES - GENERAL

1490.   National Middle School Association. (1995). *H.E.L.P. - Get ready for
changes...Spanish Edition.* Columbus OH: Author.

The Spanish version of H.E.L.P. (How to enjoy living with a preadolescent)
which can be distributed to families.

1491.   National Middle School Association. (1995). *What is a middle school?*
Columbus OH: Author.

A resource brochure that can be distributed to the public during the planning
and implementation of middle level programs.

E. PARENT INVOLVEMENT - RESEARCH

1492.   Dauber, S. L., & Epstein, J. L. (1989). *Parent attitudes and practices of parent involvement in inner-city elementary and middle schools.* (CREMS Report No. 33). Baltimore, MD: Center for Research on Elementary and Middle Schools. (ERIC Document Reproduction Service No. ED 314 152).

Reports the results of a study designed to examine the extent of parental involvement, the extent to which middle level schools attempted to involve parents, and methods used by schools to achieve increased parental involvement.

1493.   Davenport, J. S. (1991). The role of parents in the transition to a middle school organization: A case study (Doctoral dissertation, University of Minnesota, 1991). *Dissertation Abstracts International, 52,* 753A.

High parental participation, particularly in areas related to policy, was found to be significant in assuring the success of the middle school transition process. Administrative leadership, particularly from the superintendency, was found to be a critical factor.

1494.   Horn, L., & West, J. (1992). *A profile of parents of eighth graders.* Washington, DC: U. S. Department of Education. 106 pp.

Conducted by the National Center for Education Statistics under the auspices of the U.S. Department of Education, this report had two main goals: to provide a profile of the characteristics of the eight graders' families, focusing on the sociodemographic characteristics of the students and their families and the relationship between selected family background and parental involvement in their children's education; and to provide a closer look at the influences that specific types of parental involvement have on academic achievement and on whether or not American eighth graders drop out of school between the 9th and 10th grades. In addition to the introduction (which delineates the goals and limitations of the study) the report is comprised of the following chapters: 1. The Families of Eighth Graders, 2. How Parents Participate, 3. Parents' Expectations and Beliefs, 4. School Type and Parental Involvement; 5. Parent Involvement and Student Outcomes, and 6. Summary and Conclusions.

1495.   Myers, J., & Monson, L. (1992). *Involving families in middle level education.* Columbus, OH: National Middle School Association. 48 pp.

One section of this primer on family involvement at the middle level addresses some of the research findings on family involvement in schools.

F. PARENT INVOLVEMENT - PRACTICAL

1496.   Domino, V. A., & Carroll, K. (1994). Back to basics: Celebrating the family schoolwide, curriculumwide. *Inside Schools in the Middle, 4*(2), 13-17. Describes one middle school's efforts to reduce substance abuse through a focus on the positive aspects of the families in their school. Events include a teen theater group, professional storyteller, sock hop, and family lunch hour. Family themes are also the focus in various content areas. Suggestions for future celebrations are offered along with ideas for funding such events.

1497.   Garlington, J. (1993). *Helping dreams survive: The story of a project involving African American families in the education of their children.* Washington, DC: National Committee for Citizens in Education.

This report "relates in personal, poignant detail the struggle to help black parents in a poor Baltimore community learn to shape their children's educational experiences." In doing so, it describes the With and For Parents program that worked for three years with about 150 families in a Baltimore middle school. The key purpose was to prevent the students from dropping out of school. The report describes the intervention efforts, what worked, what did not work, and the successes of the program. "The report gives sound advice on how to reach — and learn from — parents such as those at this inner-city middle school."

1498.   Gennaro, E. D. (1982). Science courses selected by middle school children and their parents to take together. *School Science and Mathematics, 82*(2), 127-131.

Reports on a program in which parents and their middle level children learn science together. Details of a zoo course are provided. Data from a survey designed to find other courses that could be taught in a similar manner are included.

1499.   Georgiady, N. P., & Romano, L. G. (1982). Parent teacher conferences: Indispensable for the middle school. *Middle School Journal, 14*(1), 7, 30-31.

Begins with a parent-teacher conference program list of beliefs, including "the welfare of the pre-adolescent is the common concern of both the teacher and the parent." Suggests that students be active members of the conference as they need input into their own behavior. Guidelines are listed for preplanning conferences and for conducting conferences. An outline for preparing a parent conference guide is offered.

1500.   Hagborg, W. J. (1992). A counseling report card: A study of parental satisfaction. *The School Counselor, 40*(2), 131-135.

The Counseling Report Card was rated as useful or very useful by 90.9% of parent respondents. Includes a copy of the report card in an appendix. As a guard against possible confidentiality violations, students were allowed to preview their counseling report card and given the option of not having their parents view the card.

1501.   Huhn, R., & Zimpfer, D. G. (1984). The role of middle and junior high school counselors in parent education. *The School Counselor, 31* (4), 357-365.

Previously most parent education was directed toward parents with young children or children with special needs. Today, many parents of adolescents also find themselves in need of education. Parents, students, and schools can benefit through counselor-provided parent education.

1502.   Hunter, D. D. (1994). Parent involvement, business partnerships promote student achievement. *Inside Schools in the Middle, 4*(2), 22-23.

Brief overview of how parents and businesses are involved in one West Virginia middle school. Attributes improvements in attendance and other academic indicators to their parent program.

1503.   Johnston, J. H. (1994). Home-school partnerships: Shall we dance? *Inside Schools in the Middle, 4*(2), 5-8.

Criticizes the lack of shared responsibility for parenting all children evident in society today. Calls for a renews effort to bring community support into schools.

1504.   Lewis, A. C. (1992). Parents care, do schools? A look at the research. *Schools in the Middle: Theory into Practice*, 2(2), 10-11.

Discusses the need for middle level programs to make a greater effort to involve parents in their children's education and provides some recommendations as to how schools can link up with inner city families.

1505.   Marguardt, J. (1991). Keeping parents informed. *The Transescent, 16*(1), 22-23.

Discusses the importance of communicating with parents of middle-level students. Suggests that a newsletter is a time-efficient, effective way of establishing and maintaining open communication. Includes examples of newsletters.

1506.   Schurr, S. L. (1992). Fine tuning your parent power increases student achievement. *Schools in the Middle: Theory into Practice*, 2(2), 3-9.

Argues that administrators need to take the initiative to create an environment that invites, rather than discourages, families of all types and socioeconomic levels into the school. In doing so, Schurr initially delineates seven common elements that have been identified with "promising parent involvement programs" and then lists and discusses sixteen proven parent involvement strategies.

1507.   Schurr, S., & Hunt, K. (1991). Nuts and bolts of a middle school. *The Transescent, 16*(1), 24.

Although only one page in length, the information is essential for middle level educators who must communicate with "upset" parents. Includes suggestions for parents to become collaborators in the educational process. Also addresses key components of a problem solving parent-teacher conference. Parents and teachers of middle level students will find the advice both practical and useful.

1508.   Stinson, K. (1993). Strategies to improve parent-teacher conferences. *The AIMS Journal*, *8*(1), 46-49.

Presents a five-step plan for arranging and conducting effective parent-teacher conferences: (1) Focus on the students' academic and social progress, (2) Write a brief non-judgmental description of problems, (3) Prioritize other concerns and issues, (4) Suggest possible strategies, and (5) Provide a list of questions. Includes examples of a parent conference communication form.

1509.   Strickland, B. L. (1991). ET phone school. *Becoming*, *2*(2), 20-22. Emphasizes the need for communication among parents, teachers, and students.

Offers a variety of practical suggestions for using technology to increase communication.

1510.   Swap, S. M. (1993). *Developing home-school partnerships: From concepts to practice*. New York: Teachers College Press.

Discusses the importance of parental involvement in the educational process. Offers suggestions for establishing and maintaining meaningful relationships between parents and educators. Focuses on the benefits of parental involvement, barriers to parental involvement, three models of home-school interaction, and practical suggestions for creating effective partnerships.

1511.   Waggoner, J. E., & Loucks, H. (1993). Successful parental involve-ment programs in rural Illinois middle schools. *The AIMS Journal*, *8* (1), 54-58.

Addresses the need to re-engage families in the education of young adolescents. Presents an overview of eight model programs operational in Illinois public schools, including the Friendship Carousel Big Buddy Program, Parent Pair, and Project C.A.R.E.S.

1512.   White, G. P., & Matz, C. (1992). Steps to success: Parents as true partners in middle level education. *Schools in the Middle: Theory into Practice*, *1*(4), 15-19.

The authors discuss the benefits of a home-school partnership, types of home-school programs, and an actual parent involvement program that has been implemented at Upper Perkiomen Middle School which is located in a rural district in Pennsylvania.

1513.   White-Hood, M. (1994). Enriching adolescent lives: Focus on changing family structures. *Inside Schools in the Middle*, *4*(2), 9-10.

Offers suggestions for how educators can establish partnerships with families including "create summer academies and weekend enrichment options...expose adolescents to real-life role models...develop parenting seminars" (p. 12).

XXIII

Middle Level Teacher Preparation Issues

A. CERTIFICATION

1514.   Ervay, S. B., & Wood, D. E. (1979). Middle school teacher certification and education: An update. *The Clearing House*, *53*(3), 143-144.

Examines national trends in state certification requirements from 1975-1978. Also provides a overview of teacher education with middle level education as an area of emphasis. Although the focus is in the mid- to late-70s, the information is useful for comparing that data with current data.

1515.   National Middle School Association. (1986). *Professional certification and preparation for the middle level*. Columbus, OH: National Middle School Association.

A paper outlining the position of the National Middle School Association with regard to professional preparation and continuing education of middle level educators. Provides brief guidelines for personal and professional competencies of effective middle level educators.

1516.   Roberts, M. (1985). The credentialing squeeze for schools in the middle. *Thrust*, *15*(1), 22.

Argues that since middle schools have special staffing needs, the credentialing system in California needs to be more flexible.

1517.   Seitz, L. F. (1993). Transescent-centered middle level education: Is middle level teacher certification the answer? *Current Issues in Middle Level Education*, *2* (2), 27-36.

Reports on the status of middle level teacher certification programs as of 1991. Emphasizes the need for prospective teachers to receive training in meeting the needs of young adolescents. Argues that teacher education institutions should assume most of the responsibility for providing appropriate content and field experiences for prospective middle level teachers.

1518.   Valentine, J. W., & Mogar, D. C. (1992). Middle level certification —
An encouraging evolution. *Middle School Journal*, *24*(2), 36-43.

The purpose of this study was to "chronicle the history of special certification
requirements to teach or administer at the middle level." Among the key issues
addressed in this study were: The number of states that had standards prior to
the position paper that the Board of Directors of The National Middle School
Association adopted that emphasized the importance of specific certification
standards for middle level teachers, the states that established standards since
the publication of the original plus a second position paper (*Professional
Certification and Preparation for the Middle Level*) by NMSA, the grades that
are covered for certification, renewal requirements, whether principals of
middle level schools are required to have specific training in middle level
education, and whether there is a historical pattern for middle level certification
standards evolving.

B. TEACHER EDUCATION - RESEARCH

1519.   Bartos, R. B., & Smith, J. (1980). Priorities of needs, competencies
and training of middle grade teachers. In *Middle school research: Selected
studies 1980* (pp. 17-26). Fairborn, OH: Research Committee and Publications
Committee of the National Middle School Association.

The sample in this study was comprised of two groups of teachers (51
elementary and secondary teachers from a county, public school system in a
mid-sized city in the southeastern part of the United States and 204 middle grade
teachers from four counties in the greater metropolitan area in the southeastern
U.S.). The responses of the two groups were compared. "Teachers were
questioned as to which competencies they perceived necessary for effective
teaching, how proficient they perceived themselves to be in these competencies,
and, finally, where they believed these proficiencies had been developed (if
indeed they had been developed)." Among the competencies listed in the
questionnaire were: "Ability to construct performance/behavior objectives in
your particular subject area, ability to interpret and report student performance
on teacher made tests; ability to maintain order in a classroom and to assist
students in the development of self-discipline, ability to utilize audio-visual
equipment and material in teaching, and ability to prepare teacher-made tests.
Many of the items were extremely general, and the questionnaire was also bereft
of specific items probing instructional procedures or the teacher's knowledge
base vis-à-vis his/her subject area.

1520.   Hubert, J. B. (1973). On preparing teachers for the junior high and
middle school: The teacher input. *The Clearing House*, *47*(9), 553-54.

Reports the results of a study designed to gather factual and attitudinal data from
middle level teachers with regard to teacher preparation programs. Includes a
discussion of components perceived to be vital to a well-rounded program.

1521.   Krinsky, J., & Pumerantz, P. (1972). Middle school teacher preparation programs. *The Journal of Teacher Education*, *23*(4), 468-470.

This is a report based on a survey that the authors conducted of 241 NCATE-accredited teacher training institutions in the U.S. in order to ascertain the current extent and nature of middle level teacher preparation. "The survey revealed that in 1969-70 only 37 (23 percent) of the 160 accredited teacher-training institutions responding had middle school teacher preparation programs."

1522.   Lesh, R. A., & Schultz, K. A. (1983). Teacher training in applied problem solving: A study in metacognition. In Thomas Owen Erb (Ed.), *Middle school research: selected studies 1983* (pp. 86-96). Columbus, OH: Research Committee of the National Middle School Association.

The authors describe a study which was designed to examine "the relationships between pre-service middle school teachers' ability to accurately characterize the problem solving episodes of middle school children and their own problem solving ability. For both populations problem solving involved using elementary mathematical ideas to solve problems in realistic everyday situations."

1523.   McEwin, C. K., & Scales, P. C. (1994). *Growing pains: The making of America's middle school teachers.* Chapel Hill, NC, and Columbus, OH: Center for Early Adolescence and National Middle School Association.

Examines the preparation and perspectives of 2,139 middle level teachers in five states (Georgia, Kentucky, Missouri, North Carolina, and Virginia) which contain 57% of the nation's middle grades teacher preparation programs. Finds that comprehensive programs are better than add-on programs.

1524.   Sage, M. E. (1989-1990). Preservice teachers' attitudes toward middle level prior to student teaching. *Action in Teacher Education*, *11*(4), 19-23.

This focus of this study is on the rationale of preservice teachers who were allowed to select middle school or high school sites for their initial student teaching experience. The sample included 85 preservice secondary student teachers. The article describes the purpose of the study, the population, methodology of the study, findings, and implications. One problem with the study is that the researcher does not differentiate between junior high and middle level programs.

1525.   Scales, P. C. (1992). Improving the preparation of middle-grades teachers. *Educational Horizons*, *70* (4), 208-215.

Reports the findings of a study by the Center for Early Adolescence designed to evaluate the preparation of middle-level teachers. Also includes a variety of practical suggestions for improving the preparation of middle level teachers.

1526.   Scales, P. C. (1992). The effect of preservice preparation on middle grades teachers' beliefs about teaching and teacher education. *Midpoints*, *2*(2), 1-12. (Available from the National Middle School Association, 4807 Evanswood Dr., Columbus, OH 43229-6292).

In this occasional paper published by the National Middle School Association, Scales discusses a study that he conducted (a random sample survey of 439 fifth through ninth grade teachers from Arkansas, California, Florida, Georgia, Indiana, New York, North Carolina and Washington) in regard to the following: the kind of teacher preparation they received, how they rated that preparation, the relationship of having had special preparation to ratings of preservice program adequacy, professional beliefs about middle grades teaching, and recommendations for improving the preparation of middle grades teachers. In this paper, he discusses the sample, presents an overview of the results and closes by discussing the implication of the findings.

1527.   Scales, P. C. (1992). *Windows of opportunity: Improving middle grades teacher preparation*. Carrboro, NC: Center for Early Adolescence of the University of North Carolina at Chapel Hill. 185 pp.

In this book, Scales presents the findings of a study that was conducted "in response to a growing realization that many teachers are coming out of school unprepared to address the special academic, psychological, and social needs of their adolescent students." The study involved a review of the literature and data collection from "a large sample of randomly selected middle grades teachers in eight states where middle-grades were a relatively high priority." The states were Arkansas, California, Florida, Georgia, Indiana, New York, North Carolina and Washington.
        Data were also collected from the deans of teacher education programs and the chief state school officers in those states. Scales discusses the purpose and organization of the study, presents a review of the literature, discuses the design of the study as well as the results, and concludes with a set of recommendations.

1528.   Stahler, T. M. (1992). A comparative analysis of specifically prepared and generally prepared middle school preservice teachers (Doctoral dissertation, The Ohio State University, 1992). *Dissertation Abstracts International*, *53*, 3877A.

Scores of specifically prepared preservice teachers were higher in all areas measured, with the greatest difference being that of attitude about middle level teaching. 100% of specifically prepared vs 30% of generally prepared teachers intended to teach in middle school. All subjects in the study agreed that teachers should be prepared, specifically, for middle level teaching.

1529.   Strahan, D. B. (1993). Preservice teachers reflecting on young adolescents as students and themselves as teachers. *Current Issues in Middle Level Education*, *2*(2), 37-52.

Presents the results of a study designed to investigate the evolution of reflection on instruction among four student teachers. Methodology included collecting data from interviews and journal entries. Findings support the importance of clinical experiences in promoting reflecting practice. Also offers suggestions for encouraging reflection in teacher education programs.

1530.   Swain, J., & Stefanich, G. (In progress). *Meeting the Standards: Improving Middle Level Teacher Education*. Columbus, OH: National Middle School Association.

Focuses on "best practice" responses to individual program elements of recognized national middle level standards. Uses the NMSA Curriculum Guidelines as its basis.

C. TEACHER EDUCATION - PRACTICAL

1531.   Bosch, K. A., & Manning, M. L. (1993). Imperatives for early field experiences in middle school. *Current Issues in Middle Level Education, 2*(2), 82-91.

Argues that the quality of early field experiences depends upon appropriate design, implementation, and evaluation of the experiences and that teacher educators must change their own attitudes toward the experiences. Presents five suggestions for improving the quality of early field experiences for prospective middle level teachers.

1532.   Brough, J., Hoffman, M., & Martini, A. (1995). Practicing what you preach: Preparing teachers for an interdisciplinary curriculum. *Inside Schools in the Middle, 4*(4), 10-13.

Highlights the efforts of one teacher preparation program to provide meaningful field experiences early in the student's professional program. Key concepts of the experience include reflection, collaboration, and conceptual thinking.

1533.   Butler, D., Davies, M. A., & Dickinson, T. A. (1991). *On site: Preparing middle level teachers through field experiences*. Columbus, OH: National Middle School Association. 71 pp.

This interesting and useful booklet is comprised of four parts: 1. "The Power of Good Middle Level Experiences," 2. Models of Early Field Experiences at the Middle Level," 3. Models of Student Teaching at the Middle Level," and 4. "Building Effective Field Experience Programs."

1534.   George, P. S., & McEwin, L. K. (1978). Middle school teacher education: A progress report. *The Journal of Teacher Education, 31*(5), 13-16.

This is a fascinating article by two well known middle level pioneers who discuss the status of teacher education programs as of the late 1970s. The authors discuss both undergraduate and graduate programs as well as provide a list of ten recommended program components.

1535.   Goerss, K. V., & Associates. (1993). *Letters from the middle*.
Columbus, OH: National Middle School Association.

Experienced middle level teachers write to novice teachers, giving advice on topics such as discipline, cooperative learning, advisory programs, and homework.

1536.   Lewis, A. C. (Ed.). (1989). Teachers [Special issue]. *High Strides*, *1*(4).

Focuses on teacher preparation and continued professional development.
Includes five guidelines for effective program development for middle level
teachers. Also includes suggestions for long-term support of inservice teachers.

1537.   McEwin, C. K., & Dickinson, T. S. (1995). The professional
preparation of middle level teachers: Profiles of successful programs.
Columbus, OH: National Middle School Association. 208 pages.

Successful teacher preparation programs for middle level are profiled. An
interesting appendix contains several course syllabi.

1538.   Scales, P. C. (1992). Improving the preparation of middle-grades
teachers. *Educational Horizons*, *70* (4), 2, 8, 215.

Discusses the need for middle level teachers to receive adequate training in
middle level concepts and processes. Suggestions for improving teacher
preparation programs include (1) providing in-depth exposure to and discussion
of middle-level philosophy and concepts, (2) allowing opportunities for
development and enhancement of leadership skills and interpersonal
communication skills, (3) revising the teacher preparation curriculum to include
middle level strategies, (4) requiring prospective students to successfully
complete appropriate field experiences at the middle level, (5) recruiting
candidates who have a genuine desire to teach middle level students and to serve
as advocates for young adolescents, and (6) identifying those candidates who are
risk-takers and who want to participate in meaningful school reform.

1539.   Scales, P. C. (1994). Strengthening middle grade teacher preparation
programs. *Middle School Journal*, *26*(1), 59-65.

While middle school have become the most common and fastest-growing form
of school for young adolescents, only 20 percent of middle grades teachers
undergo special preparation for teaching at the middle level. By early 1993,
only 14 middle grade teacher education programs had unconditionally met
NMSA developed/NCATE approved program guidelines. Responses from 175
faculty from half of the nation's middle grades teacher education programs
provide the most detailed picture yet of what resources are being used and what
are needed in those teacher preparation programs.

D. TEACHER EDUCATION - GENERAL

1540.   Alexander, W. M., & McEwin, C. K. (1984). Solving the dilemma—

Training the middle level educator—Where does the solution lie? *NASSP Bulletin: The Journal for Middle Level and High School Administrators,* 68(473), 6-11.

The authors discuss the issue of teacher education programs in regard to middle level education; and in doing so, they address the following points: why middle level education was neglected for so long, certification and teacher education issues, the type of preparation that is needed in order to teach at the middle level, and whether or not middle level education can succeed.

1541. Arth, A. A., & Weiss, T. M. (1977). University of Wyoming: Middle school teacher education. *The Journal of Teacher Education,* 28(1), 32-36.

Succinctly describes the rationale and component of the University of Wyoming's middle level teacher education program, which was one of the earliest programs to be developed.

1542. Burke, P. J., & Stoltenberg, J. (1979). Certification for the middle grades. *Action in Teacher Education,* 1(3-4), 47-52.

Groups junior high, middle school, and intermediate schools, and then briefly discusses such issues the characteristics of such schools, the characteristics of young adolescents, learner styles, and teacher styles. Concludes by calling for the development of teacher education programs that meet the needs of young adolescents, and discusses the implications for certification.

1543. Hart, L. E. (1995). Statewide processes for improving middle level teacher education. *Middle School Journal,* 26(5), 37-40.

Presents processes for improving middle level teacher education across the State of Georgia. Describes the initiative called Principles of Educating Teachers (POET). The goal of POET is to improve middle level teacher education at Georgia colleges and universities that prepare middle level teachers. Discusses barriers to teacher education improvement.

1544. Lauritzen, C., & Jaeger, M. (1994). Language arts teacher education within a transdisciplinary curriculum. *Language Arts,* 71(8), 581-587.

Discusses the importance of a transdisciplinary teacher preparation curriculum in the preparation of pre-service language arts teachers. Emphasizes that inclusion of a transdisciplinary curriculum at the college level models the need for such a curriculum at the middle level. Also stresses that a transdisciplinary curriculum demonstrates the interrelatedness of context and meaning found in real-world situations.

1545. Lounsbury, J. H. (1992). Teacher certification and middle level education. *Current Issues in Middle Level Education,* 1(1), 79-81.

Lounsbury asserts that the major concern of middle level teacher education preparation programs should be on personal development of the future teachers. More specifically, he says that "It is not just a matter of adding components of information in methodology and content to an already formed person, but rather it involves changing the person himself or herself. ...' [A]n understanding of early adolescents, which is the foundation for all middle level education, must be ingrained in one's being sufficiently to be reflected in attitudes and appreciations."

1546.   Manning, M. L. (1989-1990). Contemporary studies of teaching behaviors and their implications of middle level teacher education. *Action in Teacher Education, 11*(4), 1-5.

A rather general piece that initially provides a brief review of Bruce Joyce's research on training and preservice teacher education, Brophy's synthesis of research on motivating students to learn, Walberg's synthesis research on time and learning, Porter and Brophy's research on "good teaching," and Brophy and Good's research on teacher behavior and student achievement. It concludes with a short section on the implications of these studies/research for middle level teacher education, and a list of possible research questions.

1547.   McEwin, C. K. (1977). The middle school. An institution in search of teachers. In P. S. George (Ed.), *A look ahead* (pp. 116-127). Columbus, OH: National Middle School Association.

Discusses several issues related to professional preparation of middle level teachers and administrators. Specifically discussed are undergraduate and graduate degree programs, certification components, and professional development needs and opportunities.

1548.   McEwin, C. K. (1984). Preparing teachers for the middle school. In John H. Lounsbury (Ed.), *Perspectives: Middle school education* (pp. 109-119). Columbus, OH: National Middle School Association.

Discusses the following issues: the neglect in the past of the middle level by teacher preparation programs, middle level certification, the nature of middle level teacher preparation programs in the early to mid 1980s, essential components for effective middle level teacher preparation programs, and the need for more middle level teacher preparation programs.

1549.   McEwin, C. K., & Dickinson, T. S. (1995). *The professional preparation of middle school teachers: Profiles of successful programs.* Columbus, OH: National Middle School Association.

Offers fourteen "best practice" pictures of teacher preparation programs. Provides significant insights into program development and design, middle school courses and field-based experiences, and collaboration with public schools. Includes over 50 pages of course syllabi drawn from various programs.

1550.   McEwin, C. K., Dickinson, T. S., Erb, T. O., & Scales, P. C. (1995). *A vision of excellence: Organizing principles for middle level teacher preparation*. Columbus, OH: National Middle School Association. 52 pages.

A document of interest to teacher preparation programs who want to assess their current program or develop a new track for middle level. Answers the question: How are middle level teachers unique?

1551.   Totten, S. (1994). University/college round tables on middle level education. *Current Issues in Middle Level Education, 3*(2), 77-84.

The author discusses the purpose and focus of university round-table sessions that are held bi-annually in the state of Arkansas.

1552.   Totten, S., Pedersen, J., Wilson, S., & Nielsen, W. (1995). Turning the corner: The University of Arkansas' new middle level teacher education program. *Current Issues in Middle Level Education, 4*(1), 94-107.

The authors describe and discuss the development stages and programmatic components of a new middle level teacher program that they were instrumental in designing.

1553.   Ullrich, W. J., Putbrese, Sartell Middle School Staff, & St. Cloud Junior High School Staff. (1993). The early adolescent block: Meaningful school/university collaboration in Minnesota. *New Mexico Middle School Journal, 3*, 10-13.

Describes unique features and courses of the middle level teacher education program at St. Cloud State University.

1554.   Walzer, P. (1994). Teacher education misses the middle. *High strides, 7*(2), 1, 4-5.

Argues for the development of teacher preparation programs with an emphasis on middle level. Identifies the lack of distinct certification for middle level in most states as a problem. Cited two recent studies on teacher preparation as the basis for the recommendation.

1555.   Webb, C. A. (1994). Ten principles of in-service. *English Journal, 83*(7), 109.

Lists ten principles of effective professional development programs for middle level and high school teachers. Emphasis is upon reflective practice, ownership in the teaching/learning process, collaboration among all stakeholders, partnerships, and resources. Although written for an audience of English teachers, the article is useful and appropriate for teachers in all content areas.

XXIV

Middle Level Teacher Inservice and Staff Development

A. INSERVICE AND STAFF DEVELOPMENT - RESEARCH

1556.   Nye, B. A. (1993). Examining the relationship between process-oriented staff development and classroom practices using integrated mathematics and science instructional modules. *Journal of Elementary Science Education, 5*(1), 10-26.

This study found that hands-on, cooperative learning format and the process-oriented activities and content of an intensive one-week AIMS science and mathematics institute created a high degree of teacher satisfaction. Teacher perception of student understanding, as well as that of their own personal skills needed to implement instructional change, may be the key to implementation. One hundred forty-two teachers (K-9, including four middle level) from urban and rural school systems participated in this study.

1557.   Steer, D. R. (1983). Inservice education/professional development for middle school teachers: A national perspective. In Thomas Owen Erb (Ed.), *Middle school research: Selected studies 1983* (pp. 23-32). Columbus, OH: Research Committee of the National Middle School Association.

Reports on a questionnaire sent out to 500 individuals (160 responded for a response of 32%) who were members of the National Middle School Association in order to ascertain perceptions regarding components perceived as most important for inclusion in middle school teacher inservice programs. While most of the suggested topics were perceived to be at least moderately important by most of the respondents, those rated highest were characteristics and needs of the early adolescent, philosophy and rationale of the middle level, and enhancement of student self concept.

1558.   Youngblood, S. R. (1980). Middle level staff development needs: A survey of middle level educators. *NASSP Bulletin: The Journal for High School and Middle School Administrators*, 73(515),102-105.

The author discusses a study of administrators (superintendents, directors of staff development, directors of middle level education programs) in 298 school districts in Washington on the effectiveness of middle level education staff development programs.

B.   INSERVICE AND STAFF
DEVELOPMENT - PRACTICAL

1559.   Clarke, S. (1972). The middle school: Specially trained teachers are vital to its success. *The Clearing House*, *46*(4), 218-222.

Discusses the unique role of middle schools and the importance of preparing middle level teachers to meet the needs of young adolescents. Offers suggestions for revising teacher education courses to include instruction in the academic and social needs of middle level students.

1560.   Epstein, J. L., et al. (1991). Staff development for middle-school education. *Journal of Staff Development, 12*(1), 35-41.

Offers four components to guide the purposes, distribution, content, and structure and organization of staff development of middle school faculty.

1561.   Merenbloom, E. (1984). Staff development: The key to effective middle level schools. *NASSP Bulletin: The Journal for High School and Middle School Administrators*, *68*(473), 25-33.

Merenbloom describes that which constitutes an effective staff development program. In doing so, he addresses such issues as putting theory into practice, characteristics of an effective staff development program, those who are responsible for staff development, a process/content approach to staff development (including examples of process activities and examples of content topics), and ways to evaluate staff development.

1562.   Merenbloom, E. Y. (1990). *Developing effective middle schools through faculty participation*. Columbus, OH: National Middle School Association. 122 pp.

Written by a noted middle school administrator, this booklet provides a component by component (e.g., goals; programs that respond to cognitive, social/emotional, physical needs of young adolescents; a specialized curriculum; teachers who are interested in and capable of meeting the unique needs of young adolescents; an advisory/advisee program; flexible scheduling; teaming; involvement of parents; regular evaluation that is used to strengthen current programs) description and plan of action for developing an effective middle school.

1563.   Nelson, S. L. (1995). Mentoring new teachers: One middle school's experience. *Middle School Journal, 26*(5), pp. 41-45.

Describes an induction program designed to help first-year teachers successfully ease into their first teaching position. Formal mentoring meetings provided support and an opportunity for mentors to teach skills and share experiences. The informal portion of the program concentrated on individual needs of new teachers. Includes suggestions for helping the beginning teacher's transition into the first week and possible topics for after-school conferences. Stresses the importance of commitment by the principal.

1564.   Parkay, F. W., & Damico, S. B. (1989). Empowering teachers for change through faculty-driven school improvement. *Journal of Staff Development, 10*(2), 8-14.

Assists teachers in designing staff development programs based on their own needs through use of a seven-step school improvement model. Includes a case study.

1565.   Prosise, R., & Heller, M. (1993). Mentoring for beginning middle level teachers. *Schools in the Middle, 2* (4), 20-22.

Discusses the need for mentoring programs that offer support to beginning middle level teachers. Includes a list of the most common challenges faced by beginning middle level teachers. Also lists characteristics of an effective mentoring programs. Concludes with suggestions for designing and implementing an effective program.

1566.   Sills, T. (1981). Socrates was executed for being innovative. *English Journal, 70*(7), 41-42.

Practical list of suggestions for beginning teachers or student teachers.

1567.   Stephen, V., & Varble, M. E. (1995). Staff development model: Thematic units in the middle level school. *Inside Schools in the Middle, 4*(4), 23-26.

Provides an outline for introducing middle level teachers to the value and mechanics of thematic units through six sessions.

1568.   Stephens, D. M. (1995). Framework for instruction: Staff development for teachers. *Inside Schools in the Middle, 4*(4), 14-19.

Highlighted one middle school's staff development framework that focused on sources of information used by students, skills needed and appropriate assessments. Describes a four-step planning process.

1569.   Totten, S. (in review). The development and implementation of a middle level summer institute.

The author describes and discusses the design, implementation, evaluation, and revision of a middle level summer institute undertaken by the University of Arkansas' Center for Middle Level Education, Research, and Development.

1570.   Underwood, B., & Underwood, R. (1978). Concerns of junior high school and middle school teachers: A framework for in-service. *The Clearing House*, *51*(1), 36-37.

Discusses the need for relevant professional development and inservice opportunities for middle level educators. Includes suggestions for developing and implementing inservice programs designed to meet the professional needs of teachers who interact with young adolescents.

1571.   Whitfield, E. L, Whitfield, C., & Purkeson, R. (1983). Middle school staff development. *The Clearing House*, *56*(5), 230-231.

Argues that the principal should assume primary responsibility for providing relevant professional development opportunities for middle school teachers. Includes practical suggestions for developing and implementing meaningful programs.

C. INSERVICE AND STAFF DEVELOPMENT - GENERAL

1572.   Aichele, D. B. (Ed.). (1994). *1994 Yearbook: Professional development for teachers of mathematics*. Reston, VA: National Council of Teachers of Mathematics. 248 pp.

Reports on outstanding teacher training programs at all the K-12 grade levels. Details how creative math teachers, administrators, and teacher educators are using the NCTM Standards to change their preservice and in-service programs.

1573.   Holland, H. (1994). Staff training gets a second look. *High strides*, *7*(2), 6.

Promotes the use of sustained support models of staff development to ensure lasting change.

1574.   Johnston, W. F. (1994). Staff development for rural middle schools through regional conferences. *Middle School Journal, 26*(1), 15-17).

Distance, isolation, and financial restrictions seriously restrict staff development for middle level rural educators. Johnston suggests a variety of regional and state conferences to meet the challenge of providing adequate support.

1575.   Mancini, G. H. (1994). Meeting a higher standard. *High Strides, 7*(2), 10-11.

Describes the contribution and experience of teachers who participated in the pilot test of national certification procedures. Comments on the pros and cons of the process are included.

XXV

Middle Level Resources

A. ORGANIZATIONS

1576.   *Center for Early Adolescence* (University of North Carolina at Chapel Hill, D-2 Carr Mill Town Center, Carrboro, NC 27510).

The Center for Early Adolescence, a component of the School of Medicine at the University of North Carolina at Chapel Hill, was founded in 1978 to promote the healthy growth and development of young adolescents. It fulfills this mission by advocating for young adolescents and providing information, service, research, training, and leadership development for those who can have a positive impact on the nation's 10- to 15-year olds. The Center's programs include major initiatives in adolescent literacy, urban middle-grades reform, the preparation of middle-grades teachers, promotion of adolescent health, community collaborations for youth, and leadership development for the nation's youth workers. Individuals should contact the Center for information services, research (the Center conducts original research that advances knowledge about young adolescents and how policies and programs can best respond to their needs), training/leadership development, consultation, presentation, and publications (the Center has published more than 30 resources — curricula, books and monographs, pamphlets and articles — in the areas of early adolescent development, school improvement, teacher preparation, literacy, parent education, program planning, adolescent health and sexuality, and public policy analysis).

1577.   *Center for Middle Level Education, Research, and Development* (University of Arkansas, College of Education, Fayetteville, AR 72701).

Established in 1992, the Center for Middle Level Education, Research and Development conducts research into various facets of middle level education, provides technical assistance to schools and school districts that have either developed or are in the process of developing middle level programs, conducts annual university and college teacher education roundtables, and holds an annual summer institute on middle level education. It also has a resource center.

1578.   *Center for Research on Effective Schooling for Disadvantaged Students* (c/o Center for Social Organization of Schools, Johns Hopkins University, 3505 N. Charles St., Baltimore, MD 21218).

"The mission of the Center for Research on Effective Schooling for Disadvantaged Students (CDS) is to significantly improve the education of disadvantaged students at each level of schooling through new knowledge and practices produced by thorough scientific study and evaluation." One of its main program areas is "The Middles Grades and High Schools Program." Among its key reports are: "How Equal Are Opportunities for Learning in Disadvantaged and Advantaged Middle Schools?"; "A National Description of Report Card Entries in the Middle Grades"; "Two Reports: Implementation and Effects of Summer Home Learning Packets in the Middle Grades"; "Helping Students Who Fall Behind: Remedial Activities in the Middle Grades"; "Motivating Disadvantaged Early Adolescents to Reach New Heights: Effective Evaluation, Research, and Recognition"; "Opportunities to Learn: Effects on Eight Graders of Curriculum Offerings and Instructional Approaches"; "Using Student Team Reading and Student Team Writing in Middle Schools: Two Evaluations."

1579.   *Center for Youth Research (Social Science Research Institute*, 2500 Campus Rd., Honolulu, HI 96822).

"The Center for Youth Research (CYR), situated at the University of Hawaii, engages in research, program development and management and program evaluation, concerning youth-at-risk." Topics of special interest include crime and delinquency, substance abuse, youth gangs, child abuse, delinquency prevention and educational and health programs.

1580.   *Center of Education for the Young Adolescent* (128 Doudna Hall, University of Wisconsin at Platteville, 1 University Plaza, Platteville, WI 53818).

The Center's associates conduct research, hold seminars, sponsor and conduct a summer seminar, develop resources on various facets of middle level education, provide consultants to school districts, and offer inservice programs on a wide array of middle level concerns. It publishes a "newsmagazine" entitled the *Middle Link.*

1581.   *Colorado Middle Level Interdisciplinary Education Center (*University of Northern Colorado Laboratory School, University of Northern Colorado, Greeley, CO 80639). (303) 351-2369.

Serves as a repository for interdisciplinary units of study developed by middle level teachers.

1582.   *Community Service Learning Center* (258 Washington Blvd., Springfield, MA 01108).

The Community Service Learning Center (CSLC) provides assistance to school people interested in organizing, developing and implementing community service learning (CSL) projects. Through individualized consulting, small workshops and comprehensive conferences, CSLC facilitates the understanding of CSL philosophy, process and programs. CSLC also publishes curriculum which focuses on the middle level.

1583.   *Edna McConnell Clark Foundation* (250 Park Ave, Suite 900, New York, NY 10177-0026).

The Clark Foundation strives to improve conditions for people who are poor and disadvantaged. The current interests of the Foundation focus on five carefully defined program areas, one of which the Program for Disadvantaged Youth. The Program supports inner-city school districts to develop and provide an education of high expectations, high content, and high support for disadvantaged young adolescents. The Program's mission is to encourage initiatives that are likely to result in systemic changes necessary to improve the education of large numbers of disadvantaged youth in grades through nine. Since June 1989, the Program has been collaborating with the Baltimore, Louisville, Milwaukee, Oakland, and San Diego school systems to reform their middle schools. In September 1992, the Program helped to initiate middle school reform efforts in Chattanooga, TN, Jackson, MS, and Long Beach, CA. The Program is also involved with a variety of national organizations that provide support, technical assistance, and evaluation services to the eight school systems named above, and/or build a national infrastructure for middle school reform. Among the Foundation's key publications are *Making It in the Middle: The Why and How of Excellent Schools for Young Urban Adolescents*, *Gaining Ground: The Highs and Lows of Urban Middle School Reform 1989-1991*, and *Changing the Odds: Middle School Reform in Progress 1991-1993*.

1584.   *Harvard Project on the Psychology of Women and the Development of Girls* (Harvard University, Graduate School of Education, 503 Roy E. Larsen Hall, Appian Way, Cambridge, MA 02138).

The Project is a feminist research collaborative consisting of women and men who are affiliated with the Graduate School of Education at Harvard University. It conducts research that focuses on gaining an empirically grounded understanding of girls' and women's psychological development. The Project is a continuation of work begun in the early 1970s by Carol Gilligan at Harvard. Working Papers of the Harvard Project are available from the Project's headquarters.

1585.   *Middle Grades Support Services Office* (California Department of Education, 721 Capitol Mall, P. O. Box 944272, Sacramento, CA 94224-2720).

The Middle Grades Support Service is responsible for coordinating the statewide implementation of California's middle grades task force report, "Caught in the Middle." The report details one hundred recommendations for improving middle grade education in California, including the development of "state of the art middle grades schools." The Middle Grades staff works in partnership with networks of schools, universities, county offices of education, and other organizations.

1586.   *National Association for Core Curriculum* (404 White Hall, Kent State University, Kent, OH 44232). (216) 672-2792.

Provides teacher-constructed interdisciplinary units, results of research studies, newsletters, and a variety of other resources in the area of curriculum.

1587.   *National Association of Secondary School Principals* (1904 Association Dr., Reston, VA 22091).

The National Association of Secondary School Principals (NASSP) represents 43,000 middle level, junior high, and high school principals and assistant principals in both public and private education. In addition to the regular NASSP services all of its members receive, it provides a variety of services which address the unique needs of its members who are in middle level schools, including but not limited to: a subscription to *Schools in the Middle*, professional development opportunities including conferences and workshops that address areas of concern to middle level educators, the Middle Level Council (a committee of nationally recognized middle level professors, writers and researchers who meet three times each year to advise the association on critical concerns in middle level education), the Middle Level Committee (which is comprised of middle level principals, one from each NASSP region, who advise the association about the needs and concerns of the association's members), a complete middle level program during the NASSP convention, and major research studies that focus on middle level concerns.

1588.   *National Center for Effective Schools* (Maryland Student Service Alliance. Maryland State Department of Education, 200 West Baltimore Street, Baltimore, MD 21201-2595).

Provides technical assistance to school systems for the development of effective service-learning programs. Provides access to videos, teacher-training materials, and curricula appropriate for middle-level programs.

1589.   *National Center for Service Learning in Early Adolescence* (Center for Advanced Study in Education - Graduate School and University Center of the City University of New York, 25 West 43rd St., Suite 612, New York, NY 10036-8099).

"The National Center for Service Learning in Early Adolescence's mission is to make service learning a possibility for every young person." The Center serves as a resource for educators, youth workers, and policy makers seeking to meet the developmental needs of young adolescents. It promotes service for young adolescents through program development, research, advocacy, and information-sharing. Model service programs are developed and piloted through the Early Adolescent Helper Program. The central staff and field associate network provide training and technical assistance on planning, curriculum development, and evaluation to schools and agencies through the country. Among its many publications are *Connections: Service Learning in the Middle Grades*; *The Learning Helper Program: A Guide for Program Leaders and Teachers*; *The Partners Program: A Guide for Teachers and Program Leaders*; *Reading, Writing and Reviewing: Helpers Promoting Reading*; and *Reflection: The Key to Service Learning*.

1590.   *National Middle School Association* (2600 Corporate Exchange Dr., Suite 370, Columbus, OH 43231).

Established in 1973, the National Middle School Association's (NMSA) main goal is addressing the unique needs of middle level students—young adolescents between the ages of ten and fifteen years old. More specifically, it is dedicated to improving the educational experiences of young adolescents by providing vision, knowledge, and resources to all who serve them in order to develop healthy, productive, and ethical citizens. Membership in NMSA is open to all persons interested in, and concerned about, middle level education. Teachers, administrators, parents, teacher educators, college students, and other educational professionals are well represented in NMSA's membership.

1591.   National Resource Center for Middle Grades/High School Education (University of South Florida, College of Education, EDU-118, Tampa, FL 33620-5650).

The Resource Center staff and its advisory board members provide a wide range of "how-to" consultative services to educators throughout the United States and Europe. Among the Center's specific areas of expertise are development of middle level programs, the establishment of teaming and interdisciplinary instruction in the middle grades, development and implementation of advisory programs, the development of flexible scheduling of core curriculum and exploratory programs, methods for differentiating instruction in heterogeneous classrooms, the improvement of classroom management procedures, the incorporation of higher level thinking skills into the curriculum, strategies for working with the at-risk student, ways to build an effective school/community public relations program, and the evaluation of middle level programs. It also has a detailed products brochure available.

1592.   *New England League of Middle Schools, Inc.* (460 Boston St., Suite 4, Topsfield, MA 01983-1223).

The purpose of the League is "to foster excellence in education for emerging adolescents." In doing so, it sets out "to network information between middle level schools, serve as an advocacy group for the middle school concept, establish research studies, provide services for school evaluation, update current activities, be a clearinghouse for resource materials, develop conferences, and arrange for inservice work." Among its members are not only middle schools in title, but junior highs, elementary schools, and intermediate schools representing twenty-one different grade level configurations. It publishes a journal, a newsletter, and monographs.

1593.   *SerVermont* (c/o Cynthia Parsons, Coordinator, P.O. Box 516, Chester, VT 05143).

"SerVermont is a statewide privately-funded initiative whose purpose is to assist all the schools in Vermont—including those serving the early adolescent—to integrate community service with academic coursework to fulfill four goals: 1. To teach school children to be small 'd' democrats through hands-on lessons in civic rights and responsibilities; 2. To carry out the John Dewy principle of 'learning through doing"; 3. To improve community health, environment, and welfare; and 4. To provide students with lessons in 'giving' and 'getting' support for making positive, spiritual, and moral decisions."

B. STATE REPORTS

1594.   Bureau of Elementary and Secondary Education. (1988). *Florida progress in middle childhood education program (PRIME).* Tallahassee, FL: Program Development and Analysis Services, Bureau of Elementary and Secondary Education, Florida Department of Education-Division of Public Schools.

PRIME, the Florida Progress in Middle Childhood Education Act, was passed in 1984 to improve middle level education within the state of Florida. Provides technical assistance to school districts that have implemented PRIME as well as to those districts that want to improve their middle level programs.

1595.   California State Department of Education. (1987). *Caught in the middle: Educational reform for young adolescents in California public schools.* Sacramento, CA: Author. 162 pp.

This early and significant state report on middle level education "presents a reform agenda for grades six, seven, and eight...." Twenty-two principles of middle grade education are addressed in great detail. The discussion of each principle concludes with specific recommendations which have implications for legislative initiatives, educational policies, administrative guidelines, and professional practices. As the discussions proceed, the authors clearly delineate that which constitutes an exemplary middle level program, the unique needs and characteristics of young adolescents as well as specific programs that need to be developed to meet those needs, the type of professional preparation need for teachers and administrators in order to develop and implement sound middle level programs, a description of the catalysts needed for such educational reform, and a bibliography.

1596.   Connecticut State Departments of Education, Health Services and Human Resources. (1991). *Right in the middle: A report of the Connecticut Task Force on the Education of Early Adolescents.* Middletown, CT: Connecticut Middle Grade School State Policy Initiative Project. 34 pp.

This report provides a summary of the efforts of the Connecticut Task Force on the Education of Early Adolescents which was convened to make recommendations for reform policies in the area of middle grades education. The contents include the following: 1. Response to Carnegie Challenge, 2. Task Force Activities, 3. Assessing and Restructuring Schools, 4. Preparation and Professional Development, 5. Connecting Schools with Parents and Communities, 6. Middle Grade Curricula, and 7. Coordinating Health and Social Services.

1597.   Council of Chief State School Officers. (1990). *Critical thinking in the middle grades: State initiatives for improved teaching and learning.* Washington, D. C.: Council of Chief State School Officers.

1598.   Delaware Department of Public Instruction. (1991). *Guidelines for middle level education in Delaware: An agenda for success.* Dover, DE: Author. 46 pp.

The authors of this report state that "the policy and supporting guidelines in this document are intended to help schools prepare young adolescents to develop the characteristics associated with being an effective human being. As stated in *Turning Points*, these characteristics are: an intellectually reflective person, a person enroute to a lifetime of meaningful work, a good citizen, a caring and ethical individual, and a healthy person." The report goes on to delineate the following: the State Board's education policy as it relates to middle level education; ideas on the administration of the middle school; agency, community, home partnerships; school climate; health and wellness issues; curriculum; staff development; and certification.

1599.   Florida Bureau of Elementary and Secondary Education. (1989). *Assessment of school programs: A comparison of the Carnegie Report recommendations and the state of Florida's policies in middle childhood education.* Tallahassee, FL: Program Development and Analysis Services, Bureau of Elementary and Secondary Education, Florida Department of Education-Division of Public Schools.

Provides a comprehensive comparison of the Carnegie Report recommendations and middle level practices in Florida. Concludes that the state of Florida provides programs that effectively meet the unique developmental needs of middle level students.

1600.   Florida House of Representatives. (1984). *The forgotten years.* Tallahassee, FL: Speaker's Task Force on Middle Childhood Education.

Contains recommendations for implementing an exemplary program in middle level education. Included are a philosophy, goal statements, and strategies for implementation.

1601.   Georgia Board of Education. (1993). *Linking services for Georgia's young adolescents.* Atlanta, GA: Georgia Department of Education. 82 pp.

Georgia's report is divided into five parts: 1. The National Picture, 2. The

Georgia Task Force, 3. Middle Level Education in Georgia, 4. Excellence in Operation, and 5. A Call to Action. Particularly interesting are the following components: an overview of various middle level programs around the state, the "Middle School Program Criteria" adopted by the State board of Education in 1990, a section entitled "Converting from Junior Highs to Middle Schools," and the richness and wide variety of different types of programs in the state that are addressing the unique needs of young adolescents (e.g., the use of technology to enhance student learning, the use of student/teacher progression, parent conferences at the parent's worksites, an after-school study group, an adventure-based counseling program, a county-wide interdisciplinary unit, and school-based health clinics).

1602.   Governor's Task Force on Early Adolescence. (1991). *Bridges for young adolescents in North Dakota*. Grand Forks, ND: BRIDGES PROJECT, Center for Teaching and Learning, University of North Dakota. 23 pp.

This report delineates the special needs of young adolescents and then addresses the sorts of bridges that need to be developed and built by various parties in order to address those special needs. Among the "bridge builders" focused on are families, communities, local school districts, middle grade educators, the department of public instruction, health and human service agencies, colleges and universities, and state government.

1603.   Illinois State Board of Education. (1992). *Right in the middle*. Springfield, IL: Author. 17 pp.

Right in the Middle is "the planning document for the transformation of education for young adolescents in Illinois." Among the topics it succinctly discusses are the following: early adolescence today, a profile of today's students, what it means to be "right in the middle," a rationale for middle level education, principles guiding middle level education, and the various recommendations of the Illinois Middle Grades Task Force.

1604.   Indiana Department of Education Middle Grades School State Policy Initiative Project Task Force. (1991). *Betwixt & between*. Indianapolis, IN: Author. 53 pp.

This report is a study of Indiana's present practices and task force recommendations (as of 1991) for restructuring education for middle level learners. It includes an overview of the needs of young adolescents; the cognitive, physical, and social emotional characteristics of young adolescents, a progress report check-list, a host of recommendations concerning social and health care services, appropriate curriculum for the middle level, preparation standards for middle level educators, and staff development ideas.

1605.   Kentucky Department of Education. (1991). *"Middle" Morphosis: Kentucky's plan for young adolescents*. Frankfort, KY: Author. 62 pp.

As stated in the introduction to this report: "'*Middle' Morphosis* presents state policyholders and agencies serving young adolescents a blueprint for change in Kentucky's middle grades. The document highlights each recommendation of *Turning Points*, states the link to the Kentucky Education Reform Act (KERA), analyzes the current status of Kentucky's middle level practices, and suggests strategies to align middle grade education with each recommendation. The strategies are primarily written to assist individual schools or local districts in their alignment efforts."

1606.   Louisiana Middle Grades Advisory Committee. (1989). *Turning Points for Louisiana: A blueprint for quality middle schools*. Baton Rouge, LA: Louisiana State Department of Education. 29 pp.

The authors state that this "report is intended to guide the adoption of the Carnegie Task Force recommendations [as set out in *Turning Points*] and to highlight areas where resources are needed, program development must occur, and policy must be reviewed for possible additions and/or changes in order to transform middle level schools and make them more effective in meeting the needs of students."

1607.   Maryland Task Force on the Middle Learning Years. (1989). *What matters in the middle grades: Recommendations for Maryland middle grades education*. Baltimore, MD: Maryland State Department of Education. 82 pp.

This detailed report contains the following: Maryland's perspective on middle level education, the developmental characteristics of students ages ten to fourteen, and a set of recommendations that address the following concerns. Also discusses expected outcomes of middle grades education, the various parties/agencies that should be involved in the welfare and education of young adolescents, organization and delivery of middle grades instruction, types of assistance that should be provided to support middle grades students and teachers, the administration of middle level programs, issues concerning the implementation of the recommendations set out herein, and issues concerning the evaluation of the eventual impact of the recommendations.

1608.   Massachusetts Department of Education. (1993). *Magic in the middle: A focus on Massachusetts middle grade schools.*. Malden, MA: Massachusetts Department of Education, Division of School Programs.

1609.   New Mexico Middle Level Education Advisory Committee, The. (1991). *Moving into action: Middle level education in New Mexico*. Santa Fe, NM: Author. 45 pp.

Subtitled "A Report for the State Board of Education, and A Call for Action from The Middle Level Education Advisory Committee," this report presents "findings and recommendations which underscore the compelling need and urgency for middle level educational reform in New Mexico schools." It includes a glossary of key terms, a call for action, and a description of desirable attributes of middle level programs.

1610.   North Carolina Department of Public Instruction. (1991). *Last best chance: Middle Grades Task Force report*. Raleigh, NC: Author. 56 pp.

This booklet highlights a series of concerns regarding the education of middle level education (e.g., school organization, curriculum, instruction, student success, health concerns, teacher preparation, technical assistance, professional staff, parents, and communities); and in doing so, it addresses the following: 1. The focus of the concern, 2. The rationale and current situation vis-à-vis the concern, and 3. Recommendations for addressing the concern. It concludes with a glossary of key terms and a short bibliography of key works on the education and needs of of middle level students.

1611.   Oregon Department of Education. (1992). *Middle Level Task Force report - Draft*. Salem, OR: Oregon Department of Education. 27 pp.

This draft is comprised of a mission statement, description of the characteristics of young adolescents, and the recommendations of the task force.

1612.   Rhode Island Middle Level Educators (RIMLE). (1992). *From the margins to the middle: A call for reform*. Providence, RI: Author. 10 pp.

While this report was not issued by the Rhode Island State Department of Education, it should be noted that RIMLE was formed in 1991 with the encouragement of the Rhode Island Department of Education and a grant from the Carnegie Foundation. It includes a set of general recommendations as well as a discussion of how these recommendations dovetail with the *Turning Points* agenda. Basically this report urges the Rhode Island Board of Regents for Elementary and Secondary Education to examine the Carnegie Foundation's *Turning Points* agenda and to endorse its philosophy for all schools encompassing middle school age (10-15 years old) children throughout the state of Rhode Island.

1613.   Texas Education Agency. (1991). *Spotlight on the middle: A source book of notable Texas middle school programs developed for the Texas Task Force on Middle School Education*. Austin, TX: Author. 127 pp.

Provides information on more than 100 Texas programs for middle grade students. Each description includes a program contact, a descrip-tion of the program and a summary of its objectives as well as the type and amount of training needed to implement the program, and program evaluation methods. It also includes a "Glossary of Middle School Program Concepts," and an index. Among the various programs that are highlighted are teaming, advisor/advisee, author visits, cheerleading, computers and collaborative learning, cooperative learning, homework, integrated curriculum, parental involvement, etc.

1614.   Texas Education Agency. (1991). *Spotlight on the middle: Report of the Texas Task Force on Middle School Education*. Austin, TX: Author. 64 pp.

This booklet, which is both a call for the need to restructure middle schools in

Texas as well as a plan of action, delineates a set of strategies which educators are encouraged to consider and use when implementing and/or strengthening a middle level program. The strategies are organized by the nine goals areas which were previously outlined in *Quality, Equity, Accountability: Texas State Board of Education Long-Range Plan for Public Education, 1991-1995*. An executive summary of the report is available.

1615.   Vermont Middle Grades Task Force, The. (1991). *The middle matters: Transforming education for Vermont's young adolescents.* Montpelier, VT: Vermont Department of Education. 86 pp.

This document was developed in order to provide direction for the development of middle grades (5-8) programs in all of Vermont's schools. It includes the Vermont Middle Grades Mission Statement, a set of goals for middle level students, a scenario of a "responsible middle level school," a set of conceptual frameworks (e.g., student-responsive curriculum and pedagogy; success-oriented learning environments; innovative assessment of students and programs; coordination of education, health, and social services, etc.), task force recommendations, a selected bibliography, information and ideas on school/program self-assessment, and a resource guide.

1616.   Virginia Department of Education (n.d.). *Framework for education in the middle school grades in Virginia.* Richmond, VA: Author. 27 pp.

The primary purpose of this document is set out the "desirable educational practices for grades 6, 7, and 8 in all schools in Virginia" and to specify twenty-two recommendations "which can be implemented in every school division where there is a genuine concern that early adolescents receive the best education that can be provided." Among the issues that are addressed are education and developmental needs, organizational structure of the school for grades 6-8, school climate, various curricular issues (e.g., knowledge and skills across the disciplines, the expanded core, learning rates, grouping and tracking, remediation, scheduling), gifted education, staffing and staff development, computers and technology, student's health and fitness, and students at risk.

1617.   Virginia Department of Education. (1991). *Restructuring education in the middle grades.* Richmond, VA: Author. 75 pp.

This document focuses on Virginia's decision to restructure education in the middle school grades and delineates the goals and means to do that. In the introduction the authors state that the "goals of restructuring are related to student outcomes [that] focus on positive self-esteem, on meaningful learning and achievement, and on successful transition to further education and productive adulthood." The major headings of the table contents are Restructuring Education in the Middle School Grades; The Restructuring Process: An Overview; The Restructuring Process at the Individual School; Role of the Department of Education; and Congruence with the Original Restructuring Process.

1618.   Wisconsin Department of Instruction. (1990). *The middle level grades: Where we are; Where we need to be.* Madison, WI: Bureau for Teacher Education, Licensing and Placement, Wisconsin Department of Public Instruction. 59 pp.

This document was developed in order to serve as a "research tool for schools districts to examine their middle level practices and programs." It includes the results of a survey that was administered to assess the extent of middle level practices and programs in Wisconsin's public schools, a description of the principles and characteristics of the ideal middle level school, and a set of strategies for developing stronger middle level programs. Also included is a copy of the survey that was used.

C. JOURNALS

1619.   *AIMS JOURNAL, The* (Dr. Mary Polite, Southern Illinois University-Edwardsville, Box 1125, Department of Educational Leadership, Edwardsville, IL 62026-1125).

The AIMS JOURNAL is "devoted to the promotion of the middle school concept, both in Illinois and nationally. The journal is intended to serve teachers, counselors, and administrators who have daily contact with early adolescents, college and university middle-level teacher educators and pre-service students, parents of early adolescents, and interested members of the general public."

1620.   *Becoming* (Ronnie Sheppard, Editor, Georgia Southern University, Landrum Box 8134, Statesboro, GA 30460-8134).

Published in November and April, *Becoming* is the official, refereed journal of the Georgia Middle School Association and the Georgia Association of Middle School Principals. The journal is intended to serve teachers, counselors, and administrators who have daily contact with early adolescents, college and university middle level teacher educators, and their students, parents of early adolescents, and interested members of the general public. Articles that deal with teaching the early adolescent, promising programs and practices of an all-school nature, solutions to educational problems, thought provoking essays, and current research are published by the journal.

1621.   *CROSSROADS: The California Journal of Middle Grades Research* (California League of Middle Schools-CROSSROADS, 18012 Cowan, Suite 110, Irvine, CA 92714).

CROSSROADS is published semi-annually and is a benefit of membership in the California League of Middle Schools. "The primary focus of CROSSROADS is offering applied research findings to middle grades school practitioners and scholars of the middle level philosophy. It is hoped that CROSSROADS will be the vehicle used to publish the findings of middle level teachers and administrators who have joined hands with one another in order to engage in conducting site level research which informs middle grades practice."

1622.   *Current Issues in Middle Level Education* (West Georgia College, School of Education, Carrollton, GA 30118).

A refereed journal, *Current Issues in Middle Level Education* "is aimed at professors of middle level education and others with an interest in middle level philosophy, curriculum and instruction, and research. It provides a forum for the discussion of new ideas and issues related to the middle grades." It is published twice a year.

1623.   *In Focus* (Wabash College, Teacher Education Program, Baxter 29, Crawfordsville, IN 47933).

The editor of *In Focus* states that this journal is "refereed and scholarly, [and that it] is the official publication of the Indiana Middle Level Education Association. The journal is published annually in the spring, and it prints articles that consider issues and aspects of middle level education and the development of young adolescents." It includes a good number of practical pieces by and for practitioners at the middle level.

1624.   *In Transition* (Dr. Charles Fallon, New York State Middle School Association, 385 New Castle Road, Rochester, NY 14610).

Published tri-annually, *In Transition* "contains articles, research reports, and special features that focus on classroom or all-school activities, effective teaching strategies and current research on middle level education."

1625.   *Instructor Middle Years* (P.O. Box 59297, Boulder, CO 80322).

A quarterly published by Scholastic, this journal includes articles on all facets of middle level education (including interdisciplinary projects, advisory activities, adolescent development, hands-on "teacher ready" projects and activities, and multicultural and multiethnic ideas).

1626.   *Journal of Adolescent Research* (Sage Publications, Inc., 2455 Teller Rd., Newbury Park, CA 91320).

This refereed quarterly includes "empirical research and theoretical papers on all aspects of adolescent development." It focuses on individuals between ten and twenty years of age. Among the issues/topics it addresses are the following: psychology, public education, health education, public health, public welfare, social work, treatment programs, and school counseling.

1627.   *Journal of Early Adolescence, The* (Sage Publications, Inc., 2455 Teller Road, Newbury Park, CA 91320).

This refereed journal's main purpose is to contribute to the understanding of individuals ages ten to fourteen years old. "The *Journal* is designed to present major theoretical papers, state-of-the-art papers, and current research, as well as reviews of important professional books, and early adolescent films and literature." It is published four times annually.

1628.   *Journal of Research on Adolescence, The* (Lawrence Erlbaum Associates, Inc., 365 Broadway, Hillsdale, NJ 07642).

Published four times a year, this is the official journal of the Society for Research on Adolescence. "Multidisciplinary in scope, this journal is designed to significantly advance knowledge about the second decade of life. Employing any of a diverse array of methodologies, it publishes original research that includes intensive measurement, multivariate-longitudinal, and animal comparative studies; demographic and ethnographic analyses; and laboratory experiments. Articles pertinent to the variety of developmental patterns inherent throughout adolescence are featured."

1629.   *Journal of the Texas Middle School Association, The* (Linda Robinson, Texas Middle School Association, P.O. Box 494984, Garland, TX 75049-4984).

Published twice a year (once in the spring and once in the fall), the purposes of the journal are: "to facilitate the exchange of ideas common to Texas middle schools; to inform middle school members of trends on the national and state level; to provide the membership with ideas to improve the performance of middle school students and staff; and to advocate quality, excellence, and equity for middle level students."

1630.   *KAMLE Karavan: Journal of the Kansas Association for Middle Level Educators* (c/o Thomas Erb, Editor, KAMLE Karavan, 207 Bailey Hall, University of Kansas, Lawrence, KS 66045).

KAMLE Karavan is published by the Kansas Association for Middle Level Education. "It exists to provide a forum for the discussion of ideas related to the education of early adolescents. It publishes articles describing educational practices at the middle level, accounts of research into middle level education, and theoretical articles which raise questions about research or practice in middle grades education." It is published annually.

1631.   *Kentucky Middle School Journal* (P.O. Box 3062, Frankfort, KY 40603).

The Kentucky Middle School Journal is sponsored by the Kentucky Middle School Association. It includes articles that "describe successful programs, stimulating projects, exemplary teaching techniques, unique team concepts, action research, and memorable student anecdotes."

1632.   *League Journal: The Journal of the North Carolina League of Middle Level Schools, The* (North Carolina League of Middle School, PO Box 1222, Salisbury, NC 28145-1222).

Published annually, this journal publishes "a wide range of articles related to middle level practice, theory, commentary and research. School-based articles are especially encouraged."

1633. *Louisiana Middle School Journal* (Bob Gillan, Director of Education Technology Center, Northwestern State University, Natchitoches, LA 71497).

The Louisiana Middle School Journal is published by the Louisiana Middle School Association and "serves a readership of teachers, administrators, counselors, college and university personnel who are involved with teacher education, parents, and others concerned with the education of adolescents. Articles focusing on integrating technology in the classroom, teaching techniques, and curriculum design for schools serving adolescents are of particular interest to the journal.

Such articles may be based on empirical research, experiences in program development and implementation, review and analysis of current literature and research, or may be an exposition of the author's observations or views on issues in middle level education."

1634. *Mainely Middle* (Dr. Julia Phelps, Editor, Wells Junior High School, P. O. Box 310-Route One, Wells, ME 04090).

Mainely Middle is an official publication of the Maine Association for Middle Level Education. It publishes general interest articles that promote middle level education and contribute to an understanding of the educational and developmental needs of youth between the ages of 10 and 14. Articles submitted should specifically relate to the theory and practice of middle level education and should speak directly to practitioners in the field.

1635. *MAMLE Journal* (c/o Fred Sanford and Dave Larkin, Co-Editors, Bemidji Middle School, NW, Bemidji, MN 56601).

The *MAMLE Journal* (Journal of the Minnesota Association of Middle Level Educators) highlights practical suggestions for middle level classroom teachers and teacher educators.

1636. *Mathematics Teaching in the Middle School* (National Council of Teachers of Mathematics, 1906 Association Dr., Reston, VA 22091-1593). A quarterly magazine, *Mathematics Teaching in the Middle School* is touted by NCTM as a "practical journal that focuses on issues, teaching concepts, and practical ideas for teachers working with the middle grades. Articles cover how math matters in the real world, students insights, and turning technology into math teaching power."

1637. *Michigan Middle School Journal* (Michigan Association of Middle School Educators, Michigan State University, College of Education, 419 Erickson, East Lansing, MI 48824).

Includes practical and research-based pieces by educators (teachers, administrators, counselors, professors) from across the nation whose focus is middle level education.

1638.   *Mid-South Middle Level Education Journal* (c/o Samuel Totten, University of Arkansas, College of Education, Fayetteville, AR 72701).

A publication of the Arkansas Association of Middle Level Education, this refereed journal's focus is middle level education in the "mid-South" (e.g., the states of Arkansas, Louisiana, and Mississippi). Published annually, its goal is to produce a journal that is evenly divided between practical pieces and research reports. The editor is particularly interested in receiving pieces by teachers, administrators, counselors, professors, and others that focus on significant aspects of middle level education germane to the "mid-South" region.

1639.   *Middle Level Educator* (University of Northern Iowa, Department of Curriculum and Instruction, Education Center 618, Cedar Falls, IA 50614).

Primarily written by and published for educators in Iowa, the *Middle Level Educator* highlights "middle school teaching strategies, curriculum, research, program and policy innovations, opinions."

1640.   *Middle Link* (The Center of Education for the Young Adolescent, University of Wisconsin-Platteville, 1 University Plaza, Platteville, WI 53818-3099).

Includes descriptions of exemplary middle level projects, articles by middle level teachers and students, synopsis of research findings, interviews with leading middle level practitioners, etc.

1641.   *Middle School Journal* (National Middle School Association, 2600 Corporate Exchange Dr., Suite 370, Columbus OH 43231).

The *Middle School Journal* is NMSA's premier publication. Generally it contains fifteen to twenty articles by middle level teachers, middle level administrators, and teacher educators on a wide array of topics. Two regular columns are entitled "Teacher to Teacher," and "Out of Research—Into Practice."

1642.   *NCMSA Journal, The* (North Carolina Middle School Association, Box 37748, Raleigh, NC 27627-7748).

The NCMSA Journal includes articles on innovative middle level programs, research, and book and media reviews. It includes pieces by teachers, administrators, teacher educators, university and college students in teacher education programs, and middle level students.

1643.   *New England League of Middle Schools Journal, The* (The New England League of Middle School, 460 Boston St., Suite #4, Topsfield, MA 01983-1223).

"Addressed primarily to the practitioner in the field, *The New England League of Middle Schools Journal* seeks to further the understanding and implementation of quality middle level education throughout New England and the nation."

1644.   *New Mexico Middle School Journal* (c/o Jim Burns, Editor, New Mexico Middle Level Publications, 2121-B Thirty-Third St., Los Alamos, NM 875444).

Published by the New Mexico Middle School Association, this journal exists to provide a forum for the dissemination and discussion of ideas related to middle grades education. It is published annually.

1645.   *Ohio Middle School Journal* (Ohio Middle School Association, P.O. Box 39005, Solon, OH 44139).

Primarily written by and published for educators in Ohio, this journal includes ideas on teaching, classroom practices, curriculum development, and programs.

1646.   *Research in Middle Level Education* (a publication of the Research Committee of the National Middle School Association, 2600 Corporate Exchange Dr., Suite 370, Columbus OH 43231).

A major refereed journal. It focuses on all types of research that examines various facets of middle level practices, various middle level components (e.g., interdisciplinary team organization, advisory/advisee) school- and community-based programs designed to meet the needs of young adolescents, the unique needs of and problems faced by young adolescents, teacher education programs and practices, etc.

1647.   Scholastic Network. (1995). *Press Return*. America Online. 1-800-827-6364.

Middle level students are the editors and contibutors of a new magazine available by computer through America Online, one of the commercial vendors for on-line computer services.

1648.   *Schools in the Middle* (National Association of Secondary School Principals, 1904 Association Dr., Reston, VA 22091-1537).

Prior to 1991, *Schools in the Middle* was a bi-monthly newsletter that kept middle level educators up-to-date on important issues, trends, and practices. No longer published, NASSP sells back issues that are still available.

1649.   *Spectra* (Nebraska Association for Middle Level Education (c/o Glenn Schanou, Millard North Middle School, 2828 South 139th Plaza, Omaha, NE 68144).

Spectra is published annually for the sole purpose of providing information pertinent to middle level issues to the members. In addition to news about the Nebraska Association for Middle Level Education, *Spectra* generally includes several articles on instructional and/or curricular issues.

1650.   *TAMS Journal* (Dr. Art Garner, Editor, Memphis State University, Memphis, TN 38152).

The official journal of the Tennessee Association of Middle Schools, *TAMS Journal* publishes practical pieces that are germane to all aspects of middle level education.

1651.   *Transescent Trails* (Colorado Association of Middle Level Education, P.O. Box 447, Greeley, CO 80632-0447).

Transescent Trails, an annual publication, publishes "articles that promote middle level education." It welcomes submissions from locations other than Colorado.

1652.   *Transescent, The* (Susan Rumer, Hixson Middle School, 630 S. Elm, Webster Groves, MO 63119).

The Transescent is the official journal of the Missouri Middle School Association. It is published four times a year (September, November, February, and May) and is comprised of pieces by educators (most of whom, but not all, are from Missouri) that address instructional, curricular, classroom management, extracurricular, and other issues germane to the education of early adolescents.

1653.   *VAMLE Journal* (Vermont Association for Middle Level Education, P. O. Box 664, Middlebury, VT 05753).

"The VAMLE Journal is an official publication of the Vermont Association for Middle Level Education. Addressed primarily to practitioners in the field, the *Journal* seeks to further the understanding of exemplary middle level education throughout Vermont, New England, and the nation. It is published annually in September." Among the types of articles published by the *VAMLE Journal* are those which describe classroom or all-school activities, offer solutions to educational problems, report effective teaching strategies, relate new ideas and current research to middle level education, and those that pertain to middle level curriculum and parent-community involvement.

1654.   *Youth and Society* (Sage Publications, 2455 Teller Rd., Newbury Park, CA 91320).

For both the researcher and the practitioner, this journal provides an interdisciplinary forum vis-à-vis the latest scholarship on child-youth socialization. It presents original research (both quantitative and qualitative) from a variety of disciplines. Among the many topics it has addressed are drug and alcohol abuse, delinquency, gangs, sexual attitudes, athletics, career choices, stepfamilies, youth and work, and black youth in America.

D. NEWSLETTERS

1655.   *AIMS Newsletter* (Newsletter of the Association of Illinois Middle-

Level Schools, P. O. Box 11076, Champaign, IL 61826-1076).

Provides up-to-date information on both the national middle level movement as well as the movement in the state of Illinois. Features programs at specific middle schools, includes recommended readings and short annotations of key publications, association news, information about institutes and conferences, etc.

1656. *Arkansas Association Middle Level Education Newsletter* (AAMLE, Box 8, Springdale, AR 72764).

Includes information on AAMLE activities, a president's letter, an executive director's corner, feature articles by middle level educators, efforts of AAMLE zones across Arkansas, and other relevant notices/announcements.

1657. *Community Roles for Youth* (c/o National Center for Service Learning in Early Adolescence, CASE: The Graduate School and University Center of CUNY, 25 West 43rd St., Suite 612, New York, NY 10036-8099).

The newsletter of the National Center reports on the Center's activities and successful service learning programs. Additionally, the newsletter provides a forum in which current issues in middle level reform and service learning may be addressed.

1658. *Connections* (National Middle School Association, 2600 Corporate Exchange Dr., Suite 370, Columbus, OH 43231).

The purpose of this NMSA newsletter is to "link together NMSA and its 48 affiliate organizations dedicated to middle level education." It includes information about grants, new publications, membership campaigns, upcoming NMSA and regional conferences, et al.

1659. *Courier: The Newsletter of the New England League of Middle Schools, The* (New England League of Middle Schools, 460 Boston St., Suite 4, Topsfield, MA 01983-1223).

1660. *Crucial Link - Newsletter of the Virginia Middle School Association, The* (c/o Tom Gatewood, Editor, Virginia Tech, 2990 Telestar Ct., Falls Church, VA 22042).

Includes notes on the association's business, a column entitled "Practical Ideas for Middle School Teachers," pertinent research on various aspects of middle level education, resources for middle level educators, and various articles on different aspects of middle level education.

1661. *CSLConnection* (Community Service Learning Center, Inc., 258 Washington Blvd., Springfield, MA 01108).

This newsletter provides updates to the unique programs and efforts of the Community Service Learning Center as well as ideas and tips for the practitioner.

1662.   *Focus - A Newsletter for the South Carolina Middle School Association* (South Carolina Middle School Association, P.O. Box 664, Columbia, SD 29202).

Includes information on: upcoming conferences, regional reports, unique projects undertaken by middle level programs in South Carolina, and pertinent publications.

1663.   *Forum: Newsletter of the Texas Middle School Association, The* (Texas Middle School Association, P.O. Box 494984, Garland, TX 75049-4984).

Includes the following: announcements of forthcoming conferences, reports on recently held conferences, short articles on key issues related to middle level education, announcements pertinent to association business and/or middle level issues pertinent to the state, and updates regarding middle level activities around Texas.

1664.   *Foundation for the Mid South Newsletter* (Foundation for the Mid South, 633 North State Street, Suite 602, Jackson, MS 39202).

Highlights efforts of the Foundation and its partners, which are seeking regional solutions to the common concerns (including the unique needs of early adolescents) of communities throughout Arkansas, Louisiana, and Mississippi.

1665.   *Georgia Middle School Association Newsletter* (c/o Dori Marshall, Editor, Bibb County Public Schools, 1062 Forsyth St., Macon, GA 31201).

Includes information about the Georgia Middle School Association, forthcoming conferences, higher education's involvement in middle level education, middle level education efforts undertaken by the state education department, and articles by teachers about middle level concerns.

1666.   *High Strides: The Bimonthly Report on Urban Middle Grades* (EWA, 1001 Connecticut Ave., N.W., Washington, DC 20036).

An outstanding publication, *High Strides* is regularly published five times a year with funding support from the Edna McConnell Clark Foundation. It addresses a wide array of issues germane to urban middle grade programs.

1667.   *IAMLE* (Iowa Association of Middle Level Educators, Department of Curriculum and Instruction, University of Northern Iowa, Cedar Falls, IA 50614-0606).

Basically includes information about the activities of the Iowa Association of Middle Level Educators and announces forthcoming conferences.

1668.   *In The Middle: The Newsletter of the Ohio Middle School Association* (c/o Marie W. Strayer, Editor, St. Boniface School, 215 Oak St., Oak Harbor, OH 43449).

Contains information on news pertinent to the Ohio Middle School Association, upcoming conferences, etc.

1669.   *Ka Pu Olo Waena - News from the Middle* (Hawaii Association of Middle Schools, 4967 Kilauea Ave., Honolulu, HI 96816).

Highlights activities and projects of its members, announces conferences and upcoming events, etc.

1670.   *Louisiana Middle School Association Newsletter* (Louisiana Middle School Association, Caddo Public Schools, 1961 Midway St., Shreveport, LA 71108).

 Highlights forthcoming conferences, news of special projects in Louisiana middle level programs, pertinent announcements, and thebusiness of the Louisiana Middle School Association.

1671.   *Mid Sports* (Available from National Middle School Activities Association, P. O. Box 207, Pittsburg, KS 66762).

A bi-monthly publication that focuses on age-appropriate activity programs for middle level students. Provides practical ideas for developing, administering, and coaching middle level activity programs. Also provides a forum for promoting the positive effects that age-appropriate activities have on middle level students.

1672.   *Middle Ground—News of Middle Level Education* (National Middle School Association, 2600 Corporate Exchange Dr., Suite 370, Columbus, OH 43231).

Includes information about the various initiatives, programs, conferences and publications either sponsored by and/or available from NMSA as well as announcements of programs/institutes offered by other bodies; highlights special and unique programs in middle level schools and/or that are appropriate for middle level programs; and spotlights positions available in middle level education.

1673.   *Middle Level News, The* (California League of Middle Schools, 18012 Cowan, Suite 110, Irvine, CA 92714).

One of the more extensive middle level newsletters in the nation, this publication is published in September, November, January, March and May. It includes updates, notices, and short articles by teachers and administrators on various facets of middle level education. Readers are invited to submit articles and comments.

1674.   *Middle School "Messenger," The* (New York State Middle School Association, Queensbury Middle School, 75 Aviation Rd., Queensbury, NY 12804).

Includes short articles about various facets of middle level education, announcements about conferences and meetings, and updates on the New York State Middle School Association's activities.

1675.   *Middling Around* (Indiana Middle Level Education Association, c/o College of Education, Butler University, Indianapolis, IN 46208).

Contains information about the efforts of the Indiana Middle Level Education Association, upcoming conferences, articles about various aspects of middle level education, pertinent announcements.

1676.   *Midpoints* (Colorado Association of Middle Level Education, P. O. Box 447, Greeley, CO 80632-0447).

Highlights upcoming conferences, mini-grant competition, articles on various aspects of middle level education, and other pertinent information.

1677.   *MLA News* (Oregon Middle Level Association, c/o Confederation of Oregon School Administrators, 707 13th St., Salem, OR 97301-4035).

Published four times annually, the MLA (an organ of the Oregon Middle Level Association) includes information on middle level education in the state of Oregon, short articles on various facets of middle level education, and information about middle level conferences and other events.

1678.   *MLE* (c/o AMLEND/BRIDGES, University of North Dakota, PO Box 8158, Grand Forks, ND 58202-8158).

MLE (Middle Level Education) is the newsletter of the Association of Middle Level Education of North Dakota (AMLEND) and the BRIDGES project. It not only includes news pertinent to the focus and activities of AMLEND, but also articles on various middle level concerns by middle level and university-based educators.

1679.   *NAESP Communicator* (National Association of Elementary School Principals, 1615 Duke St., Alexandria, VA 22314-3483).

"Published to serve elementary and middle school educators," this newsletter includes the following: information on upcoming conferences, a box that lists requests for assistance concerning specific problems faced by one's school, a legislative corner, and articles on various concerns pertinent to elementary and middle schools/programs.

1680.   *NCMSA Connection* (National Collegiate Middle School Association, c/o University of Northern Colorado, McKee Hall #213, Greeley, CO 80639). The *NCMSA Connection* is the official publication of the National Collegiate Middle School Association.

Its purpose is to highlight the work and focus of NCMSA, an affiliate

organization of NMSA. The organization's primary focus is the development
of strong middle level teacher preparation programs.

1681.   *Network Spotlight* (The Publication of the Texas Middle School
Network: A 21st Century Investment, c/o Texas Education Agency, 1701
N.Congress Ave., Austin, TX 78701-1494).

Provides information on the Texas Middle School Network, including "Mentor
School" profiles, the efforts of the various schools in the Network, exemplary
programs implemented in the Network's schools, information about institutes
and seminars, state efforts in regard to the development of sound middle level
programs, ideas in the areas of curriculum and instruction, etc.

1682.   *New Mexico Middle School Educator* (c/o Jim Burns, New
Mexico Middle Level Publications, 2121-B Thirty-Third St., Los Alamos,
NM 87544).

A quarterly newsletter that highlights the activities of the New Mexico Middle
School Association.

1683.   *News from The Kentucky Middle School Association* (Kentucky Middle
School Association, P.O. Box 3062, Frankfort, KY 40603).

Includes information about upcoming conferences, pertinent resources, articles
by teachers, articles about specific middle level programs developed by and/or
implemented in schools, pertinent notices.

1684.   *Newsletter, The* (Minnesota Association of Middle Level Educators,
714 Victoria, Fairmont, MA 56031).

The Newsletter is published bi-monthly from September to June. It provides
middle level educators in Minnesota with the latest information in regard to
Association business.

1685.   *Oklahoma Middle Level Education Association Newsletter* (c/o Mike
Hacker, Madison Middle School, 4132 W.Cameron St., Tulsa, OK 74147-0208).

Provides an update of OMEA's activities, including a region-by-region update.
Also includes information about publications that are available on various
aspects of middle level education, upcoming conferences and institutes, etc.

1686.   *Schools in the Middle: Theory into Practice Magazine* (National
Association of Secondary School Principals, 1904 Association Dr., Reston, VA
22091-1537).

Prior to 1991 this magazine was a newsletter entitled *Schools in the Middle*. In
1991, the NAASP's newsletter (*Schools in the Middle*) evolved into this
quarterly magazine which focuses on important trends, issues, and practices that
are pertinent to middle level education.

1687.   *South Region Newsletter* (School of Education, University of North Carolina, Greensboro, NC 27412).

Includes information (upcoming conferences, meetings, publications) on middle level education that is pertinent to its constituents—states in the South.

1688.   *Spectrum* (Nebraska Association for Middle Level Education, c/o Glenn Schanou, Millard North Middle School, 2828 South 139th Plaza, Omaha, NE 68144).

Includes information about upcoming conferences, articles by middle level teachers and administrators on various aspects of middle level education, highlights key research on middle level education, and other pertinent information.

1689.   *TAMS Tidbits* (Tennessee Association of Middle Schools, 4317 Emory Rd., Knoxville, TN 37938).

TAMS Tidbits is the official letter of the Tennessee Association of Middle Schools. It includes information about forthcoming middle level conferences, institutes, and inservices; efforts of the state department of education in regard to middle level education; and highlights programs in specific middle schools and middle level programs.

1690.   *Target: Newsletter of the National Middle School Association* (NMSA, 2600 Corporate Exchange Dr., Suite 370, Columbus, OH 43231).

Includes information on NMSA business, grant opportunities, new publications on middle level education, both proposed as well as adopted resolutions by NMSA, and other pertinent announcements.

1691.   *Toward a Community of Learners : A Regional Newsletter on Authentic Instruction for the Middle Grades* (Far West Laboratory for Educational Research and Development, 730 Harrison St., San Francisco, CA 94107).

Toward a Community of Learners is published twice a year and distributed to middle grade schools and curriculum specialists in Arizona, California, Nevada and Utah. It highlights exemplary methods for implementing outstanding instructional practices in the middle grades. Highly recommended.

1692.   *Turning Points State Network News: A Newsletter of Carnegie Corporation of New York Middle Grade School State Policy Initiative* (Council of Chief State School Officers Resource Center on Educational Equality, One Massachusetts Ave., NW, Suite 700, Washington, DC 10002-1431).

Highlights efforts of the Carnegie Corporation of New York Middle Grade School State Policy Initiative, various states' middle level projects, key publications and conferences, and a monthly calender of events.

1693.   *WSAMLE Newsletter* (Washington State Association for Middle Level
Education, P. O. Box 3647, Kent, WA 98032).

Highlights projects, institutes, programs, conferences on middle level education
in the state of Washington; spotlights exemplary middle schools and/or middle
level programs; includes short pieces by middle level teachers and administrators
in which they share useful ideas; and offers other pertinent information.

E. BOOK REVIEWS

1694.   Haas, R. (1995). [Review of *History alive: Engaging all learners in
the diverse classroom*]. Middle Ground, 8.

Highly positive review of the philosophical underpinnings of a resource for a
"hands-on" (p. 8) curriculum. Critical of the sales pitch for supplemental
materials available from the publisher.

1695.   Haskvitz, A. (1995). [Review of *The peopling of America: A timeline
of events that helped shape our nation*].

A positive review of a resource that illustrates the contributions of "Native
Americans, African-Americans, Mexican-Americans, Puerto Ricans, Asian-
Americans and European-Americans" (p. 9) for social studies classrooms that,
according to the reviewerl, is limited by the lack of an index.

1696.   Totten, S. (1993). *A Matter of Time: Risk and Opportunity in the
Nonschool Hours:* An essay review. *Current Issues in Middle Level Education*,
2 (2), 53-61.

Describes the report of the Carnegie Council on Adolescent Development
published in 1992 as a "must read" for people involved in middle level
education. Outlines the key points of the report and concludes that the document
is an excellent resource for use in developing and implementing programs for
young adolescents in areas where opportunities for positive activities are not
readily available.

F. TEXTBOOKS

1697.   Allen, H. A., Splittgerber, F. L., & Manning, M. L. (1992). *Teaching
and learning in the middle level school.* New York: Merrill/Macmillan. 448 pp.

Among the many features of this text are: case studies of actual learners,
exploration sections in each chapter, and a chapter on home-school-community
connections. It is comprised of the following twelve chapters: 1. The
Exemplary Middle School, 2. The Evolving Middle Level School, 3. Middle
Level Student: Physical and Psychosocial Emotional Development; 4. Middle
Level Student: Cognitive Development; 5. The Middle Level Teacher; 6. An
Integrated Approach to Middle Level Curriculum; 7. Middle Level Curriculum:
Language Arts, Social Studies, Science and Mathematics; 8. Middle Level

Curriculum: Exploratory, Elective and Career Education Options; 9. Middle
Level Organization for Teaching and Learning; 10. Guidance in the Middle
Level School; 11. Home, Community and the Middle Level School; and 12.
Implementing the Middle Level School.

1698.   Bushman, J. H., & Bushman, K. P. (1992). *Using young adult
literature in the English classroom.* New York: Merrill/Macmillan. 288 pp.

The express purpose of this text is to provide middle level and high school
teachers with ideas and methods on how to use young adult literature effectively
in the English classroom. Theories of Piaget, Havighurst, Kohlberg and Carlsen
are discussed, as is literature that builds on these constructivist theoretical
frameworks. The authors provide ideas on how to organize literature lessons
when teaching a single book to an entire class, groups of books to a single class,
or thematic units. Also included is a concise history of young adult literature, an
extensive list of titles and literature awards, and lists of sources for reviews of
such literature. The nine chapters in the book are: 1. Young Adults and the
Literature that Meets Their Needs and Interests; 2. Young Adult Literature in
the Classroom; 3. The Reading/Writing Connection; 4. The Language
Connection; 5. Young Adult Literature and the Classics; 6. Diversity in Young
Adult Literature: Ethnic, Cultural, National; 7. The Censorship Issues; 8.
Young Adult Literature: A Brief History; and, 9. Support for Teaching Young
Adult Literature.

1699.   Forte, I., & Schurr, S. (1993). *The definitive middle school guide.*
Tampa, FL: National Resource Center for Middle Grades/High School
Education. 352 pp.

Excellent general resource book for middle level education. The *Guide* is
accessible, comprehensive, and organized into independent modules for ease of
use in workshops and in-service programs. It provides the perfect overview for
middle school teachers, administrators, and others concerned with middle school
success. Each of the seven modules includes an overview, questions to be
answered, a glossary, findings from the published literature, informational pages
in a convenient "Top Ten" format, and "teacher activities" keyed to Bloom's
taxonomy. A comprehensive index and bibliography are provided.

1700.   Fuhrmann, B. (1986). *Adolescence, adolescents.* Boston: Little,
Brown and Co.

A comprehensive text on adolescent development.

1701.   George, P. S., & Alexander, W. M. (1993). *The exemplary middle
school.* New York: Harcourt Brace Jovanovich College Publishers. 550 pp.

Written by two of the most respected educators in the field of middle level
education, this is a basic textbook for students who are studying to become
middle level educators. The authors state that the purpose of the book is to
bridge "the gap between theory and practice, aiming toward a significant

increase in the number of exemplary schools and of exemplary practices in schools." They provide a mix of theory, research and illustrative practices to assist the reader to come to a more thorough understanding as to what constitutes exemplary programs and practices. The book is comprised of ten chapters: 1. The Middle School Student, 2. The Middle School Movement and Concept, 3. Middle School Curriculum, 4. Instruction, 5. The Teacher as Advisor, 6. Interdisciplinary Teaming Organizations, 7. Grouping Students in the Middle School, 8. Organizing Time and Space in the Middle School, 9. Planning the New Middle School, and 10. Middle School Leadership.

1702.   Kellough, R. D., Kellough, N. G., & Hough, D. L. (1993). *Middle school teaching: Methods and resources*. New York: Merrill/Macmillan. 400 pp.

This methods text is comprised of six parts and fifteen chapters: Part I. Orientation to Middle School Teaching (Chapters 1. "What Do I Need to Know About Today's Middle School?"; 2. "What Are the Expectations of Me as a Middle School Teacher?"); Part II. Planning for Instruction (Chapters 3. "What Do I Need to Know About the Middle School Curriculum?; 4. "How is Middle School Curriculum Developed?"; 5. "How Do I Prepare Lesson Plans for Instruction?"; 6. "What Do I Need to Know About Planning for Instruction That Attends to Individual Differences?"); Part III. Choosing and Implementing Instructional Strategies for Middle School Teaching (Chapters 7. "What Are the Basic Teacher Behaviors That Facilitate Student Learning?"; 8. "What Are the Guidelines for the Use of Specific Instructional Strategies?"; and, 9. What Other Aids and Resources Are Available to the Middle School Teacher?"); Part IV. Classroom Management, Control, and Legal Guidelines (Chapters 10. "What Do I Need to Know to Cope with the Daily Challenges of Middle School Teaching?"; 11. What Are the Approaches to Classroom Control?"); Part V. Evaluation of Student Achievement and Teacher Performance (Chapters 12: "How Do I Evaluate and Reports Student Achievement?; 13. "How Can I Continue to Evaluate My Developing Competency as a Middle School Teacher?"); and Part VI. What Do I Need to Know About the Middle School Student Teaching Experience and Beyond (Chapters 14. "What Do I Need to Know About the Middle School Student Teaching Experience?"; 15. "What Do I Need to Know That May Help Me in Getting and Keeping a Middle School Teaching Job?"). Every chapter includes practical exercises and questions for discussion.

1703.   Klingele, W. E. (1979). *Teaching in Middle Schools*. Boston: Allyn and Bacon. 296 pp.

An early and popular textbook on middle level education. It is comprised of three units: The Middle School Concept, Foundations for Instruction, and Selected Instructional Strategies. Unit three includes information on learning centers, instructional packets, instructional games, values-clarification activities. It is interesting to compare this text with some of the latest textbooks in order to compare and contrast how far the field has come in just over a decade and a half.

1704.   Maxwell, R., & Meiser, M. J. (1992). *Teaching English in middle and secondary school.* New York: Merrill/Macmillan. 350 pp.

Maxwell and Meiser advocate a process approach to English instruction which is interactive and developmental and one that is learner—rather than teacher-centered. The text is comprised of thirteen chapters: 1. Teaching and Learning English Language Arts; 2. Oral Language: The Neglected Language Arts; 3. Teaching Literature; 4. Selecting Literature; 5. Teaching Composition; 6. Evaluating Composition; 7. Improving Writing Skills: Usage, Syntax, Mechanics; 8. Understanding Grammar; 9. The Nature of Language; 10. Varieties of American English; 11. Understanding Curriculum and Instruction; 12. Planning for Classroom Instruction; and 13. Developing Thematic Units.

1705.   Messick, R. G., & Reynolds, K. E. (1992). *Middle level curriculum in action.* White Plains, NY: Longman. 260 pp.

This textbook is comprised of eleven chapters: 1. Introduction to Middle Level, 2. Evolution of Middle School Level Schooling, 3. The Middle Level Student, 4. Curriculum-Building Basics, 5. Basic Subjects of Curriculum, 6. Basics of Exploratory Curriculum, 7. The Affective Curriculum, 8. Core Curriculum Implementation, 9. Instruction at the Middle Level, 10. Evaluating Student Progress, and 11. Interdisciplinary Units of Instruction.

1706.   Moore, D. W., Moore, S. A., Cunningham, P. M., & Cunningham, J. W. (1994). *Developing readers and writers in the content areas K-12.* New York: Longman.

Designed for teachers at all levels, this book shows how literacy and subject matter instruction can be integrated. Includes excellent examples to illustrate each teaching theory and practice. Major sections in the book are Content Area Reading and Writing, Reading Materials, Learning Independence, Comprehension, Writing, Student Research, Meaning Vocabulary, and Issues in Content Area Organization and Instruction. Also discusses the importance of keeping a journal for both students and teachers and offers suggestions for journal entries. Ideal for use as a textbook in teacher preparation programs or as a guide for professional development activities.

1707.   Muth, K. D., & Alvermann, D. E. (1992). *Teaching and learning in the middle grades.* Needham Heights, MA: Allyn and Bacon. 426 pp.

This textbook is comprised of three parts and fifteen chapters: Part I. Young Adolescents (Chapters 1. Introduction: Young Adolescents and Schools, 2. Young Adolescent Development, 3. Providing for Individual Differences). Part II. Middle-Grades Content (Chapters 4. The Middle-Grades Curriculum, 5. Middle-Grades Academic Core Content). Part III. Instruction in Learning (Chapters 6. Teachers as Decision Makers, 7. Instructional Planning: Year, Unit, Weekly, and Daily Planning, 8. Instructional Planning: Lesson Planning, 9. Classroom Assessment, 10. Using Technology to Improve Instruction, 11. Teaching Strategies, 12. Learning Strategies, 13. Classroom Questions, 14. Classroom Interaction, and 15. Classroom Management).

1708.   Stevenson, C. (1992). *Teaching ten to fourteen year olds*. White Plains, NY: Longman. 338 pp.

Of this textbook, John Lounsbury, one of the major figures and pioneers of the middle level movement, states the following in the book's foreword: "Here is a book that breaks new ground, that departs significantly from the traditional textbook pattern. Chris Stevenson's book is the most exciting, nonstandard education text that I've seen in more than forty years in education.... Here...is a book with an engaging style that is solidly grounded in human growth and development and never departs from that proper foundation no matter what the topic. It is thoroughly and consistently kid-centered." The text is comprised of three parts and eleven chapters: Part One. About the Kids. Chapters 1. A Rationale for Responsive Schooling, 2. Awareness through Shadow Studies, 3. Understanding through Inquiries, 4. Teacher's View of Development; Part Two:About Responsive Teaching. Chapters 5. Developmentally Responsive Pedagogy, 6. Choosing Curriculum, 7. Organizing for Responsibility and Harmony, 8. Evaluation and Assessment: Understanding What's Happening. Part Three: About Being a Teacher. Chapters 9. Success and Satisfaction through Teaming, 10. Advocacy and Alliance through Advisories, and 11. Partnerships with Parents.

1709.   Szymanski, C. S., & Haas, M. E. (1993). *Social studies and the elementary/middle school student*. New York: Harcourt Brace Jovanovich College Publishers. 369 pp.

The authors are strong advocates that the study of social studies should begin in kindergarten and continue through twelfth grade. In their preface the authors state that this textbook was "designed to illustrate the following: 1) the processes (strategies) for teaching social studies, 2) the structure of the knowledge to be learned, and 3) the theory and research that explain learning in social studies." They go on to note that "The research literature on constructivism and information processing has contributed heavily to the approach taken in this book." The volume is comprised of fourteen chapters: 1. Introducing Social Studies, 2. The Learning Cycle: A Framework for Teaching Social Studies, 3. Teaching Process Skills in Social Studies, 4. Developing Social Studies Concepts, 5. Constructing Generalizations in Social Studies, 6. Planning for Teaching, 7. Instructional Strategies and Materials for Teaching Social Studies, 8. Using Audio-Visual and Electronic Media in Social Studies, 9. Evaluating and Meeting Student Needs in Social Studies, 10. Psychology, Sociology and Values Education, 11. Geographic Education, 12. History Education, 13. Economic Education, and 14. Political Science, Civics, and Law Education.

1710.   Wiles, J., & Bondi, J. (1992). *The essential school*. New York: Merrill/Macmillan. 432 pp.

Written specifically for future middle school teachers and administrators, it includes the following chapters: 1. Rationale for the Middle School, 2. The Middle School Student, 3. The Teacher in the Middle School, 4. A Program

Design for the Middle School, 5. Organizing for Instruction in the Middle School, 6. Instructional Leadership in the Middle School, 7. Developing Creative Instructional Activities, Materials, and Learning Environments in the Middle School, 8. Planning Considerations for Middle School, 9. Implementing the Middle School, 10. Evaluating the Middle School, and 11. Future Directions of the Middle School.

G. VIDEOTAPES AND FILMSTRIPS

1711.   *Adolescent development* (30-min video). Available from Insight Media, 121 West 85th Street, New York, NY 10024.

Describes the physical, social, and psychological changes faced by young adolescents. Includes a discussion of Kohlberg's theory of moral development and the development of conscience. Produced in 1991.

1712.   *Adolescent health: Nursing implication series* (Series catalog number: 881-VI-033S) (Each video is 30 minutes in length). N. Davidson & J. Smith, 201 Silver Cedar Court, Chapel Hill, NC 27514: Health Sciences Consortium.

An eight volume set of videotapes focused on adolescents. The series covers the following topics: adolescent physical and psychosocial changes, nutritional needs and obesity, anorexia, sexuality, pregnancy, intrapartum, parenting, and long-term health problems. Highlights the nurse's role in providing care. Produced in 1988.

1713.   *Among equals*. (57-min. video). Available from Insight Media, 121 West 85th Street, New York, NY 10024.

Analyzes how peers provide support for solving moral dilemmas and problems arising in social relationships. Also contrasts the interactions and types of relationships formed by males and females. Produced in 1991.

1714.   Author. *Van Til, Vars and Lounsbury: A historical perspective on the middle grades curriculum*. [Videotape]. Columbus OH: National Middle School Association.

Videotape of a panel discussion by three middle level experts.

1715.   *Boy to man* (Videodisc). Available from distributor at 12210 Nebraska Ave., Los Angeles, CA 92225-3600.

Third edition of a videodisc on the changes of puberty for boys. Includes discussion about physical and psychosocial issues. Produced in 1993.

1716.   Burns, J. (1994, Fall). A documentary, but much more. [Review of In the game.]

A review of "Frontlines's documentary on Coach Tara VanDerver and her

Stanford University Basketball Team" (p. 8). The reviewer suggests using the videotape with middle level students in an effort to reinforce positive role models.

1717.   *Child's mind, The* (30 minute video). Available from Insight Media, 121 West 85th St., New York, NY 10024.

The program explores the concrete operational stage of the Piagetian approach as well as the information-processing approach to understanding cognitive development. David Elkind demonstrates the differences between children's concepts about the physical world and morality and adults' concepts. Memory capacity, strategies for remembering, interferences with the memory process, and creativity are also examined.

1718.   *Cognitive development* (30-min. video). Available from Insight Media, 121 West 85th Street, New York 10024.

Explains stages of cognitive development through a discussion of Piaget's theory and examples of skills development at various levels. Produced in 1990.

1719.   *Conflict resolution curriculum module: Grades 5-9* [Vidotape series No. 2428-AA]. Available from Sunburst Communications, 39 Washington Ave., Pleasantville, NY 10570-0040.

This curriculum package covers issues of communication with friends and parents using conflict resolution. Also includes role-play scenarios and staff development video.

1720.   *Development of self, The* (60-minute video). Available from Insight Media, 121 West 85th Street, New York 10024.

Focuses on self-concept, self-esteem, and self-worth by exploring the Perceived Competence Scale for Children, a scale designed to assess self-concept in a variety of domains including academic performance, athletic competence, popularity, and physical appearance. Examines the developmental factors that often influence feelings of self-worth in young adolescents, discusses three methods for improving one's self-worth, and describes disorders often associated with low self-worth. Produced in 1991.

1721.   *Early adolescence: A time of change* (13-minute VHS videotape). Available from: National Association of Secondary School Principals, 1904 Association Dr., Reston, VA 22091-1537.

Examines the physical, emotional, and social changes that take place during early adolescence. Useful for use by adolescents, parents, teachers, and administrators. Produced in 1988.

1722.   *Education with a heart*.. Available from the National Resource Center for Middle Grades/High School Education and Incentive Publications,

University of South Florida, College of Education-EDU 118, Tampa, Florida 33620-5650.

Focuses on the social, physical, intellectual, psychological, and moral development of early adolescents. Presents in a visually appealing way the essential elements of advisory programs.

1723.   *Elementary mind, The* (30 minute video). Available from: Insight Media, 121 West 85th St., New York, NY 10024.

Developmental psychologist Jean Piaget's theories on the logical operational period are examined in this program, which features interviews with such experts as Robert Sternberg and Rochel Gelman. It shows experiments that demonstrate how conceptualization becomes easier in middle childhood. The importance of memory strategies in learning situations is explained and elaboration tests that measure mental effort under interference are described. The controversy over intelligence and diagnostic testing is also discussed.

1724.   *Getting along* (30 min, video). Available from Insight Media, 121 West 85th St., New York, NY 10024.

Psychologists explain how children begin to understand people's differences during middle childhood. The program discusses how empathy may be a core factor in successful social interactions, and considers how children need to learn to disagree in socially acceptable ways. Why certain children do not get along with others is explored and the role of both the family and television in shaping development is studied. An experiment which monitors the physiological reactions of children during parental conflict is described and long-term effects of living in such stressful situations are discussed.

1725.   *Girl to woman* (Videodisc). Available from distributor at 12210 Nebraska Ave., Los Angeles, CA 92225-3600.

Third edition of a videodisc on the changes of puberty for girls. Includes discussion about physical and psychosocial issues. Produced in 1993.

1726.   *Helper Program: Getting started, The* (20 minute video). Available from the National Center for Service Learning in Early Adolescence, c/o Center for Advanced Study in Education, Graduate School and University Center of the City University of New York, 25 West 43rd Street, Suite 612, New York, NY 10036-8099.

"Describes the process of starting a service learning program based on the Early Adolescent Helper Program model. It is an invaluable way of introducing teachers, administrators, and youth workers to the specifics that constitute a quality service learning program." Produced in 1991.

1727.   Johnston, J. H. (1994). *Raising standards, raising children: An agenda for middle schools in the 21st Century.* [Videotape]. Columbus OH:

National Middle School Association.

Videotape of remarks by inspirational speaker at the keynote address of the 1994 NSMA annual conference.

1728.   *Jump start*. (3 videos, 7 minutes each). Available from Southern Media Design and Production, Inc., Chapel Hill, NC.

Encourages middle level students to take education seriously. Features student-athletes from the Atlantic Coast Conference discussing problems and other issues (including goals, dreams, academic concerns, peer pressure, and decision-making) relevant to middle level students. Has a sound track and graphics that will appeal to middle level students.

1729.   *Me and my friends* (30-min. video). Available from Insight Media, 121 West 85th Street, New York, New York 10024.

Noted psychologists discuss characteristics of middle level students with an emphasis on friendship development. Addresses a wide variety of issues, including what makes a student popular and why certain students are rejects by their peer groups. Produced in 1992.

1730.   *MGAP Videotape* (25 minute video). Available from Center for Early Adolescence, University of North Carolina at Chapel Hill, D-2 Carr Mill Town Center, Carrboro, NC 27510.

Reviews early adolescent development and school responsiveness. It also shows assessment team members how to sharpen their observation and interviewing skills when conducting a middle school assessment.

1731.   *Modern middle school, The* (60-minute, 4-tape series). Available from Teacher Education Resources, P. O. Box 206. Gainesville, FL 32602.

A four-part video series with a written script appropriate for professional development sessions. The first part explores the nature of young adolescents, presents an overview of the "middle level" concept, and outlines characteristics of effective middle level teachers. Part two focuses on the basic goals of effective middle level schools from a parental perspective. Part three focuses on the organizational and leadership issues involved in establishing and maintaining an effective middle level school. Part four provides a tour of a model middle level school, emphasizing its growth and development since the 1970s.

1732.   National Middle School Association. (1994). Sexual harassment: It's hurting people. [Videotape]. Columbus, OH: Author.

"This 17 minute video is accompanied by a 68 page instructional manual" (NMSA Annual Report, #6).

1733.   *Partners Program: Helping hands, The* (11 minute video). Available from the National Center for Service Learning in Early Adolescence, c/o Center for Advanced Study in Education, Graduate School and University Center of the City University of New York, 25 West 43rd Street, Suite 612, New York, NY 10036-8099.

"Describes the benefits and activities of the Partners Program, the National Center's model of intergenerational service learning. It is an effective way to introduce such programming to teachers, administrators, youth, and elders." Produced in 1991.

1734.   *Peers in development* (60 minute video). Available from Insight Media, 121 West 85th St., New York, NY 10024.

Probing the importance of peer relationships in social and emotional development, this program examines the growth of peer relationships from the social interest of infants though the groupings of adolescence. It considers the importance of play in cognitive development, as explained by Piaget and Vygotsky, and describes Parten's six categories of social participation. It explores how peer attachments shift from those based on concrete, observable characteristics to those based on abstract, dispositional characteristics. Commentary from children of different ages provides insights into the way the idea of friendship develops with age. Produced in 1991.

1735.   *Planning programs for young adolescents: What works and why videotape* (20 minute video). Available from the Center for Early Adolescence, University of North Carolina, D-2 Carr Mill Town Center, Carroboro, NC 27510.

Describes the characteristics of effective afterschool programs for 10- to 15-year olds, as well as a model for successful planning. Interviews with youth workers and examples from effective programs provide insights in regard to what is working in communities nationwide.

1736.   *Self esteem* (25 minute video). Available from Insight Media, 121 West 85th St., New York, NY 10024.

This video explores the components of the self—self concept (cognitive awareness of personal attributes), self-control (behavioral conduct), and self esteem (feelings of worth). It outlines the five criteria for self-perception and relates the way an individual ranks these five criteria to feelings of self-worth. It concludes with an explanation of how adults can enhance self-esteem in children.

1737.   *Success with discipline: The trials of Jenny Tippet* (3-part series, each 2 2/3 to 3 hours, video). Available from the National Middle School Association, Columbus, OH.

Designed for use in professional development sessions. Focuses on fundamentals of classroom behavior management in middle level settings.

1738.   Teacher Education Resources. *Interdisciplinary team organization.*
[Videotape]. Gainesville, FL: Author.

Presents developmental stages of team organizations and methods on successful
teams.

1739.   Teacher Education Resources. *The 21st Century middle school: A
school improvement plan.* [Videotape]. Gainesville, FL: Author.

An inside look at one middle school's experience.

1740.   Teacher Education Resources. *The case for the middle school.*
[Videotape]. Gainesville, FL: Author.

Presents the rationale and research for middle level programs.

1741.   Teacher Education Resources. *The modern middle school.*
[Videotapes]. Gainesville, FL: Author.

A set of four videos especially developed for districts planning for
implementation of middle level programs

1742.   Teacher Education Resources. *The teacher-advisory program.*
[Videotape]. Gainesville, FL: Author.

Presents purpose of advisor-advisee programs and offers several suggested
activities.

1743.   Teacher Education Resources. (1995). Becoming the very best team.
[Videotapes]. Gainesville, FL: Author.

Three tapes that cover characteristics of strong teams, building blocks for
success, and leadership tasks.

1744.   *Teaching in the middle school* (10 minute filmstrip). Available from
the National Educational Association Professional Library, P.O. Box 509, West
Haven, CT 06516.

"Full color filmstrip with audiocassette narration and printed guide. It explores
the curriculum which the middle school format makes available, and looks at
some of the qualities of those teachers who can best guide students in this
environment." Produced in 1987.

1745.   *Teenage body and mind* (30-min. video). Available from Insight
Media, 121 West 85th Street, New York 10024.

Examines the differences between teenagers' abilities and interests and parents'
expectations with an emphasis on cognitive and physical development. Also
discusses Piaget's "formal operations" stage by investigating how teenagers

engage in the thinking process, and investigates the ability of teenagers to cope with moral dilemmas as explained in Kohlberg's model. Produced in 1992.

1746.   *Teenage relationships* (30 minute video). Available from Insight Media, 121 West 85th Street, New York 10024.

Examines the social development of teenagers from the perspective of psychologists, parents, and teenagers themselves. Explores how teenagers cope with change, how parenting practices can enhance competence and self-esteem, and how the attention of teenagers often turns from the family to peer groups. Produced in 1992.

1747.   Video Outreach. (1994). *Go for it!*

Career video highlighting manufacturing jobs in tooling and machining that don't require a college degree. Available from the author at (516) 436-7490.

1748.   *Why a school in the middle?* (16mm film or VHS). Available from National Association of Secondary School Principals, 1904 Association Dr., Reston, VA 22091-1537.

Filmed in middle schools in Maryland and Georgia, "Why a School in the Middle?" is a concise presentation of the need for a middle school. It is suitable for use at parent orientations, at community group meetings, and at preservice and inservice sessions for administrators and teachers.

H. BIBLIOGRAPHIES

1749.   Center for Early Adolescence. (1986). *Resources for youth workers and program planners*. Carrboro, NC: Author. 40 pp.

Describes resources that are helpful to individuals who work with 10- to 15-year olds in out-of-school settings. Topics covered include program development and implementation, model programs, funding, youth participation, community collaboration, social trends and public policy, racial, ethnic, and gender differences, and promoting physical and emotional health.

1750.   Center for Early Adolescence. (1987). *Families with young adolescents: A resource list.* Carrboro, NC: Author. 53 pp.

An extensive listing of books and other print materials for parents and professionals on topics ranging from adolescent alcohol abuse to puberty to shyness. Entries are fully annotated and indexed.

1751.   Center for Early Adolescence. (1989). *Early adolescent sexuality: Resources for professionals, parents, and young adolescents.* Carrboro, NC: Author. 58 pp.

Lists books, films and videos, journals, curricula, difficult to locate pamphlets, and organizations for those needing information on specific topics or a general treatment of early adolescent sexuality. Entries are fully annotated and indexed. Covers AIDS, decision making, homosexuality, menstruation, parent-teen communication, puberty, pregnancy prevention, etc.

1752. Center for Early Adolescence. (1992). *Early adolescence: A resource directory*. Carrboro, NC: Author. 58 pp.

Comprehensive list of organizations and journals that focus on topics affecting the early adolescent age group, including education, adolescent development, religion, family, community, health, and sexuality. Entries are fully annotated and indexed.

1753. Center for Early Adolescence. (1993). *Early adolescence: A resource directory*. Carrboro, NC: Author.

A comprehensive directory of resources for middle level educators and parents. Includes an annotated listing of 143 organizations and 43 journals with a focus on the development of young adolescents. Also includes a helpful subject index.

1754. Lawton, E. J. (1989). *A journey through time: A chronology of middle level education resources*. Columbus, OH: National Middle School Association. 27 pp.

This bibliography on middle level education resources is comprised of four chapters: 1. Historical References: 1920-1964; 2. Transitional References: 1965-1975; 3. Modern Middle School References: 1976-1988; and, 4. Current Resources. The first chapter primarily focuses on the topic of "the junior high." The last chapter does not so much list current resources, but rather states where the latest resources (as of 1989) can be found. More specifically, the chapter provides annotations of (1) key middle level organizations and centers and (2) middle level journals. The bibliography has over 90 citations.

1755. Nielsen, L. L., & Nielsen, G. R. (1990). Preparing for the Columbian Quincentenial: An annotated bibliography. *Social Studies and the Young Learner*. *3*(1), 13-15.

Prepared to encourage teachers to plan activities celebrating the five hundredth anniversary of the voyages of Columbus. Limited to books written about the voyages of Columbus, the bibliography contains annotations of books appropriate for a wide range of readers, including preschoolers through students in middle level grades.

1756. Sensenbaugh, R. (1991). Developing strategies for reading, writing, and critical thinking: The intermediate grades. *Reading Research and Instruction*, *31*(1), 77-80.

An annotated bibliography of ten documents available through the ERIC database. Emphasis of each of the documents is upon strategies for addressing issues and concerns involved in middle level education.

1757.   Totten, S., Sills, T., Digby, A., & Russ, P. (1991). *Cooperative learning: A guide to research*. New York: Garland Publishing. 390 pp.

This annotated bibliography is comprised of over 800 annotations on various facets of cooperative learning (e.g., different strategies; use in different subject areas; and, research on a host of issues such as cooperation, effectiveness of certain cooperative learning strategies, classroom climate, cultural and ethnic differences, friendships, etc.). It includes listings of essays, articles, books, films, games, newsletters, and organizations.

INDEXES

Author Index

Subject Index

ability grouping, 481
academic achievement, 188, 315, 360, 480, 625, 1035-1036, 1110, 1112, 1162, 1210, 1212, 1215, 1218, 1506; programs, 232; standards, 242
accelerated learning, 237, 260, 603
Achievement, 1209-1219
active learning, 999
active teaching, 26
activity programs, 11, 575
administration, 213, 276
Adolescent Health Survey, 1344
advance organizers, 605
adventure education, 573
advisement, 1302
Advisor-Advisee, 384-411
advisory groups, 17, 24, 357
advisory guide, 405
advisory programs, 51, 59, 70, 105, 176, 220, 384-388, 392, 394-397, 399, 400-403, 407-408
aerobics, 580
affective education, 300, 382, 966
African Americans, 224, 1110, 1184, 1214, 1369, 1465, 1497
after-school programs, 147-149
aggressive behavior, 153
AIDS, 1382-1388
AIMS Journal, 1619
Alcohol Misuse Prevention Study (AMPS), 1426

alcohol education, 1296
alcohol, 1322, 1421, 1423, 1425-1426, 1428-1429, 1454
Algebra Project, 565
algebra readiness, 485
algebra, 522, 529-530, 535, 538, 565, 567
alienation, 196
alternative grading, 1201
anger management, 1222
anxiety, 1310
archaeology, 784
arithmetic errors, 476
Arkansas, 1656
art curriculum, 901, 903-904; education, 907, 914; institutes, 910; museums, 905; programs, 908-909, 911-913; writing, 906
assertive discipline, 1236-1237
Assessment, 1188-1208
Assessment authentic, 1190, 1192-1193, 1197, 1200; middle level programs, 12, 41, 66, 107, 205-206, 208, 211, 217, 239, 306, 308, 506, 1191; middle school, 242, 294, 454, 1189, 1191, 1195-1196, 1200, 1202, 1204-1206, 1208, 1219; reading, 623, 659; science, 732, 770; students, 203; writing, 1164
astronauts, 755
at-risk gifted, 1155; math, 560;

About the Authors

SAMUEL TOTTEN is Associate Professor of Curriculum and Instruction at the University of Arkansas, Fayetteville, where he is also the Director of the Center for Middle Level Education, Research, and Development. His publications include *First Person Accounts of Genocidal Acts Committed in the Twentieth Century: A Critical Annotated Bibliography* (Greenwood, 1991).

TONI SILLS-BRIEGEL is Assistant Professor of Middle Level Education at Southwest Missouri State University at Springfield. She has written numerous articles and has coauthored a book on cooperative learning.

KATHLEEN BARTA is an Assistant Professor in the Department of Nursing of the University of Arkansas College of Education. Her clinical background is in the care of children.

ANNETTE DIGBY is Associate Professor and Assistant Dean for Professional Education at the University of Arkansas, Fayetteville. She has published two books and has written numerous articles on cooperative learning, middle level education, and university/public school partnerships.

WILLIAM NIELSEN is Regional Coordinator for the Arkansas Math, Science, and K-4 Crusades. Prior to his current position, he taught math methods to elementary preservice and inservice teachers at the University of Arkansas.

ISBN 0-313-29002-4

EAN

HARDCOVER BAR CODE